RESEARCH
IN PHYSICAL EDUCATION,
EXERCISE SCIENCE, AND SPORT:
AN INTRODUCTION

RESEARCH
IN PHYSICAL EDUCATION, EXERCISE SCIENCE, AND SPORT: AN INTRODUCTION

CHARLES F. CICCIARELLA
West Texas A&M University

GORSUCH SCARISBRICK, PUBLISHERS
SCOTTSDALE, ARIZONA

Publisher:	Gay L. Pauley
Editor:	A. Colette Kelly
Consulting Editor:	Robert P. Pangrazi
Developmental Editor:	Katie E. Bradford
Production Editor:	Ann Waggoner Aken
Cover Design:	Kevin Kall
Typesetting:	John Wincek/Aerocraft Charter Art Service

Gorsuch Scarisbrick, Publishers
8233 Via Paseo del Norte, F-400
Scottsdale, Arizona 85258

10 9 8 7 6 5 4 3 2 1

ISBN 0-89787-631-8

Library of Congress Cataloging-in-Publication Data

Cicciarella, Charles F., 1950–
    Research in physical education, exercise science, and sport : an introduction / by Charles F. Cicciarella.
        p.   cm.
    Includes bibliographical references and index.
    ISBN 0-89787-631-8 (alk. paper)
    1. Sports sciences—Research—Methodology. 2. Physical education and training—Research—Methodology. 3. Exercise—Research—Methodology.   I. Title.
    GV558.C53 1997
    613.7'1—dc20   96-24644
                                                         CIP

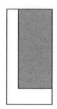

BRIEF CONTENTS

For a complete table of contents, see page vii.

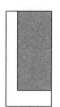

CONTENTS

PREFACE

The concepts, resources, tools, and ethics of research are widely accepted as fundamentally important for graduate level preparation of professionals in exercise science, physical education, coaching, sport management, and related fields of endeavor. Additionally, there is increasing recognition of a need for exposure to the skills required for intelligent consumption of research in undergraduate training. At the same time there is a trend toward a broader view of what constitutes scholarship, one that is inclusive of a wide range of kinds and methods of inquiry. There is a need, therefore, for a textbook in research methods applied to sport-related fields of study that provides skills relevant to both the production and consumption of research, that is cognizant of the many dimensions of sport-related professions, and that recognizes a very broad interpretation of what constitutes research. *Research in Physical Education, Exercise Science, and Sport: An Introduction* is written to meet these needs.

This book is designed for use as a text in academic programs preparing students either for professional practice in exercise science, physical education, sport management, coaching, and related professions, or for subsequent advanced graduate work. Portions of this book may also find use as a reference by those occasionally engaging in research or as a text in programs requiring a baccalaureate thesis or other major exposure to research/inquiry concepts.

This book is distinguishable from most other research methods texts in several important ways. First, great care has been taken to produce a text that is clear and concise, particularly in discussions of topics students frequently find quite difficult. Second, complex topics are supported by examples, illustrations, metaphors, and similar devices based on experiences that should be already familiar to most students. Many illustrations of statistical tools and concepts, for example, use data that might reasonably be generated within the world of sport.

Third, this book defines research and scholarly inquiry quite broadly, thus recognizing the interdisciplinary, or perhaps more properly *multidisciplinary,* nature of our field. Along these lines, the first chapter discusses the wide variety of projects that may be classified as research. Fourth, an entire chapter is devoted to ethical conduct in research, including the more subtle issues involving conflicts of interest, misuse of research, and the risks faced by researchers willing to stand up for unpopular truths, as well as more obvious issues such as human and animal subject rights and scientific misconduct. Finally, significant effort has been made to take advantage of the widespread availability of computer technology for the teaching of research. In addition to coverage of electronic database searching and the Internet, for example, the statistical tables generally provided in the appendices of similar texts have been replaced by computer programs, available on disks to instructors, capable of performing computations directly. Rather than look up the significance of an F value in a table, for example, the student can now compute areas under the F curves directly.

Chapters 1 through 3 introduce the student to scholarly inquiry and a variety of its forms, the role of the research requirement in academia, and the purpose and structure of research reports. Chapters 4 and 5 cover the researcher's basic tools: the research library and concepts and issues of measurement. Chapters 6 through 10 discuss the research designs and methodologies associated with descriptive, experimental, historical, and exploratory and qualitative studies. Tools for data presentation and statistical analysis are presented in Chapters 11 through 14. Chapter 15 deals with a wide range of ethical issues faced by the producer and consumer of research.

I would like to express my appreciation to the reviewers, who read the manuscript in various stages of completion and offered suggestions for its improvement. Special thanks to Mark Ricard, Brigham Young University, and Deborah Johnston, Baylor University.

Statistical Computer Programs

Many textbooks of research methods or statistics include appendices reproducing lengthy mathematical and statistical tables. Such tables are a method by which complex computations may be avoided by providing the results of repeated computations using a wide range of trial values. Computers, however, provide a more modern and more accurate alternative to such tables. In short, the tables are no longer needed because the computer can perform the computations quite easily. Appendix C provides several templates for use using the program Mathcad®, and Appendix D provides several computer programs written in the BASIC language. (Mathcad® is a program, classified as an equation solver, that reads files containing mathematical equations and performs mathematical operations.) Each of these programs is available for textbook adopters at no cost from Gorsuch Scarisbrick, Publishers on MS Dos format diskettes (3.5"), and they may be easily copied onto your computer. Some adaptation may be needed to use the BASIC programs with specific BASIC interpreters or compilers or to use the Mathcad® programs with different equation solvers.

THE PRACTICE OF RESEARCH

Research is not something done by only absentminded, mad scientists with white laboratory coats, mismatched shoes, and trifocal glasses. Just about everyone can and does do research, at least at some level. Research is finding answers. It is finding answers by asking questions, by looking things up in books, by playing with and manipulating ideas and things, or simply by being mentally engaged in what is going on around us. However, though research may be defined as finding answers, merely *finding* answers is *not* research: Research is a self-directed effort to find answers. When a student (or anyone else) begins to seek answers because of a desire to know rather than because of a desire to pass a test or course, then that student has crossed the boundary into research.

For the human species, learning is a life-long, continual process. It does not, and should not, end at graduation from high school or college. Indeed, one might make a good case that genuine learning really begins at graduation from school. One of the fundamental goals of higher education, therefore,

> Being "taught" is passive. "Learning" is active. The unmotivated student will not learn in spite of the best teaching. The student who wants to will learn in spite of the worst teaching.

is to prepare students to be fully independent learners. That is, persons who, for the rest of their lives, will not have to rely on external direction from a formal educational system in order to learn. Such persons will more easily adapt to our rapidly changing world. As a means of enabling students to demonstrate that they have become independent learners, many institutions of higher education require them to complete some kind of culminating project involving research. At the graduate level, such a project is usually called a thesis or a dissertation and generally requires a research effort designed to demonstrate in-depth mastery of a field of study. Doctoral dissertations are intended, as well, to advance the frontiers of knowledge. At the undergraduate level, such a project may be designed more flexibly to demonstrate the ability to learn independently and effectively communicate what has been learned to others. At the undergraduate level such a project may be called a bachelor's thesis, or senior paper, project, or theme.

Research is also an integral part of professional practice in every profession. Professionals are expected, at the very least, to be continually aware of new developments and to be self reflective in order to maintain their own practice at a state-of-the-art quality. Ideally, professionals should also be continually involved in advancing the state of the art of their chosen profession. In some professional positions, research is a principal focus and may even be a condition of continued employment.

A RESEARCHER'S ATTITUDE

Children and great scientists are not afraid to be wrong. The late Nobel laureate Richard Feynmann was widely recognized as a brilliant scientist and as a genuinely original thinker. In a television interview he said that he was once asked by a student, "Mr. Feynmann, how do you come up with so many good ideas?"

"That's easy," Feynmann answered. "You just come up with a lot of ideas and throw out the bad ones."

Research can also be profitable. Although the funding of research through government and private grants is cyclic, there are always opportunities for freelance research, especially in product marketing. Further, the information that is the product of research can often be sold by the researcher.

Feynmann's point was not that you need a lot of ideas or some magic ability to tell good ideas from bad ones. His point was really that good ideas are generated by a kind of mind set or attitude that is willing to play with ideas and is not afraid to be wrong. Scientific discovery, after all, is frequently the result of someone recognizing a connection or relationship among ideas that has not previously been noticed. Such connections are rarely made by those who fear being wrong.

If there are any psychological characteristics that distinguish the researcher (or the researcher likely to be successful at research), the first is surely a high degree of curiosity. Curiosity is a critical attribute in at least two ways. First, the researcher must be curious about the subject he or she chooses to investigate. The researcher is more likely to succeed in a research effort when that research is driven by a genuine and intense desire to know rather than by external forces such as the desire to complete a degree, the promise of financial reward, or the fear of tenure denial. Second, the researcher with a high degree of inherent curiosity is more likely to notice the kinds of small details that often provide the key to major discoveries. The genuinely curious researcher, for example, will notice, wonder, and speculate on reasons for small differences between observed phenomena and the predictions of theory while the less curious will fail to notice the difference or dismiss it as unimportant. The inherently curious researcher is also likely to have a broader base of knowledge outside of his or her chosen specialization, from which new ideas or methods of inquiry may be drawn.

A second critical psychological attribute for a researcher is that of playfulness. Research, after all, may be described as a self-directed process of discovery, and no human beings are better at self-directed discovery than young children. Lacking the encumbrance of preconceived notions about what is appropriate or correct, young children explore their environments with great intensity. They put objects and ideas together in unusual and unexpected ways, constructing in their minds their own models of the world and increasing their knowledge at a phenomenal rate. As children get older, becoming more self-conscious and encountering the need to conform to societal norms, their willingness to be playful seems often to be suppressed or lost altogether, and their learning tends to become more passive. The ability to return to playfulness by examining problems or ideas from different or unusual perspectives without fear of appearing foolish will often permit the researcher to make connections among elements of a research problem that others will miss.

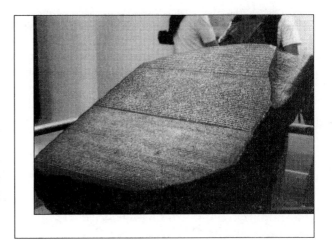

FIGURE 1.1   The Rosetta Stone. Sometimes a seemingly small and unimportant discovery turns out to be of monumental importance. This desk-sized stone slab, discovered in Egypt by an officer in Napoleon's army, became the key to deciphering the hieroglyphics of ancient Egypt. (British Museum)

THE RISK OF SUCCESS

The practice of research can, on occasion, prove dangerous. Research, in perhaps its simplest sense, is a search for truth (scientific truth, at least) and the truth can often be unpopular—sometimes extremely so. Those who speak the truth or what they honestly believe to be the truth sometimes risk vilification, ridicule, loss of security, loss of professional reputation, and even serious physical harm, especially when their statements threaten widely or deeply held views or undermine established institutions. There is no shortage of historical examples of attacks on those who dared to contradict establishment ideas, nor are such examples limited to the distant past. Galileo, in 1613, reported using the newly developed telescope to observe that there were dark spots that appeared occasionally, moving across the surface of the sun. His observations, which today can easily be confirmed using a simple lens and a sheet of paper, were in conflict with the religious doctrine that declared the sun and other celestial bodies to be perfect. After several years of controversy, as well as a few other publications seen as heretical, Galileo was placed under house arrest where he remained until his death. In the mid-nineteenth century, when Charles Darwin offered the theory of evolution as the explanation for the origin of the many species of plants and animals, such severe sanctions could no longer be imposed, but the attacks on Darwin and his theory were extremely hostile, often personally directed, and continue to this day.

Contradicting religious ideas is not the only way research may lead to difficulties for the researcher. The scientific community itself has occasionally been guilty of censorious behavior. In the early twentieth century, the theory that continents slowly drift around across the surface of the earth—the theory of continental drift—was proposed by a meteorologist named Alfred Wegener. As this theory was contrary to current thinking in the field of geology, the theory and Wegener were ridiculed and his career was ruined. Today, of course, we not only know the continents move, but we also have measured the rate at which they do so. Ocean scientists have even observed magma emerging from the sea floor along the boundary between crustal plates that are gradually moving apart.

Attacks on scientists for their work are not limited to the past. Very recently there have been cases in which the motivation, competence, and even national loyalty of scientists have been questioned after their having expressed scientific opinions such as a prediction that continued use of certain chemicals could result in the depletion of the ozone layer, that cigarette smoking is carcinogenic, or that blood products should be screened for the HIV virus.

Publication of research findings on topics that are controversial or that threaten vested interests can sometimes be hazardous, but good scientific practice demands that the researcher be willing to accept such risks. Indeed, to some extent the researcher ought to welcome such attacks as a sign of the importance attached by others to his or her work, as work considered trivial is usually ignored irrespective of how outrageous or controversial it may be. The self-correcting nature of the scientific method should result in eventual vindication of ideas or theories that are correct and the discreditation of those that are wrong or incomplete, although not necessarily as quickly as the researcher might like. The victims of each of the examples mentioned above, with some exceptions among the most recent cases, are now almost universally recognized in the scientific community as having been correct, and some are counted among the historical giants of science.

Although important or revolutionary discoveries and their discoverers are sometimes treated with disdain by establishment institutions, such reactions by the establishment do not mean an announced discovery or theory is important, revolutionary, or even reasonable. Just as establishment institutions sometimes attack scientists whose ideas they find threatening, scientists and others purporting to be scientists sometimes use the accusation of such attacks as a smoke screen to cover poor science. Incidents of this type in recent years have included claims about the cancer-fighting efficacy of Laetrile, claims about psychokinesis and other paranormal phenomena, and the theory that lines on the plain of Nazca and the statues of Easter Island were made by extraterrestrial visitors. When the validity of such claims has been questioned, they have been defended by such tactics as lawsuits for slander (Alexander, 1991), dismissal of the questioners as jealous or protective of some conflicting interest, or the invention of claims of phenomena that are inherently untestable (Randi, 1984), rather than through scientific arguments or demonstrations. Ultimately, scientific questions must be settled by the methods of science, not by popular opinion, force of will, or political pressure. Scientific ideas or theories that are correct will prevail and those that are not will fail in the end.

THE RESEARCH ENVIRONMENT

The type of research that is conducted in any setting, as well as its quantity and quality, is almost certain to be affected by the environment under which it is attempted. A clinical setting, where professional services of some kind (medical treatment, rehabilitation, instruction, coaching, conditioning, and so on) are offered to clients, usually for a fee, is likely to be supportive of research of a practical nature, and probably less supportive of purely theoretical investigation. A purely academic setting, one unconnected to any program of clinical practice, would probably produce more research of a theoretical nature, although that research might eventually find plenty of practical application. An institution that provides its researchers with efficient infrastructure support, such as secretarial service, easy access to computer and library support, modern laboratory equipment, and so on, is likely to produce a greater volume of research than one that fails to provide such support or that makes its access cumbersome. Similarly, there is likely to be an inverse relationship between research productivity and the demands placed on researchers for other responsibilities such as teaching and committee work.

Other than transferring to a different school or seeking another position there is not often much a student, faculty member, or other professional can do to rapidly change many aspects of the research environment within a given institution. The resources allocated to the support of research are an expression of the value placed by the institution on the conduct of research, and not all institutions of higher education assign a high value to it (often unless it can be paid for by external funds). However, there are some aspects of the research environment than can be modified fairly easily even by students so as to increase the quantity and quality of their research productivity. Two such aspects of the research environment are the opportunities for cross fertilization of ideas and for a team approach to research problems.

It is an old saw that "two heads are better than one" for solving any sort of problem. Though it is also said that the camel was the result produced by a committee assigned to design the horse, it is generally true that a group effort is likely to produce more rapid progress toward solving a problem than an individual effort. To take advantage of this, it is not uncommon for graduate students reaching the thesis stage of their degree programs to form small symposia groups to help each other in their research projects, and there is no reason undergraduate students cannot do the same. Such groups usually meet on a regular, but extremely informal, basis, often in the evening, for the purpose of unstructured discussion of their research problems. Meetings typically last for several hours and may be held once or twice per week. Faculty members sometimes participate as well (or they may have their own such groups), but everyone involved is an equal participant—this is not a classroom activity. Although symposia groups of this type are informal, they are not parties or social events. The focus is clearly on the sharing of ideas, problems, and solutions related to the actual or potential research projects of the participants.

In most academic institutions, research in physical education, recreation, sport, and related areas is done largely on an individual basis. This is especially so for student research projects done to meet degree requirements. It is not necessarily a desirable situation, but it is hard to avoid when enrollments are small and the faculty is composed of only one person in each of the various specializations within a major. In industry and in many larger academic departments, research is more often conducted using a team approach. Typically, a large scale research program is established by a team of several faculty members and graduate students, and smaller components of that program are then assigned to team members. The common student problem of trying to identify a research topic may be eliminated by simply joining a team of this sort and being assigned a topic by the team leader or being allowed to select one from a list of approved topics. In most cases each team member is then expected to conduct an investigation of an assigned component. However, that investigation is likely to be significantly facilitated by interaction with the other researchers. In other cases, and particularly when the restrictions of granting academic credit are not involved, such as in industry, the project may really be a team effort. In smaller academic institutions where such large scale projects are not readily available, small groups of students may still gain the advantages of the group approach simply by forming small teams of their own to work on different but related aspects of a larger research problem or by choosing research topics with some common theme. For example, a team of five students interested in doing descriptive work in sport biomechanics might decide that each member will do an analysis of a form of bipedal locomotion using cinematographic analysis and a force platform, but each with a different form of locomotion. If such a group chooses a topic that is within the interest of a faculty member, its members should find little difficulty in persuading that person to work with them as an advisor or even as the team leader. One potential pitfall that participants in such a group must carefully avoid is the tendency to share too much. In most academic institutions certain aspects of a student's thesis project, especially the written thesis itself, are expected to be a solo effort.

THE METHOD OF SCIENCE

Science is a method of inquiry, not a subject of inquiry (except, of course, to the extent that science itself is studied scientifically). The *sciences* of physics, chemistry, biology, psychology, and so on are so called because of the methods by which they are studied, not because their subject matter makes them different from non sciences. Chemistry studied without science is alchemy; astronomy so studied is astrology.

Human beings have a strong drive to make sense of the universe. Indeed, the human mind may be described as a mechanism driven to creating and maintaining a mental model of its universe—so driven, in fact, that it will sometimes perceive patterns where none exist. Over the centuries people have created many such models or systems for making sense of their world, including mythology and religion, magic and witchcraft, and astrology. Another system, of more recent vintage and of greater success for most applications, is science.

Science, as a method of inquiry, rests on two very basic assumptions. First, science assumes that the world is deterministic—that is, that there are elemental laws of nature that all objects or phenomena inescapably must obey. Second, science operates under the assumption that the elemental laws of nature can be understood only through observation, and that what is ultimately beyond the possibility of observation is outside the domain of science.

Although it would be a mistake to assume that all scientists proceed in a common, linear sequence of steps, or even that they are conscious of such a sequence, the general approach to inquiry in science may be described in diagrammatic form as such a sequence (see Figure 1.2). The method of science begins with the identification of a problem. Based on what is already known relevant to the problem, a process of reason is used to develop a proposed or theoretical solution to the problem. For a somewhat whimsical but historically genuine example, the problem of explaining the long necks of giraffes might lead to the theory that constant stretching to reach food high in trees leads to a lengthened neck that is then passed on to subsequent generations. (This idea, known as the Lamarkian theory of evolution, was quite recently believed to be the truth.) Based on this theoretical solution, a *prediction* or **hypothesis** is made

FIGURE 1.2   The method of science. The actual practice of science is, of course, rarely as simple or direct as is suggested here.

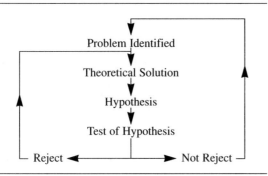

that will be confirmed if the proposed solution is correct or contradicted if it is false. If the theory of giraffe neck growth is correct then after a few generations the babies of giraffes raised in zoos and fed with food spread on the ground ought to have shorter necks than those whose parents have to reach for their food. The hypothesis is tested as rigorously as possible. If it fails the test, that is, if that which is predicted to occur based on the proposed solution does not occur, then the solution is incorrect or incomplete. If it passes, then the proposed solution is tentatively accepted as consistent with available evidence. In the giraffe example, the theory that stretching for food affects neck length in giraffe offspring would prove false or inadequate. A different theory would then be proposed and tested, perhaps that giraffes with longer necks would be able to find more food and thereby survive to bear more offspring than those with shorter necks. Note that the proposed solution is never accepted as *correct*, but only as *not demonstrated as incorrect*.

There is sometimes a tendency for those seeking attention, or perhaps for authors seeking to sell more books, to propose hypotheses that are very unlikely to be correct. Given a small island with a number of very large sculptures and people who do not appear to have heavy machinery (such as Easter Island) the hypothesis is developed that the sculptures must have been built by space aliens. This is not science. The scientist will seek first the most likely explanation and will only move on to less likely hypotheses when the first is shown to be false. This scientific approach is humorously but aptly summarized by the so-called *duck test:* "If it looks like a duck, waddles like a duck, and quacks like a duck, then most likely it's a duck."

RESEARCH PROJECTS IN ACADEMIA

Most academic institutions above the secondary or junior college level expect their faculty to engage in research, and many require their students to demonstrate the ability to conduct at least elementary research and to report their findings in written form. Nearly all doctoral, most master's, and an increasing number of bachelor's degree programs require some form of culminating research or creative project for graduation. Although research is widely expected of both faculty and students, the definition of what qualifies as research is highly varied. Some insist that research must be an activity that attempts to advance the frontiers of humankind's knowledge. Others apply a broader definition that includes a wider variety of scholarly pursuits. Thus, pursuits such as the development of a new type of computer program, the creation of a musical score, or the design of a new or improved commercial product may be accepted as research in some locations and not in others. Similarly, the kinds of scholarly or creative work that will be accepted as meeting an academic requirement may vary substantially among institutions or even among departments within an institution. One institution may require students in a particular program of study to perform a research project involving the collection and analysis of original data, whereas another may allow students in a comparable program to complete a more flexible project such as a literature review or the development of teaching materials. In any case, it is the students' responsibility to ascertain, understand, and comply with the requirements of a particular institution.

REDEFINING SCHOLARLY INQUIRY

Throughout the 20th century, and increasingly in the last 50 years, research has come to mean a form of scholarly inquiry conducted to discover new knowledge. The emphasis on such research has produced outstanding progress in many fields of study. American institutions of higher education in particular have achieved worldwide reputations for excellence in such inquiry. Many academic leaders, however, have quite recently begun to recognize that an ever-increasing emphasis on this view of inquiry, what Boyer (1990) called the scholarship of discovery, is a narrow one that has led to the increasing denial of attention and resources to problems best addressed through other methods. In his landmark 1990 book, *Scholarship Reconsidered,* Boyer proposed four major categories that should be recognized as equal forms of scholarly inquiry:

- Scholarship of discovery—the traditional view of research as the original discovery of knowledge for its own sake.
- Scholarship of integration—efforts concerned with the integration of knowledge and often involving interdisciplinary study. The scholarship of integration includes the interpretation of findings from the scholarship of discovery and their placement into larger and larger contexts in order to provide broader understanding.
- Scholarship of application—attempts to use scholarship as a tool in solving social problems. Just as medicine attempts to solve problems of illness through the tools of scholarship, so other fields of inquiry attempt to address problems of endemic poverty, substance abuse, or prejudice. It is not the problem addressed that makes an inquiry one of application, but the attempt to address a genuine problem in a scholarly way.
- Scholarship of teaching—the kinds of effort required to be an effective teacher, including projects such as the scholarly development of teaching materials or instructional experiences. The scholarship of teaching does not refer only or even predominantly to the study of pedagogy, which falls, for the most part, into the realm of scholarship of discovery.

THE RESEARCH PROJECT AND ACADEMIC DOCUMENTATION REQUIREMENTS

Most universities with a formal research requirement also require that students produce written documentation of their research and submit that documentation to the university faculty in a formal document called a dissertation, thesis, or senior paper, project, or theme. Although most colleges and universities that require students to complete a research project tend to be quite flexible with respect to the types of research that may be done, they tend to be much less flexible in their requirements for written documentation of that research. Typically, this documentation is expected to conform to certain guidelines and standards regarding structure, content, and writing style. Standardization enables the university to maintain a coherent archive of completed projects. It also provides a structure under which the student can demonstrate mastery of subject matter and the ability to communicate effectively in writing, which are often also principal purposes of the research requirement. Sometimes, however, this standardization may force the student into a writing format that may not seem appropriate for the type of research that has been done. If this conflict seems bothersome, it may be helpful to try to view the research requirement as consisting of two distinct, though related, requirements, one to do research and one to document that research. In some cases it may be appropriate to produce two separate documents: the research itself, and documentation of the procedures and/or problems encountered in completing the research. For example, a project to gather data and produce a directory of graduate programs in an emerging specialization might be better produced as two documents: the directory itself and a document justifying the project, describing the research procedure, and summarizing the results.

RESEARCH PRODUCERS AND CONSUMERS

There is sometimes a tendency, especially in higher education, to make a distinction between the producers and consumers of research, as if an individual must be one or the other but never both. Many often complain of a lack of communication between producers and consumers of research. Those who see themselves as producers complain that those who should be consumers act as if they were unaware of the producer's findings. Those who see themselves as consumers complain that the researchers study irrelevant topics or publish their findings in a form readable only by a few other researchers. Such a conceptual division between producers and consumers may be realistic under the rather narrow view of research as scholarship of discovery. If, on the other hand, one accepts a broader view of research, such as Boyer's, then the distinction fades to one merely of emphasis or degree of involvement. To some extent, everyone who seeks to solve problems or do things more effectively is engaged in both the production and consumption of research.

In any event, everyone involved in the practice of a profession, including physical education, coaching, fitness leadership, and so on, has, by the very fact of that practice, certain obligations with respect to the production and consumption of research. Of those practicing a profession, probably the most fundamental obligation concerning research is to conduct their practice in a manner consistent with the best available relevant information.This means the practitioner has an obligation to maintain a basic familiarity with current research relevant to his or her practice. The practitioner must know where to find relevant research results, as well as be able to read research results with understanding, differentiate between research done well or poorly, and recognize the practical implications of research results.

Although often seen as a consumer of research, the practitioner also has an important role to play as a producer, either directly as a principal investigator carrying out specific research projects, or indirectly, by identifying practical problems that need formal study or by otherwise assisting others in the conduct of formal studies.

Just as the practitioner of a profession has certain obligations concerning research, so the researcher has obligations concerning professional practice affected by his or her research. In addition to conducting research in a careful and ethical manner, these include the obligations to disseminate, and to interpret and clearly communicate the practical implications of the researcher's findings.

TYPES OF RESEARCH STUDIES

The following sections describe a wide variety of categories of research studies. Except where noted otherwise, most meet academic requirements in the majority of academic institutions. However, although the decision rests with the faculty, the responsibility for finding a project that meets academic requirements lies solely with the student.

It is not generally desirable to select a method of study prior to the identification of a research problem. It is far more desirable to select a method of study that will match the demands of a particular problem. Nevertheless, some researchers do seem to focus on a preferred method of study regardless of the problem.

Literature Review

Most types of research studies require the researcher to review the literature relevant to the topic of study. New knowledge is built upon a foundation of existing knowledge. In a typical graduate thesis one chapter is nearly always devoted to reviewing the literature and nearly all scientific articles include some type of literature review. Sometimes, however, a literature review can be a complete piece of research in itself.

A **literature review** intended to stand by itself (as opposed to one that serves as a foundation for a larger study) should generally be *a comprehensive review of the current literature on some topic*. It should serve as a descriptive statement of the current knowledge on that topic. A literature review should be such that reading it would be sufficient to give the reader (assuming the requisite competence) comprehensive knowledge of the chosen subject. For some student projects it may be acceptable to limit the review to materials available locally, though this would rarely be acceptable for a graduate thesis or dissertation.

In order to make a free-standing literature review feasible as a student project, the topic of the study must be defined narrowly enough so that the body of literature to be reviewed is reasonable in size. The volume of literature available today is so vast that too broad a topic definition can cause the volume of

FIGURE 1.3   Topics that are too broadly defined have such huge volumes of related literature that a comprehensive review is impossible. This edited and simplified printout from a computerized library reference search shows the number of items found for two keywords entered separately, then combined to form a more narrow search. It illustrates the importance of specificity in defining a topic for research.

1. Research	15,572 items
2. Ethics	7,184 items
3. Research and Ethics	283 items

relevant material to quickly balloon into thousands of items. The topic of a review should, however, not be so narrow as to be trivial or silly.

Meta-Analysis

The traditional literature review requires the researcher to integrate the findings from many different studies, which may differ from each other in a very wide variety of subtle ways, and to make judgments about those studies in ways that are often subjective. A **meta-analysis** is *a type of literature review in which much of the subjectivity of the review process is reduced by the application of statistical and standardized procedures.* Those procedures enable the researcher to examine the results of multiple studies using two basic approaches: integrative and discriminatory.

In an **integrative meta-analysis,** the *data resulting from various studies with a common dependent measure are mathematically transformed into a common form called an* effect size *using statistical techniques.* These effect sizes are then used as if they were individual data points in a single study. Because the original studies used in a meta-analysis tend to have variations in subject characteristics, the combined study may be more easily generalized than any of the original ones. For example, several studies of the effects of exercise on blood pressure, each using relatively homogeneous groups (with respect to age, gender, race, or other characteristics) might be combined in a meta-analysis to form a study of exercise effects on a more generalized population.

In a **discriminatory meta-analysis,** *the outcomes of different studies, along with information about the characteristics of each (such as subject demographics, status of publication, experimental design used) are used to attempt to explain differences in the results among studies in terms of differences in study characteristics.* In the previous example, a discriminatory meta-analysis might explain differences in results among studies of the effects of exercise on blood pressure as being attributable to study characteristics such as experimental design or to subject characteristics such as gender.

Bibliography

A **bibliography** is *a comprehensive listing of citations of literature on a topic.* It differs from a reference list found following some studies in that it attempts to include everything relating to the topic rather than everything actually used in a study. Well done and with an appropriate topic, a bibliography can be a useful contribution to a discipline or profession. When a bibliography can be prepared by simply ordering a literature search through a computerized service such as DIALOG (discussed in a later chapter), it is probably not appropriate as a student research project. It would probably be far from complete, as most computerized databases are still incomplete in their coverage. However, a bibliography may be very appropriate, not to mention quite useful to other researchers, when the materials listed in the bibliography are rare, obscure, or otherwise difficult for the ordinary researcher to find. For example, a bibliography of some famous person's private papers recently donated to a university library might be a very appropriate student project and a very valuable professional service as well.

Annotated Bibliography

An **annotated bibliography** is *a bibliography of materials relevant to some topic in which each citation is accompanied by a brief critical review or notation.* An annotated bibliography is similar to a review of literature except that it is formatted as a series of bibliographic citations followed by annotations rather than as a well-integrated discussion (see Figure 1.4). Because there is no need to prepare an integrated discussion the annotated bibliography is very much easier writing than a review of literature. The number of items that must be identified, read, and annotated is likely to be substantially higher than the number necessary for a good literature review. As with the simple bibliography, the annotated bibliography is probably most useful and appropriate as a student project when it involves obscure, unusual, rare, or highly specialized items.

FIGURE 1.4   Sample entries in an annotated bibliography.

Edwords, F. (1984). New evidence for Noah's Ark. *The Humanist, 44,* 34.
   A brief but very readable exposé of the truth behind certain claims regarding the existence of Noah's Ark. This article provides a good example of what tends to happen when people attempt to use what they think is science to prove what they already believe to be true.

McIntyre, L. (1975). Mystery of the ancient Nazca lines. *National Geographic, 147*(5), 716–728. Background reading concerning the Nazca lines.

Roberts, R.M. (1989). *Serendipity: Accidental discoveries in science.* New York: John Wiley & Sons, Inc.
   Dozens of stories of serendipity and pseudoserendipity in science and industry. This book makes it very clear that serendipitous discoveries in science result from open minds and careful observations more than sheer luck.

Van Andel, T.H. (1985). *New views on an old planet: Continental drift and the history of the earth.* Cambridge, England, Cambridge University Press.
   A very readable review of the continental drift theory. See pages 85-86 for a brief discussion of the treatment of Alfred Wegener by the community of geologists when he first proposed the theory.

Directory/Reference Publications

A directory is a publication designed to be useful in finding information or resources in some domain. Some familiar examples include the telephone directory, the *Yellow Pages*™, the *Directory of Higher Education*, a library's directory of periodical holdings, *Peterson's Field Guide to the Birds,* and Ulrich's *International Periodicals Directory.* As a rule, directories are alphabetical listings although other forms of ordering may be used in some cases. For example, *Peterson's Field Guide* is arranged according to taxonomic classification. In a sense, therefore, even dictionaries and encyclopedias are forms of directories. A well-conceived directory can be a significant professional service. If a directory is truly useful to enough users, then preparing and publishing it can be quite profitable.

Directories have traditionally been published as printed volumes. Recent developments in computer technology, however, have made feasible the publication of directories in the form of computer databases. Software products such as dBase, Oracle, Paradox, and HyperCard, and mass storage hardware such as video disk drives, CD-ROM (compact disk read only memory) drives, and magneto-optical disk drives make it possible for computerized directories or databases to include materials which could never be included in a printed book. For example, a field guide to birds can be published in a computerized form that includes video sequences showing behaviors of each bird, audio recordings of the calls of each bird, and animated graphics showing the migration patterns of each bird.

Survey

In the practice of research, a **survey** is *an effort to gather and/or infer information in order to gain a general overview of some subject.* For example, a survey may be used to gain an overview of public opinion on how tax money ought to be spent. Another survey might attempt to gather information about trends in the salaries of professional athletes.

There are many ways of conducting surveys but typically a questionnaire is administered to the members of the population under study, either by mail, phone, or face-to-face interview. Data may also be collected by observing subjects who are unaware they are being studied (note that a study of this kind may not be acceptable as a student project because it may violate the rights of the subjects). An example of this kind of study is the measurement of automobile traffic flow, which is usually done by placing a device across the road that increments a counter every time a vehicle rolls over it.

Some surveys involve collecting information from all or most members of the population under study. For example, data for the *Directory of Periodicals in Sport* (Cicciarella, 1992) was gathered by sending a questionnaire to the editor of every sports related periodical that could be identified. Other surveys are conducted by sending a questionnaire to or interviewing a rather small but carefully selected *sample* of members. The election exit polls which have

Proper selection of the sample to be studied is critical in survey research work. In the presidential elections of 1936 and 1948, the predictions from the public opinion polls were grossly inaccurate. In both cases it has been clearly demonstrated that the procedures used to select the sample to be questioned were defective.

FIGURE 1.5   A sample page from the *Directory of Periodicals in Sport,* an example of a directory or reference publication.

(The) Olympian
ISSN No. 0094–9787
Issue reviewed was volume 18, No. 1, July/August 1991

Content

Magazine; 10 issues per year

Olympian is the official magazine of the United States Olympic Committee. Its contents consist mostly of news and articles about the Olympics and athletes in or preparing for the Olympic Games.

Editorial Information

Editor: Bob Condron

1750 E. Boulder St., Colorado Springs, CO 80909 Tel: (719) 578–4529

Readership: Athletes training for Olympic, Pan American, or similar competition, coaches, parents of athletes, spectators, and supporters of the Olympic movement.

Submissions: Submit 2 copies of the manuscript. Types of materials include Olympic related news, competition results, biographies, autobiographies, and interviews of Olympic competitors. Associated Press style. Editorial review.

Blanket permission to reproduce articles, with appropriate credit, is given in each issue unless articles are accompanied by notice of copyright. Review time varies.

Subscription Information

Address: Olympian, Box 1699, Colorado Springs, CO 80909

Individuals $19.92   Institutions $19.92

No information was provided in indexing or availability in micro or electronic forms.

Advertising Information

Display, including covers.   Circulation data not provided.

Olympian, H. O. Zimman Co., Seaport Landing, 152 The Lynnway, Lynn, MA 01901

Tel: (617) 598–9230   Fax: (617) 599–4018

---

been able to predict the winner of every presidential election since 1952 within minutes of the close of the polls are of this type. As long as the sample is properly selected, extremely accurate results can be obtained from a sample size that is only a tiny fraction of the population size.

Surveys can be relatively simple to conduct and are a popular type of research for the fulfillment of academic research requirements. However, they are not as simple as making up a list of questions and collecting answers from the nearest 50 or 100 people. Questions must be very carefully written to avoid confusing, antagonizing, or influencing subjects, as well as to avoid any unnecessary invasion of subjects' privacy. Also, questionnaires must be designed to gather information useful to some purpose other than the mere completion of a course requirement.

Description/Documentation

There are many fields of study in which a substantial body of research consists essentially of a description or documentation of some phenomenon or entity.

For example, many biologists are involved in the preparation of scientific descriptions of new species of plants and animals collected in the field. Another example is a study conducted by an economist that attempts to describe the relationship between economic infrastructure and the long-term prospect of economic growth. A researcher in sports management might want to examine the relationship between customers' satisfaction with such factors as the cleanliness of rest room facilities at athletic events and their likelihood of future attendance at such events.

A descriptive study is not an exercise in creative writing. While the writing in such a study should be neither boring nor simplistic, heavy emphasis should be placed on the accuracy and precision of language and not on entertaining the reader. Such writing constructs as metaphor, alliteration, and simile should be used only with great caution if at all.

Experiments

An **experiment** is *a carefully controlled procedure designed to test a hypothesis.* Somewhat simplistically stated, a true experiment always involves conducting at least two sets of trials that are identical except for one factor, so that if the results of the two sets of trials are different, the difference can only be due to the one differing factor or to random chance.

An experimental study, of course, involves more than simply conducting an experiment and reporting results and conclusions. The experiment itself may be a small part of the project. Before any experiment can be carried out or even designed, the researcher must develop a hypothesis for the experiment to test. This demands substantial preliminary work, including comprehensive reading and logical analysis of relevant literature, participation in discussion or debate with other researchers, and/or careful observation of relevant phenomena.

Experimental studies have a widespread reputation among students and non-scientists as being extremely difficult and complicated, but this reputation is undeserved. In reality, provided the researcher has sufficient background knowledge as well as a good grasp of experimental design, and can exercise good control of experimental procedures, an experiment may be the easiest of all types of studies. Typically, theses and dissertations based on experiments are among the shorter of such reports.

A Simple Experiment

Suppose a medical researcher has developed the hypothesis that a certain chemical called XYZ found in tobacco smoke should cause skin cancer in mice. The researcher would want to conduct an experiment to test that hypothesis. The researcher might start by obtaining 100 laboratory mice. The mice would then be divided randomly into two groups of 50 mice. All the mice would be raised under identical conditions except that the mice in one group would have the XYZ chemical painted on their backs every day. If the hypothesis is correct, then skin cancer should occur much more frequently in the group exposed to the chemical than in the other group.

Beta Test

A **beta test** is *a systematic, thorough, independent evaluation of a product or service.* While products are being developed, they are subjected to a substantial amount of testing and evaluation by their developers. For example, the designers of a new computer software product would probably prepare a series of prototypes and test each in a variety of ways, using each set of results to modify the construction of the next prototype. Such testing is sometimes called **alpha** or *primary testing.* Alpha testing helps to eliminate most of the problems in a new product. However, because the designers of a product are perhaps overly familiar with it, and are perhaps not well informed about some of the unusual ways their product might be used, they often overlook or miss certain defects. This problem is analogous to trying to proofread one's own work. The obvious mistakes will probably be corrected but the more subtle ones will probably be missed. For this reason, new products are often subjected to a secondary or beta test.

Fourteen of the 33 articles in the July 1992 issue of Byte Magazine were product reviews or previews.

A beta test is usually conducted prior to release of the product so that any detected problems can be corrected in the final product. Similar studies, however, may also be conducted, with or without approval from the manufacturer, on products already available for purchase. Such studies are commonly known as product reviews and are often published in such magazines as *Consumer Reports.*

Case Study/Report

A **case study** or report is *a detailed description of an event or incident of some kind, most typically an unusual one.* Some simple examples include accident reports, insurance claims, and statistical reports of athletic events. A newspaper play-by-play account of a basketball game might be called a case report except that in a real case report the wording and writing style should be done in a way that promotes accuracy and precision of meaning rather than to entertain the reader.

Case reports are commonly used in research in medicine, athletic training, law, and many other fields to report unusual incidents or events to others who may have encountered similar incidents or events. For example, athletic trainers regularly submit reports of athletic injuries to a central clearinghouse where they can be compared with other such reports. Through such research it was discovered several years ago that artificial playing surfaces in football were contributing to a higher incidence of certain injuries, and this resulted in some changes in athletic footwear to correct the problem.

In a research context, a case report should be designed to accomplish two principal objectives. First, a case report should provide as much detail as possible about the incident, using language that is as accurate and precise as possible. For example, in an automobile accident report, the words "the car screeched to a halt leaving an uninterrupted, 70-foot skid mark under all four tires," is preferable to "the car screeched to a halt leaving a long skid mark." Second, a case report should present an analytical, objective discussion of the incident from the point of view of the observer reporting it.

Invention/Design

Although the design or invention of a new or improved product or service is not a common approach to completion of a student research requirement in most fields of study, such research is as valid as any other. If the student has the requisite ability and has access to the necessary resources, such research should be encouraged.

A project to design or invent a new product need not be limited to development of products in the form of machines or other physical objects. In the fields of health and physical education the development of such things as a new game or new game strategy, or a new type of computer program is more likely than an improved design for a football helmet or a more powerful tennis racket.

A research project ought to make some kind of genuine contribution to knowledge, particularly a project in the category of invention or design. The true test of any invention, at least in the marketplace, is whether it serves any practical purpose. Thus, a project such as a new game should be one that attempts to produce a genuinely new game, not just a minor change in an old game. The invention of basketball in 1891 would qualify as a valid research project but a mere change in the rules, such as the adoption of a smaller ball for women's basketball, would not qualify.

> ### An Improved Method for Overnight Mail Delivery
>
> The design of an improved product or service can be profitable as well as a valid student research project. In the 1960s a business student at Yale named Frederick Smith wrote a paper describing an overnight mail delivery system in which planes loaded with packages from all over the U. S. would converge on a single city, be reloaded after all the packages were sorted, and then fly back in the early morning with packages for their home cities. The idea was judged as "not feasible" and given an average grade. Despite this and other criticism, Smith started a company in 1973 to test his idea. Having overcome some early difficulties, his firm is still around. It's called Federal Express (Ketteringham, 1987).

Artistic Work

The creation of a work of art is certainly just as valid a form of research as a scientific investigation, although it may be much harder to evaluate academically. Artistic work obviously includes painting, sculpture, choreography, musical composition, dramatic script writing, poetry, and many other traditional fields of expression. Among the less obvious or less traditional forms of artistic expression are photography, creative writing, and architecture. In the field of sport the creative use of video for purposes of education or entertainment can also be considered as artistic research even though the value of much of our sports television may be questionable.

Few would argue that the creation of a work of art is not valid research, at least for those whose field of endeavor is artistic creation. However, defining just what constitutes a work of art is much more difficult. A sheet of canvas covered with paint does not, per se, qualify as a work of art. Such an object could be made by a machine or even accidentally by a gust of wind knocking over some cans of paint. At what point does paint applied to a canvas become a work of art? We cannot even apply the test of market acceptance (if people are willing to buy it, then it is art). The paintings of Van Gogh were never commercially accepted in his lifetime, though now they sell for millions. "Art is in the eye of the beholder" may be a trite statement, but it is quite true.

Restorative Work

Restorative work involves *the repair or reconditioning of works of art, artifacts, or important documents.* The mere repair of ordinary items does not fall into the category of restorative research. Although not common in the field of sport and

Electronic Textbooks

In the near future, some printed textbooks could be replaced by computerized multimedia textbooks. Such books would display text and illustrations on a computer screen just as regular books do on paper. However, illustrations could turn into full motion video with stereo sound, or animated graphics at the click of a mouse.

exercise science, restorative research is a very important and very technical form of research in a wide variety of fields of study including the arts, archaeology, and library science.

Biography

A **biography** is *a personal history of some person written by another person.* Biographies of famous persons, particularly sports stars, film personalities, and political figures fill many shelves in bookstores and are quite popular. Usually such books are written and published with the aid and consent of the subject, although not always. Like any good work of history, a good biography is not just a recitation of dates or a simple narrative of events, but an attempted explanation as to how and why things happened the way they did as well as the impact of those events.

A biography undertaken as research should conscientiously seek the truth and scrupulously avoid the innuendo, hyperbole, and other insupportable claims often found in popular literature. The biographer may, of course, venture into interpretations of the evidence or even into speculation, but these passages should be clearly identified.

Position Paper

A **position paper** is *a statement or essay describing the views of an individual or organization on some issue.* For example, the American College of Sports Medicine has published several position papers dealing with recommended policies for exercise testing and prescription and the safe conduct of athletic events. However, a position paper should do more than simply state an opinion. Certainly if it is to be accepted as research, the bulk of a position paper should serve to set forth the reasoning behind the opinion being expressed.

Learning Resource Development

The development of learning resources refers to the authorship of materials that facilitate learning, including textbooks, instructional videos, computer assisted instruction (CAI) software, instructional films, and other materials. It also refers to the creation of information retrieval systems and similar archival resources commonly found in libraries.

New technological developments are opening up new opportunities for the development of learning resources in the domain of *multimedia*. **Multimedia** is *a combination of computers, television, CD-ROMs, and other media into a single, integrated system.* Materials can now be published that combine computer displays of text with synthetic speech, computer graphics, television displayed on the computer's screen, and stereo sound.

Exposé/Investigative Report

An **exposé** is *a detailed, carefully documented report of an investigation of some event or situation, often done surreptitiously or without consent of the* *persons involved.* On June 17, 1971, there was a break-in of an office in a building in Washington, DC. At first no one took much notice but the fact that the victim of the break-in was the headquarters of a major political party involved in a presidential campaign did attract some notice. After a few months it was determined that some of the people involved in the break-in had connections inside the White House with the Nixon administration, but they were minor officials and most reporters lost interest. Two reporters at the *Washington Post* did not lose interest. Against all odds they continued to investigate and to report their findings in the *Post.* More than two years later dozens of senior officials of the Nixon administration were disgraced and on their way to jail, and President Nixon himself was forced to resign in what became known as the Watergate scandal. The work by reporters Woodward and Bernstein of the *Washington Post,* a shining example of dogged investigative reporting, won them a Pulitzer Prize.

The topic of an investigative report need not be as grand as the Watergate scandal. Recently, for example, a Charlotte, North Carolina, television station used a video camera to record city employees doing personal business while they were supposed to be working for the city. Several years earlier, another television station in the same city used a camera with a telephoto lens to document and expose racial discrimination at a Veterans of Foreign Wars (VFW) swimming pool.

An investigative report is well worth considering as a method of research. However, such projects should be undertaken with full understanding of the risks. Persons or organizations exposed as having been engaged in unethical, immoral, or illegal activities can sometimes respond in a violent manner. Also, an accusation of wrongdoing that is inadequately documented can lead to a lawsuit for libel.

Longitudinal Study

A **longitudinal study** is *any study examining a phenomena over an extended period of time.* The Framingham Heart Study, which has studied the development of heart disease in selected individuals over more than 20 years, is an excellent example. Similar studies looking at factors that may affect educational outcomes over the course of 12 years of public schooling probably ought to be conducted, as well.

The longitudinal study is a very important method for detecting and measuring subtle, long-term relationships. Because of the extended period of time required, longitudinal studies are generally a poor choice for student research projects, even at the advanced level. For some kinds of research questions, however, information of a longitudinal nature can often be obtained using historical methods. For example, the annual growth rings of trees can be used for estimating annual rainfall where the tree grew. Although the hypothesis that rainfall varies cyclically could be experimentally tested with a longitudinal study lasting 200 or 300 years, it would be much more efficient to examine past rainfall patterns by looking at cross sections of 200- or 300-year-old trees. Similarly, hypotheses concerning climatic or geologic history over millions of years may be tested by examining layers of sedimentary rocks in cliffs or oil well core samples, or in core samples from the ocean bottom or glacier ice.

TERMS

alpha test	hypothesis
annotated bibliography	integrative meta-analysis
beta test	literature review
bibliography	longitudinal study
biography	meta-analysis
case study	multimedia
discriminatory meta-analysis	position paper
experiment	restorative work
exposé	survey

EXERCISES

1. Make a list of 10 different ideas or attitudes that interfere with scientific or professional creativity. Discuss with classmates how these might be avoided.

2. Prepare a set of at least 10 index cards, each identifying a possible question for research that you might be interested in answering. Share and discuss these with classmates.

3. Identify all of the documentation requirements for one or more type(s) of student research project(s) at your institution and obtain samples of all necessary forms or checklists for that documentation.

4. Locate in your library and other nearby places at least one example of each type of research study described in this chapter.

5. Form groups of five to eight classmates. Hold an informal meeting outside of class hours for the purpose of sharing ideas or problems for research.

6. Interview one or more faculty member(s) engaged in current research projects regarding ideas for additional research topics.

ADDITIONAL RESOURCES WITH ANNOTATION

American College of Sports Medicine (1993). ACSM position stand: Physical activity, physical fitness, and hypertension. *Medicine and Science in Sports and Exercise, 25* (10), i–x.
An example of a research-based position statement.

Charlson, C. (Producer). (1993). *Secrets of the Psychics.* [Video]. Boston, MA: WGBH Educational Foundation.
An episode of the NOVA television program concerning claims of psychic and other paranormal phenomena and the debunking efforts of James Randi. A transcript is available through Journal Graphics, Grant St., Denver, CO.

Edwords, F. (1984). New evidence for Noah's ark. *The Humanist, 44,* 34.
A brief but very readable exposé of the truth behind certain claims regarding the existence of Noah's Ark. This article provides a good example of what tends to happen

when people attempt to use what they think is science to prove what they already believe to be true.

McIntyre, L. (1975). Mystery of the ancient Nazca lines. *National Geographic, 147* (5), 716–728.
Background reading concerning the Nazca lines.

Roberts, R.M. (1989). *Serendipity: Accidental discoveries in science.* New York: John Wiley & Sons, Inc.
Dozens of stories of serendipity and pseudoserendipity in science and industry. This book makes it very clear that serendipitous discoveries in science result from open minds and careful observations more than sheer luck.

Van Andel, T.H. (1985). *New views on an old planet: Continental drift and the history of the earth.* Cambridge, England: Cambridge University Press.
A very readable review of the continental drift theory. See pages 85–86 for a brief discussion of the treatment of Alfred Wegener by the community of geologists when he first proposed the theory.

2

COMPLETING THE ACADEMIC RESEARCH REQUIREMENT

Though all students may not agree, many institutions of higher education include a research or investigative requirement in their degree requirements with very good reason. Such a requirement enables students to demonstrate, as can no other curricular component, that they have become independent learners and that they have the ability to communicate effectively in writing.

In an ideal world, the role of the university and its faculty in each student's research project might be very simple and limited. A faculty member would simply say to the student, "Here are the keys to the library and the laboratories; now go do some research." The student would then be left to sink or swim, relying solely on the skills gained during the preceding years of education. Unfortunately, ours is not an ideal world, and the method just described would be unlikely to produce success for more than a small minority of students. Thus, even though a principal objective of the research requirement is to demonstrate the capacity for independent learning, the student is not expected to work entirely without guidance.

To assist the student in completing a research project successfully, a certain support structure is provided. Although the exact nature of that support structure varies among institutions and even among departments within institutions, it generally consists of some combination of research seminars, faculty advisory committees, consultation services on research design and statistics, and a schedule of target dates and deadlines for completion of each step of the research and documentation process. Available support may also include access to computers, laboratories, and other physical facilities, as well as the opportunity for interaction with other students and faculty. Details about the general purpose and nature of some of these support structures at any specific institution must, of course, be obtained locally.

TARGET DATES AND DEADLINES

When students fail to meet research requirements the cause is far more often than not a failure to *finish* one or more aspects of the project. A disappointingly high number of students at the doctoral level, in fact, complete all of their course work and comprehensive examinations and then never quite seem to get around to their dissertations. They seem to just get stuck on some part of the project, or the pressures of working or other interests get in the way, until the time limit for completion of the project runs out.

In order to trigger intervention when progress slows down, academic departments may provide students with a schedule of target dates and deadlines by which each phase of a research project should be completed. Target dates should be regarded as guidelines. They are established through experience that students who have not completed each phase of the project by approximately the corresponding target date are unlikely to complete the research requirement in time to complete their degree and graduate on schedule. Failure to meet a target date does not preclude finishing the project on time, nor does meeting any target guarantee timely graduation. Deadlines, on the other hand, are not estimates of when project phases should be completed, but firm boundaries. Particularly when they apply to the submission of the final research report, deadlines are necessary to ensure that there will be time for materials to be reviewed or processed. In addition to the final review by the supervising faculty member or committee, for example, student research papers, especially theses and dissertations, often must be reviewed by library personnel for compliance with archival requirements. The student who misses a deadline should expect that graduation will be delayed by at least one semester.

FINDING A TOPIC

Finding a topic is essentially a process of identifying a problem that is of interest to the student, acceptable to the supervising faculty, and has a reasonable prospect for success with the time and resources available to the student.

There are at least two important characteristics the student should look for in a potential research topic. First, the topic should be something of significant interest to the student. While an important factor in any research project, even a simple, library-based term project, a strong personal interest in finding the answer to a research question is critical in a project of the duration and intensity of a thesis. A lack of interest can turn what should be a passionately exciting and intensely rewarding academic experience into one of insurmountable drudgery and failure. Second, the project needs to be *do-able* in a reasonable amount of time and with the resources available to the student. A student may have an abiding interest in designing an experiment to go aboard the space shuttle but unless he or she has access to a large grant or is personally rather wealthy the resources for such a project will not exist. Similarly, a student may want to study the effects of a new approach to education in the public schools, but while such research is needed very much, the length of time required—12 years or more—is not reasonable for a student project.

> It is a good practice for students to assemble and maintain a small database of potential ideas for research. A pack of index cards or a simple computerized database can be used to record ideas as they occur and then to sort through ideas when a topic is needed. Following the advice of Dr. Feynmann (see Chapter 1) the student should try to record every idea that occurs—the bad ones can be discarded later.

Ideally, a research topic should be derived from a genuine problem encountered by the student in the course of preliminary study, professional practice, or reading of the professional literature. However, it is not at all uncommon for students, even those at the advanced graduate level, to do their research on a topic obtained from a supervising faculty member. Such topics might be selected by the student from a list

---

Reducing a Research Topic to a Do-able Project

Student: I'm having trouble defining my thesis topic.

Professor: What do you think you want to study?

S: I want to do my thesis on learning to swim.

P: That seems rather broad. Can you be a bit more specific?

S: Well, really on the teaching of swimming; how to teach people to swim.

P: That's still an awfully large, complex topic.

S: I want to find out the best way to teach people to swim.

P: What do you know about the subject?

S: I know what is taught about teaching swimming doesn't seem to work very well. Not just for me, either; a lot of swimming instructors I know feel the same way.

P: What else do you know?

S: I've read a lot of studies of swimming instruction. All sorts of teaching methods have been tested but the results seem inconclusive. It doesn't seem to matter how the instruction is presented. Maybe it's not how we teach but what we teach.

P: You could have something there. Tell me more!

S: Beginning swimmers seem to get disoriented when they have to put their faces in the water and only come up looking sideways. Also, I wonder about raising the arms out of the water; those with marginal buoyancy don't really need to lift all that weight out of the water all the time. Maybe if they were taught the breast stroke or the backstroke they wouldn't have so many problems.

P: I think you just came pretty close to stating a testable hypothesis for an experimental study!

S: I did?

P: Sure. You just said you wanted to teach two or three groups to swim—one using the current crawl stroke and the others using the other strokes you mentioned. You just said you would expect one of the latter to produce better results than the former.

S: Gee, I guess I did!

P: If you can design and set up an experiment where you control for other factors that might affect the results, you'll have your thesis just about finished.

S: Thank you, I guess that wasn't so hard after all!

Although the above conversation illustrates the process of narrowing down a general interest to a do-able study, the process more commonly takes place over a much longer period of time—perhaps several months or more—and may include more steps as well as one or more reversals of thought.

---

of possible topics offered by the faculty member or they might simply be assigned without option. That research topics might be readily available from and even willingly given by a faculty member should not be surprising. University faculty members who have developed a significant research program of their own typically will have identified a long list of research questions in the course of developing that program and usually find that every question answered generates several additional questions. The availability of ready-made research topics from a faculty member may vary according to the faculty member's field of study or to the type of research being conducted. Indeed, the availability of one or more faculty members who can and will make such topics available may be a very important factor to consider in selecting a graduate school.

It can be argued that what distinguishes the fully educated from the partially educated person is that the fully educated person has learned that there is much he or she has yet to learn. For the established professional engaged in daily practice, finding a topic in need of research should rarely be a problem. Potential topics are encountered almost daily as part of the difficulties and questions encountered in everyday practice. A more likely problem is, in fact, deciding which of dozens of research ideas to pursue first. For the student whose experience is confined by the limits of the theoretical, classroom environment, however, identification of an appropriate research topic may sometimes require a bit more effort. Still, if the student is genuinely interested in his or her own chosen field of study and is reasonably knowledgeable of the fundamental ideas, concepts, and controversies of that field, a systematic approach to identifying and selecting a topic should not be too difficult.

For the person engaged in an active professional practice, there is often no need to *look* for a research topic at all. Rather, research projects are initiated constantly in the attempt to find solutions to the day-to-day problems such practice encounters. The student's own experience, limited though it may be, should be the first place to look for a research topic. Even if the student has no direct, practical experience in a relevant field of study, the academic curriculum in most fields will have provided some degree of simulated experience in the form of field observations, laboratory exercises, practica, and so on. If the student is fully engaged in such experiences and questions or difficulties are noted, these experiences should provide a rich source of at least general areas in need of study that can be gradually refined into a research topic.

The next place to look for possible research topics is the literature of the student's field of study—in current and very recent issues of the professional and semi-professional journals serving the field of study. As knowledge is gained in a field of study one discovers more and more that much is still to be learned. Regular, careful reading of articles in journals followed by reflection on the implications of those articles is a very important part of one's professional education, whether formally required as part of a curriculum or not. Articles that report the findings of research will often include recommendations or suggestions for future research, and occasional articles may be found that focus exclusively on suggesting directions for future research. Simple familiarity with current research and with the issues and controversies discussed in non-research professional journals may also lead to many ideas for new lines of study. Review or exploration of data from sources outside the student's immediate professional domain may provide inspiration. Huge volumes of data are collected on a regular basis by governmental agencies, businesses, educational institutions, and other organizations. The census, public records of real estate transactions, polling data, licensing records, stock market listings, and court records are but a few examples. Most such data is readily open for public inspection and can offer rich sources for researchers. Exploratory examination of such data may reveal or suggest relationships or trends that can be examined more formally.

Familiarity with new devices, instruments, methods of analysis or inquiry, technological advances, and other new developments may also provide a rich source of research ideas. Old, intractable problems often succumb unexpectedly to fresh approaches.

A third source of ideas for research is free and extended discussion with active professionals and other students. Students and faculty in many of the larger or more active graduate schools often form study groups for this purpose. The opportunity for such discussion is, for many, one of the highlights of attendance at many professional conferences. Student study or discussion groups need not be formally organized, take minutes, elect officers, or engage in any of the trappings of formal clubs or organizations. Merely meeting on a regular basis in a voluntary, informal setting that encourages uninhibited discussion is often enough. Study groups can often be very productive, not only of ideas for research, but as sources of assistance in executing the research as well.

On-line conferences and similar computerized services may offer another tool for topic identification, as well as for sharing research findings. Most such conferences may best be described as computerized bulletin boards devoted to messages concerning specific topics. Conference participants may read items contributed by others—often in their sequence of contribution—post comments or suggestions, ask questions, and post their own contributions. Such conferences are different from real conversations in that the dialogue is not in real time and is conducted through the intermediary of a computer keyboard and screen.

In addition to providing a vehicle for discussion with others sharing common interests, on-line conferences can sometimes be used to distribute useful research materials, including executable computer programs. For example, a researcher needing a program to calculate an estimation of body fat from skinfold measures might be able to download such a program from an on-line conference dealing with a closely related subject. However, the researcher should be very careful in handling such matters as the downloading of copyrighted materials without the permission of the copyright owner is illegal. Also, the downloading of computer programs is frequently the vector by which computer viruses (programs that damage other programs and files) spread from computer to computer.

Through such systems as the Internet, on-line computer conferences can be conducted quite easily among people from all over the United States and most of the world, often at little or no cost other than that of access to the telephone system.

Finally, attendance and active participation at research and professional meetings can be a rich source of research ideas. As such meetings tend to be highly focused on specific areas of study, they are attended by large numbers of the most creative researchers with related interests. Such researchers are often more than happy to discuss ideas with genuinely interested students. Sessions at such meetings may be called by different names. A **free paper session** refers to *a series of brief, rather formal presentations of papers, usually on closely related*

Although scientific symposia tend to be much more formal, the term originally referred to an informal get-together for conversation and good times. The word itself derives from a Greek phrase meaning *drinking together.*

topics. A **symposium** is *a presentation of one or two papers followed by several responses or critiques by other presenters, although the original meaning of the word implies a more freewheeling, unrehearsed discussion.* A **poster session** consists of *a setting in which several, often several dozen, research projects are presented in poster displays. Those in attendance are free to move around, observe the displays, and freely question the researchers.*

SELECTING AN ADVISOR AND ADVISORY COMMITTEE

Procedurally, the selection of a faculty advisor and/or committee for supervising a student research project is controlled by rules determined by each academic institution. Such rules may specify matters such as which faculty members are eligible to serve on or chair committees, whether and how many committee members may come from departments other than the student's department of enrollment, upper or lower limits to the size of each committee, and how replacements are to be handled when necessary. The committee may be appointed by the student's academic advisor, by the department chairperson, by a director of student research, or in some other manner. The student may or may not have any influence in the matter. Usually, however, it is largely a matter of arriving at a consensus among the student, department head, and those asked to serve as advisor (chair) or as committee members.

Typically, a student research project is conducted under the supervision of a committee of at least three (almost always an odd number) faculty members and/or other resource persons, one of whom serves as chairperson. This committee has at least two important roles. First, perhaps with the chairperson acting in its name, the committee supervises the progress of the project, approving the student's research proposal and any requested variances from the approved proposal which become necessary during the course of the project, and certifying when the project and supporting documentary report have been completed satisfactorily. Second, members of the committee serve as expert advisors to the student on matters relevant to the conduct of the project, such as research design, statistical treatment of data, computer usage, or manuscript editing, and they should be selected at least partially for their ability to provide such advice.

As a rule, at least one committee member—probably the chairperson—should be a faculty member who is highly knowledgeable of the research subject matter and who has a strong interest in the outcome of the project. This person will usually serve as the chairperson if he or she has sufficient research experience and has, in some cases, the appropriate academic rank. If such expertise is known or anticipated to be needed the student should not be shy about requesting the assignment to the committee of persons with requisite capabilities.

THE RESEARCH PROPOSAL

The research proposal is a written document submitted by the student to the student's advisory committee for the dual purposes of describing the research to be undertaken in fulfillment of the student research requirement and requesting approval to proceed. When the proposal is approved it becomes an agreement between the student and the advisory committee as to what will be done and what will be accepted for the student research requirement. The research proposal may be a brief series of statements identifying the research problem and the method of inquiry or a substantially more lengthy document demonstrating the student's knowledge of the topic as well as describing the problem. The proposal may be required to be divided into two or three chapters following a traditional thesis format, or the elements usually assigned to different chapters may be allowed to be combined into a single chapter. If two chapters are required, the first will probably be composed of a formal problem statement combined with a review of related literature, and the second will describe the investigatory methods to be used. If three chapters are required, the first two will be a formal problem statement and review of literature, and the third will be methodology.

A successful research proposal will clearly and unambiguously communicate to the advisory committee what it needs to know in order to make a decision to approve the project. Put simply, the committee needs to know what the student intends to do, whether the project is worth doing, what methods the student will use, and whether or not the student has the knowledge and resources to successfully complete the project.

The student research proposal and the portions of the final research report dealing with corresponding information (i.e., the problem statement, review of literature, and methods) are essentially the same except that the problem statement and methodology sections of the proposal are written in the future tense, and the corresponding portions of the research report are written in the past tense. This is done in order to accurately reflect the truth of what is going to be done and what has been done. Details of the structure and content of the research proposal are provided in Chapter 3.

THE PROBLEM HEARING

As a rule, once a student research proposal has been approved by the student's research advisory committee, the agreement between the student and the committee cannot be unilaterally changed. The student has formally stated what is to be done and the committee has agreed that that will be acceptable toward the student research requirement.

Sometimes, after a research proposal has been approved, a change becomes necessary or desirable. Proposed subjects may become unavailable, vital equipment may cease to function, or perhaps a better research design or statistical treatment of data may be identified. If such changes are extremely minor, the chairperson of the advisory committee *may* have the standing to approve them without consulting other committee members. The student, however, has no such authority. Deviations from the approved proposal *might* be retroactively approved, but the student has no assurance of such approval.

If changes to the approved proposal are needed, the most common procedure is to hold what is usually called a **problem hearing**. This is *a meeting of the advisory committee in which a proposed change and rationale for the change are presented.* The committee will then approve, disapprove, or approve with modifications or conditions the requested change. The problem hearing may be formal or informal. If the request is simple and unlikely to require clarification or discussion, the student may be able to submit a request in writing and not actually attend the problem hearing.

Although changes are generally requested by the student for approval by the committee, there is no reason changes cannot be requested by the committee for approval by the student.

HANDLING DATA

Whether the method of inquiry is experimental, historical, descriptive, or of some other approach, most student research projects involve the collection and/or analysis of data. Data may consist of direct, numerical measurements, responses to survey questions, the text of an interview or manuscript, the content of articles in the literature, or any of a hundred other forms of information.

If data is poorly handled, many months of hard work may be transformed into worthless trash. The details of precisely how data should be handled depend significantly on the kind of research being done and the conditions under which data is collected. However, the following suggestions should apply generally:

- Keep an up-to-date research notebook or log.

  Even if data is not recorded directly into a notebook, one may be used as a sequential record of progress and may be very helpful in tracing the source of problems or errors identified later.

- Never throw data away.

  Even if data is known to be in error and cannot be used, it should be kept. If defective data is thrown away or lost it leaves the remaining data open to question.

- Never make erasures.

  Erasures in original data could be interpreted as falsification of data. When mistakes are made in recording data they should be crossed out neatly but left readable. Anyone suspicious of the data can then analyze the errors. Genuine errors will usually show no systematic pattern.

- Handle the data as little as possible.

  Every time data is handled, such as when it is transcribed from handwritten notes into a computer file, errors may be introduced.

- Keep a backup copy in a safe place.

  If there is no backup and the original data is lost, there is no alternative to starting over by collecting new data. Keep a backup copy of data in a place safe from loss, theft, fire, and all other hazards. Remember that even if the loss of data is someone else's fault, the data will still be lost.

- When manually recording data, be very careful with handwriting.

  Data that is in doubt because of difficult handwriting cannot be used. Pairs of characters such as "O" and "0", "Z" and "3", "l" and "1", and "i" and "j" are often confused when handwritten.

- Always keep original data forms or records.

  Original data forms and records can be used to correct mistakes made in transcription and sometimes to verify that the data is genuine. For the protection of subjects, names and other information that could identify subjects may have to be destroyed, isolated and kept in a separate location, or encrypted in some manner.

TECHNICAL ASSISTANCE

Though a student may receive substantial training through course work in research design, statistical analysis, computer usage, or other technical areas related to research, a need for technical assistance is to be expected. Even faculty members in research universities who spend most of their time engaged in research frequently need such assistance. Technical assistance may be available through special services offered by academic departments, or it may have to be aggressively sought out. It is not at all uncommon to find statistical consulting offered by the mathematics department, computer assistance offered by the computer science department, and help in locating archival material offered by the library. The student may be expected to pay for such assistance, especially when obtained from outside the department or university. Technical assistance may also be available from a faculty member whose own work provides expert technical knowledge in a domain other than that normally associated with his or her department. For example, many faculty members will have advanced knowledge of certain aspects of computing even though they may not be in the computer science department.

THE ORAL PRESENTATION

Most student research requirements include an oral presentation of the project at its conclusion. The oral presentation serves several important purposes. Formally, it serves as a final check on the quality of the student's work and as a chance for members of the committee to examine the student's work and interpretation of that work. Particularly at the graduate level, this presentation is often called an **oral defense** because *the presentation is followed by questioning designed to challenge the work.* The oral presentation is also an opportunity for the student to share newly discovered knowledge with others. Particularly at the doctoral level, by the time the oral presentation is given the student should be more knowledgeable about the topic (at least in a narrow sense) than anyone and is therefore obligated to enlighten others.

Normally, the presentation portion of the defense will be brief and very direct, concentrating on a concise review of the rationale of the study, an outline of the design or procedures employed, and an explanation of the results. The student should not try to include every detail of the study. Such details will be included in the written documentation and should have been read by the student's committee in advance. Well-prepared slides or other visual illustrations are often helpful. Chapter 12 offers suggestions regarding the preparation of such materials.

The student should avoid making a presentation by reading a prepared text. Presentations which are read are difficult to follow unless the presenter is an excellent speech writer and speaker. Reading a paper may even suggest to listeners that the presenter doesn't understand the material.

Do's and Don'ts for Oral Presentations

Do

1. speak from brief notes
2. use simple, easy-to-read visual aids
3. rehearse beforehand
4. try to maintain good eye contact with listeners

Don't

1. try to read your paper verbatim
2. try to present too much
3. exceed the time limit
4. mumble

FINAL MATTERS

The student should not expect that submission of the final draft of a research paper and the oral presentation will complete the academic research requirement. Assuming the advisory committee accepts the paper, there will still be several matters to take care of to complete the research requirement. These may take a substantial amount of time if they are not anticipated. Though such final details may vary among institutions, they are likely to include some or all of the following:

Preparation of the Final Manuscript

Typically, an academic institution requires the submission of one or more copies of the final manuscript to its library or to the student's department. Any spelling errors, punctuation mistakes, and other minor problems detected by the advisory committee will have to be corrected in this manuscript. Also, in order to prevent deterioration over time or to maintain consistency with other materials, a particular type of paper, certain typefaces, or other special requirements may be specified.

The use of "acid free" paper helps prevent yellowing of the paper over time.

Binding

Because unbound or softbound documents do not last long, students are usually required to submit one or more *hardbound* copies of the final research manuscript for archival storage. The actual process of binding the student's manuscript is generally handled by the university library or by an outside vendor under contract to the university, although the cost of binding is borne by the student. Typically, the student must simply deliver the final manuscript along with payment or proof of payment of the binding fee to the appropriate librarian.

Extra Copies

Universities generally require a specific number of bound copies of a student's research paper for archival storage, usually from one to three. The student, however, may want to have additional copies bound as personal mementos or for use as gifts. Especially in the case of a doctoral dissertation or master's thesis, for which the student has invested a tremendous amount of effort, having a few bound copies as keepsakes will probably be well worth the additional cost. Also, it is a common tradition (and perhaps politically astute) to present a bound copy of a thesis or dissertation to the advisory committee chairperson, particularly in cases in which the chairperson has made a substantial or extraordinary contribution toward completion of the project.

Publication in Microfilm

Nearly all doctoral dissertations and many master's theses are made available for use by other scholars through University Microfilms International (UMI) or similar services. Listings and abstracts of available dissertations are published in Dissertation Abstracts International and complete documents may be ordered through UMI. In order to permit these services to fill requests, the author must provide the service with a complete, unbound copy of the manuscript along with a signed copyright release form or letter. If submission of such materials is part of the student research requirement, information on where to obtain forms and submit materials should be obtained from the student's advisory committee chairperson.

Electronic Storage

Some universities may require the student to submit copies of the research report in the form of a computer-readable document, such as a diskette file. Storage of such reports in computer-readable form makes their use by future scholars more flexible. Such a requirement may be in addition to or in lieu of the submission of bound, paper copies to the library.

In order to be useful, computer-readable documents must be in a form compatible with the system that will be used for retrieval. Details of compatibility should be obtained from the student's advisory committee chairperson and may include specifications for type of media, storage format of the media, and digital code used to encrypt the text. Since conversion from one media or format to another may be difficult, the student would be wise to determine such requirements very early in the research project—probably in the proposal stage—so that compatible materials can be used and no conversion will be necessary.

 ## TERMS

free paper session   problem hearing
oral defense   symposium
poster session

EXERCISES

1. Obtain or assemble a list of all deadlines and target dates for the kind of research you are required to complete.

2. Prepare a statement outlining who among available faculty members would be best to serve as your research advisor and why.

3. Interview one or more faculty members in your department to determine the kinds of research in which each is interested and the purposes of projects currently under way.

4. Obtain information regarding the kinds of technical assistance, if any, currently available to students engaged in research at your institution. Find out what must be done to request such assistance.

5. Attend one or more sessions of research presentations at a nearby conference. Take notes on at least one presentation and then attempt to summarize the reported study.

3

THE RESEARCH REPORT

According to most history textbooks, the continents of North and South America were *discovered* by an Italian named Christopher Columbus. Those books say little about a Viking named Leif Eriksson who beat Columbus by several hundred years, and nothing at all about millions of Native Americans who had long established complex civilizations when Columbus (or Eriksson) arrived and whose ancestors predated Columbus by tens of thousands of years. Why does Columbus get the credit? Certainly a Eurocentric viewpoint in those giving the credit explains why it is given to a European, but why Columbus over Eriksson? There may be many reasons, but certainly an important one is that Eriksson's "discovery" was kept a secret by the Vikings while that of Columbus quickly became widely known. In effect, Columbus *published* his discovery and Eriksson did not.

The principal purpose of research, regardless of the field of study, is to find the *truth* and thereby advance the *body of knowledge*. That is, not the body of knowledge held by the researcher but the body of knowledge held by humankind. It is, therefore, not enough to *do* research and make discoveries. It is necessary *to make public* or **publish** the results of research. Publication, whether formal or informal, serves two purposes that are critical to advancing the body of knowledge. First, for the results of research to become part of the body of knowledge, they must be transmitted from the original researcher to others. Second, the details of a research project must be made available to others so that they may be critically reviewed, replicated, or otherwise challenged in order to detect and correct mistakes.

A research report is a story about the conduct of a research project, including the purposes of the project, the details of conduct of the project, results, and interpretation of those results. However, though it may be characterized as a story, a research report is not a piece of informal writing such as a novel or short story. It is, instead, a very formal and structured piece of writing, requiring a very high standard of accuracy and precision of wording, an avoidance of misleading figures of speech or exaggeration, and an attention to accuracy and detail not necessary in most other kinds of writing.

"Once upon a time when the world was young and the earth was ruled by dinosaurs . . ."

This kind of writing may be appropriate for a bad novel but does not belong in a research report.

It is fairly common for introductory textbooks on research procedures to attempt to describe *the* way to write a research report or paper. Generally, these publications describe a model based on the historical format of a dissertation or scientific paper. It is becoming increasingly obvious, however, that such a model is inappropriate in many cases. A rigid model for research papers is inadequate for any but the most narrowly defined application because no one model can meet the reporting needs of all areas of study or all approaches to research. A model appropriate for an experimental study leads to endless confusion when applied to a report of a creative research project. Even different sciences have different traditions with respect to the structure of reports of experimental studies. Also, a rigid model is inappropriate as an academic exercise because it cannot meet the different and often contradictory requirements for research reporting for which the student is being trained, which might involve several different areas of study or approaches to research.

This chapter, therefore, does not attempt to prescribe a rigid format for theses or other research reports. Indeed, it counsels against such a practice and instead provides a general description of the structure and various elements of such documents. The prescription for the precise composition of a research paper for academic purposes is left with the supervising faculty where it belongs.

PRELIMINARY PAGES AND APPENDED MATERIALS

Some types of very detailed research reports, principally the thesis and the dissertation, are composed of three distinct parts: preliminary pages, the main body of the report, and appended materials. Other forms of research reports, such as papers published in journals, may consist of only the main body or may include portions of the other parts in abbreviated form.

Preliminary material is not essential to the research report in the sense that understanding of the report would be impaired without it, but it does serve a purpose. **Preliminary pages** *include the title page and may include such items as table of contents, list of figures, list of illustrations, acknowledgments, dedication page, and abstract.* When the report is submitted to an academic institution as a dissertation, thesis, or even as a term paper, there is usually also a page for supervising faculty to certify acceptance of the report or to assign a grade. Preliminary pages serve as guides to locating the essential components of the report and as a way to recognize major contributions toward completion of the work. The preliminary pages of an academic paper also provide a place for items that are important in linking the research report to a course or degree requirement, such as a signature page.

The appended pages of a research report are those pages that follow the main body of the report. Appended pages may include such items as a reference list, bibliography, annotated bibliography, index, tables of raw data, copies of tests, forms, or correspondence used in the study, and any other material which does not properly belong in the main body but which serves as documentation of the study.

A **reference list** is nearly always included. *It is a listing of correct and complete bibliographic citations for all published materials cited as references in the main body of the report.* A **bibliography** is included far less commonly than a reference list. *It is a listing of correct bibliographic citations of all published materials matching the criteria defined for the bibliography, whether used as citations in the main body of the report or not.* An **annotated bibliography** is *a bibliography in which each entry is enhanced by a summary of or commentary on its contents.* If an index is included it is given its own heading and is the very last element of the paper. Any *other items appended to a research report* are called **appendices** and are arranged in sequence following the reference list.

THE MAIN BODY OF THE REPORT

The main body of a research report constitutes the formal report of the research project. The purpose of the study is explained, the background of knowledge leading to the study is reviewed, the methods and procedures used are reported in detail, and the results are summarized and commented upon.

The order of content of a research report varies quite widely depending upon several factors. Traditionally, a thesis or dissertation has been divided into five chapters: Introduction, Review of Literature, Methods and Procedures, Results, and Conclusions. Each chapter is then divided into a series of sections based largely on the needs of scientific research. Recently, many schools have begun allowing (or even requiring) students to combine certain chapters such as the Introduction and Review of Literature or the Results and Conclusions so that the structure more closely matches that of journal articles in the student's field of study. Research reports published in journals usually include most of the elements found in a thesis but in much briefer form and certainly not divided into chapters. These differences are due largely to the differing purposes of each format. The principal purpose of the thesis is to serve as a culminating and integrating academic experience and as an opportunity for the student to demonstrate knowledge of an area of study and competence in doing research. The purpose of a journal article, on the other hand, is primarily to communicate research findings and ideas to others in order to facilitate the advancement and dissemination of new knowledge.

Whether separated into distinct chapters with headings and sub-headings, or combined into a less formal format, there are certain elements that should be present in almost all research reports. These elements are described and summarized in the following sections.

The Introduction

The introduction of a research report should briefly and concisely inform the reader of what the report is about, why the research project was conducted, and what results were expected. The purposes of an introduction, whether as a separate chapter in a thesis or dissertation or as a few opening paragraphs of a journal article, are twofold. The first purpose is to inform the reader about the nature of the research project so that a decision to continue reading can be made. Many consumers of research articles in journals, after all, may receive several journals containing hundreds of articles every month and there is not time to read each in its entirety. The second purpose is to set the stage for the rest of the report. A research report is, as suggested earlier, a story about a particular piece of research. A well organized and presented introduction places the research project in a context regarding what is known and unknown about a problem and makes the story of the research effort much more understandable to the reader. In the case of a thesis or dissertation, it may be argued that a third purpose is to ensure that certain key steps of the research process, such as the formulation of a testable hypothesis statement, have been carried out. Still, it is not uncommon for students to be unable to clearly and unambiguously articulate the purpose of their research project even after data has been collected. Often, this is the result of attempts to do research for the purpose of complying with academic expectations rather than for the purpose of solving a genuine problem.

FIGURE 3.1   An introduction and statement of purpose. This introductory paragraph begins with a statement of fact about the state of the art in the teaching of swimming. This would be followed by statements, documented where necessary, indicating a problem, followed by the logical development of a possible solution. This would then be followed by a concise statement of the purpose of the study. (The above is paraphrased from Cicciarella, 1983.)

It is well known that in nearly all beginning level instruction in swimming in the United States the focus of instruction centers around the front crawl stroke. Even though instruction may include a few skills unrelated to the crawl stroke or may involve highly modified forms of the crawl stroke, the first form of aquatic locomotion taught is clearly the crawl stroke. An exhaustive review of the literature associated with swimming instruction, however, failed to identify any study supporting the choice of the crawl stroke except one (Cureton, 1939) for the reason that the crawl stroke was most commonly taught first. Additionally, no studies were found of the relative effects of variations in the first stroke taught on the achievement of pupils in beginning swimming classes.

There is reason to expect other strokes, particularly the breast stroke, might be preferable as a first stroke to be taught to beginners. The breast stroke does not require the swimmer to rotate the head so as to face in a direction other than the direction of intended travel, making it likely to be less disorienting when the eyes are closed (a typical preference for novice swimmers) and does not require the swimmer to sacrifice buoyancy by maintaining an arm above the water surface at nearly all times. Therefore, it is the purpose of this study to experimentally compare the achievement of initial non-swimmers taught the breast stroke to a comparable group taught the crawl stroke.

Statement of purpose

With few exceptions all research reports should include a statement of purpose or purposes. Sometimes such a statement is a simple, very explicit sentence such as "The purpose of this study was to . . . ." More often, a statement of purpose is built into an introductory paragraph that places the study in a context of a problem in need of investigation as is shown in Figure 3.1. Depending upon the type of research, the purpose may be to test a hypothesis; assemble information of some kind; create a new product or prototype for a product; create a work of art such as a dance score, musical score, painting, or sculpture; describe an object, organism, event, or idea in detail; or explain and defend a legal, philosophical, or political point of view. Regardless of the type of research, the statement of purpose should be unambiguous and as brief and simply stated as possible.

Limitations

Outside of the "pure" sciences it is rarely possible, even in experimental studies, to design or carry out a research project that does not contain a weakness in design, sample selection, or subject mortality, or some other problem. Obviously, major weaknesses should be eliminated at the planning stage, but some problems are inevitable. *Weaknesses sometimes develop after a study has begun as the result of unavoidable occurrences such as the loss of subjects or equipment failures.* Weaknesses are called **limitations** and should always be acknowledged by the researcher in the research report. For example, in a report of a study suffering an unavoidable loss of subject, the limitation should be acknowledged with a statement such as, "The results of this study are limited by an excessive subject mortality." Failure to report limitations in a research report is unlikely to get past a critical review of the report and suggests that the researcher is either unaware of them or attempting to conceal them. Both situations are unacceptable.

Delimitations

The **delimitations** of a research study are *the limits placed on interpretation of its results by its design or by other aspects of its execution.* Delimitations are not weaknesses and do not necessarily suggest that elements of the study ought to have been done differently. For example, suppose an exercise physiologist were to use a group of college students to compare two different approaches to aerobic conditioning. The interpretation of the results of such a study would be delimited to college students at best and, quite possibly, only to students in colleges demonstrably similar to that from which the subjects were selected. If all or most of the subjects in the study were male, then the study would also be delimited to males. One could infer from the results that the conditioning method shown to be best in the study would also be best for any group of males in similar colleges, but that inference could not be extended to female students, to students in dissimilar colleges, or to non-students anywhere. Such an inference might, in fact, be correct but the study itself would provide no basis for making the inference. Although a delimitation is not a weakness in the design of a study, it is a mistake to unnecessarily delimit a study when a more generalized approach is possible and practical. An excessively delimited study may be quite valid within the restrictions imposed by the delimitations but will also be quite meaningless beyond those boundaries.

Definition of terms

It is important in research communication that there be no confusion between what was intended and what is understood by the reader. Such confusion can easily be caused when the researcher coins new terms or uses terminology or technical jargon in an unusual or unconventional manner. Obviously, the easiest way to avoid such confusion is to avoid using potentially confusing terms, but this is not always possible. When potentially confusing terms must be used, **operational definitions** must be provided in the introduction to the research report. *An operational definition is a definition of a term as it is used in the research report.*

Hypotheses

Literally, a **hypothesis** is *a proposition formulated for purposes of argument or study.* In the context of a research study a hypothesis is a prediction or expectation regarding the outcome of the study. A statement of the hypotheses or expected outcomes of a research project at the time the project was initiated should always be included as part of the introduction to the research report. It is

FIGURE 3.2   Statements of Hypothesis. Alternate forms of the hypothesis for a study of the effectiveness of two methods of teaching swimming. The null form (A) is appropriate if there is no theoretical basis for expecting either method to be superior. The directional form (B) is appropriate when there is a theoretical basis for expecting the results to be as hypothesized.

A. It is hypothesized that the breast stroke sequence and the crawl stroke sequence are not significantly different as determinants of swimming achievement as measured by the maximum swimming distance test.

B. It is hypothesized that the breast stroke sequence is significantly superior to the crawl stroke sequence as a determinant of swimming achievement as measured by the maximum swimming distance test.

---

usually quite straightforward in the report of an experimental research project and will generally make some kind of prediction regarding the dependent variables of the study. Although the term **dependent variable** is discussed more fully in a later chapter, it may be understood here to refer to *the measured outcome of an experiment.* Typically, the two or more groups of subjects in the experiment are predicted to be different or not different on a dependent variable at the conclusion of the experiment, whereas they would have been expected to be the same before the experiment or if the experiment were not conducted. In addition, a hypothesis statement will include an indication of the statistical level of confidence with which a judgment will be made regarding the attribution of differences in the dependent variable to real causes or to chance.

In any study following an experimental format there are two possible forms in which the hypothesis may be written. The traditional form is a *prediction that no difference will be found between experimental groups, even when the researcher expects that a difference really will be found.* This form, called the **null form** or **null hypothesis**, is used to put all of the hypotheses of a study into the same form whether differences are expected or not, and to permit the standardization of application of the statistical tests used to assess whether differences are real or due to chance. Use of the null form of hypothesis is not required (except by some academic institutions) and it may be less confusing to avoid the null hypothesis when there is reason to expect a particular outcome.

In studies of other than experimental type, a statement of hypothesis is often informal or may be implied rather than explicitly stated. In a descriptive survey, for example, there may be hypotheses dealing with the results to be found or the hypothesis may simply be that the data called for in the survey *can* be collected. In various forms of creative research, the hypothesis is very likely to be that the object of the research can, in fact, be created as planned. In some creative kinds of research, such as the creation of a computer program or a work of art, the hypothesis may be that it will be accepted in the commercial marketplace, by critics, or by some other measure.

The Literature Review

With rare exception, research is conducted in a context of existing knowledge resulting from prior research. The research report must reflect that context. A

Figure 3.3   Two drafts of a literature review.

First Draft

Several recent studies have found the part method more effective than the whole method. Jones (1986) found the part method slightly but significantly more effective for teaching basketball defensive systems at the high school level. The part method also proved more effective than the whole method in the teaching of water polo (Smith, 1987), tennis doubles strategy (Brown, 1987), and canoe-sailing (Green, 1989).

The whole method has also been reported as significantly better than the part method in several studies. Murphy (1987) found the whole method more effective for each of seven different swimming strokes with a wide range of student ages and both genders. The whole method was also reported as superior for teaching basic tumbling (Smith, 1990), baseball and softball pitching (Johnson, 1990), and bicycle riding (Jackson, 1991).

Revision

At least eight recent studies have compared the effectiveness of the part and whole methods for teaching motor skills with apparently contradictory results. In each case subjects were randomly assigned to be taught by one method or the other, given an equivalent amount of instruction, and then tested to measure how much had been learned. The part method was found superior for basketball defensive systems (Jones, 1986), water polo (Smith, 1987), doubles tennis strategy (Brown, 1987), and canoe-sailing (Green, 1989). The whole method was reported as superior for seven different swimming strokes (Murphy, 1987), basic tumbling (Smith, 1990), baseball and softball pitching (Johnson, 1990), and bicycle riding (Jackson, 1991). The contradiction, however, may be explained by differences in the complexities of the eight different types of skills involved. The part method consistently proves superior for highly complex skills which might be better described as integrated sets of many simpler skills, and the whole method consistently proves better with more fundamental skills.

Comments

The first draft shows very limited integration of the findings from the reviewed materials. The two paragraphs each describe several articles with similar findings but there is no connection to the articles with contradicting findings. Notice that there is no attempt to explain or even point out the contradictions in the two paragraphs. The writing in the second paragraph is also somewhat repetitive of the first. This is not too distracting with only two repetitive paragraphs but could make the writing rather boring and dry if many more paragraphs continued the repetition.

The revised draft integrates all eight articles, which are all very similar studies, into a single paragraph. This eliminates the problem of repetition. The revision also calls the reader's attention to the apparent contradiction in research findings and then proposes an explanation for that contradiction.

Note: Both review drafts and all citations are fictitious.

literature review is *a report and discussion of previously published research reports and other materials relevant to the research project being reported.*

The literature review should not be a mere recitation of previously published facts. The researcher, after all, does not (or should not) read such materials as isolated, unconnected bits of information, nor should the information be read uncritically. The researcher reads such materials in the context of the contribution the work can make toward the solution of some problem. Toward that end the researcher takes note of consistencies and inconsistencies among findings, makes informed judgments about the strengths and weaknesses of the methods employed in various studies, and tries to synthesize or combine findings from them. All of this should be reported in the literature review.

The scope of the literature review varies tremendously depending on the type of research report. In an article to be submitted to a research journal the literature review is typically brief and highly focused on the immediate topic. Space in research journals tends to be expensive, and it is generally assumed that both writer and readers are familiar with the general area of study being reported. In a thesis or dissertation, on the other hand, the literature review is usually longer and more broad in scope. This is because the thesis or dissertation serves as a vehicle for the student to demonstrate breadth and depth of knowledge about the general area of the study being undertaken as well as knowledge of the literature immediately relevant to the study itself.

If a literature review is lengthy, as is particularly likely in a thesis or dissertation, it may need some internal organization to keep the flow of the text from wandering or becoming convoluted and confusing. Depending on such factors as the subject matter, the method of inquiry, and the preferences and writing ability of the researcher, there are several possible approaches to such organization.

A topical arrangement may be most appropriate for reports in which several different subjects or aspects of a study must be reviewed. In a thesis, for example, the student may need or be required to provide a review dealing with general background, measurement instruments used in the study, or other matters in addition to the immediate topic of study. If the research is a historical study or if the study is built upon a foundation of a series of previous studies, it may be most appropriate to use a chronological form of organization, one in which the literature is reviewed in the sequence of its publication. Alternatively, the researcher may want to follow a reverse chronological structure, beginning with the most recent findings and working backward in time. Other possible approaches include a geographic structure, point-counterpoint structure, evolutionary structure, or some combination of these.

Methods and Procedures

One of the critical portions of a research report is the methods and procedures section in which the actual conduct of the study is described. This section, which may be called Methods, Procedures, Methods and Procedures, or something similar, is a *detailed* report of every method and/or procedure employed in conducting the research, including the details of selection and protection of subjects, experimental treatments, data collection and analysis, equipment used, and similar matters.

A report of methods or procedures is adequate if it is sufficiently detailed so that another, equally qualified researcher could perform a faithful replication

FIGURE 3.4   An example of why it is critical to keep careful documentation of research procedures and results. Whether or not proper documentation was actually kept in this case may never be known, but the inability or unwillingness to produce such documentation invites skepticism and very careful scrutiny of a researcher's work.

Cold Fusion: The Case of the Missing Documentation

The need for detailed reporting of methods and procedures was well demonstrated by the relatively recent controversy over "cold fusion."

In March of 1989 two scientists at the University of Utah announced that they had performed an experiment in which nuclear fusion took place using simple apparatus that cost less than one hundred dollars. If true, such a discovery would almost instantly eliminate worldwide dependence on fossil fuels, make energy abundantly available everywhere in the world, and probably eliminate poverty. Within weeks similar results were being reported from other laboratories. The State of Utah appropriated five million dollars for further research. The Utah scientists, however, were rather vague and even evasive in describing their methodology, claiming they had to be vague to protect their patent rights. Many scientists were skeptical and began to look very carefully at the procedures that had been reported. Soon the apparently confirmatory results being reported by other laboratories began to be retracted as those scientists detected errors in their own procedures. After a year or so of controversy involving the expenditure of millions of dollars, it became clear that cold fusion had not been achieved.

---

of the study. If any detail is left out that would prevent such a replication or that would leave a researcher in doubt on any aspect of procedure, then the report is inadequate and should be corrected. Replication of research studies by other researchers is an important component of scientific and professional practice. It allows each researcher's work to be challenged by others and either verified or refuted and is an essential part of the self-correcting nature of science.

Results and Conclusions

The results of a study and the conclusions derived from those results are frequently presented as separate parts of a research report or they may be combined under a single heading. In either case, however, the writer must be careful not to confuse the purely factual reporting of results with the somewhat interpretive conclusions or inferences made from those results.

The presentation of research results should present a summarized form of the data. Tables, graphs, and statistics should be employed rather than raw data. **Raw data,** which is the unanalyzed data in the form in which it was originally collected, should always be kept, of course, and made available to any qualified researcher requesting access to it, and may be included in an appendix if desired. The text of the results section should describe the results concisely and with absolute accuracy and honesty. The text should complement rather than repeat the information presented in graphic form.

The conclusions of a research study should be limited to a presentation and discussion of what the results indicate about the hypotheses of the study. In an experimental study each hypothesis will be accepted, rejected, or, perhaps due to failure to complete some part of the study as planned, left undecided.

Following the presentation of conclusions, there should be some very carefully considered follow-up discussion addressing such issues as implications for action based on the findings of the study and general suggestions for additional research. Such discussion should be limited, however, to areas clearly indicated by the results of the study and should never be extended to include the personal opinions of the researcher.

TENSE IN RESEARCH WRITING

In all research writing, the verb tense of each part of the report should reflect the *truth* of what is being said.

In a research proposal, the portions dealing with procedures and any elements dealing with what is planned or expected to occur, such as the hypotheses and delimitations, should be written in the future tense. Most of a review of literature, on the other hand, should be written in the past tense because all of the items reviewed are about studies that have already been done. Observations on or interpretations of items reviewed, however, should be written in the present tense.

In a final research report those portions written in the future tense in a proposal should be changed to past tense because they will then be in the past. Sections dealing with methods and results are also written in the past. Conclusions, implications, and suggestions, however, should usually be written in the present tense.

AVOIDANCE OF SEXIST AND OFFENSIVE LANGUAGE

Authors of research reports and other forms of professional literature should make every effort to avoid using language that might be interpreted as biased according to gender, race, or ethnic, religious, or other characteristics. With respect to gender, for example, the writer should avoid the generic use of the pronouns "he" or "him" in reference to subjects who may be of either gender. Gender-specific pronouns are correct, however, in reference to subjects of all one gender. When referring to persons of specific races, ethnic backgrounds, religions, sexual preference, or other characteristics, the researcher should avoid using terms such persons would likely find offensive, inappropriate, or inaccurate. For example, the term "Indian" is appropriate in reference to a person from India but inappropriate in reference to a Native American. Bear in mind, however, that the acceptability of certain terms tends to change over time and what is the preferred term today may be considered inappropriate at some time in the future.

STYLE AND MANUSCRIPT PREPARATION

For a variety of reasons, there is a need for standards regarding the writing style and, more particularly, the details of manuscript preparation of a research report. A very direct, uncomplicated, and precise writing style, for example, helps to avoid confusing the reader. Conformity in format details such as the style of references, the hierarchy of headings and sub-headings, the size and style of type, line spacing, and the size of margins would not be of much importance if the report were meant to stand in isolation. Research reports,

FIGURE 3.5 Formats for text citations and reference lists from three different style manuals.

STYLE	TEXT REFERENCE	REFERENCE LIST ENTRY FOR JOURNAL ARTICLE
APA	The recent study by Jones (1993) determined . . . or One recent study (Jones, 1993) found . . .	Jones, J. (1993). Fungus among us. *Journal of Toadstools, 7*(3), 22–30.
MLA	The recent study by Jones (1) determined . . . or One recent study (Jones 1993) found . . .	Jones, J. "Fungus Among Us." *Journal of Toadstools*. 7 (1993): 22–30.
University of Chicago Press	The recent study by Jones (1993) determined . . . or One recent study (Jones, 1993) found . . .	Jones, J. "Fungus Among Us." *Journal of Toadstools*. 7 (1993): 22–30.

however, are usually combined with many others in research journals, conference proceedings, and other forms of publication. A single issue of a research journal may have from a few to a hundred or more separate articles. It would be very confusing if the author of each article operated independently with regard to preparation of the manuscript.

There is not, however, a single standard that can be prescribed for matters of style or for the details of manuscript preparation. Rather, there are several, depending mainly upon the field of study. Most fields of study are served by national associations composed of researchers and practitioners engaged in those fields. The members of several of these associations have established sets of guidelines for the preparation of manuscripts to be submitted to journals they publish and have published detailed manuals in which those guidelines are specified. Some of the style manuals in current use include those of the American Psychological Association (APA), the Modern Language Association (MLA), and the University of Chicago. Many other associations and learned societies have adopted one of these manuals for use in their publications. Publications in education, for example, generally specify use of the APA guidelines. Fields that integrate aspects of other fields, such as physical education—which integrates aspects of education, business, medicine, and the physical sciences—may use different style manuals at different times depending upon the nature of a study. Always refer to the most recent, up-to-date editions of style manuals. See Figure 3.5 for a comparison of the different formats specified for in-text citations and reference lists by three style manuals.

Research reports written in fulfillment of course or degree requirements, principally theses and dissertations, generally must conform to the style manual most closely associated with the student's field of study or major. Quite often, however, there will be additional or different specifications imposed by the academic institution or department. Such requirements typically involve such matters as the inclusion of special pages or documentation, type of paper used, method of binding, and number of copies required to be submitted, and may include matters of style as well. Wherever style manual and academic institution specifications conflict, those of the academic institution take precedence for academic papers and those of the style manual take precedence for journal submission. In any case it is the *student's* responsibility to obtain the appropriate specifications and style manual, to be familiar with all academic requirements and expectations, and to prepare a paper in accordance with all requirements.

PUBLISHING THE RESULTS

Anyone who has completed a research project and has obtained results that contribute to the body of knowledge in any way should prepare a research report for public dissemination. Submission of an article to a journal or presentation of a paper at a conference does not require possession of an advanced degree or a position as a professor. Even a student in junior high school is eligible to do these things if genuine research has been conducted. Publication of a research report does require, in addition to completion of a valid and meaningful study, the preparation of a manuscript that is reasonably well written, free of grammatical, spelling, and other technical errors, and is in accordance with the topical and technical requirements of the journal to which it is submitted.

For most purposes the preferred and most prestigious method of dissemination of completed research reports is publication in a refereed journal. Although this method can sometimes result in a delay of a year or more between submission and publication, the use of a journal results in a permanent, written record of the research report, to which scholars can refer whenever they wish. Journal publication also may be less expensive (to the researcher) than a conference presentation or other methods and may provide wider dissemination of the research results.

The submission requirements (style, number of copies, topical interest) of a journal can usually be found somewhere inside each issue or they may be requested from the editor. Many journals are highly focused on specific areas of study and will not accept articles outside that area, so it is very important to check the topical appropriateness of a journal prior to submission. All manuscripts should be prepared in *exact* conformity to the technical requirements of the journal, as it is not uncommon for manuscripts not in conformity to be rejected automatically. Fortunately, most journals use one of the well-known style manuals for all matters of style so only a few items, such as the number of copies to submit, need special attention.

Professional journals do not pay authors for publication rights though many commercial magazines do. In fact, some journals *charge the author by the page for publishing an article.* While journals which assess **page charges** will often waive or reduce those charges if the researcher lacks funds to cover them, they are not obligated to do so. Reading the *information for authors* or *submission requirements* usually printed somewhere inside each issue will reveal whether the journal assesses page charges.

The most prestigious journals in which to publish a research report are those which use what is called a **blind peer review** process to decide which manuscripts to accept for publication. This means that the decision to accept or reject a submitted manuscript is made by a review panel of members who meet two very important criteria. First, the *members of the panel are the peers of the researcher submitting the manuscript.* That is, they are experts in the same field of study and have a professional interest in encouraging advancement of that field through publication of quality research and rejection of poor quality research. Second, the *members of the panel are "blind" to the identity of the author.* The journal editor will remove the cover letter, title page, and any other information that could identify the author or authors before the manuscript is sent to the reviewers. This way, the reputation, or lack thereof, of the researcher cannot influence the decision to publish or reject.

An alternative form of dissemination of research is presentation of a paper at a conference. While not as prestigious as a journal article, this form of publication is preferred by many researchers for several reasons. First, the time delay between submission of a proposal and presentation is often much shorter than that experienced with journals. Second, the live presentation of a paper encourages a degree of interaction with other researchers unavailable using printed media. Third, conferences often permit presentation of reports of work in progress. The sometimes critical but always (well, almost always) constructive criticism that can follow such presentations can be invaluable in fine tuning or revitalizing a research project, and many researchers find the intellectual exercise quite stimulating. Others, of course, are intimidated by the possibility of criticism.

Copyright Matters

The right to make copies of any original work in tangible form, from a novel to a class report, initially belongs to the author, except in cases such as a "work made for hire" in which a prior agreement has been made transferring those rights. When a research report or other materials resulting from a research project are to be published in a journal, book, or report, the author is generally expected (and required) to transfer the copyright to the publisher. As a rule, the publisher will provide the necessary forms and will handle all details of copyright registration and the deposit of necessary copies and fees with the Copyright Office, a department of the Library of Congress. However, when the results of a research project are to be sold or distributed without the intermediary of a publisher, it may be necessary for these matters to be handled by the author. Information and necessary forms may be obtained by contacting the Copyright Office of the Library of Congress in Washington, D. C.

Copyright applies to all forms of creative work fixed in tangible form, including sound recordings, computer software, magnetic tapes, microfilms, photographs, and works of art. Trade names and trademarks are not copyrightable but are protected by similar laws. Inventions and some other creations such as hybridized or genetically engineered organisms are protected by patents. Legal assistance should always be sought in applying for a trademark registration or patent.

 TERMS

annotated bibliography   delimitations
appendices   dependent variable
bibliography   limitations
blind peer review   literature review

null form   preliminary pages
null hypothesis   publish
operational definition   raw data
page charge   reference list

EXERCISES

1. Identify the style manual used for student research papers in your department.
2. Determine what requirements or expectations are required concerning the structure of student research papers in your department.
3. Identify several of the research journals in your field of interest and obtain copies of the submission requirements for each.
4. Determine what computer resources, especially software, are available to you as aids to the preparation of a research report manuscript. Possibilities include software for typesetting, spell checking, reference list generation, equation typesetting or solving, drawing, and graphing.
5. Identify the purpose statement, hypotheses, and delimitations of several research reports from journals in your area of interest.

ADDITIONAL RESOURCES WITH ANNOTATION

Cicciarella, C.F. (1992). *Directory of periodicals in sport.* Charlotte, NC: Persimmon Software.
    Provides information on more than 100 English-language periodicals in the physical education/sport field, including information for potential authors.

Library of Congress Copyright Office (1980), *Copyright basics.* (Publication No. 1980-311-426/5). Washington, D. C.: U. S. Government Printing Office.
    Information for authors who may wish to maintain the copyright to their work. Includes information regarding requirements for obtaining or registering a copyright.

4

LIBRARIES AND RELATED RESOURCES

For most of the history of humankind, knowledge was shared among individuals and passed from generation to generation through oral transmission. Facts and ideas were simply told by one person to another, often in the form of stories, which tended to change as each storyteller added embellishments or left out details. The knowledge available to any one person was severely limited to that person's access to persons with the ability and willingness to share information. Many discoveries were certainly made independently by people isolated from each other and then lost. Indeed, much potentially vital knowledge held by tribal cultures around the world is *still* being lost today as tribal elders die out without passing on their knowledge to younger generations who have moved to the developed world.

With the invention of writing some 5,000 or so years ago it became possible for knowledge and ideas to be preserved in a tangible form and transmitted indirectly. Any literate person could transmit information or ideas to any similarly literate person even though separated by hundreds of miles or thousands of years. A story carved into a clay tablet 4,000 years ago in Egypt is exactly the same story today.

When information can be recorded permanently and recalled at will a tremendous increase in the rate of discovery of new information becomes possible. A discovery which originally took a lifetime of observation and contemplation can be passed on in the time it takes to read about it to an entire generation of younger people who can then use their lifetimes to make new discoveries instead of re-discovering the old ones. Access to the accumulated knowledge of past generations is arguably the key that permits a culture to adapt to the changing demands of its environment and opens the possibility of avoiding the mistakes of the past.

The idea that knowledge is power, and that accumulated knowledge is accumulated power, is not new. Since ancient times, literate cultures have attempted to build and maintain storehouses of knowledge in the form of libraries, as a means of spreading and preserving their knowledge and that of cultures with which they have had contact. Ancient Egypt, Babylon, and Assyria all had large libraries of written materials inscribed on thousands of clay tablets, many of which still survive and can be studied by scholars. In the Roman period, when books could be handwritten on paper scrolls, there was a great library at Alexandria which reportedly contained more than a half million scrolls. At about the same time, there was a large Imperial Library in the Korean and Chinese Empires. If the construction and maintenance of great libraries is almost universally associated with the flourishing of great or powerful cultures, the destruction and loss of such resources is similarly associated with the decline of those cultures. The great library at Alexandria, for example, was completely and deliberately destroyed by religious fanatics bent on eliminating anything that contradicted or questioned their ideas. Accounts differ whether early Christian or Islamic zealots were involved in this destruction (Canfora, 1989). The great library in Korea met a similar fate. In our own era, governments and other groups with rigid, dogmatic ideas have attempted to force their ideas on others by denying access to and even burning books, punishing those who read them, and preventing people from learning to read. Even today there are frequent attempts to ban controversial books and sometimes to intimidate their authors with threats.

In our modern culture libraries represent an enormous resource of knowledge and ideas. For all practical purposes, the libraries of the world contain the total knowledge of humankind. It must be admitted, of course, that libraries also contain much junk. If the answer to any question is known to humankind, the chances are good that it can be found in a library somewhere. With few exceptions, furthermore, the information found in libraries is freely available to anyone. All one has to do is enter the library (physically or electronically) and locate the information that is needed. Locating the information that is needed, however, is not always a simple matter. Libraries in the modern world are often enormous and may contain a tremendous range of different kinds of materials in addition to the usual collections of books and periodicals. The Library of Congress in Washington, D. C., for example, contains more than 20 million volumes, including books, periodicals, tape recordings, videotapes and disks, government documents, computer disks, and many other kinds of materials. Familiarity with the systems and techniques for finding and using the materials in research libraries is an essential skill for anyone expecting to function effectively in any professional role.

This chapter, therefore, is intended to serve as an introduction to some of the systems and techniques used to find and utilize information in a research library. Reading each section carefully should give the student a general understanding of those systems and techniques. However, *there can be no substitute for actually visiting one or more libraries and using each system or technique.* The student is strongly urged to find a topic of personal interest and then use each of the systems in the library to search for and locate materials relevant to that topic. Also, because there may be slight variations in certain systems among different libraries, the astute student should consider undertaking the exercise of using each system in at least two different libraries.

WHAT IS A LIBRARY?

Any collection of books or a building containing a collection of books meets the dictionary definition of a library. A modern library, however, is much more than a collection of books. It is much more in several ways.

First, the collections in a modern library are *organized.* The books in a library are not just lined up randomly on the shelves or piled on a table, they are arranged by subjects and other criteria according to a specific set of rules. Anyone who knows and understands the rules used to organize a library will immediately, without ever having visited that library, be able to locate the books on any subject.

Second, the collections in a modern library are *indexed*. An **index** is *an alphabetical listing that serves as a key to locating specific items in a collection of some kind.* In addition to the **card catalog,** *an index of the book holdings of a library,* most large libraries have whole sections containing dozens or hundreds of general purpose and specialized indexes designed to assist library patrons to identify and locate materials in the library or in other libraries. Any patron able to use these resources should be able to identify the library's holdings on any topic or combination of topics without actually entering the areas of the library used to house those materials.

Third, the holdings of a modern library include collections of far more than just books. Nearly every library also contains, for example, an extensive collection of magazines, newspapers, and specialized periodicals. The largest university libraries may subscribe to tens of thousands of different periodicals. Also, large libraries often maintain collections of government documents of all kinds, dissertations and theses, sound recordings on various media, video recordings on tape or disk, computer software, personal papers of important historical figures, and many other materials.

LIBRARY-LIKE RESOURCES

In addition to libraries, civilizations typically maintain a variety of other resources that also serve as repositories of materials and information that may be of interest to researchers as well as members of the public in general. For example, located a very short distance from the Library of Congress in Washington, D. C., with well over 20 million volumes one of the largest libraries in the world, is one of the largest and best museums in the world, the Smithsonian Institution. Occupying numerous buildings on both sides of the Capitol Mall in Washington, D. C., the Smithsonian displays vast collections of art, American inventions, natural history, aviation, and American history. Similar institutions in the Washington area maintain collections of living organisms. The Smithsonian Institution itself, for example, maintains several exhibits and collections of living organisms including insects and reptiles. Institutions with collections of living organisms include zoos (animals of all kinds), aquariums (marine animals of all kinds), botanical gardens (plants), herpetariums (reptiles), aviaries (birds), and so on.

Like libraries, these institutions maintain collections of materials, such as works of art, historical artifacts, fossils, animals and plants for public display and as reference resources for scientists and other researchers. Some such institutions, such as the Smithsonian, may serve a broad range of interests, whereas others, such as the National Herb Garden or the Baseball Hall of Fame, may focus their attention on specialized topics. Also like libraries, such institutions usually provide systems for identifying and locating the materials in their collections, and usually make extensive efforts to assist researchers (including qualified students) in using their resources for study. The collections of most museums, in fact, are very commonly far more extensive than the items put on display; most of the items in a museum's collection are stored in archives for use on demand by researchers. Although the remainder of this

FIGURE 4.1   The entrance to the Museum of the Holocaust in Jerusalem, Israel.

FIGURE 4.2   The Palm House at the Royal Botanical Garden in London, England.

chapter deals with use of the resources found in libraries, the student involved in a research study should not overlook or ignore the resources of library-like institutions.

A LIBRARY RESEARCH PLAN

A substantial portion of the time devoted to most types of research projects involves reviewing library materials relevant or possibly relevant to the topic under study. In the case of an experienced researcher this is an ongoing process that will probably have begun during graduate or even undergraduate training and that continues from study to study. In the case of a student project, the research is more likely to begin with a general review of library materials in an effort to find and refine a topic for study.

Library research involves more than just going to the library with a pad of note paper and looking up and reading materials. A library research effort should be planned so that it can be as systematic and focused as possible.

Planning a library research effort should probably begin with consideration of the question or questions for which answers are to be sought. For example, a

FIGURE 4.3   An exhibit at the Panhandle-Plains Historical Museum in Canyon, Texas.

researcher might be interested in studying the effectiveness of a school's basketball team against each of the various forms of defense that it might face under game conditions. Specific questions that could be answered through library research might include the following:

- "What are the different forms of defense used in basketball?"
- "Has the effectiveness of teams against different defenses been studied before and what did such studies reveal?"
- "How can basketball effectiveness be measured?"

Once a small set of such questions has been formulated the next step is to decide on a strategy for finding information to help answer each question. For example, information about different basketball defenses would probably be found in a book about basketball strategy. Information about previous research on the effectiveness of teams against different defenses would probably be found in research journals dealing with sports or in the proceedings of conferences at which sports-related research is presented.

NOTE TAKING

Of course, library notes can be written on notebook paper, typing paper, a legal pad, or anything else, but most students will find it more efficient, unless they have access to a portable computer, to use index cards. Index cards stand up to repeated handling much better than ordinary paper and they can be sorted and neatly stacked, characteristics that will make the process of writing a paper or literature review much easier. Most students will find either the 4×6 or 5×8 size useful, although those with very limited note taking experience will find the larger size preferable. The larger size provides plenty of room for errors as well as for recording needed information and will minimize instances in which notes for a reference must be continued onto a second card.

It is highly recommended to prepare an index card for *every* item identified as *potentially* useful even if that item is eventually determined not to be useful. At the minimum, record a complete bibliographic entry, according to the guidelines in the required style manual, as well as whatever local information—such

FIGURE 4.4   A Model Index Card Record. One index card is used for each item reviewed. Extra cards may be added if needed but multiple items should *never* be recorded on a single card.

Complete bibliographic citation.   Library

Call No.

Summary of item cited. Design, subjects, variables, results, conclusions, important quotations, etc.

Critique of item cited. Strengths, flaws, ideas for improvement, etc.

as a call number or shelf location—is needed to locate the item again. This will prevent wasting time finding and reading the item a second time if it should be identified through some other source and will make it easier to relocate the item if it should be needed for further review or for another project.

The content of the notes recorded for each item reviewed will vary considerably depending upon the type of material being examined, the purpose of the literature review, and the skill of the researcher (the student) doing the review. In an academic setting, advice on this matter should be sought from the student's course instructor or thesis advisor. In the absence of specific information about a particular project, the best advice that can be given is to read carefully the full text of the item and then reflect on its relevance—however obscure—to the purpose of your project. Then, if any possible relevance is identified, record in your notes everything that might be needed to explain that relevance to someone else. If the item being reviewed is a research report, then the essential details of the research, including the method or design used, the subjects studied, and findings should be recorded. If the item reviewed is an essay or editorial, the information recorded should include the views expressed, the main points of supporting and opposing reasoning, if expressed, and background data about the author. Direct quotations should generally be kept to a minimum but if any quotations are recorded they must, of course, be surrounded by quotation marks. This is extremely important even in notes taken purely for personal use in order to prevent any chance of accidentally plagiarizing the material. It may also be helpful, for later relocating such a quote, to record the page and line number as well.

The note-taking process of a review of literature is not just an exercise in which one compiles materials on a topic of study. The note-taking process should be one of reflection, comparison, criticism, and synthesis of published materials on a topic of interest. Thus, the notes recorded on each item reviewed in a literature search should include comments by the reviewer. It is not at all uncommon for a reflective undergraduate (or even high school) reader to observe defects in an author's reasoning or to detect unreported faults in research methods. Such observations are, in fact, the very essence of a good literature review and often form the basis of new research.

CRITICAL REVIEWING

As discussed in Chapter 3, the principal purpose of a literature review, as part of a large research project or a simple term paper, is to identify and summarize what the literature has to say that is relevant to the current project. It is not enough merely to identify and summarize each of the relevant items in the literature. Rather, what must be identified and summarized is what the literature itself, as a whole, has to say. This requires that the researcher have at least two skills that do not tend to come easily.

First, the researcher must be able to synthesize findings, concepts, and ideas from different sources and different kinds of sources into new knowledge, at least in the form of new or refined ideas and concepts. Synthesis in a review of literature is the integration of smaller, less refined, less useful, or less comprehensive pieces of information or ideas into a larger, more refined, more useful, or more comprehensive whole. The researcher's task may be seen as analogous to that of solving a jigsaw puzzle. If the literature is seen as a huge collection of parts from many different jigsaw puzzles, the researcher must first identify those parts that belong to the puzzle and then attempt to put them together correctly to assemble the puzzle. Just as a difficult jigsaw puzzle may be solved systematically by searching for common relationships (parts with common features such as edges, corners, colors or straight lines), the researcher's task may be accomplished by seeking out relationships or patterns in the literature. While much of the effort of synthesis is largely that of absorbing and understanding details from many different sources and combining that information using reason and intelligence, the process may be aided by simple, organizational techniques. For example, one could make charts showing results of related studies in graphic form, or sort cards or computer records of articles into groups with contradictory results and then look for characteristics that correlate with the results.

Second, and essential to the first, the researcher must be able to evaluate the relative merit or worth of each relevant item, assigning more weight to items that are well done or carefully reasoned and less to those with obvious shortcomings or biases. Rather than accepting the results, conclusions, or rationale of each item in a review at face value, the researcher must attempt to skeptically consider those results, conclusions, or rationale in the light of experience, common sense, and reason. For items reporting research results, critical evaluation involves such processes as the review of experimental or data collection procedures, re-examination of the authors' interpretation of their own results, and consideration of alternative explanations of the results. Critical evaluation of opinion or advocacy items involves consideration of such factors as possible biases or vested interests of the author, possible biases of the journal or publisher, and biases related to sources of funding, as well as a review of the soundness of the author's reasoning.

COPY MACHINES

Most libraries offer patrons access to one or more kinds of photocopying machines, operated either by coin or debit card. These almost always include standard type copiers which can be used to copy pages from journal articles, books, and other printed materials, but may also include machines to make paper copies from microfiche, microcards, microfilm, or various forms of digi-

FIGURE 4.5   A copy machine operated by debit card. The card is purchased from and recharged by a specialized vending machine. Charges for copies are then deducted from the card's balance as it is used.

tal document storage. Although the charge for using such machines is often unreasonably high in comparison to similar services at commercial copy centers (often twice the charge or more), making copies of materials likely to be important in a study is often well worth the price. Stinginess regarding making copies of important materials is most often a false economy. Making a copy of important documents allows the document to be studied at one's convenience and without the necessity of returning to the library.

Library users who take advantage of copier services must, of course, be familiar with applicable copyright regulations. **Copyright** is *the legal ownership of a creative work in any tangible form, including the right to control the act of copying that work in any form.* In general, researchers, including students engaged in research projects, may make single copies of relevant journal articles or small portions of other materials for personal use in conducting their research. Making multiple copies, making copies for distribution to others (except in severely limited education circumstances) or copying of entire or major portions of books, is not legal without the permission of the copyright holder. As the copyright law is changed or reinterpreted from time to time, guidelines for acceptable uses of copy machines are usually displayed near them in a prominent location.

FINDING THINGS: LIBRARY RESOURCES

As suggested earlier in this chapter, the difference between a pile of books and magazines and a library is that the library is organized and indexed so that materials can be located efficiently and without the necessity of browsing through irrelevant items. Libraries have many different and powerful systems for locating different kinds of materials. The following sections describe a selection of the major indexing tools that may be encountered. Many of these systems will already be familiar to the student whereas others may be new.

The Library Card Catalog

A **card catalog** is *an index of the book holdings of a library.* Although many libraries have converted to a computerized catalog system and may or may not

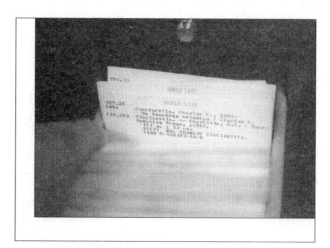

FIGURE 4.6   A sample card from physical card catalog. The library here uses the Dewey decimal numbering system.

continue to maintain a physical card system, some libraries have a catalog in the form of a set of index cards housed in cabinets of drawers and usually placed in a central location within the library. The cards of a library catalog are always arranged in alphabetical order. For every book catalogued there are always at least three cards: one for the author's name, one for the title of the book, and at least one (usually several) for the subject(s) of the book. Each card will contain a bibliographic citation for the book (note that this citation may not be in the form required for an academic assignment or manuscript submission), a call number, and possibly other information as well. The call number is the key to locating the item in the library. All of the numbers and/or letters of the call number should be written down exactly as they appear on the card.

When conducting a literature search it is important to understand that only the *book* holdings of a particular library will be found by using a card catalog. Journal articles, newspaper stories, government documents, dissertations, and other items in the library, many of which may be much more important in a literature review than books, must be found by other means. Also, a card catalog will not contain any information about books that may be available through other libraries, bookstores, or other sources.

Call Numbers

The materials on the shelves of a library are arranged according to *a topical numbering system* known as **call numbers.** If the card catalog is used to find the call number of a desired item in the library it is not necessary to have any understanding of the meaning of the numbers and/or letters of a call number in order to locate an item—one need only find the desired call number in its numeric or alphanumeric order. Most older and smaller libraries use *a topical, alphanumeric numbering system invented by Melvil Dewey* known as the **Dewey Decimal System.** Most university and larger research libraries use *a more flexible system* known as the **Library of Congress, or 'LC' system.** A book or other item held by two libraries using the same numbering system will have the same number in both libraries (this is not always the case with periodical holdings). All of the various indexes in the local library, such as the card catalog or the Index to Periodical Holdings, will list the call numbers assigned to each item.

FIGURE 4.7   Call numbers on the aisles help in locating items in the library stacks. This library uses the L.C. system.

FIGURE 4.8   This library uses the older Dewey decimal system.

ISBN, ISSN, and Other Numbers

Although Library of Congress call numbers provide an efficient means for locating books (or other materials) in a library, there are occasions when books must be obtained from sources other than a library, such as a bookstore or from the publisher. In such instances the **ISBN,** or *International Standard Book Number,* is usually a more efficient means of identifying the needed book than the Library of Congress number. Whereas the Library of Congress numbers are assigned according to a book's subject matter and serve to facilitate placement of the book within a library, the ISBN number is assigned according to the book's country of publication, publisher, and order of publication and serves to facilitate acquisition of the book from the publisher. Unique ISBNs are assigned by publishers to every different book they publish, including every revised edition, type of binding or cover, translations, or editions released in different countries.

ISBNs are composed of four parts. The first three parts identify, in sequence, the country of publication, the publisher, and the book. The fourth part, the last letter or digit, is used to check the accuracy of the first three parts when numbers are transmitted or transcribed. Although ISBNs are assigned to books by

FIGURE 4.9 Books on a library's shelves are arranged in alphanumeric order of the Library of Congress or Dewey decimal call numbers, which are found on the catalog card and on the spine of the book. Here the Dewey decimal system is used.

Public Library Public Access Catalog

The card catalogs of many public libraries can be automatically searched by computer from any location. Additionally, anyone with a modem-equipped personal computer can access such public library catalogs. Information needed to do this is usually available from the library or on line.

The public library catalogs generally contain listings on the holdings of the main library plus all branch libraries, including books, films, sound recordings, and video recordings, but *not* periodical holdings.

Searches may be conducted by subject, exact title, title keywords, author, and other criteria. Search criteria often cannot be combined because the search is alphabetical but it is often possible to find items using a different term or even using an approximate spelling. For example, materials on water polo, water pollution, water ballet, and water exercise could all be found in a search using "swim" as a keyword.

Using the system is a very simple matter of following instructions printed on the screen and making choices from menus of options. In addition to listing available items matching the search criteria, the system also usually identifies the type of item (book, audio recording, video recording, etc.), displays the call numbers, and notes the availability of items in the various branch libraries.

Public library catalogs also often provide access to a bulletin board containing announcements of current and forthcoming events and other services at the public library or branch libraries. Typical announcements may include diverse events, such as special film screenings, reading programs for children, sales of old books, and small business management seminars. Access may also be available to a wide range of other services such as Internet access, searches of large periodical databases, or access to the catalogs of other libraries.

individual publishers, the numbers themselves are assigned to the publishers by the R.R. Bowker Company of New York in order to avoid the possibility of conflicting number assignments. ISBNs are assigned to and printed on the covers of nearly all books, but are not used with other types of materials. Periodical materials are covered by a similar system of *International Standard Serial Numbers* (**ISSN**), and music materials by *International Standard Music Numbers* (**ISMN**).

PERIODICAL INDEXES

A typical college or university library will contain hundreds or even thousands or periodical publications, ranging from general readership and juvenile magazines to highly specialized research journals. Faced with a course requirement to conduct some kind of literature review, students often attempt to go directly to the shelf holding a prominent journal in their field and begin looking at the table of contents of issue after issue looking for material to review. Such an approach is almost certainly doomed to failure and is a colossal waste of time.

Most periodical publications do not provide indexes in each issue but do provide them on an annual basis and occasionally publish cumulative indexes for several years (commonly 10) as well. When a research topic is so narrowly focused that there are only a few journals likely to publish relevant articles, these annual and cumulative indexes can be very useful. However, most studies are not so tightly focused, so there may be dozens or even hundreds of journals to be searched for relevant material. To address this problem, most professions and academic disciplines have one or more publications that serve as cumulative indexes of all or most of the journals in that field of study. Such indexes are published in monthly and/or annual printed volumes, on CD-ROM disks purchased by individuals or local libraries, or stored in large computer data banks that can be remotely accessed by anyone with a microcomputer and an account number.

Some examples of periodical indexes serving specific areas of study and published in printed form are *Index Medicus, Biological Abstracts, Education Index, Physical Education Index*, and *Psychological Abstracts.* General readership magazines are also indexed in the *Reader's Guide to Periodical Literature.* The precise details of use for each index may vary somewhat, but may be learned by studying the opening pages of any volume in a few minutes. Generally, each contains separate alphabetical listings of author's names and keywords or phrases. The latter is by far the most extensive portion of the index. The **keywords** are *terms gleaned from the title of each article or supplied by the authors as representative of the topics addressed in the article.* Most periodical indexes can be used in a variety of ways but the most common method is to look up keywords that seem closely related to the topic of study. For example, a researcher interested in the training of athletes in aquatic sports might try looking up the possible keywords *swimming, water polo, diving,* or *synchronized swimming.* The index provides listings of bibliographic citations of articles under such keywords. Often, of course, not all of the listed citations will be found to be useful. In many indexes, the keyword *swimming* is likely to turn up articles about fish and whales as well as about competitive swimming.

Some indexes merely provide bibliographic information on each article listed. In such cases, the next step after locating a title that appears useful is to locate and read the article itself. Other indexes, however, also serve as a key to a collection of **abstracts** or *summaries of articles.* The index and abstracts may be printed in a single or separate volumes. *Biological Abstracts,* for example, annually publishes in excess of 100,000 abstracts of articles in biology and may

---

Some Selected Indexes

Current Periodical Holdings
Usually a computer printout listing the periodical holdings of the library.
Use it to find out if the library subscribes or has ever subscribed to a particular periodical.

Current Contents
A monthly compilation of the tables of contents of a large selection of
journals. Different versions exist for the sciences and social sciences. Use
it to browse for articles of interest each month.

Dissertation Abstracts
An index and abstract collection for virtually all doctoral dissertations.
Two versions exist for the sciences and other areas of study.

Books in Print
A listing of virtually all published books still available for purchase from
publishers. Use it to see what is available on a topic, by a particular
author, or from a publisher.

Forthcoming Books
A listing of books expected to be published in the next six months. Use it
to obtain advance information about books about to be published.

Encyclopedia of Associations
An alphabetical listing of organizations in all sorts of fields. Includes current address and phone numbers, membership size, publications, meetings,
names of executives, and a brief description of each organization.

Ulrich's International Directory of Periodicals
A listing of thousands of periodical publications in every subject. Includes
a brief description of content, addresses, names of editors and publishers,
and other data.

---

require a dozen or more volumes, each two to three inches thick. A search of
Biological Abstracts and similar resources usually begins with a keyword
search of the index section, which yields an abstract number rather than a bibliographic entry. The abstracts themselves include a brief description of the
contents of the article as well as bibliographic information and are arranged in
numerical order in the abstract section.

OTHER INDEXES

The reference sections of most libraries contain a significant number of indexes and index-like reference works which the student or researcher will
frequently find useful for locating books, periodical articles, and other
resources. A few minutes of exploration will reveal the resources available in
any particular library, and the use of most can be learned in a few minutes.
Typical resources of this type may include a listing of periodical holdings of the
library, indexes to periodical holdings of nearby libraries, reference books listing books or periodicals currently available from publishers, the tables of
contents of current journal issues, listings of journal articles cited as references

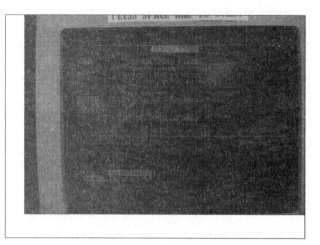

FIGURE 4.10   Computerized card catalog display. Computerized card catalogs have libraries. This display is the entry for the same book as the physical card in Figure 4.6. Notice that the computerized display includes substantially more information than the older style cards.

in other journal articles, indexes of doctoral dissertations or master's theses, directories of available films or videos, directories of periodicals serving particular fields, and many others.

COMPUTERIZED INDEXES

Recently, many computerized indexing systems have been installed in most libraries. In some cases such systems have been added alongside existing printed indexes in order to provide improvements in efficiency and flexibility, whereas in others the computerized systems have entirely replaced the older, printed versions. Computerized catalog systems can be searched by title, author, and subject just as the manual card systems are searched but may offer more sophisticated searches as well. For example, it may be possible to search for books according to words in the title, call number, publisher, or other criteria. It may even be possible to perform searches using logically combined criteria (such as a search for two alternative subject words) or using an approximate spelling of an author or title. Similarly, most libraries have one or more computerized indexing systems for periodical material which also offer more sophisticated searching capabilities than the printed indexes. Most research and university libraries also have computerized services for searching through various kinds of databases located in computer systems throughout the world. Computerized indexing systems offer several very important advantages over the older systems. From the point of view of the library itself, computerized indexing systems occupy much less space than printed indexes and the problem of wear and tear on the printed indexes is eliminated. From the user's point of view, computerized indexing systems are a tremendously more efficient method for searching the literature. A search through many years' worth of issues of hundreds of publications, which could take weeks or months using the older systems, can be reduced to *seconds*. Additionally, the computerized system is much more powerful in the types of searches that may be conducted. For example, manual systems can be searched using only one keyword at a time whereas two or more keywords can be combined on the computerized systems using logical operations (see math appendix). Articles dealing with the teaching of swimming, for example, could be located by conducting a single search using

FIGURE 4.11   Selected On-line Databases. Most libraries can access these and other on-line databases through services such as DIALOG. Some are also available locally in CD-ROM form. Note that there may be some variation between the on-line, print, and CD-ROM versions. In particular, the on-line versions are likely to be more complete and more up to date.

ON-LINE	COVERAGE	PRINT VERSION	CD-ROM VERSION
MEDLINE	Medicine	Index Medicus, Index to Dental Literature, & International Nursing Index	MEDLINE
BIOSIS Previews	Biology	Biological Abstracts & BioResearch Index	—
Dissertation Abstracts Online	Doctoral Dissertations	Dissertation Abstracts	—
SPORT	Sport & Exercise	—	—
PsycINFO	Psychology	Psychological Abstracts	PsycLIT
Sociological Abstracts	Sociology	Sociological Abstracts	Sociofile
ERIC	Education	Resources in Education	ERIC
Current Contents Search	Tables of Contents	Current Contents	—
Academic Index	Magazines	—	—
LC MARC-BOOKS	Library of Congress Catalog 1968–	—	—

the keywords *swimming* and *teaching* combined using the AND logical operator. Only a small number of articles, all dealing with both swimming and teaching would be found, whereas either keyword used alone would produce thousands of articles, nearly all of which would not be useful.

Another powerful feature found in most computerized indexes is the ability to search more thoroughly for articles that may be relevant to a topic. Whereas non-computerized indexes only allow the researcher to search using keywords attached to an article by the author or publisher and, perhaps, by elements of the bibliographic citation, most computerized indexes can search for a keyword match anywhere in the index's database. For example, with a computerized index, the keyword *Proposition 48* could be used to find every article in which *Proposition 48* appears anywhere in the title, bibliographic citation, or abstract, as well as those to which it is attached by the author as a keyword. Some systems would even identify articles in which *Proposition 48* appears anywhere in the article text.

FIGURE 4.12   The InfoTrac system, a self-contained computerized database for periodical literature. Bibliographic information and brief abstracts are stored on CD-ROM disks and may be searched in a variety of powerful ways.

ON-LINE INDEXES

Around the country and the world are hundreds if not thousands of computer databases containing bibliographic citations, abstracts, and even the complete texts of journal articles with some common theme. *Biological Abstracts,* described earlier in this chapter as a printed index for biology, is also available as a computer database under the name BIOSIS®. Another printed index of major importance, *Index Medicus,* is available as a computerized database called MEDLINE®. These computerized databases exist in the storage devices attached to large computers in many different places. They are available everywhere in the country, however, because they are designed to be accessed over telephone lines. *Any properly equipped personal computer can be connected over a telephone to such databases and used to search through them for information.* Resources accessed in this manner are said to be **on-line resources.**

Learning to use even a small proportion of the available on-line databases would be a daunting, if not impossible, task. Each has its own unique characteristics and limitations. Fortunately, most libraries subscribe to one or more additional on-line services, such as DIALOG®, which serve as a front-end to the various on-line databases so that they can all be accessed through a single telephone number, a single account number, and in essentially the same way.

Although it is possible for anyone with a personal computer to obtain a DIALOG® account number and use its on-line services directly, doing so efficiently does require a certain amount of training. Therefore, most university libraries offer DIALOG® services through the intermediary of a research librarian. The student or researcher is merely required to request that a search be done and

---

Logical Operators

Most computerized searching systems allow keywords to be combined using any or all of these operators. Some systems permit even more complex searches to be designed combining two or more operators and using parentheses to control the sequence of operations.

AND

Restricts or narrows a search. Only materials matching both keywords will be selected.

OR

Broadens a search. Materials matching either keyword will be selected.

NOT

Broadens or narrows a search. Materials matching the first keyword will be selected unless they also match the second keyword.

InfoTrac

InfoTrac is a computerized access system for a database of periodicals called *Academic Index*. It contains a wide variety of materials covering psychology, sociology, current events, political science, education, economics, literature, and religion. It does not provide coverage of journals in medicine, business, or the sciences except those listed above. Most of the information available consists of bibliographic citations but some abstracted information is also available for some materials.

InfoTrac searches are conducted using a hierarchical system of topical keywords. For example, materials on steroid abuse by athletes might be located by entering the keywords *Drug Abuse* and *Athletes,* but these would be entered in sequence rather than combined with a logical AND operator. Information is extremely easy to find because following entry of one keyword, available subtopics are displayed on the screen.

Bibliographic citations and even abstracts located using InfoTrac can very easily be printed using a printer attached to the system. Another very important feature of the InfoTrac system is that it contains information about the host library's periodical holdings and marks each citation as available or not available as part of its built-in display.

InfoTrac is also available at many public libraries, so any materials identified that are not in the host library very likely are available at other libraries in the area.

ProQuest™ Periodicals

ProQuest™ Periodicals is a computerized, *full text* database of periodicals, published by University Microfilms International (UMI). The system consists of a personal computer equipped with several CD-ROM drives, a large screen display, a printer, and a large and growing collection of CD-ROM disks containing images of each page of the journals in the system. For the hundreds of periodicals included in the database it can provide keyword searches of articles, titles, and abstracts. Keywords can be used singly or may be combined with the AND, OR, and AND NOT and other logical operators. In addition to the use of keywords, searches may be limited to certain fields of the database, such as the journal name.

For many of the journals in the database the system can display an image of the actual journal page on the computer screen and, where needed, print that image on paper. Some articles may not be available in this manner, usually because the copyright holder has not given permission for copies to be distributed without payment of royalties. In such cases, it is possible to order copies from UMI using a check or credit card for payment or the article may be available in paper form in the library stacks or from another library. Complete instructions for using the system are available using a menu-driven help system built into the system itself.

The system permits the user to search the entire contents of the database and to read the full text of most of the articles identified as relevant from a single location.

explain, as precisely as possible, what information is desired. This will almost certainly involve filling out a form specifying the keywords and other constraints to be placed on the search (such as limiting the search to the most recent five years or to materials in a specific language only) or limiting the amount of money that may be spent conducting the search. The librarian may also want to interview the researcher as well for clarification of the search parameters before the search is conducted. As a rule, the costs of conducting searches on systems such as DIALOG® are based on actual long-distance telephone charges, a basic fee for connection to the system, and a small charge for each bibliographic citation, abstract, or article received, and are borne by the student or researcher requesting the search. In some cases, there may be special reduced rates for students conducting searches as class exercises. The student should contact the reference services librarian for assistance in conducting an on-line search.

> Note that many materials are not yet included in on-line databases. Also, many materials relevant to a research topic may not have full-text searchability. Therefore, an electronic search should not be considered exhaustive.

INTERLIBRARY LOAN AND VISITING SCHOLAR SERVICES

Few libraries can even come close to offering complete collections in a field of study, let alone across many fields of study. At the same time, even most small college libraries own special collections that may be unavailable elsewhere. For this reason most libraries cooperate by providing interlibrary loan services to the clients of other libraries. The reference librarian at the student's home library should be consulted for assistance in the process of identifying the nearest library with a specific holding and of ordering such materials.

Interlibrary loans can, of course, be somewhat expensive as the user of such materials will have to pay for shipping costs in both directions, photocopying and copyright fees if any photocopying of copyrighted materials is involved, and possible charges for special handling by cooperating librarians. Therefore it is wise to be certain that materials really are needed before placing an order. The student should also be aware from the beginning that the interlibrary loan process can take as long as several weeks—another reason to begin early on any literature review project.

When the library with the needed materials is not too far away it may be both more efficient and less expensive to travel to that library and use the needed materials on site. In some cases, visiting scholars and students may freely walk in and use the resources of a library without any special permission or notice, although borrowing privileges may be another matter. More often, however, access to some or all resources of a library, especially rare or specialized collections, may require identification or a letter of introduction from the user's home library. A telephone call to the library to be visited should be enough to determine the procedures to be followed.

MICROFORM RESOURCES

Printed and bound materials—books, journals, dissertations, and so on—have been a dominant form for library resources for centuries and are still preferred

FIGURE 4.13   Microform reading devices. Above is a reader for sheets of film known as microfiche. On the right is a reader for 35mm rolls of microfilm. The microfilm reader is also equipped with a card-operated printer for making paper copies of film images.

by many, if not most, readers. However, such materials are expensive, take up substantial amounts of valuable storage space, and are not durable over long periods of time. In recent decades all major libraries have replaced large portions of their collections with miniature forms which require far less storage space and maintenance. In addition to saving storage space, miniaturization permits the information in rare and valuable materials to be casually studied by many clients while the original is kept safely stored in a vault.

Because technology is constantly evolving, most libraries have collections stored on a variety of different miniaturized media. These include *positive-image, photographic prints* called **microcards;** *negative-image, photographic sheet film* called **microfiche;** *negative-image, 35mm rolls of film* called **microfilm;** and various, newer electronic forms of document storage. Each format is essentially the same thing—a photographic image of the original pages of a book, journal, or other document. Up to 96 pages of an original document can be stored on a typical 4- by 5-inch microfiche. Because the images of each page are too small to be read by the unaided eye, a special machine called a reader is needed to enlarge the stored images to a readable size.

To use resources stored in microform one must locate the correct microcard, microfilm, or microfiche, usually in a cabinet or rack of some kind, correctly mount the microform in the reader, turn on the lamp, and advance the form to the desired series of images. A few minutes of experimentation or instruction should be sufficient to learn how this is done.

Often it is desirable to be able to make a paper copy of a microform image, particularly a chart, graph, or table of data. For this purpose, many libraries offer microform readers with the ability to produce a photocopy of whatever image is displayed. Such devices are typically operated by coin or debit card.

INTERNET RESOURCES

The Internet is a giant computer network of computer networks across which an enormous variety of information may be transmitted. Millions of computers are connected to this network, ranging in size from giant supercomputers to personal computers. The kinds of information that may be transmitted include personal text correspondence, computer software, photographic images and sequences of such images, and sounds. In the future, even full length movies may be transmitted across the Internet. Information may be transmitted from user to user in virtually any format understood by both users. The format of transmitted documents and their interpretation are controlled by software tools such as the following.

WWW. Provides access to extremely complex documents that may include photographic images, "hot text" links that provide access to additional documents, and sequences of images, in addition to simple text.

GOPHER. Provides a hierarchical menu system for locating, viewing, and obtaining a wide variety of documents. Documents are placed by providers on GOPHER servers which may be accessed by GOPHER clients.

VERONICA. An index of materials available through GOPHER servers. Hundreds of official GOPHER servers are indexed on a weekly basis. VERONICA permits Internet users to search for GOPHER documents using keywords rather than by accessing individual GOPHERs.

ARCHIE. An indexing system similar to VERONICA but designed to permit searching for documents by title words rather than by keyword.

FTP. A system specifically designed to permit computer software to be downloaded from one computer to another. Many useful shareware programs, including products for searching the Internet, can be obtained through FTP.

TELNET. A program permitting the Internet user to connect directly to any other computer on the Internet. Many computers, of course, may not allow access to anything without entry of a valid user account name and password.

E-MAIL. A system for sending, receiving, and archiving mail electronically. Mail may be sent to or received from individuals or entire lists of people at once.

USENET. A system for accessing thousands of discussion groups on nearly any topic. Participants can ask questions and receive answers, respond to questions or comments by others, and do anything that one might do in a group discussion of some topic.

MAJOR REFERENCE TOOLS

With few exceptions, students are generally familiar with such reference books as the encyclopedia, dictionary, atlas, and thesaurus. A good reference library, however, has many more research tools about which some students seem quite unaware. Time spent browsing through the reference section of a student's college library to discover such resources will be well spent. The following are some useful reference tools that may be of interest.

Dictionaries

Everyone is familiar with standard dictionaries as references for the correct spellings and definitions for words. However, the reference sections of most libraries will often have a good collection of specialized dictionaries that can be useful references as well as interesting to browse through. These may include a variety of dual language dictionaries, dictionaries of jargon related to specific professions or areas of interest, dictionaries of slang terms, and dictionaries of names. Unabridged dictionaries are also very useful for tracing the origins and original meanings of words. The term *dictionary* is also applied to many encyclopedia-like works which consist of alphabetically arranged articles on topics related to some theme. Examples of this type of reference book include the *Dictionary of American Biography* and the *Dictionary of American History.*

Atlases and Maps

Most people have used road maps and maps of countries or geographic regions such as those commonly found in *National Geographic* magazine. Maps are a very high-density form of information presentation and can be fascinating to browse through as well as educational. The reference sections of most libraries will almost always include a collection of atlases and maps. Of particular interest might be such items as local topographic maps, road maps, economic resource maps, or antique maps. In the future it may be practical (it is already possible) to use computerized, three dimensional maps and virtual reality environments to simulate walking, driving, or flying through buildings, cities, national parks, or virtually anything else, real or imaginary.

Encyclopedias

Every library reference section offers its patrons access to one or more encyclopedias, which are often extremely extensive collections of topical articles arranged in alphabetical order. Such materials are useful for very general background information on a wide variety of subjects. However, materials from encyclopedias are unlikely to provide more than a very superficial overview of a topic and, because of the time required to prepare an encyclopedia for publication, can never be viewed as fully up to date in coverage.

Almanacs

Originally, an almanac was a collection of information relating to the calendar—principally dealing with the cycles of the sun and moon as they related to the seasons for planting and harvesting. The word itself is derived from the arabic *al-manakh* which means *calendar.* Today an almanac, which is sometimes also called a *yearbook,* means an annually published collection of statistics, facts, tables of data, or other kinds of information, usually concerning a particular year but sometimes also including cumulative data for several or many years. Almanacs typically contain special feature or filler articles of various kinds as well. Most libraries offer an extensive collection of almanacs in their reference sections, some offering a broad range of general interest kinds of information and some focusing on a particular area of interest. For example, such information as the current addresses of charitable organizations, a list of the worst earthquakes in history, a list of Olympic medal winners, or pictures of the current national flags of the world's nations would very likely be found in a general-interest almanac. A complete listing of world records for most sports would very likely be found in an almanac focusing on sports.

Directories

Directories are listings or compilations of some kind of data. Telephone books, organizational membership lists, listings of governmental officials, and museum exhibit guides are all directories. The reference sections of most research libraries typically offer hundreds if not thousands of specialized kinds of directories. Indeed, all of the indexing and catalog systems of the library itself are types of directories. Browsing through the stacks containing these resources may even be useful in the process of identifying a research topic as the availability of the information contained in them may suggest opportunities for research.

 TERMS

abstract	ISSN
call number	keywords
card catalog	Library of Congress system
copyright	microcard
Dewey Decimal System	microfiche
index	microfilm
ISBN	on-line resources
ISMN	

EXERCISES

1. For a topic of your own choosing or one assigned by your instructor use the resources of your library to assemble the following:

   a) a list of at least 10 books dealing with some aspect of your topic, including correct and complete bibliographic citations and the library call numbers.

   b) a list of up to 10 titles of journals likely to provide coverage relevant to your topic.

    c) a printout of at least 10 citations from a computer search of your topic. Also include details of the search itself.

    d) a list of at least 5 journal articles or similar material actually available in the library and an order form for interlibrary loan of at least one article not locally available.

2. Identify the indexes, on-line services, microfilm collections, and other resources of your library and attempt to use each one to find material related to a topic of your own choosing or one assigned by your instructor.

3. Using a local, computerized index, such as ERIC, Humanities Index, Social Science Index, or a similar system, generate a bibliography of a topic of your choice. Broaden or narrow the search specification as necessary to produce a bibliography of no fewer than 20 and no more than 50 citations.

4. Repeat exercise #3 using an on-line access database such as DIALOG®.

5. Locate, obtain, read, and summarize selected items from the bibliographies produced in exercises 3 and 4 to produce annotated bibliographies of at least 10 items each.

6. For a topic of your own choosing or one assigned by your instructor, review at least 8 journal articles, portions of books, and similar material and write a separate summary or abstract (in your own words) for each.

7. Write a review of at least two pages in which the separate items summarized in item #2 above are integrated.

ADDITIONAL RESOURCES WITH ANNOTATION

Cicciarella, C.F. (1992). *Directory of periodicals in sport*. Charlotte, NC: Persimmon Software.
A directory of information for authors, potential subscribers, and advertisers concerning more than 125 periodicals related to sport or physical education, including research and professional practice journals.

Delia, D. (1992). From romance to rhetoric: the Alexandrian library in classical and Islamic tradition. *American Historical Review, 97* (5), 1449–1467.
A very readable summary of the history of the Alexandrian library and of various theories of its fate.

DIALOG Information Services (1993). *DIALOG database catalog*. Palo Alto, CA: Author.
Descriptive catalog of databases accessible through DIALOG.

Library of Congress (1994). *Library of congress subject headings*. Washington, DC: Author.
An annually published guide to the Library of Congress indexing system.

5

MEASURING

Everyone uses measurement. We use a yardstick or tape measure to measure distances. We use a bathroom scale to measure our weight, usually hoping to find less than we had before. We use a speedometer to measure how fast we drive a car and we use the meter in a pump to measure how much gasoline we put into the car. For ordinary quantities or qualities, such as length, weight, or volume, measurement is very simple and straightforward. For more complex constructs, however, measurement can become more difficult. Measuring the height of a basketball player is easy but how can we measure the potential talent of a basketball player, or a child's fear of the water at a beach? Also, in the contexts of scientific research and the assessment of students in a classroom, the process of measurement requires a bit more understanding than reading the dial on a bathroom scale. This chapter is intended to introduce the basic concepts of measurement that must be understood to appropriately use measurement in these more complex settings.

DEFINITION

Measurement may be defined as the process of equating or associating a number or quality to an attribute or characteristic of a person, thing, or other phenomenon. *Measurement in which the result is a number representing some kind of quantity* is called **quantitative** measurement whereas *measurement which uses words to describe an attribute* is called **qualitative** measurement. Some readers may prefer to restrict the definition of measurement to quantitative measurement and to use an alternative term such as assessment or evaluation to mean qualitative measurement. However, evaluation is usually used to refer to the application of a value judgment to something rather than just making a qualitative description.

FIGURE 5.1   Five black dots. "Five" is a quantitative measurement. "Black" is a qualitative measurement.

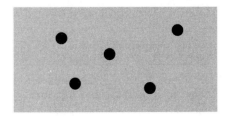

Measurement may be exact as is the case when the members of a class or group of persons or objects are counted. More often, however, measurement is an inexact process of *estimation*. This form of measurement always involves the comparison of the characteristic or attribute to be measured to a known, common standard. For example, when the length of a football field is measured using a tape measure, the yards, feet, and inches marked on the tape are the known, common standard to which the field is compared. The markings on the tape are actually representations or approximations of the real, known, common standard, and are themselves, in fact, estimates of that standard.

In the past, standards used to define measurements were rather crude and even subject to substantial variation over time. For example, such measures as the foot and the inch were once based on the length of a man's (or perhaps the king's) foot or the length of three grains of wheat laid end to end. Today measurement standards are derived from physical phenomena or characteristics of objects known to be highly stable. The meter, for example, is based on the wavelength of a portion of the spectrum of the element Krypton-86.

ERROR

It is very important in measurement to understand that most measures are estimates of the true quantity or quality being expressed. Estimates may be extremely accurate (or even, by chance, perfectly exact) but it is *never* possible to know exactly how much deviation from the true value may be present. Careful measurement technique, quality measurement equipment, and diligent calibration of that equipment all serve to improve the accuracy of a measurement but never to the point where error is entirely eliminated.

Measurement errors may be either random or systematic. Random errors are unavoidable but, by their very nature, vary at random around the true value. Therefore, they tend to cancel each other if multiple measurements are made and their average taken. That is, the average of several measurements will tend to be closer and closer to the true value as the number of measurements taken increases. Systematic errors are those that occur as the result of some consistent problem during the measurement process, such as external factors that affect the responses of subjects or measurement instruments that are out of calibration. Because systematic errors tend to vary consistently from the true value, taking multiple measurements or increasing the number of subjects being measured does not result in their elimination or reduction. The careful control of biasing influences and careful attention to measurement instrumentation and technique are the only means of eliminating or minimizing systematic errors.

THE INTERNATIONAL SYSTEM OF UNITS

Many students, particularly those lacking a strong background in science, may find certain parts of the *International System of Units* (**SI**)—formerly and commonly called the Metric System—somewhat unfamiliar and awkward, but its use is becoming increasingly desirable and necessary in all fields of endeavor. There is now only one remaining country (the U.S.A.) in the developed world that has yet to adopt it as the official system of weights and measures. The International System is used almost exclusively in the sciences and almost all scientific journals require that manuscripts report all measurements in SI units.

FIGURE 5.2   The International System of Units (SI). These are the base units of the system used throughout most of the world. Other units of the SI system are derived from them.

PARAMETER	BASE UNIT
length	meter
force	newton
mass	kilogram
time	second
volume	liter
frequency	hertz
temperature	kelvin

The International System is a modernized and expanded version of the metric system. For the most part it is a decimal system, like our system of money and the original metric system. All measurements are expressed in terms of one or more *base units* plus prefixes that represent decimal fractions or multiples of ten. The term **base unit** *refers to simple units of measurement that are not defined in terms of other units of measure.* For example, distances are expressed in base units called meters, masses are expressed in base units called grams, and volumes are expressed in base units called liters. Quantities of 10, 100, and 1,000 base units are given the prefixes deca, hecto, and kilo, respectively. The prefixes deci, centi, and milli are used as prefixes to signify 1/10, 1/100, and 1/1000 base units.

COMPOUND AND DERIVED UNITS OF MEASURE

Meters, grams, liters, and seconds are all *base* units of measure. Respectively, these are used to express length, mass, volume, and time. Some phenomena, however, cannot be measured or expressed so simply. Measurement or expression of the velocity of an automobile, for example, requires the combination of two base units, one for length or distance and one for time. Automobile velocity is commonly expressed in miles per hour or feet per second (kilometers per hour or meters per second in the SI system). The two base units are combined to form a ratio (that is, one measure divided by another). Whenever *two or more base units are used together as a ratio or as a product* the result is a **compound unit** of measure. Liters per minute, kilograms per square inch, dollars per acre, and revolutions per minute are all examples of compound units of measure in which two base units are combined as a ratio. The combination of two (or more) base units as a product results in compound units such as the foot-pound, man-hour, and acre-foot. Base units and compound units can also be combined with additional base units or compound units to produce new compound units such as the foot-pound per hour, acre-foot per day, or even the acre-foot per man-hour.

When compound units of measure are used frequently, a new unit is sometimes created to simplify the terminology. For example, 550 foot-pounds per second is given the new name *horsepower.* Measurement units of this type are called **derived units.**

FIGURE 5.3   Prefixes used in the SI system of measures. The prefix attached to a unit of measure multiplies the unit by the associated value from the table below.

MULTIPLIER	PREFIX
.000000000001	pico
.000000001	nano
.000001	micro
.001	milli
.01	centi
.1	deci
1	———
10	deka
100	hecto
1000	kilo
1,000,000	mega
1,000,000,000	giga
1,000,000,000,000	tera

The International System of units is not consistently decimal. Time, for example, is expressed using the hours, minutes, and seconds we all find familiar, although fractions of seconds, such as milliseconds, microseconds, and so on, are all decimals. Angles are expressed in radians.

CONVERSION OF UNITS OF MEASURE

Measurements should always be recorded or expressed in research reports in the units in which they were originally made, even if they were not made in SI or metric units. If measurements are not in SI units then the SI equivalents should also be reported but these must be placed in parentheses. (If measurements are made in SI units then the equivalent non-SI units may be reported in parentheses or left unreported.)

Conversions to or from SI units are made by multiplying the actual measurement by the appropriate conversion factor. Conversion factors may be obtained from tables of equivalent measures which can readily be found in almanacs and other reference books. Many calculators and computers can also make measurement unit conversions. When making such conversions, however, one must be careful to avoid inadvertently inflating the apparent precision of a measurement. For example, although 2.54 is the usual factor for conversion of inches to centimeters, it is not correct to convert a measurement of 1 inch with a precision of 1/16 inch to a measurement of 2.54 inches with a precision of 1/16 centimeter. The correct converted measurement is 2.54 centimeters with a precision of 2.54/16 centimeters.

Many hand calculators offer built-in conversion functions.

FIGURE 5.4   Selected SI-English measurement conversions. Note that all such conversions are approximate. Units of time and frequency require no conversion.

SI UNITS		NON-SI UNITS	NON-SI UNITS		SI UNITS
1 meter X	=	1.093613 yards	1 yard	=	0.9144 meters
1 liter	=	1.056688 quarts (liquid)	1 quart (liquid)	=	0.946353 liters
1 kilogram	=	2.204623 pounds	1 pound	=	0.453592 kilograms
1 newton	=	7.33717 poundals	1 poundal	=	0.136292 newtons
1 degree Kelvin*	=	1.8 degrees	1 degree F	=	0.555556 degrees K

*For the temperature conversion note that the Kelvin scale is a ratio scale measurement whereas the Fahrenheit scale is only interval in scale. Thus the above conversion is only for the unit of measurement and not for actual temperatures. To convert a Kelvin temperature to Fahrenheit, subtract 273.2, multiply by 1.8 and then add 32. To convert a Fahrenheit temperature to Kelvin, subtract 32, multiply by .55556, and then subtract 273.2. To perform such conversions involving the Celsius scale rather than the Kelvin scale omit the step above involving the addition or subtraction of 273.2.

MEASUREMENT INSTRUMENTS

The term **measurement instrument** is applied to *any apparatus, system, or material used for the purpose of obtaining a quantitative or qualitative measurement.* Although the word *instrument* seems to suggest machines or laboratory devices, such things as a classroom test, a survey questionnaire, the 40-yard dash, or a live interview are also measurement instruments.

MEASUREMENT PROTOCOLS

The best and most expensive measurement instrument is completely useless if it is not used properly. *The procedures for using a measurement instrument* are called the **measurement or test protocol.** For example, the protocol for estimating body composition using skin fold measurements specifies the sites from which measurements must be taken, how the skin fold caliper should be held, and the amount of pressure to be applied to the skin by the caliper. The protocol for a treadmill stress test specifies the exact sequence of changes in speed and elevation of the treadmill, when physiological measurements should be taken, and when the test should be aborted.

A measurement protocol serves to standardize the measurement process, eliminating variation in the way measurements are taken as a possible source of variation in the measurement data. In the use of skin fold measurement for the estimation of body composition, for example, skin fold measurements could be taken from slightly or even substantially different sites on the body without affecting the usefulness of the technique, as long as everyone using the technique uses the same sites. But if everyone doing skin fold measurement uses different sites, the technique is rendered nearly useless. The same is true for academic examinations. Teacher-created, non-standardized examinations are fine for use within a single class, but cannot be used to make comparisons between classes because their non-standardization means that there may be variations in the instructions or exam conditions used with each class.

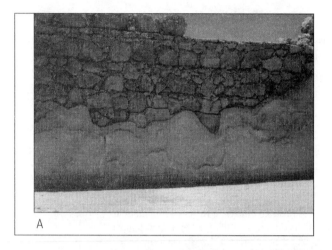

FIGURE 5.5   The meaning of precision is illustrated in the fit between the stones above. A) Relatively low precision of fit between stones in the walls of an ancient fortress at Masada, Israel. B) Relatively high precision of fit between stones in the walls at the Sphinx near Giza in Egypt.

PRECISION

The precision of a measurement instrument is the capacity of that instrument to resolve small differences in the parameter or quality being measured. A measurement instrument that has a greater ability to resolve small differences than another instrument is said to have greater precision or to be more precise than that other instrument. Consider two classroom examinations, for example: one with 100 questions and a second with only 50 questions. Theoretically (that is, ignoring the fact that no test is a perfect measure), if these tests are both given to a student who understands 50 percent of the test content, the student should correctly answer 50 percent of the test items. On the 100-item test 50 items should be answered correctly, and 25 should be answered correctly on the 50-item test. Suppose, however, that another student given the test actually understands 51 percent of the test content. This student's raw score should be 51 on the 100 item test. On the 50-item test, however, the student's raw score should be either 25 or 26 because 51 percent of 50 is 25.5. Both tests should produce raw scores within 1 item of the student's true score, but 1 item represents an expected error of 1 percent on the 100-item test and 2 percent on the 50-item test. Therefore, the 100-item test has greater resolving power or precision than the 50-item test.

VALIDITY

The **validity** of a measurement instrument is *the degree to which the instrument actually measures what it is supposed to measure.* For most kinds of measurement instruments, validity is relatively obvious and unlikely to be challenged or questioned. For example, few would dispute that a tape measure is a valid instrument for measuring lengths or that a balance scale is valid for measuring weight. Validity that is obvious or self evident is called *face* or *logical* validity. Note, however, that even face validity may rest on the truth of assumptions upon which the instrument is based. For example, an essay examination item which most everyone would agree is valid nevertheless rests on certain assumptions such as the ability of students to read and write in the language used in the examination, the availability of sufficient time to respond, and the motivation of students to score as well as they can on the test.

A measurement instrument may be highly valid for one purpose and highly invalid for another. For example, a thermometer is a highly valid instrument for measuring the current air temperature but a calendar would be of considerably more use in predicting the temperature two months in advance. Similarly, the Scholastic Aptitude Test (SAT) faced by most students applying to enter college is generally accepted as a relatively valid predictor of success in college but is a very poor indicator of intelligence, attitude, or motivation. The following terms refer to specific aspects of the validity of measurement instruments.

Content Validity

Content validity is a term usually applied to tests and examinations. It is *the degree to which the content or subject matter of a test actually represents the content or subject matter of the course or instructional unit to which it applies.*

Construct Validity

The term *construct* is used to refer to attitudes, personality characteristics, values, and other abstract concepts that are generally rather hard to define. For example, **locus of control** *is a construct that refers to the figurative location, internal or external, from which an individual perceives him- or herself to be controlled.* **Construct validity** is *the degree to which an instrument measures some such construct.*

Predictive Validity

Predictive validity refers to *the use of a measurement instrument to predict something in the future.* An aptitude test is a test that should have a high degree of predictive validity. Odds makers use a variety of methods to try to predict the outcome of sports and other events. Obviously no method is 100 percent accurate.

Concurrent Validity

Concurrent validity refers to *the degree to which an instrument measures the status of something at the time the measurement is made rather than predicting a status in the future.*

FIGURE 5.6   Validity and Reliability. The left target shows the target hits from a rifle with a valid sight (as well as a competent marksperson). The right target shows the result of an invalid sight. The tight clustering of hits on both targets shows that both sights are reliable. Note that if the sight were unreliable the hits would be scattered all over the target (or possibly completely off the target) and no judgments could be made concerning validity.

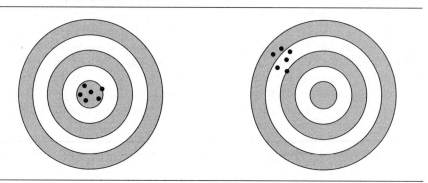

RELIABILITY

Reliability should be understood as *consistency of performance*. An automobile that always starts and runs without trouble is said to be reliable. One that frequently breaks down or fails to start is unreliable. A reliable measurement instrument is one that gives consistent results. It is *one in which the error introduced by the instrument itself,* called **instrument error**, is small.

EFFICIENCY

The **efficiency** of a measurement instrument may be conceptualized as *the ratio between the benefits and the costs of using the instrument.* Efficiency increases when the value obtained through use of the instrument increases, and decreases when the cost of using the instrument increases. The value obtained through use of a measurement instrument is the utility or usefulness of the measurement data. The cost of using a measurement instrument is what must be sacrificed in order to obtain a measurement.

$$Efficiency = \frac{benefit}{cost}$$

Costs may include fees charged for the use of test or survey materials, the time required to conduct the measurement, the cost of equipment, and even the potential discomfort or risk to persons or materials involved.

Decisions in which efficiency may play a role must sometimes be made regarding the selection of a measurement instrument. For example, there are several alternative instruments available for estimating body composition, including underwater weighing and skin fold measurement. Of these two, the cost of underwater weighing is substantially higher. Underwater weighing takes much longer, requires special equipment and facilities, and is uncomfortable to some subjects. On the other hand, the value of the data obtained by underwater weighing is potentially much higher than that obtained by skin fold measurement because its precision is higher. Thus, the decision to use one method or the other must be made by considering both the benefit and the cost of each alternative.

FIGURE 5.7   Beauty is in the eye of the beholder. The measurement of some things is highly subjective.

OBJECTIVITY AND SUBJECTIVITY

The **objectivity of a measurement instrument** is *the degree to which use of the instrument does not require special knowledge or the use of judgment.* **Subjectivity** is the degree to which use of an instrument does require special knowledge or the use of judgment. Instruments such as a tape measure, balance scale, stopwatch, or a multiple choice examination or questionnaire are usually considered highly objective. Instruments such as essay examinations, psychoanalysis, or the rules for judging gymnastics, figure skating, or diving involve a substantial degree of subjectivity. That a measurement instrument is highly complex or can only be used by an expert does not cause the instrument to lack objectivity. For example, the instruments that monitor conditions inside a nuclear power plant certainly must be used by persons with special training but they are considered highly objective. The kind of special knowledge that makes an instrument low in objectivity is the kind of intuitive, impossible-to-define, "gut" knowledge that comes only with experience. In fact, it may be argued that it is this very indefinability of the knowledge needed that makes the use of a measurement instrument subjective.

The scoring of an essay test item can be made at least partially objective by defining the criteria, such as a list of points to be made, a description of standards for grammar, spelling, and other factors, to be used in scoring the exam.

One means of judging the objectivity of a measurement instrument is to determine the degree to which scores or readings can be determined by a machine or computer. A multiple choice examination, for example, is 100 percent objective by this standard because a computer, properly equipped, can easily compare a student's answers with an answer key to determine the student's score. Some subjective judgment may still be needed at times to decide when items are misleading or ambiguous. An essay examination, on the other hand, is much less objective because no computer algorithm has yet been written that can judge all aspects of a student's essay.

The above paragraph notwithstanding, many measurement or assessment-like procedures traditionally thought to require both expert knowledge and judgment have been computerized with substantial success to create what is known in the computer field as an *expert system*. An expert system is a piece of software that combines a specialized knowledge base with a usually complex set of rules for decision making within the domain of the knowledge base. For

FIGURE 5.8   The numbers on a license plate are nominal in scale.

example, expert systems consisting of databases of symptoms, signs, and diseases combined with diagnostic rules have proven remarkably successful in making medical diagnoses and are now widely used by medical practitioners to assist in diagnosing difficult cases. Successful expert systems are examples of situations in which the knowledge needed to make assessments or measurements, previously thought to be indefinable, has been defined.

VARIABLES AND SCALES OF MEASUREMENT

Anything that can be different from case to case is a **variable**. Adult body height, for example, is a variable among the human population because it differs from individual to individual. The exercising heart rate of an athlete is also a variable because it changes as the work being performed changes. The ratio of the circumference of a circle to its diameter is *not* a variable because it is always equal to pi. Pi is a *constant. Anything that remains unchanged from case to case is a* **constant.** *When the quantity or quality of a variable is measured or assessed for a group of cases or subjects the results* constitute what is referred to as a *set* of data or as a **data set**.

Even variables themselves commonly vary in different ways. Some, such as gender, can take only two possible values. Others can have many different, but only particular, values while others may have any value. Also, it is possible for a variable to vary in one way but to be measured as if it varied in another. Understanding the information in a data set, including the correct application of statistical analysis tools, requires an understanding of the type of variables and their measurement in the set. The following sections describe several types of commonly encountered variables and the corresponding measurement scales.

Nominal Data

To *nominate* someone for public office is to *name* that person as a candidate. **Nominal data** is *data, often but not necessarily in numeric form, that identifies a subject or case within a data set.* When nominal data is in the form of num-

FIGURE 5.9   House numbers constitute ordinal scale data.

bers, those numbers serve as labels or substitutes for names. For example, the numbers on the jerseys of a team of baseball players are nominal in scale. The numbers themselves represent no numeric quantity or meaning of any kind—they merely serve to identify the players. If those same players were asked their preference in bats, their responses of "wood," "metal," or "plastic" would also be nominal in scale.

Ordinal Data

Consider a data set consisting of the ranks of a group of military personnel. The data, words such as general, colonel, lieutenant, corporal, and private, indicate the order or sequence of command. A general ranks higher than a colonel, a colonel outranks a lieutenant, and so on. However, the data does not contain any information about the relative difference between each rank. The data does not show whether the difference between a corporal and a private is the same or different than the difference between a general and a colonel. *Data that varies only in sequence* is called **ordinal.** (The term *ranked* data is also sometimes used.)

Sometimes a variable that is not ordinal is measured or recorded as if it were ordinal. For example, the performance of the competitors in a cross-country foot race might be recorded as first, second, third, and so on. This results in the loss of information about the relative difference in performance, but it does permit the performance of the runners in several races to be compared even when those races are performed under different conditions.

Interval and Ratio Data

The last column of Figure 5.11 gives the actual times of each runner in a 100-meter race. In addition to information about who finished first, second, third, and so on, this data also shows the relative margin of difference, or interval between any two runners. *Data that shows relative difference in addition to relative standing or rank* may be **interval** or **ratio** in scale. Such data is called ratio in scale if the zero point of the scale actually represents the quantity of zero. It is called interval if the zero point does not represent a true zero quantity. For

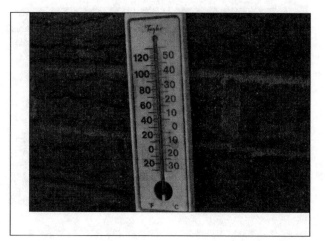

FIGURE 5.10   A dual scale thermometer showing temperature in both Fahrenheit and Celsius. Fahrenheit and Celsius temperatures are interval in scale because the zero point does not represent a true absence of heat. Kelvin or absolute temperatures are ratio data because a temperature of zero represents the total absence of heat.

FIGURE 5.11   Race Results. Place of finish and times (in seconds/hundreds of seconds) for runners in a 100-meter run. These three columns of data contain nominal, ordinal, and ratio data, respectively.

RUNNER NO.	PLACE OF FINISH	TIME
12	2	20.12
11	3	20.18
6	1	19.32
4	6	21.01
22	5	20.32
3	4	20.25

example, the temperature of 0° on the Celsius scale is not a true zero point. It is certainly possible to be colder than 0° Celsius. On the other hand, 0° is a true zero point on the Kelvin scale. Therefore, temperature measurements using the Celsius scale result in interval data and measurements using the Kelvin scale result in ratio data.

Dichotomous and False Dichotomous Data

Any variable that can have only two possible values or states is called a **dichotomy**. Gender, pass/fail grades, the on/off status of simple electric circuits, and the fair/foul status of a batted baseball are all examples of dichotomous variables.

If a variable is genuinely dichotomous it is said to be a *true* dichotomy. On the other hand, if a variable actually varies continuously or has more than two possible states but is measured or expressed in the form of a dichotomy, then it is said to be a *false* dichotomy. For example, the data in the "status" column of Figure 5.12 represents a true dichotomy. Each player can only be classified as a starter or as a substitute. The "Height for Position" column, on the other hand, is a false dichotomy. "Tall" and "Short" imply a dichotomy but height, whether relative to some standard or not, varies continuously.

FIGURE 5.12   Basketball Player Scoring Statistics. This table of scouting statistics illustrates data of a variety of types. The player numbers are nominal in scale. The player status and height for position data are dichotomies, the former a true dichotomy and the latter a false one. Height is interval in scale and points scored are ratio in scale. The player positions constitute categorical data.

PLAYER	STATUS	HEIGHT	HEIGHT FOR POSITION	POSITION	POINTS SCORED
2	starter	76	tall	guard	17
3	starter	68	short	guard	11
11	sub	70	short	guard	3
12	starter	78	tall	center	10
13	sub	77	short	center	6
1	starter	80	tall	forward	10
10	starter	75	short	forward	5
14	sub	66	short	guard	0
22	sub	72	short	guard	4

Continuous and Discrete Data

A variable or data that is interval or ratio in scale may also be classified as continuously or discretely variable. A **continuous** variable is *one for which there is no smallest unit of variation.* That is, regardless of how precisely the variable is measured, it could still theoretically be measured with even greater precision. A **discrete** variable is *one that does have a smallest unit of variation.* If a discrete variable is measured with a precision such that it is resolved to its smallest unit of variation, then an even more precise measurement would yield no further information. In a basketball score, the variable "points scored" is discrete. Points in basketball can be scored in units of 1, 2, or 3, but one can never, under current rules, score a fraction of a point. The "player height" variable, however, is continuous. Height is continuously variable even though it may be measured or expressed with no greater precision than the nearest inch or centimeter.

It is important to recognize that the terms "discrete" and "integer" do not mean the same thing. The smallest unit of variation in the set of integer numbers is 1, whereas a discrete variable may vary in units of any fixed amount, including fractional values (see Appendix A1 for a discussion of integer numbers).

USE OF SIGNIFICANT DIGITS

The number of **significant digits** in any decimal number is defined as *the number of digits from the first or leftmost non-zero digit to the last or rightmost digit.* The number 123.4, for example, has four significant digits. There are also four significant digits in the number 1.234, 0.1234, and .0001234.

When numbers are used to record or express measured quantities the number of significant digits used should not have the effect of overstating the precision of measurement. The result of any measurement is an *estimate* of the exact dimension. Times written as 10 seconds, 10.0 seconds, and 10.00 seconds are *not* the same. The first case means 10 seconds within a tolerance of .5 second, often stated as 10 seconds plus or minus one-half second. The actual time could be anywhere within one-half second of 10 seconds. The second case means 10 seconds within a tolerance of .05 second and the third case means 10 seconds within a tolerance of .005 second.

When measurement data is used in any computation it is not possible to improve the precision of the original measurements. Thus, results should generally be of the same precision as the *least precise* measurement in the original data. When measurements are added or subtracted the number of significant digits in the result should be the same as in the least precise measurement. For example, if three segments of a cross-country footrace were measured with an odometer and recorded as 1,500 feet, 1,250.7 feet, and 1,780.25 feet, then the total distance should be recorded with a precision of 4 significant digits (4,531 feet) because the least precise measurement (1,500 feet) has 4 significant digits.

When measurements are multiplied or divided the result should have the same precision *relative to its magnitude* as the least precise original measurement. For example, consider an object with a measured mass of 10.500 kilograms that is lifted a measured distance of 2.0 meters. The mass measurement is precise to approximately 1 part in 10,000, and the distance measurement to 1 part in 20. The work performed is the product of the mass and the distance and is expressed in kilogram-meters. The work performed should be expressed as 21 kilogram-meters because such a figure has a precision of about 1 part in 20. On the other hand, if the distance had been measured as 2,000 millimeters, then the work performed would be expressed as 21.00 kilogram-meters.

When recording measurement data it is very important to do so in a manner that does not distort or misrepresent the measurement precision. For example, if the distance between two points on a road is measured as 5.4 kilometers using an automobile odometer, then it is correct to record the measurement as 5.4 kilometers. It is not correct to record the distance as 5,400 meters, because such a figure implies precision to within a half meter and the original measurement is really only precise to within .05 kilometer or about 50 meters. If it is necessary to express such a measurement in meters, then scientific notation should be used to avoid confusion. The 5.4 kilometer distance would be written as 5.4×10^3 meters.

MEASURING THE HARD TO MEASURE

Properties such as length, mass, time, and volume are all relatively easy to measure. Once the property to be measured has been defined and a common, standard unit of measure agreed upon then comparison of that property to the common standard is simple and straightforward. Everyone is familiar with simple measurements using such instruments as a tape measure, balance scale, or stopwatch. Some properties and characteristics, however, are not so simple to measure or, in many cases, to define. For example, how can attributes such as intelligence or trustworthiness, personality characteristics such as introversion or stability, or psycho-physical traits such as susceptibility to pain or situational anxiety be measured? In most cases we do not have great difficulty in crudely classifying someone as introverted or anxious, but such classifications are often made in error and precise quantification becomes extremely difficult.

Personality characteristics, emotional and mental attributes, psychological responses, knowledge, and many other hard-to-define constructs are very often, perhaps always, impossible to measure directly. However, they can often be measured or estimated through indirect methods. Extroversion, for example, is associated with a readiness to meet and interact with other people and a willingness to express ideas openly. By directly measuring an individual's choices when given the opportunity to interact with others or to express an idea, an indirect measure of extroversion might be obtained. The characteristic that cannot be measured directly can be measured indirectly because it is associated with a characteristic that can be measured directly.

The following sections describe a selection of methods commonly used to make indirect measurements.

Knowledge Tests

Everyone who has been to school has certainly experienced a wide variety of knowledge tests, and is probably familiar with their use for the assignment of grades and motivation of students. Contrary to popular opinion among many students, however, the goal of education is not to enable students to pass exams. Rather, the goal is to help students acquire knowledge, as well as the ability to acquire more knowledge, and an exam is merely a device for *measuring* what has been learned or understood.

A knowledge test consists of one or more items such as multiple choice questions, true/false statements, fill-in items, and essays, which make some kind of request to which the student or subject must respond. Good test items are designed so that the response can be used to discriminate between students who have the knowledge or competence being tested and those who do not. Each item may be designed to test a single element of knowledge or multiple competencies may be tested by a single item. Collectively, the responses of a student to the items on a knowledge test provide a measure of that student's knowledge or competence within the domain covered by the test.

The validity of a knowledge test is frequently a source of controversy and confusion. Validity was defined earlier in this chapter as the degree to which a measurement instrument (the test) measures what it is supposed to measure. In a narrow sense it may be argued that except in the most extreme cases there is really no such thing as an invalid test. Any test, from the Scholastic Aptitude Test (SAT) and Graduate Record Exam (GRE) to the simplest pop quiz, is valid with respect to the content of the test itself. That is, any test taken seriously by the student will produce a valid measure of the student's ability to respond to the items on the test. That test A is a valid measure of a student's ability to pass test A, however, is not very meaningful. To be meaningful or useful, the validity of a knowledge test must be in reference to something external to the test, such as a domain of knowledge or competence. The validity of a knowledge test is the degree to which the test measures knowledge or competence in the declared domain of the test.

Scales

Especially in the behavioral sciences there are many attributes or characteristics, such as extroversion, situational anxiety, locus of control, or even degree of

The Likert Scale Technique

The **Likert scale,** named for its inventor, Rensis Likert, is a *rating scale that uses the sum of several ratings to attempt to quantify an attitude, feeling, opinion, or some intangible characteristic or attribute.* For each such attribute, a measurement instrument using the Likert technique will include several statements with which the subject should either agree or disagree, depending upon the attribute being measured. For example, an instrument to measure the attribute of curiosity might ask the subject to use a numerical scale of 1 to 5 to indicate agreement or disagreement with such statements as "When I see a fallen log I like to turn it over to see what is underneath," "Sometimes I do things just to see what will happen," and "There are some questions we should not try to answer." Notice that the last statement is written in a negative form. A subject who tends to agree to the first two will tend to disagree with the last. The responses to negatively worded items are reversed prior to computing the subject's score. Once this conversion has been done the subject's score for curiosity is computed as the average of the responses for the three items.

Note: The term "Likert scale" is sometimes applied to any scale in which subjects respond using a numerical scale, but such usage is not technically correct.

The Semantic Differential Scale Technique

The **semantic differential scale** *attempts to quantify the subjects' feelings toward some object*—a product, person, company, etc.—*by asking subjects to apply ratings using a series of scales that represent gradations between pairs of opposite descriptive terms.* For example, to assess subjects' attitudes toward the Dallas Cowboys football team each might be asked to ascribe values to the team on scales labeled "good/bad," "hot/cold," "up/down," or even "forward/backward." Responses can range from –3 to +3 with a score of zero representing neutrality between the two opposite terms. The negative values apply to the term in each pair generally thought of as a negative descriptor (i.e. bad, cold, down, and backward.) Each subject's feeling is then computed as the average or sum of the scores given for the set of descriptor pairs.

Semantic differential data for two or more objects may often be interpreted quite usefully as a comparative profile or as a superimposed cloud of points for selected pairs of terms. Such an interpretation is commonly used in business marketing research as a measure of market differentiation for competing products. For example, in a study of two (or more) television programs, the mean scores on each pair of terms could be plotted as a profile or pair of superimposed line graphs. If the two lines overlap, it suggests that the two programs are perceived as very similar. If they do not overlap, or if they overlap only a little, then the programs are seen as different. Similarly, subject responses on two pairs of terms can be plotted as clouds of points. With computer-generated and animated graphics this could be extended to three pairs of terms at one time.

The Rank-Order and Q-Sort Techniques

Given a small number of items or concepts, such as a set of proposed names for a school basketball team or a list of reasons for failing to pass a test, most subjects will be able to arrange the items into order according to an assigned criteria without much difficulty. To obtain the consensus ranking by a group, each member of the group could be asked to sort the items into order and then an average rank could be computed by *assigning point values of 1 for a first-place ranking, 2 for a second-place ranking, and so on.* Such a procedure is sometimes called a **rank-order procedure.**

With more than 10 or 15 items, however, it becomes increasingly difficult for most subjects to make decisions regarding the relative ranks of different items. The difference in relative value of items in the mind of the evaluator tends to become smaller and smaller as the number of items increases and more and more pairs of items are seen as tied in rank. The **Q-sort procedure** is an attempt to deal with the problem of such ties in value by assigning items to a smaller number of ranked *groups*. For example, a study of the importance of various reasons for failing a test might begin with the compilation of a list of 25 (or more) possible reasons. Each reason would then be written on an index card. Subjects would be asked to sort the cards into seven piles following a strict procedure. First, the most and least important reasons would be selected and placed into pile one and seven. Next, the three most and three least important remaining cards would be selected and placed into piles two and six. Then the five most and least important remaining cards would be put into piles three and five and the remaining cards into pile four. The consensus rank for the 25 items would then be computed as the rank order of the sums of scores by all subjects.

pain, that are impossible or extremely difficult to quantify directly but that do seem to be unidimensional and to lie on a continuum. For example, required to make a speech to 50,000 people, nearly everyone will experience some degree of anxiety. Some will remain relatively calm and some will be so nervous as to be unable to function, but everyone will be somewhere on the anxiety continuum from extremely relaxed to extremely anxious.

One approach to quantifying this kind of phenomenon is to invent a linear scale that represents the full range of possible values and find a way to ask the subjects under study to indicate where they are or where someone else is perceived to be on that scale. To quantify the anxiety felt during public speaking, each of a group of subjects who have recently had to speak publicly might be asked, "On a scale of 1 to 7 where 1 means extremely relaxed and 7 means extremely anxious, rate how you felt when you had to speak in public."

The Thurstone Scale Technique

The **Thurstone Scale** Technique attempts to *measure attitudes toward some object or idea by asking subjects to select several* (commonly three) *statements from a longer list that best correspond to the subject's attitude.* The statements have been assigned numerical values in advance by a large panel of judges although these values are not disclosed to the subjects. Scores are computed by averaging the values assigned to the statements selected by the subject.

Scales of this type are obviously completely arbitrary with regard to the actual numerical values used. A value of 7 on a 1-through-7 scale represents a greater intensity of the feeling or attribute being measured than does a 1 on the same scale, but the actual value of 7 has no quantitative meaning outside the limits of the scale itself. A scale of −3 to 3 could just as easily be used and a value of 3 on such a scale would be the same in meaning as a value of 7 on the 1-through-7 scale. However, although the meanings of these two scales are the same, the actual range of numerical values used to construct a scale may have an effect on the responses of subjects. The following are several important considerations in selecting or designing a scale.

Range

In any scale in which the subject must give a numerical response the range of the scale is the number of possible numerical responses. In the two examples described in the preceding paragraph there are 7 possible responses, but there is no requirement that all scales use a range of 7. Use of a scale with more possible values theoretically offers greater precision of measurement than a scale with a narrower range. On the other hand, some subjects may tend to become confused, misinterpret the instructions, or even decline to participate if faced with too wide a range of possible responses. Most scales that require a numerical response use a range of between 3 and 9.

Odd vs. even range

All of the scales in the examples given above use an odd number of possible subject responses, but an even number of response choices can also be used. When an odd number of response choices are offered, the middle response nearly always represents an average or neutral response. This may lead many subjects to give a neutral response even when the true response is to one side of neutral, especially if the true response is only slightly to one side. Using an even number of response choices eliminates this problem by forcing subjects to make a choice on one side of neutral. On the other hand, an even number of response choices should not be used when genuinely neutral true responses are to be expected.

Numerical vs. positional scales

Whenever a scale requires the subject to respond numerically the ability of the scale to resolve small differences is limited by problems associated with the use of too many response options. Imagine being asked to rate the taste of three different brands of strawberry ice cream on a scale of 1 through 75. On the other hand, a scale of 1 through 5 must necessarily give a very crude resolution. One method for obtaining a relatively high degree of resolution without overwhelming the subject with too many response options is to ask subjects to respond by indicating a position on a line drawn between two opposite extremes. A mark may be made on a scale printed on a sheet of paper or a scale may be drawn on a computer screen and marked by pointing with a mouse or joy-stick. The researcher can then convert these marks into numerical values by measuring the distance from one end of the line to the mark with a ruler, or the computer can perform a similar measurement automatically. Obviously, differences in the way individuals make marks on paper may sometimes influence measurements made with such scales using paper and pencil, but such problems should not occur using a computerized positional scale. However, some subjects may feel intimidated or confused by the computer apparatus.

Studies in which scales are used typically involve questionnaires or forms consisting of a series of scaled items. Nideffer's Test of Attentional and Interpersonal Style (TAIS), for example, consists of 144 items, each in the form of a statement. The subject is to use a five-point scale to indicate the degree to which each statement describes his or her own behavior. Each item may measure a separate attribute or behavioral dimension or several items may be used in combination to perform each measurement. In the TAIS, for example, the 144 items are combined into groups to measure 18 distinct dimensions of attentional or interpersonal style. When two or more items are combined in this way it is very important that each item be unidimensional. That is, each item in a group must measure the same thing. For this and other reasons the development of a measurement device using scaled items requires considerable care and careful validation of the final instrument before it is used.

TERMS

base unit	nominal data
compound unit	objectivity
concurrent validity	ordinal
constant	predictive validity
construct validity	Q-sort
content validity	qualitative
continuous	quantitative
data set	rank order
derived unit	ratio
dichotomy	reliability
discrete	semantic differential scale
efficiency	SI
instrument error	significant digits
interval	subjectivity
Likert scale	Thurstone scale
locus of control	validity
measurement instrument	variable
measurement protocol	

EXERCISES

1. Measure the length and width of a building of your choice using an invented unit of measurement.

2. Identify several tests or measurements used in research articles and describe the measurement protocol to your classmates in a paragraph of no more than 200 words or orally in no more than three minutes.

3. Discuss with your classmates the relative efficiency of the skin-fold and underwater weighing methods for estimating body fat.

4. Construct a knowledge test of at least ten items for estimating knowledge of the terminology presented in this chapter. Share the test with your classmates and discuss or debate its validity.

ADDITIONAL RESOURCES WITH ANNOTATION

Auter, P.J. & Davis, D.M. (1991). When characters speak directly to viewers: Breaking the fourth wall in television. *Journalism Quarterly, 68* (1/2), 165–171.
An interesting example of a study using a semantic differential scale.

Edwards, A.L. & Kenney, K.C. (1946). A comparison of the Thurstone and Likert techniques of attitude scale construction. *Journal of Applied Psychology, 30* (1), 72–83.
A good discussion of the strengths and weaknesses of the Likert and Thurstone methods. Although this article may be difficult to locate it should be less so than the original Likert monograph or the book by Thurstone and Chave.

Tetlock, P.E., Peterson, R.S., McGuire, C., Chang, S., & Field, P. (1992). Assessing political group dynamics: A test of the groupthink model. *Journal of Personality and Social Psychology, 63* (3), 403–425.
This is a good example of a study using the Q-sort technique.

MATTERS OF DESIGN

Producers of movies and television programs often depict scientists as absent minded, sloppy, and possibly "playing in a different key," but this "mad scientist" image is far from truthful. While a good scientist or researcher may have a messy desk or difficult handwriting, good research is characterized by careful consideration and planning of methodology and rigorous attention to procedural details. Although flashes of insight or serendipitous discoveries may sometimes occur, research is usually successful by *design*. That is, success is the result of planned methodology specifically designed to answer unambiguously the research question being asked. This chapter is designed to introduce the student to a wide range of methodological or design issues commonly encountered in research. It is followed by several chapters dealing with techniques and methods usually associated with particular approaches to research, including descriptive research, experimental research, historical research, and other methods of inquiry. However, it should be understood that the various research methods described in each of those chapters are associated with but are not exclusive to any particular method of inquiry.

VALIDITY IN RESEARCH

On the Nazca Plain in Peru there are several large drawings and long, straight lines etched in the ground that can only be seen in their entirety from an aerial vantage point. Noting that from above some of these lines bear a resemblance to an airport landing strip, a noted writer once concluded (and apparently still maintains) that the lines *are* landing strips and the drawings must have been made by or with the aid of visitors from another world. Such conclusions make excellent fiction but hardly stand up as scientific conclusions. It is true that the lines *look* like landing strips from above and it is true that the drawings can only be seen fully from above but such facts hardly support the hypothesis of visitors from space. Furthermore, there is an abundance of evidence that explains the lines and drawings in a more plausible way, but that evidence was either unknown or ignored in arriving at the space visitor idea. Invalid research can lead to invalid conclusions. In genuinely scientific research one must be constantly aware of conditions and factors that threaten validity, and strive to employ methods that eliminate or minimize those threats.

Internal vs. External Validity

The validity of research studies, and the various threats or challenges to validity, are classified as either internal or external. **Internal validity** refers to *the degree to which the results of the study may be attributed to differences in the* *independent variable(s).* The term independent variable may be taken here to include classification and attribute variables and interactions among such variables (see the section "Input Variables" later in this chapter). If the conduct of a study is so sloppy or poorly controlled that differences in the dependent measures can be explained in alternative ways, then the study has poor internal validity and there is little point in considering external validity. **External validity** refers to *the degree to which the results of a study may be extended or generalized beyond the limits of the study itself.* Poor external validity does not completely negate the value of a research study but does limit the interpretation of the findings of a study.

Complete elimination of all threats to validity is impossible, especially when human subjects are involved. Indeed, techniques designed to control one type of threat may have the effect of producing another. For example, internal validity may be increased by rigidly tight control of all external factors that might affect the outcome, but imposing such a laboratory environment may threaten the validity of the results in the larger world outside the laboratory.

The principal internal and external threats to the validity of research studies are discussed in general terms in the sections that follow. For a more complete discussion of such threats, refer to the classic work by Campbell and Stanley's *Experimental and Quasi-Experimental Designs for Research,* and Chapter 9.

THREATS TO INTERNAL VALIDITY

Subject Expectancy: The Placebo Effect

When patients complaining of pain are given a pill containing nothing but sugar or an injection of a harmless solution, but which they believe is a powerful pain killer, their subjective reports of pain sometimes decrease almost as much as if a real pain killer is given. This effect disappears if the patients are told the true nature of what they are being given. This effect is called the *placebo effect* and *the pill, injection, or other "treatment" that contains no pharmacologically active ingredient* is called a **placebo**. Today the term placebo is extended beyond its medical meaning to include any effect of a treatment of any kind caused by the subjects' belief that an effect should be expected. For example, athletes sometimes breathe pure oxygen before competing in the belief that it will give them greater endurance. Even though there is no scientific evidence of the reality of such an effect, their belief may give them a psychological lift. Also, curses have been known to lead to illness and even death among individuals who believe in witchcraft or magic.

In any study in which the placebo effect may be a problem, it should be controlled by keeping subjects *blind* with respect to the treatment they are receiving. Rather than *no* treatment, subjects in control groups should receive an *apparent* treatment. That is, a treatment which is no treatment but which appears to them to be the same as the treatment given to those in other groups. In drug efficacy studies this is usually very easily done by giving control group subjects a pill (or injection, etc.) that looks just like that given to other subjects even though it contains no drug and not telling subjects whether they are getting the real drug or the placebo. In other kinds of studies, control of the placebo effect may require more ingenuity or may be impossible.

Researcher Expectancy: The Pygmalion Effect

Pygmalion is a story from Greek mythology about a sculptor who builds a statue of a woman so beautiful and lifelike that he falls in love with it. He wishes that the statue would come alive and his wish is granted. The story is about wishes coming true through the power of the wish. The story of Pygmalion is fiction but the phenomenon it describes allegorically has a very real basis. In experiments in which classroom teachers were given false information about the ability or behavior of pupils in prior classes, the performance and behavior of those pupils soon conformed to what the teachers had been told. Without any intention on their part to treat the pupils differently, the teachers' expectations for their pupils had somehow been sensed by the pupils and somehow affected their performance or behavior. A similar effect has even (and previously) been reported (Rosenthal and Lawson, 1964) when the "pupils" were laboratory rats!

The term **Pygmalion effect** is used in connection with research to refer to *effects caused by subjects' perceptions of the expectations of the researcher.* The Pygmalion effect can occur in any research situation in which the wishes or expectations of the researcher (or others involved in the study) might be detected by the subjects, or when those wishes or expectations might affect the judgment of those collecting or interpreting study data. For example, in a study of the effects of a new pain medicine, the expectations of the researcher are very likely to be detected by members of both treatment and control groups even though these subjects are not explicitly informed of their status as treatment or control subjects. This could easily affect (through the placebo effect) the subjects' perception of their pain. Furthermore, as the interpretation of pain is somewhat subjective, the researcher's expectations could affect judgments made by the researcher about the subjects' reports of pain.

Whenever such effects are likely to be a problem, they may be controlled by use of procedures in which everyone administering treatment or otherwise interacting with subjects during the study is kept unaware, or *blind*, regarding the treatment given to each subject. Because subjects must also be kept blind to their treatment, such studies are described as using a **double blind** procedure in which *neither subject nor those administering treatment is aware of the actual treatment being given.* This is relatively easy in many medical studies in which look-alike placebo pills can be used in place of the real thing and a numbering system used to keep track of the treatments given to each subject. However, control of the Pygmalion effect is more difficult in cases in which a plausible placebo is not possible. In a study of the effects of exercise versus no exercise, for example, there is no reasonable way to make subjects unaware of which treatment they are receiving.

The Hawthorne Effect

The Hawthorne effect is named after the Hawthorne works of the Western Electric Company in Chicago and Cicero, Illinois, where it was first recognized as a serious potential source of bias. In a study of environmental circumstances and methods of payment as factors affecting worker productivity at the Western Electric factory in the 1930s, researchers (Roethlisberger and Dickson, 1939) noticed that every environmental change they introduced produced an improvement in productivity *even when conditions were reversed* from those previously tested. Eventually it was determined that the increases in productivity were not due to the variations in the work environment or method of payment at all but instead to the very fact of being involved in an experiment. The workers selected to serve as subjects in the study felt special and more interested in what they were doing just because they were participating in a research study and that resulted in the productivity increases. Thus, *simple participation in a research study can sometimes produce an effect in human subjects* and such an effect is known as a **Hawthorne effect.**

Other than replacing human subjects with animals or doing studies without the knowledge of the subjects (an unethical and probably illegal practice in most cases) there is not much that can be done to control Hawthorne effects. However, complete, accurate, and above all, consistent informing of subjects about the nature and purpose of the study should be helpful in minimizing such effects.

Regression Effects

Any measurement that is unbiased (not affected by any form of systematic error) is still likely to involve some error. In a series of measurements the frequency of errors of varying magnitudes will be normally distributed around the true value, so most measurements will include a relatively small error and a few will include larger errors. If one measurement is made and includes a large error, it is much more likely that the next measurement will include a smaller error than an even larger one.

Studies are sometimes done using subjects selected on the basis of having extreme or atypical scores on some measure. For example, a new method of teaching children basic arithmetic might be tested on a group of children who have already scored very poorly on a test of arithmetic ability. Or an experimental medicine for a serious disease might be tested on a group of subjects who are sickest with the disease. In such cases, group scores should be expected to be closer to normal values (they should show improvement in both of the above examples) even if the treatment (the new method or medicine) is completely ineffective. *The tendency of repeated measurements to shift away from extreme values toward more normal ones* is referred to as the **regression effect.** In any study in which subjects are selected on the basis of extreme or atypical scores, the regression effect is likely to lead to the false rejection of the null hypothesis (that is, to the conclusion that the treatment had an effect) if it is not recognized.

The threat of regression effects to internal validity is eliminated if the vulnerability to the regression effect is the same for both or all treatment and control groups. The mean scores of all groups will be affected by regression but equally. This requires that the assignment of subjects to treatment or control groups be randomized with respect to initial scores.

Pre-Test and Repeated Measurement Effects

Particularly when research is directed toward factors that may influence change in some variable, it is common practice to use a pre-test or to repeat measurements two or more times during the course of a study. For example, in an investigation of a 12-week exercise program designed to increase muscular strength, subjects would probably be tested for strength before the program is started and then again when it is completed. Alternatively, or additionally, strength might be tested every two weeks during the exercise program.

If the pre-test or repeated measurement is one based on learning or performance, then the mere fact of having been tested before may affect performance on subsequent measurements. For example, taking a math test may, by itself, produce some learning and lead to a higher score when the same or equivalent test is taken later.

The only way to actually control pre-test or repeated measurement effects is to eliminate the pre-test or repeated measurement or to somehow use subjects who are unaware of both the fact and the results of such measurements. The latter approach is usually unethical and unlikely to be feasible in most experiments involving human subjects.

When the nature of the study dictates that a pre-test must be used, the effects of such measures cannot be controlled. However, they may at least be quantified and separated from treatment effects through use of an experimental design called the Solomon Four Groups design, but this design is not effective for dealing with learning effects caused by repeated measurement.

The Avis Effect

In studies in which subjects are not blind to their assignment to a treatment or control group, and in which their effort or level of engagement may be a factor in the outcome, those assigned to the control group sometimes tend to put in more effort than those in treatment groups. This effect is called the **Avis effect** because of an advertising campaign for the Avis car rental company that promoted the company as trying harder to please the customer because it was number two in size.

Subject Mortality

Subject mortality refers to *the loss of subjects from a study (for any reason, not necessarily through death).* People drop out of research studies for all kinds of reasons including death, illness, conflicting interests, conflicts with the researcher or other subjects, loss of interest, and so on. Human subjects in any study are legally (at least in the United States) free to drop out at any time and for any reason or no reason. If the design of a study is otherwise sound, the loss of a small proportion of subjects will usually not do too much harm to its internal validity. However, loss of a large proportion of subjects can be fatal to the validity of a study and leave no alternative but to start over with a new group of subjects.

Even a relatively small loss of subjects can have a serious effect on internal validity if that loss is systematic with respect to subject attributes that affect one or more of the dependent variables. For example, consider a study of two different approaches to coaching high school male and female basketball players. Suppose that the truth (unknown at the time of the study) is that method A works best with boys and method B is best with girls. Suppose further that there is a significant mortality among female players. Such mortality could easily render the study unable to detect the interaction effect of gender with method of coaching and the result might very well be to show method A to be superior for all subjects.

Prevention is the best way to minimize subject mortality. Carefully and completely informing all subjects about the demands of participation and the importance of completing the study should be helpful. Also the researcher should avoid making unnecessary demands on subjects or prolonging the study without good reason. Finally, provided the subject loss is not systematic, the effects of moderate mortality may sometimes be reduced by starting an experiment with a larger number of subjects.

Instrumentation Error or Drift

All measurement instruments, from the relatively crude IQ test to the most exquisitely sensitive devices used in subatomic physics, are subject to error. Step on and off an ordinary bathroom scale a few times and you are likely to get readings that vary by as much as several pounds. When such variations occur at random or if the inherent precision of the instrument is such that the errors are trivial relative to the needs of the research (if one is weighing an elephant, weighing to the nearest 10 pounds or so is probably good enough) they are not a threat to validity. Sometimes, however, some measurement instruments tend to vary over time in a systematic fashion. For example, the springs in a spring scale may tend to stretch over time producing progressively higher or lower (depending on how the scale works) readings. Subjectively scored instruments, such as many psychological tests and certainly almost all performance evaluations, also are subject to drift over time. The scoring of an essay examination item or paper, for example, may vary somewhat according to its position in a stack of such papers as the result of fatigue, frustration, self recrimination, or other factors. The *halo effect*, discussed in the following section, is really a specific type of instrumentation error.

The best control for instrumentation drift is to prevent it by regular calibration. Physical measurement instruments, such as scales, gas analysis apparatus, thermometers, and so on, should be calibrated frequently throughout the course of a study using known standards. A gas analysis apparatus is calibrated using a gas mixture of known composition. Instruments requiring subjective judgment may be calibrated by careful training and regular retraining of those whose judgment is required, again using a known standard. For example, an instrument for quantifying the interactions between a football coach and players during a game could be calibrated using a videotape of a game as a standard. Drift in the grading of a series of essay exam items or papers may be randomized to some extent by reversing or shuffling the order in which they are graded for each essay.

The Halo Effect

The **halo effect** refers to *a tendency toward evaluative bias resulting from pre-existing attitudes or opinions toward whomever or whatever is being evaluated,* even when those opinions are unrelated to the actual focus of evaluation. For example, drivers asked to evaluate a new model of automobile are likely to be lenient if they have a generally favorable opinion of the manufacturer or have some other favorable association with the manufacturer. Though the name implies a bias in favor of leniency, the phenomenon works in either direction.

The halo effect can sometimes be controlled by the selection of subjects who have no prior association with the individual (or product, company, etc.) they are to evaluate and by limiting that association subsequent to selection to things relevant to the evaluation. This is what is done in the selection of jurors for a trial when potential jurors with a prior knowledge of the case or experiences similar to those to be discussed in the case are excused from service, and those selected for service are protected from exposure to improper evidence. In research situations in which control for a possible halo effect is impossible, those effects may often be minimized by attempting to collect additional data that might indicate the direction or strength of the halo effect bias. Even if this is not feasible, the researcher must be very careful to acknowledge the possibility of such effects in the research report.

Many companies and institutions have antinepotism rules in their personnel practices as a control against the halo effect in employee evaluations.

Subject Maturation

Consider a research report of a study of 200 male, age group swimmers aged 12 to 15 asserting that a year of training had produced a significant increase in muscle strength. It seems quite a reasonable finding even though there is no control group. Suppose the report also described an increase in scores on tests of verbal and mathematical reasoning. The connection between swim training and reasoning seems much less reasonable. The truth, however, is that the increases in strength and reasoning scores are probably *both* quite real and that there is no scientific evidence from the study that *either* was due to the swim training. The truth is that increases in both strength and reasoning ability should be expected in any group of 12- to 15-year-old males. Both are expected changes resulting from the process of maturation.

In the context of a scientific experiment, **maturation** can refer to *any change likely to occur in subjects during the time period of the experiment*, not just to the physiological or psychological changes associated with puberty. Subject maturation is controlled in experiments through the use of control groups—statistically equivalent groups of subjects who do not receive the experimental treatment or who receive a different treatment. Because maturation is expected to occur in both treatment and control groups, concluding differences between groups may be attributed to differences in treatment.

History

History refers to everything that happens to subjects of a study after their selection or after the study has begun but before it has been concluded. In any experiment or quasi-experiment involving two or more groups of subjects the assumption is that the groups are initially equivalent and that any subsequent differences between or among groups must be due to differences in the treatments between or among them. Such differences can only be attributed to differences in treatment if treatment is the only *relevant* aspect of the histories of each group that varies between or among groups. Any difference in the histories of different groups is a potential threat to the internal validity of a study. If different histories are relevant to one or more of the dependent variables of a study, that is if a dependent variable is affected, then attribution of group differences to differences in treatment is invalid. The difference in group histories is an alternative explanation.

In laboratory experiments (sometimes referred to as *in vitro* experiments) in which every detail of treatment—environmental conditions, and so on—recognized as potentially relevant can be controlled, history is only a threat to validity if there are relevant factors that are not recognized or that are ignored. Many kinds of studies, however, must be conducted in real world *(in vivo)* conditions. Studies of educational methods, for example, are almost always conducted in real schools. Similarly, medical studies are almost always conducted under conditions that cannot control subject history. One simply cannot expect human subjects to submit to having every detail of their lives controlled while an experiment is carried out.

Although history cannot be eliminated as a threat to internal validity in most studies involving human subjects, that threat may often be minimized through careful monitoring of the history of each group and termination of studies in which histories are documented to have differed in relevant ways. The threat may also be reduced by replication of studies in which group histories are likely to differ, provided the differences in histories are not systematic from replication to replication.

Inter~~Intra~~-Subject Interaction

Every time there is a major election in the United States, especially a presidential election, public opinion polls are conducted and their results published on an almost daily basis. Whenever a poll shows anything advantageous to a candidate (the candidate is leading; the candidate is trailing but by less than before; the candidate is losing support but not as fast as the other one; etc.) that candidate or his or her party immediately spares no effort to publicize the results. Similarly, whenever the poll shows anything not to a candidate's advantage, everything possible will be done by the candidate to show why the poll is biased or in error. Why is there so much concern for the results of a poll which only truthfully shows how people would have voted at the time they were interviewed? The reason is that the candidates know people's decisions tend to be influenced by the decisions they perceive others to be making. These concerns are quite valid and there is a very real concern in a national election that the announcement of actual election results from east coast states before the polls have closed on the west coast might influence the votes of enough people in those western states to change the results of the election. Similar concern for this tendency to be influenced by others is seen in trials by jury in which jurors are frequently reminded not to discuss any aspects of the case with anyone, including other jurors, until the trial has been completed. In some widely publicized cases, jurors are even sequestered for the duration of the trial to protect them from outside influence, intentional or accidental.

Asch Experiment

The effects of intra-subject interaction were clearly demonstrated in an experiment by Asch in the early 1950s. "Subjects" were asked to tell which of several index cards had the longer line drawn on it, each responding in turn. In actuality, however, only the last of the supposed subjects was actually being studied; the others were all part of the experiment. At first, the decoy subjects gave correct responses. After a few trials, however, the decoy subjects began to name the wrong line and to stand by their choice when challenged by the real subject. Eventually, the real subject would acquiesce even when the decoys' choice was clearly incorrect.

In any research study in which the opinions, judgments, beliefs, etc., of human subjects are to be measured or may affect whatever is to be measured, intra-subject interaction is a potential threat to internal validity. The only method of control is prevention through procedures such as asking subjects not to discuss or express anything relevant to the study with anyone until after the study is completed.

THREATS TO EXTERNAL VALIDITY

Selection Bias

Bias in the selection of subjects is a threat to both internal and external validity of research studies. Internal validity is obviously compromised if treatment and control groups cannot be considered as equivalent at the moment of subject assignment to groups. In experimental studies such equivalence is achieved through random assignment of subjects to treatment and control groups. For example, in a study of the effectiveness of a new method of weight control, a set of 50 volunteers would be assigned to either treatment or control groups by a random process such as drawing names from a hat. In a descriptive study, such as a survey, the subjects to be studied (called the sample) must be selected by a random process from the larger population for which a description is desired. Chapter 7 contains a discussion of subject selection techniques and several examples of the consequences of selection processes that are not random.

Testing Effects (no)

Taking a pre-test or the first of several successive measurements may lead subjects to differentially alter their behavior during the course of the study in ways that affect subsequent measures. For example, in a study of an exercise or diet program on weight loss a pre-test that demonstrates their overweight condition might cause subjects in a control group—who are supposed to continue their usual behavior—to begin to exercise or diet. Subjects in treatment groups would tend not to do this since the treatment itself would seem to be an appropriate response to becoming aware of being overweight.

File Drawer Effect

Our minds are tuned to notice that which is different and ignore the familiar. A tree in a forest is not noticed but we immediately take note of a single tree in the desert or on a tiny island. Scientific experiments are usually designed to see if one or more treatments has an effect on some variable that is different from other treatments or no treatment. Because the treatments tested are usually those the researcher believes are likely to have an effect, when an effect is found it tends to be seen as a success or victory and no effect is seen as a defeat. Because of this unfortunate perception, which often seems to be shared by journal editors and reviewers, researchers are much more likely to write and submit a research report when a treatment shows a significant effect than when no effect is found, and such a report is more likely to be accepted for publication. Research data and reports showing no effect are likely to be filed away in a file drawer rather than published. Thus, the term **file drawer effect** refers to

FIGURE 6.1   We do not notice a tree in a forest but we immediately take note of a single tree in the desert or on a tiny island.

the tendency of published research reports to be numerically biased in favor of reports showing significant effects. This tendency must be taken into account during a literature review or meta-analysis of studies showing contradictory results. The researcher must always remember that scientific questions are not matters to be settled by majority vote.

METHODS OF INQUIRY AND SCIENTIFIC RIGOR

There is sometimes a tendency to think of the various methods of inquiry and the disciplines associated with each as varying predictably in rigor. Physics, chemistry, and biology are seen generally as having a high degree of scientific rigor because they are associated strongly with the experimental method. Education (including physical education), history, and anthropology are often criticized as lacking in rigor because they are associated strongly with the descriptive method of inquiry. Psychology and education are sometimes strongly criticized for using quasi-experimental or pre-experimental designs (see Chapter 8) and then treating the results as if true experiments had been done.

Though much of the criticism leveled at education, psychology, and other fields has been well deserved, it is not valid to automatically associate a lack of rigor with either a field of study or a method of inquiry. The sciences of astronomy and cosmology are principally descriptive rather than experimental but generally enjoy a reputation as highly rigorous sciences. In contrast, chemists and physicists have sometimes performed very well-designed experiments to test utterly trivial hypotheses. Good scientific inquiry does not come from the use of any particular method. Rather, good scientific inquiry comes from the rigorous application of whatever methods of inquiry are most appropriate to each particular problem.

TYPES OF VARIABLES IN RESEARCH

Anything that is free to vary among subjects or cases in a study is a **variable.** In the context of research, variables are classified according to the role played in a particular study. An understanding of the various types (or roles) of variables in research is important in the selection of some types of statistical analyses and is fundamental to the understanding of research literature. Note that the term "types of variables" is also widely used to refer to a classification of variables according to the method of measurement of the variable.

Research variables include those that serve as input to a study, those that are the outcome of a study, and those that are present within a study.

Input Variables

An experiment generally seeks to identify or quantify the effects of one or more input variables. If an experiment is conceptualized as an effort to find a "cause and effect" relationship, then the input variable is the cause.

If *an input variable is manipulated by the researcher*, it is called an **independent variable.** For example, if a fitness coach wanted to compare the effectiveness of two alternative methods of strength training, athletes could be assigned at random to one method or the other and then given a strength test after several weeks of training. In such an experiment "method of training" is the input variable. Because the random assignment of experimental subjects (the athletes) to different training methods constitutes manipulation of the input variable, method of training is an independent variable.

It is relatively common to refer to all input variables as independent variables, but to do so is not strictly correct. Some variables that serve as input to an experiment or study cannot be manipulated—such as the gender and age of experimental subjects. In the study of strength training described above, half of the subjects selected for the study could be male, and half female. Gender would clearly be an input variable but gender cannot be manipulated by the researcher. Each subject is already male or female. *Input variables of this type that constitute a qualitative or categorical distinction, such as gender or religious affiliation,* are called **classification variables.** The term **attribute variable** is *used with variables of a quantitative nature, such as age or test scores.*

Control variable is a term used to mean *variables that are likely to affect the outcome of a study but that are held constant, or controlled by the researcher.* Hence, control variables are variables that are not present in an experiment or study because they have been prevented from being present by the researcher.

Output Variables

In order to identify or quantify effects of input variables, some result of those variables must be measured. If the input variables are the "cause" in an experiment, then the output variable is the "effect." Because the output of a well-designed experiment depends upon the input to that experiment, *output variables* are called **dependent variables.**

Internal Variables

An experiment is an arrangement of circumstances that seeks to eliminate all possible sources of variation in the output variable except the input variable. However, it is very rare, especially in studies involving people, to be able to eliminate all other sources of output variation. In the study of strength training methods, for example, it is impossible to lock up all experimental subjects in a completely controlled environment as if they were laboratory rats or cultures of bacteria. Even if such a study were done in a maximum security prison, each subject brings into the study a different combination of experiences, interests, and genetic makeup. *Variables that remain present within a study* are called **extraneous, confounding,** or **uncontrolled variables.**

The presence of internal variables is usually unavoidable but is not necessarily as serious a problem as it might appear because they are not usually completely uncontrolled. Although such variables may not be controlled by the design of an experiment or study, they usually can be controlled by the statistical treatment of the data. It may seem to be a paradox but the very fact that an internal variable is uncontrolled by the design of the experiment is what allows it to be controlled statistically. At least, if an experiment or other study is designed correctly, internal variables will be present but their effects will be random and, thus, largely self-canceling relative to the input variables. On the other hand, internal variables are a very serious problem in poorly conceived studies.

RESEARCH PITFALLS

In spite of all the formalized methods and procedures of science designed to prevent errors and misinterpretations, there is still plenty of misdirected, foolish, and meaningless research being done. The student is urged to try to avoid the following research pitfalls.

Proving the Obvious

One could do an experiment comparing the relative effectiveness of gasoline and vinegar as fuel for automobiles. The author will not be responsible for the repair bill if any reader is foolish enough to actually try this. Such an experiment is sound from the point of view of experimental design (see Chapter 9) but is of little value. That gasoline is a better automobile fuel than vinegar is obvious, at least for current models.

The gasoline vs. vinegar experiment is unlikely ever to be attempted by any but the most foolish researcher, but sometimes the mistake of attempting to prove the obvious does occur. Some examples that have been observed by the author but which will be presented here without citation include studies showing that a season of conditioning in an aerobic sport results in lowering of body fat, that stretching exercises result in improved flexibility when compared to no exercise, and that geriatrics have lower cardiovascular efficiency than those of middle age.

Triviality

An experiment or other study that is methodologically valid but for which the results are of little or no interest to anyone may be described as trivial. For example, a study to evaluate the effectiveness of different techniques for teaching the two-handed set shot in basketball would generally be considered trivial because no one uses the two-handed set shot anymore.

Whether or not a study is trivial is not always superficially obvious, and depends heavily on the underlying rationale for conducting the study. In the two-handed set shot study, for example, if the purpose of the experiment is to find the best method for teaching the skill, then the study is indeed trivial because the skill itself is of little use. On the other hand, the study might be meaningful if the two-handed set shot is used merely as a novel task with which to evaluate different teaching techniques in a way that might be more broadly applicable.

Pointless Replication or Variation

Students in research design and statistics courses are taught, quite properly, that the results of a study done on a restricted subset of a population cannot be assumed to hold for the population as a whole. A study describing the physiological or anthropological profiles of Olympic class volleyball players cannot be used as a standard for Olympic gymnasts or even high school volleyball players. The only way to obtain data relevant to Olympic gymnasts is to replicate the study using a sample of Olympic gymnasts. Although the above is true, it does not hold that every study done on a restricted subset of a larger population should be replicated on every conceivable additional subset. Replications of the elite volleyball profile with other subject groups might be worthwhile but only if there is a specific reason other than the need to complete a research project or obtain a publication.

Unanalyzable Data

A very common mistake by both students and inexperienced researchers is to allow a study to proceed through the data collection stage without properly considering how the collected data will be analyzed. Seeking analytical advice after their data is collected, these researchers run the risk of having to face the awful truth that no meaningful analysis is possible or that no conclusions can be reached concerning their original hypotheses.

Sometimes things happen during the data collection phase of a study that cause analysis of the data to be more difficult or impossible. More often, however, unanalyzable data is the result of inadequate planning. Proper planning of any quantitative study includes careful consideration of the analytical treatment of the data that will be collected, and an inexperienced researcher would be well advised to include a complete analysis of a sample set of data as part of a pilot study before the collection of real data begins.

Fatally Flawed Design

The design of a research study refers generally to all the procedural and analytic aspects of the study that serve to increase validity with respect to its purpose. Such matters as random assignment or selection of subjects, use of control groups, and proper selection of statistical methods are all parts of a study's design. Studies vary in the degree to which flaws in design threaten their validity, and it is impossible to design a study, experimental or otherwise, in which all threats to validity are completely eliminated. A study may be considered to have a fatal flaw when its design (or execution) is such that its results may be explained fairly reasonably in more than one way. For example, a single-group study of the effects of a season of sports training on the body composition of 14-year-old girls is fatally flawed because the alternative hypothesis that changes in body composition are due to maturation is at least as reasonable as the primary hypothesis that changes are due to training. Studies are sometimes rendered fatally flawed by events that affect their execution, but there can be little excuse for starting a study with a fatally flawed design.

Attempting the Impossible or Impractical

Important and useful discoveries are much more likely to come from studies designed to answer simple, basic questions than from studies attempting to solve huge, global problems. Asked to identify a topic for a thesis or research paper, students and other inexperienced researchers often tend to give such broad and global responses as finding a cure for AIDS or perfecting solar energy. Though laudable, such topics are far too broad—success in either would virtually guarantee a Nobel prize—and must be greatly narrowed down before they become practical.

Disproving the Ridiculous

Scientific advancements, improved methods of doing things, refinements of ideas, and other forms of progress come about through an evolutionary process in which new ideas are compared to the current state of the art. If the new idea is shown to be more correct or more useful than the state of the art, then it becomes the new state of the art; otherwise it is discarded. Progress does not come from studies comparing new ideas to old, discredited ideas. In the field of automotive technology, for example, a car powered by a solar-powered engine or by some new type of fossil-fueled engine must be compared to traditionally powered, modern cars, not to the Ford Model T or to a donkey cart. Unfortunately, it is not uncommon to see what might be described as "donkey cart studies" proposed by inexperienced researchers or even submitted for publication or presentation.

Rationalizing Failure

Research projects do not always find the results expected or desired by the researcher. Experiments sometimes yield results contrary to expectations. When the results of a research project are in agreement with what is expected or desired, the tendency is to accept those results as correct. On the other hand, the tendency is to look carefully for weaknesses in design or execution when results contradict expectations. That is, there is a tendency to accept expected results and to rationalize unexpected results. There is no excuse for such rationalization. The researcher should behave, in fact, in just the opposite manner, making every effort to identify (and control in subsequent studies) every possible argument in opposition to results that are in agreement with expectations.

PILOT STUDIES AND REHEARSALS

The validity of any scientific undertaking is compromised if its outcome is influenced by any aspect of the study itself other than the manipulated (independent) variables. Even when a study is otherwise properly designed, such influence may be exerted by mistakes or variations in data collection or treatment protocols; questionnaire items that are misleading or confusing; variations in the wording of instructions, accuracy, or precision of measurement, or similar factors. Such difficulties often result from the researcher's inexperience with intended treatment protocols or measurement techniques or from attempts to use procedures or instrumentation that has not been properly tested.

Tainted or compromised research data is of little value, except perhaps as a lesson, and possibly an expensive one, for the researcher. If the research question is to be answered, the study must be repeated in order to obtain valid data. To avoid such mistakes it is generally wise to conduct a practice or trial run of the instruments and procedures to be used before a study is begun. Depending on the complexity of the study and the experience of the researcher and others involved in the conduct of the study, such practice may range from simple rehearsals of the procedures to be used to *a complete, small-scale run-through of major portions of the study.* Such a run-through is called a **pilot study**. In addition to rehearsing the procedures to be used in a study, a pilot study is also often used in the development or refinement of those procedures. In studies involving questionnaires, for example, proposed questions or items are often tested by administering the questionnaire to a group of subjects in a pilot study and then asking those subjects for feedback on matters such as the clarity of wording, the completeness of response options, or the introduction of bias through the phrasing or context of questions. This feedback is then used to revise the questionnaire to correct whatever weaknesses are detected. In studies involving systematic observation as a method of data gathering, for another example, the data from live observations may be compared to data obtained from repeated viewings of videotapes as a way of refining the skills of the observer.

As a rule it is also wise to include the statistical analysis of data in the piloting process. By analyzing a set of data actually gathered in a small-scale pilot study rather than inventing a purely hypothetical data set, the researcher is likely to encounter and solve most of the analytical difficulties produced by unequal treatment group sizes, missing data, smaller-than-expected treatment groups, and other problems that occur in real research but are rarely anticipated when a study is planned.

 # TERMS

attribute variable	Hawthorne effect
Avis effect	independent variable
classification variable	internal validity
confounding variable	maturation
control variable	pilot study
dependent variable	placebo
double blind	Pygmalion effect
external validity	regression effect
extraneous variable	subject mortality
file drawer effect	uncontrolled variable
halo effect	variable

EXERCISES

1. Locate several research articles in your area of interest. For each, identify all of the variables and label each according to type.

2. Advertisements sometimes make claims about results of scientific studies. Examine some such advertisements and identify any threats to their validity that are not mentioned or discussed.

ADDITIONAL RESOURCES WITH ANNOTATION

Adair, J.G., Sharpe, D., & Huynh, C. (1989). Placebo, Hawthorne, and other artifact controls: Researcher's opinions and practices. *Journal of Experimental Education, 57,* 341–355.
Results of a survey of how researchers understand and handle various threats to internal validity in experimental studies with human subjects.

Cornell, J. (1984). Science vs. the paranormal. *Psychology Today, 18* (3), 28–31, 34.
An easy-to-read account of the continuing battle between genuine and pseudo science and the readiness of the public to accept bizarre ideas camouflaged as scientific.

Dietz, R. (1983). Scientists, gamblers, and magicians: Allies against the irrational. *The Humanist, 43* (2), 9–11, 36.
A thought-provoking article suggesting that the training given most scientists may be inferior to that of gamblers and magicians with respect to recognizing and avoiding fraud and self-deception.

Gregory, G. (1989). Placebo effect: The power of suggestion. *Current Health, 2,* 23–25.
A clear, concise illustration of the phenomenon, plus an introduction to some ethical issues arising from the placebo effect.

Jenner, H. (1990). The Pygmalion effect: The importance of expectancies. *Alcohol Treatment Quarterly, 7* (2), 127–133.
An easy-to-follow explanation of the phenomenon known as the Pygmalion effect.

Jones, S.R.G. (1992). Was there a Hawthorne effect? *American Journal of Sociology, 98* (3), 451–468.
A review of the original data of Roethlisberger and Dickson (1939) (which reported the phenomenon known as the Hawthorne effect) concluding that there in fact was no such effect.

Merikle, P.M., & Skanes, H.E. (1992). Subliminal self-help audio tapes: A search for placebo effects. *Journal of Applied Psychology, 77* (5), 772–776.
A good example of an attempt to detect a placebo effect. This article also serves as an example of an experiment in which testing effects apparently occur.

Nathan, B.R., & Tippins, N. (1990). The consequences of the halo "error" in performance ratings: A field study of the moderating effect of halo on test validation results. *Journal of Applied Psychology, 75* (3), 290–296.
A study looking at the effects of the halo effect in the evaluation of clerical workers.

7

DESCRIPTIVE RESEARCH METHODS

Descriptive inquiry is any research that attempts to systematically gather or analyze information of a descriptive nature. The most common example of descriptive inquiry is probably the survey, which is the gathering of data or information about a group of people, institutions, or other entities by direct measurement of the entire population or of a smaller sample of that population. Another form of descriptive inquiry is the collection of data or information by unobtrusive or semi-unobtrusive observation. Studies of this kind are common in the investigation of behaviors of teachers and students in the classroom, animals in the wild or in contrived environments, and people in specific settings or circumstances. Descriptive inquiry can also mean the systematic, standardized description of an object or event, as might be done by a botanist describing a newly discovered plant. The following sections attempt to provide discussion of a variety of methods commonly employed in descriptive inquiry.

POPULATIONS AND SAMPLES

Descriptive research is often concerned with attempting to identify or describe attributes of some group or set. The group under study may be composed of people, organizations, animals, objects, or virtually any other discrete set that can be defined. Regardless of its composition, *the group about which information is sought* is referred to as the **population,** even though the word implies a group of people. When the study population is large, it is likely to be difficult or impossible to actually study or collect data about every one of its members. In such cases the study is usually conducted by collecting data about a small but very carefully selected portion of the population. *The portion of a population actually studied* is referred to as the study **sample**.

METHODS FOR SAMPLING

When information gathered from a relatively small sample of a population is to be used to make inferences about the population itself, it is critical that the sample be representative of the population. If the sample is not representative of the population then inferences about that population are likely to be quite misleading. Imagine, for example, the results that would probably be obtained by attempting to describe the average height of students at a college using a sample composed of students found in the gymnasium during a men's basketball practice.

Random Sampling

When *each member of a population has the same probability of being selected as part of a study sample and actual selection or non-selection is determined by chance,* the method of subject selection is referred to as **random sampling**. With random sampling, astonishingly accurate inferences can be made about a population with a remarkably small sample relative to the population size. Although random sampling is quite a simple concept, it is not always easy to achieve. If all members of a population can be identified, then random sampling can be accomplished through methods such as drawing names or numbers blindly from a container or using a table of random numbers or a computerized random number generator to select numbers matched to specific population members. (Computerized random number generators are not genuinely random but may be an acceptable substitute for most applications.) Unfortunately, identifying every member of a population is often extremely difficult or impossible. The United States Census, for example, is conducted every ten years in an attempt to identify and count every member of the U. S. population. Obviously, some people are always missed and the indisputable fact that poor people are more likely to be missed than wealthy people means that inferences about the population as a whole are biased to some degree away from the characteristics of those missing portions of the population.

Systematic Sampling

The use of any kind of non-random system to select potential subjects from a population is called **systematic sampling.** Selecting every tenth name (or any other frequency) from a directory representative of the study population, such as a telephone book or mailing list, is systematic sampling. For example, in a survey to predict how the voters of Charlotte, North Carolina, might vote in an upcoming election, subject selection might be done by picking every fiftieth name from the Charlotte telephone directory or from a list of registered voters. Interviewing the resident of every fifth house in a neighborhood and surveying every twelfth person to pass a certain point in a shopping mall are also examples of systematic sampling.

Systematic sampling is often a convenient technique but can produce quite misleading results if the system for selecting subjects produces a systematic error or if inferences are extended beyond the population actually sampled. Suppose, for example, that shoppers are systematically sampled as they pass a certain location in a shopping mall. If this location happened to be at one end of the mall, where most of the shops deal in women's clothing, then it is likely that the sample will include a much higher proportion of women than are present among all shoppers in the mall. Therefore, any inferences made about the population of all shoppers in the mall are very likely to be false.

Cluster Sampling

Cluster sampling refers to *the selection of subjects in groups composed of more than one subject.* Once a group is selected, *all* members of that group have been selected for study. Cluster sampling is useful in situations in which direct access

FIGURE 7.1 An interview of all shop operators on a street would produce biased results if it were conducted in Jerusalem on Friday, which is the Islamic holy day, on Saturday, which is the Jewish holy day, or on Sunday, which is the Christian holy day.

to individual members of the population of interest might be cumbersome or otherwise difficult but in which those potential subjects are already associated with groups that are relatively easy to approach. For example, for a researcher interested in the views of football players toward steroid drug abuse the population of interest might be all current college football players or all current NCAA Division II football players. Obtaining a list of all such players would probably be difficult, time consuming, and expensive, and attempting to directly contact each player selected as a subject would probably be very difficult. Identifying and contacting the coaches of all college or Division II teams, on the other hand, is quite easy.

If cluster sampling is used, it is very important that the selection of the clusters to be studied be a random selection. Because each selection represents the selection of several subjects for study, any bias in the selection of clusters will tend to be magnified in its effect on the outcome of the study. Furthermore, once clusters have been selected at random, it is very important to avoid introducing subject bias within clusters. Such bias will be avoided if *all* subjects within selected clusters actually serve as study subjects or if a sample of subjects within a cluster is selected at random. Although the intent is generally to use all members of a selected cluster as subjects, there is almost always some attrition for a variety of reasons. This should not be a problem if the proportion of potential subjects lost to attrition is low but it could be a serious problem if a large proportion of subjects is lost or if the loss of subjects is systematic.

Stratified Cluster Sampling

When the population to be studied is very large and members of the population are hard to reach individually but are arranged in a hierarchy of groups, then **stratified cluster sampling** may be the best method for obtaining a sample. *After a random process is used to select large groups of related subjects from the population of interest, smaller subgroups are then randomly selected from within those groups.* This process may be repeated several times until a fairly large number of relatively small clusters have been selected. If the actual study sample is composed of all members of the clusters selected in the final stage the method may also be called multiple-stage cluster sampling. If individual subjects are randomly selected in a further step then the method may be called stratified random sampling.

Quota Sampling

A quota may be conceptualized as a target or objective. If a basketball player is given a quota of 12 points per game, then that player's scoring objective is to score 12 points in every game. If 12 or more points are scored in a game, then the quota for the game has been achieved. **Quota sampling** is a method for attempting to obtain a study sample that closely matches key characteristics of the population under study. *Demographic or other characteristics of the population that are thought to be relevant are determined and then used to develop quotas to be used in selecting subjects.* For example, if a total of 100 subjects are needed and the population of interest is 60 percent female and 20 percent poor, the quotas to be filled are for 60 subjects to be female and 20 subjects to be poor.

There are at least two serious weaknesses inherent in quota sampling. First, except for the restrictions of the assigned quotas, quota sampling leaves the researcher free to select subjects as he or she sees fit. Because it seems to be a human tendency to tend to approach subjects with characteristics similar to oneself more readily than subjects who are different in some way, some selection bias is inevitably introduced into the sample. Second, it is impossible to set quotas for all of the demographic and other characteristics that may be relevant to the outcome of a study. For example, the views of the citizens of a state toward the legal status of abortion might be affected by gender, parental status, religion, economic status, education, political affiliation, race, family history, and many other factors. As the number of separate quotas increases, the minimum number of subjects needed to fill all the quotas increases rapidly to the point where it approaches the total size of the population being studied.

Screening

There are many occasions when directly obtaining a random or systematic sample of a population of interest is not possible because there is no direct way to obtain a list of people who constitute the population of interest. Suppose, for example, that a researcher is interested in behavioral characteristics of students at a particular school who are smokers. Although it might be possible, ethical questions notwithstanding, to obtain lists of students purchasing tobacco products at the school bookstore, requesting treatment for respiratory illnesses at the health center, or living in dormitories where smoking is permitted, such lists would be unlikely to include all students who smoke and would almost certainly include many who do not. When the population of interest cannot be identified or approximated directly but is known to be a subset of a larger population that can be identified, the researcher may use a **screening** process to obtain a sample of the desired population. *Any form of random sampling may be used to obtain a representative sample of the larger population and then those subjects that are not members of the desired population are screened or filtered out.* In the above example, the researcher would randomly obtain a sample of the entire student body, ask each person in the sample about smoking habits, and then not interview further or discard data from those who do not smoke. Data from such a study may be used to make inferences about students at the school who smoke but not about students at that school in general.

SAMPLE SIZE

Students faced with a requirement to complete a research project involving sampling often ask supervising faculty how large a sample they need. (Sometimes they really want to know how small a sample they can get away with.) Unfortunately, there is no simple answer to this question. It really depends upon the degree of accuracy needed in making inferences about the population being studied. Obviously, sampling only a tiny fraction of the population is not acceptable. Imagine trying to make inferences about the body fat of Americans using a sample size of one! On the other hand, a sample size of 95 percent of the population under study would yield extremely accurate results but would be extremely difficult to accomplish. For most descriptive studies a

---

The Election Polls of 1936

That samples do not have to be extremely large to provide accurate results as long as they are really representative of the population is demonstrated convincingly by the case of the presidential election polls by the *Literary Digest* magazine and Gallup polls in 1936. The *Literary Digest* had an excellent reputation as it had correctly predicted every election since it began making predictions in 1916. Gallup, on the other hand, was a new business. The *Literary Digest* used an enormous sample of 10 million people of whom nearly a quarter responded. Gallup had a sample of only about 50,000 people. The *Literary Digest* poll very confidently predicted that the Republican candidate Alf Landon would win in a landslide. Gallup not only predicted that Franklin Roosevelt would win in a landslide, but also predicted what the *Literary Digest* would predict. Gallup was correct in both predictions. The extremely large sample did not help the *Literary Digest* at all and the tremendous cost of its survey may have contributed to its bankruptcy. Differences in the make-up of the samples were responsible for these very different predictions. Response bias was also a factor. The Gallup poll used a variation of quota sampling to obtain a sample that really represented the voting public. The *Literary Digest*, on the other hand, systematically selected names from telephone books and magazine subscription lists. This had worked well in previous elections, but in 1936 the United States was in the depths of the great economic Depression of the 1930s. Many people had canceled magazine subscriptions and had even given up having a telephone to save money. Thus the *Literary Digest's* telephone and subscription lists were much more heavily weighted with people who still had money than they had been in previous elections. Because wealthy people were (and still are) much more likely to vote for Republican than Democratic candidates, especially when the economic situation is the major issue of an election, the *Literary Digest* poll tended to favor the Republican. Because there were very few people in 1936 who had much money, however, the vast majority of voters voted for the Democrat.

The Election Polls of 1948 and 1952

The power of obtaining a genuinely representative sample and the difficulty of doing so by any method that does not employ random sampling of some kind is illustrated by the stories of the 1948 and 1952 presidential election polls. In 1948, three major polls (Gallup, Roper, and Crossley) all predicted that Thomas Dewey, the Republican candidate, would win. All three polls used quota sampling to attempt to obtain a sample representative of the voting public and all three produced erroneous results. Conceptually, quota sampling would seem to be an appropriate substitute for random sampling. Quota sampling does produce a sample that is representative of the population being sampled, at least according to the criteria of the quotas used. However, it is unlikely that quotas can be specified for all of the factors likely to affect how people vote in an election. In the 1948 election poll, however, there was another problem. Within the guidelines of their quota assignments in those surveys, the selection of subjects was left to the discretion of the interviewers. There is a very natural human tendency to be more willing to approach individuals who appear similar and "safe" than those who appear different or threatening. This resulted in a slight selection bias in favor of middle class, wealthy subjects, and because such subjects were slightly more likely to be Republican than the voters in general the results of the survey were biased toward the Republicans.

The power of random sampling, especially when combined with the computer, was demonstrated on election eve of the 1952 presidential election. The UNIVAC Corporation installed a computer (also called the UNIVAC) in the election coverage studios of NBC television. The idea was to use early election returns as a sample, analyze that sample by computer, and announce the winner long before all ballots could be counted. After what appeared to be some confusion getting the computer to operate, the machine printed its result. The computer showed Eisenhower winning by such a large margin that the television reporters were certain the computer had made an error and did not announce the result. As it turned out, however, the computer, which was far less powerful than today's personal computers, was correct. Today, computers are used to announce election winners within minutes of the closing of voting places.

sample size of between 10 and 20 percent of the population size is sufficient. The student should consult expert opinion regarding the appropriate sample size for a specific study.

METHODS OF SUBJECT CONTACT

In any descriptive survey the method by which information is solicited from subjects may have important effects on the outcome of the study. The cost of the study, the rate of subject response, and even subjects' responses may be affected. The following sections discuss some of the advantages and disadvantages of contacting subjects through the mail, by telephone, in person, and through other methods.

Direct Mail Survey

When there are a large number of subjects in a study sample or when subjects are widely scattered geographically, the most cost-effective method of contact may be through the postal service. Contrary to widespread popular opinion, mail service throughout the United States is reliable and fast and the cost per piece is the same for every destination within the United States or within any other country.

The success of any mailed survey depends on the availability of a list of correct addresses for the population or sample of the population of interest. Often, the population of interest corresponds closely with the membership of some organization or with the subscribers to some publication, and use of a membership or subscription list may be a reasonable and acceptable substitute for the actual population of interest. Such lists can usually be rented either directly from the organization or magazine or from mailing list brokers.

The lack of personal contact between the researcher and subject in a mailed survey may lead to a lower and certainly slower rate of response than other methods. However, this lack of direct contact also eliminates variations in the conduct of an interview and interaction between the interviewer and subject as sources of error.

Telephone Survey

Nearly everyone with a telephone has received telephone calls from survey companies or salespeople masquerading as survey interviewers, and few people enjoy the experience. Nevertheless, telephone interviewing is the method of choice when survey data is needed quickly, as is the case with political preference surveys.

For surveys of the general adult population of any geographic area or combination of areas, one major advantage of telephone interviewing is that a list of telephone numbers is not needed. The three-digit telephone area codes and prefixes identify relatively contiguous geographic areas and numbers within prefixes can be generated randomly. (Some numbers may turn out to be businesses, computers, telephone booths, and other unwanted locations.) In any survey attempting to make inferences about the general population, it is important to remember that not everyone in the general population has a telephone. Also, not everyone in the general population is equally likely to be home to receive an interview call or as likely to agree to an interview. All these factors tend to bias the results of any telephone survey slightly against those who are not able to be reached.

Live Interview

Interviews are often conducted face to face in high pedestrian traffic areas such as shopping malls, in places where there are large numbers of persons with characteristics of interest to the researcher, and even door to door. Because the direct contact between interviewer and subject has a significant likelihood of affecting subject responses, effective live interviewing requires a substantial amount of training and practice.

FIGURE 7.2   A traffic meter is a relatively unobtrusive form of measurement device. If it can be done without violating subject rights, testing effects can often be avoided through the use of unobtrusive measurement techniques. Although drivers can certainly see the hose across the road, most are unaware of its purpose and pay no attention to its presence.

Unobtrusive Observation

In any study in which there is communication between the researcher and subjects, either directly or through some medium such as the telephone or a mailed questionnaire, there is always a potential that subject behavior (responses to questions) may be affected. (Even the behavior of animals may be affected by their awareness of human observers.) If subject-observer interaction is thought to be a serious threat to the validity of research data, the collection of data through unobtrusive observation should be considered. **Unobtrusive observation** refers to *observation by the researcher in such a way that subjects are unaware they are being observed or even of the presence of the observer.*

When the subjects of a study are people, the protection of human rights is a very important consideration. The use of unobtrusive observation may or may not be a violation of such rights as the very act of requesting informed consent from such subjects would defeat the purpose of unobtrusive observation. Such research may still be acceptable if it can be clearly shown that the data collection poses no risk to subjects or compromise of their privacy. For example, unobtrusively observing and recording the behavior of fans leaving a basketball arena would probably be found acceptable because the exit to a basketball arena is a public place where peoples' behavior is normally open to observation. On the other hand, unobtrusively observing the behavior of a group of people in a private party would probably be found unacceptable. Any researcher using unobtrusive observation of human subjects should consult with someone with substantial experience in human subjects review procedures before attempting to collect data.

Other Approaches

Other possible methods of contacting and collecting survey data include distribution and re-collection of questionnaires by fax machine or electronic mail, computer administered questionnaires, and synthesized voice telephone interviews.

MAXIMIZING THE RATE OF SUBJECT PARTICIPATION

The most careful random selection of subjects to be asked to participate in a survey or any form of research may be of little value if a large number of those selected decline or are unable to participate. Indeed, quite erroneous conclusions may be reached when even a relatively small proportion of prospective subjects do not participate, if their non-participation is systematic.

When the subjects of a research project are people or organizations composed of people, those subjects always have an absolute right (except in rare cases such as the census, in which the study is mandated by law) to decline to participate. Subjects may decline for any reason and need not give any reason. Subjects typically *will* decline if participation is perceived as hazardous, coercive, inconvenient, or burdensome in any way that is not balanced by the perceived benefits of participating. The burden of securing the participation of as many prospective subjects as possible lies with the researcher. The following sections discuss some ways the rate of subject response may be improved.

Presentation

When applying for a computer programmer's job in a bank it is better to wear a suit and bring a neatly typed résumé than to be dressed in torn jeans and have a hand-written résumé. Neither the clothes nor the method of preparing the résumé is directly relevant to the ability to program a computer but each certainly will affect the chance of being hired. The typewritten résumé and the business suit increase the chance of being hired because they improve the *presentation* of the job candidate. Similarly, the presentation of any consumer product—its packaging, that is—makes a sale more likely. For a survey, or any kind of research study, in which subjects must be asked to participate, presentation refers to the packaging of that request and of every detail of the researcher's contact with subjects.

In a live or telephone interview the presentation includes the interviewer's manner of speaking to subjects as well as the actual words spoken in approaching the subject. Subjects are not likely to respond well to an interviewer who is overly aggressive, rude, or difficult to hear or understand. The interviewer's appearance and dress are also extremely important in a live interview.

For a mailed questionnaire, the appearance, wording, and tone of the cover letter are a very important part of the presentation as is the general appearance of the questionnaire itself. Most people are unlikely to be impressed favorably by a questionnaire that arrives unaccompanied by an explanatory cover letter. Sending an introductory letter a few days or a week before a telephone survey begins or a questionnaire is mailed explaining the purpose and importance of the study can also be an effective, if expensive, method for encouraging a high rate of participation.

Incentives

Obviously, one way to persuade subjects to participate in a study is to provide reinforcement in the form of a reward of some kind for doing so. Many studies in the medical field, for example, pay subjects for participating. Persons with serious or fatal diseases may be quite highly motivated to participate in the study of a new medicine by the opportunity to try the new medicine if they feel it might provide prolonged life or even a cure. Anything that provides significant value to the potential subject may serve as an incentive to participate in a research project. Because subjects may even be tempted to participate in a study that is not in their best interest or without a full understanding of the risks involved, the researcher must be extremely careful to protect the potential subject. For example, the promise of an early release might serve as a very strong incentive to prison inmates to serve as subjects in a trial of a new medicine or in some other study that could be quite hazardous to their health and well being. Because the short-term benefit of freedom from incarceration would, in the view of the prisoner, tend to outweigh long-term health risks from participating in a study, the use of coercive incentives of this type is considered ethically very questionable.

Incentives used with simple surveys are most often relatively small tokens rather than genuine payment. Market surveys, for example, may distribute small product samples or coupons redeemable for such samples. Sometimes, the money that would be spent giving each subject a small sample is pooled to pay for a more valuable prize to be awarded through a drawing to one subject. In other cases, simply participating in the survey may be interesting enough to entice most people to become involved. Television program pilot episodes are often previewed prior to full production to audiences composed of volunteers whose only incentive is a chance to see a possible future program. Surveys of persons involved in a particular field of interest often encourage subjects to participate by offering to supply a copy of the results when the study is completed.

Avoiding Disincentives

In addition to considering the possible use of incentives, the researcher should be careful to avoid creating disincentives to participation. The most common example of a disincentive is the mailed survey in which the subject is expected to pay for the return postage. Other forms of disincentive to participation include questionnaires or interviews that are too long (10 to 15 minutes is about as much as most people will tolerate) asking for information that is too personal or invasive of privacy, calling during the dinner hour, and mailing questionnaires to "occupant" or "resident" rather than a specific person.

Follow-up

Questionnaires received through the mail are not often given a high priority by their recipients even when a response is intended. Questionnaires get put aside to be completed later and may be significantly delayed or lost completely. If a mailed questionnaire is not returned within a reasonable period (two or three weeks within the United States) a follow-up contact should be tried. A follow-up contact may consist of a second mailing with a new questionnaire and a cover letter reminding the subject of the importance of a response or it may be a phone call followed by another mailed questionnaire.

TYPES OF SURVEY ITEMS

The items on surveys, like those on knowledge tests, are often referred to as questions even though they are frequently not actually written as questions because they serve as prompts or requests for information. The choice of the type of items to use in a questionnaire should be based on the kind of information to be obtained and on the way that information will be used after it is collected. In general, one should attempt to write items in such a way as to make an accurate response as easy as possible.

Categorical Response (Multiple-Choice)

Categorical response or *multiple-choice* items are most appropriate when it is possible for the researcher to identify all possible responses in advance or when the researcher wants to limit the range of responses. Multiple-choice items also may serve to minimize the chances that subjects might misinterpret the intent of an item and give an unexpected or difficult-to-interpret response. For example, an item asking a group of baseball players their bat preferences could be constructed as an open response or as a multiple-choice item. The multiple-choice format could be used to restrict the possible responses to a) wood, b) metal, c) plastic, and d) no preference. An open-response item such as, "What kind of bat do you prefer?" might be misunderstood by some players, causing them to give answers such as "large," "Rawlings," "36-ounce," or even "fruit."

Restricting subject responses to a finite list of options tends to make the handling and analysis of the resulting data much easier. If multiple-choice items are printed on scannable forms, for example, data can be entered directly into a computer without any need for recoding. With open-response items, some degree of recoding is likely to be necessary even when sophisticated optical character recognition software is available to convert a scanned image of a data form into a form recognizable by a computer.

Dichotomous Response

Many of the questions used in surveys, especially those used for the classification of subjects, are dichotomous. Subjects are frequently classified as male or female, adult or juvenile, or owner or not of a particular product. Also, opinions are often assessed using "yes" or "no" response questions. Even when the information needed is clearly dichotomous, it is almost always advisable to construct questions in the multiple-choice format and to include response choices such as "Don't know," "No response," or "No comment" to allow for such possibilities. Great care should be taken in formulating questions in order to use a **dichotomous response** for purposes other than subject classification. It is very difficult to formulate questions that can be answered completely truthfully with *"yes or no" type responses* without some form of qualification. For example, in addition to the self-incriminating, "Yes or no! Do you still beat your wife?" even such questions as, "Do you prefer football or basketball?" obviously require more complexity of response than a simple dichotomous response allows.

Open Response

An open-response item, commonly known as a "fill in the blank" item, may be used to gather information with a finer degree of precision than is practical with categorical response items, when it is not possible to identify the full range of possible subject responses, or when the researcher wants to prevent the responses suggested by the categorical response format from influencing subject responses.

The responses to an open-response item can be generally classified as either *numerical* or *text,* although there might be studies in which subjects could be asked to respond with a sketch or drawing of some kind. **Numerical response** items are *those for which the response must be in the form of a number,* whereas **text response** *may be either text or a number.* This distinction makes little difference to the subject filling in a blank space but can have a significant effect on the way in which the resulting data is handled and analyzed. Many summary statistics, for example, can be performed directly on numerical data, although getting the data into the computer from handwritten questionnaires may be a bit complicated. Text data, however, must usually be recoded into some kind of categorical system before it can be analyzed.

Rankings

A **ranking item** is one *in which the subject is asked to arrange a set of items into a sequence according to some criteria such as ascending or descending value.* Often a ranking item can be used to gather more information than the very similar categorical response item. For example, a survey looking at preferences in pizza toppings would discover much more about secondary and tertiary preferences with a ranking item such as, "Please rank each of the following toppings from best to worst" than it would from a categorical response item such as, "Which of the following is your favorite topping?".

Scales

A **scaled response item** is one *that asks the subject to respond using some kind of scale that is built into the item or questionnaire.* Depending upon how the scaled item is written, it may be equivalent to a categorical response item or to a numerical open response item restricted to a limited range of response. An item that asks the subject to respond using a scale of 1 to 5 (or any other range) and which does not permit intermediate responses such as 3.5 is essentially the same as a categorical item in which the response choices are 1, 2, 3, 4, or 5. If intermediate responses are permitted then the item is essentially the same as a numerical open response item except that the upper and lower limits of the subject's responses are defined by the scale.

Checklists

A **checklist item** is one that asks the subject to select one or more items from a finite list. It is essentially the same as a categorical response item except that the selection of more than one response choice is possible.

SURVEY ITEM CONSTRUCTION

To the uninitiated it might seem that writing the questions for a survey should be a simple matter: just write a list of questions asking for the information needed. In practice, however, writing such items can be deceptively complex.

There are many different ways in which the wording of survey items can influence subject responses or even whether subjects respond at all. The following guidelines should be helpful in considering the construction and wording of survey items.

- Keep items as short as possible.

    Long items demand additional attention and effort and may tend to increase the rate of non- or incomplete response. Long items are also more likely to be misunderstood than shorter ones.

- Provide response choices for all possible contingencies.

    Options such as "I choose not to answer," "I don't know," or "Not applicable," should be provided even for most fill-in and open response items. Without such options it will be impossible to distinguish between items not answered by intent and items accidentally skipped.

- Word items so as to avoid influencing the responses.

    Subjects will often tend to bias their responses toward what they perceive the researcher is hoping to find. A question such as, "Should we stop wasting taxpayers' money on do-good welfare programs?" is clearly biased in favor of an affirmative response because it uses the rhetoric associated with those opposed to such programs. The question might be better phrased, "Should we spend more or less tax money for welfare programs?" Similarly, a question such as, "Should criminals be punished swiftly and severely?" is biased toward the affirmative by use of the term "criminals." Substitution of "persons who violate the law" would probably be more neutral.

- Avoid writing questions with potentially conflicting multiple responses.

    Consider the following question, for example. "Since the new coach was hired, have the Bulls improved their defense and team morale?" Suppose the subject agrees that the defense has improved but team morale is unchanged? Some subjects might answer in the affirmative because one aspect of performance has improved even though the other has not, whereas another might give a negative response because both aspects of performance have not improved even though one has. Such a question would be better split into two questions.

- When possible, avoid using the negative form.

    Consider the following question. "Do you agree that coaches should not be fired when their teams lose?" Some subjects may become confused by such questions or may even fail to notice the *not* which creates the negative form. On the other hand, writing some questions in the negative form may help to control against bulleting or giving the same response to all items without even reading them. A useful compromise may be to use **bold faced** or *italic* text to call attention to negating terms such as *not* or *disagree* when they must be used so they are less likely to be missed.

- Consider the directionality of scaled response items.

    If you are attempting to measure an attribute, for example, a greater amount or more extreme degree of that attribute should be represented by larger numbers. A typical attribute measured in this way would be "extroversion" or "courage." This is particularly important with instruments in which the attribute is to be measured as the aggregate response to several items.

- Avoid questions that threaten subjects' self-esteem.

    If the true answer to a question is embarrassing, subjects are often likely to make up less than truthful but more personally favorable responses, or they may not respond at all. For example, asked about past athletic activities, many people may tend to exaggerate their achievements.

- Avoid potentially offensive language.

    Negative, derogatory, or stereotypical terminology pertaining to political or religious affiliation, sexual behavior or identity, race, ethnic background, and similarly sensitive areas need to be carefully reviewed. It matters little if offense is unintended. If subjects fail to respond or respond in reaction to the wording of a question, the survey findings will be biased.

- Avoid ambiguity about what is being asked.

    For example, a question such as, "What kind of car do you prefer?" might be understood to be inquiring about the preferred manufacturer, size, style, or even color. Subjects who are railroad buffs might even give such responses as "hopper," "tanker," or "box." Careful pilot testing should be effective in identifying most problems of ambiguity, provided the pilot test subjects are representative of the eventual study sample.

- Consider the context of items within the survey and the survey itself.

    Responses to questions about the need for handgun control would likely be biased in favor of control if preceded by questions about children accidentally killed by handguns and biased against control if preceded by questions about rising violent crime rates. Similarly, conducting a survey about environmental matters from a location in front of a nuclear power plant would very likely produce results very different from the same survey conducted outside a state unemployment office.

- Be careful about terminology.

    Unless the population being sampled clearly has the necessary knowledge, technical terminology, jargon, slang and abbreviations are likely to cause confusion. In surveys administered in printed form there is no way to explain terms that are not understood.

- Avoid unnecessary questions.

    The term *fishing expedition* is often applied to surveys that ask a lot of questions without any clear purpose. The term refers to the idea of a fisherman casting a large net over a body of water in the hope of catching something useful. Questions should be clearly derived from the hypotheses or expected outcomes of the study. Any not related to such hypotheses or outcomes should be deleted.

- Consider the sequence and arrangement of items.

    The questions most important to the study being undertaken should generally be asked as early as possible, especially in telephone or live-interview surveys, as those placed toward the end are less likely to be answered by all subjects. Also, if survey items are of varying type—multiple response, scaled response, open response—it is usually best to group items of similar type together.

- Conduct a pilot study.

    Many expensive mistakes involving ambiguous wording of survey items, confusing response instructions, or missing response choices can be easily avoided by conducting a pilot study in which your survey is administered to a small group of test subjects. For a discussion of pilot studies, refer to Chapter 6.

- Consider the analytical treatment of the data you will gather.

  There is little point in collecting information in a manner that cannot be adequately analyzed or interpreted, or in collecting data that you do not know how to analyze. It may be very helpful to generate a set of mock data and to include a trial analysis of this data as part of a pilot study before resources are expended to collect real data.

THE DELPHI METHOD

In projects such as the formulation of an institutional position statement, the generation of a program of study leading to a degree, or the determination of long-range objectives for an organization, the task to be accomplished is essentially for a group of people to come to a consensus of expert opinion on some issue. For example, a faculty designing a new or revised major must eventually agree on the objectives and then the courses or other requirements to be used to earn that major. All, or most, of the members of a faculty involved in such a project are likely to have expert knowledge of the discipline or profession associated with the new major and are likely to have strong opinions about how the required coursework should be taught, yet they are also likely to disagree, perhaps quite sharply, among themselves on this matter. Progress toward consensus is not likely to be rapid if debate of the issue is completely unstructured. It is more likely that those with opposing views will simply keep repeating their views, louder and louder each time, or that those who are less aggressive will simply yield to those who are more aggressive or influential.

The Delphi method is a systematic approach to consensus building that may be helpful in avoiding or mitigating some of the problems inherent in such a task. To arrive at an agreement on one or more matters, a set of relevant questions is formulated by a coordinator and sent to each member of the study group or committee. Without consultation with others each member gives expert opinion on each question and these are returned to the coordinator. The coordinator then reformulates the questions and these are sent back to each member along with a summary of responses to the original questions. The identities of the authors of each response are concealed. This process is continued in a series of rounds until a consensus has been reached.

The Delphi method is appropriate for consensus building among members of a relatively small group on a matter of expert or professional opinion and when all members are equal to and independent of one another. However, the method can rapidly become quite unwieldy as the size of the group increases. Also, it is very important that anonymity be maintained with respect to intermediate responses. If anonymity is not maintained, there may be a tendency for subsequent responses to be influenced by the reputations of their authors or by relationships, professional or otherwise, that exist among group members.

Before employing the Delphi method to solve a problem the researcher would be wise to consider that a consensus, even among experts with the best of intentions, is a kind of average or compromise and is not necessarily the best solution. A college curriculum developed through consensus-building efforts among a faculty, for example, is likely to be one that offends the fewest members of the faculty, rather than one incorporating any radical new ideas. It is quite possible that one incorporating radical new ideas might be quite superior.

TERMS

categorical response	random sample
checklist item	ranking item
cluster sample	sample
dichotomous response	scaled response item
open numerical response	screening
open text response	stratified sample
population	systematic sample
quota sample	unobtrusive observation

EXERCISES

1. Define several human populations that might be of interest to a researcher doing a survey. For each, determine how a random sample of that population could be obtained.

2. From the research literature, preferably in your area of interest, identify studies using each of the sampling techniques described in this chapter.

3. Compile a list of brokers and other sources of mailing lists. For several such sources identify any restrictions placed on list use.

4. Find out how many of your classmates have been asked to participate in a phone, mail, or face-to-face survey. Discuss with these classmates the factors that influenced their decision to participate or to decline participation.

5. Write a script for a brief phone or face-to-face interview. (Include an introduction, request to participate, list of questions, and a conclusion.) Pilot test your script using yourself as the interviewer and several classmates as subjects. Discuss the effectiveness of your interviewing technique with your subjects.

6. Write a questionnaire for a written survey. (Include a letterhead or introduction, statement of purpose, and a list of questions.) Pilot test your questionnaire using several classmates as subjects to identify occurrences of ambiguity, offensive language, and other problems.

7. Write a survey instrument using one or more of the types of items discussed in this chapter or in Chapter 6. (Your instructor may want to assign each of several groups of students to produce instruments using particular types of items.) Pilot test your instrument using your classmates as subjects. Discuss problems discovered regarding item ambiguity. Save your results for possible use in class exercises with Chapters 11 and 12.

Additional Resources with Annotation

Adams, R.A., Piercy, F.P., Jurich, J.A., & Lewis, R.A. (1992). Components of a model adolescent AIDS/drug abuse prevention program: A delphi study. *Family Relations, 41*, 312–317.
An example of a study using the delphi method.

Cramer, R.H. (1991). The education of gifted children in the United States: A delphi study. *Gifted Child Quarterly, 35* (2), 84–91.
An example of a study using the delphi method.

Rathje, W.L. & Psihoyus, L. (1991). Once and future landfills. *National Geographic, 179* (5), 116–134.
A survey of landfill archaeology in which archaeological methods of research are used in still-active landfills as a method of study for modern problems. An excellent example of how established research methods for one type of study may be adapted to new kinds of problems.

8

EXPERIMENTAL
RESEARCH CONCEPTS

The essence of an experiment is the contrivance of a test of one or more hypotheses in such a way that the outcome can only be attributed, with some degree of statistical confidence, to the truth or falsity of the hypothesis or to random chance. **Experimental design,** therefore, is *the planning and construction of a procedure that eliminates or attempts to eliminate all possible sources of outcome variation except random chance and the truth or falsity of one or more hypotheses.* The sections that follow present brief discussions of the basic terminology and concepts needed to recognize and use good experimental design. A much more detailed, though rather technical, discussion of research design may be found in the classic work, *Experimental and Quasi-experimental Designs for Research* (Campbell and Stanley, 1966).

EXPLORING AND EXPERIMENTING

The term *experiment* is used by scientists to describe at least two different activities that might be better described with separate terms such as *exploring* and *experimenting* or perhaps *exploratory* and *confirmatory* experimentation.

An experiment in the confirmatory sense is a test of a hypothesis. If a scientist in a chemistry laboratory says, "Let's mix A and B and see what happens," that is not really a confirmatory experiment, even though the term experiment may be used, because there is no hypothesis being tested. On the other hand if the chemist says, "If my theory of A and B is correct they should produce C when mixed together; let's mix A and B and find out if we really get C," then that is a confirmatory experiment. The hypothesis that A and B will react to produce C will be either confirmed or contradicted.

The chemist in the first case might technically argue that the mixture of A and B really is a confirmatory experiment by creating a rather artificial hypothesis such as, "If I mix A and B I will get something else," or, in the null form, "If I mix A and B no reaction will occur." However, this is not really much of a hypothesis because it is not derived from any theory or logic; it is just an unscientific guess masquerading as a hypothesis.

The experiment described above is really just a bit of exploration. Exploration of this sort is not without value; it is essential in the early stages of inquiry when the scientist has little or nothing upon which to build a theory, but the theories eventually derived from the results of exploration must ultimately be tested by a confirmatory experiment. The complimentary activities of exploration and confirmation are also found, and sometimes confused, in the

FIGURE 8.1   An experiment in pyramid building. These are two of the oldest known pyramids of Egypt, built when the ancient Egyptians were still experimenting with pyramid design. A) The broken Pyramid was built with too steep an angle and collapsed under its own weight. B) The Step Pyramid of King Djoser was built at the correct angle. All the surviving Egyptian pyramids use the same angle.

mathematical or statistical aspects of research. The researcher may statistically explore a database looking for apparent relationships or look for systems of equations that seem to model real world phenomena, but whatever is found must eventually be accepted or rejected on the basis of a confirmatory experiment and analysis.

WHERE DO HYPOTHESES COME FROM?

As stated in the previous section, an experiment is a test of a hypothesis. In a merely exploratory experiment the hypothesis may be rather artificial and perhaps little more than a guess. In a confirmatory experiment, however, the hypothesis is a prediction derived from a proposed explanation or theory about how the world (or some part of it) works. For example, a once important theory in the field of human evolution held that the ability to make and use tools was what distinguished humans from apes and other animals. Such a theory leads to the hypothesis, "If the theory is true then no non-human animal in its natural environment will ever be observed making and using any kind of tool." Such a hypothesis can and has been tested by observing chimpanzees in the wild to see if they ever make and use tools. They do! Chimpanzees have been observed (Goodall, 1992) making probes from sticks to obtain termites as food. Thus the hypothesis has failed the test and the theory is demonstrated as false. In the words of Louis Leakey quoted by Goodall, after this discovery we must either "redefine tool, redefine human, or accept chimpanzees as humans" (p. 6).

A good hypothesis for a confirmatory experiment comes from asking a question such as, "If the theory is correct, then what does it predict will be true?" The experiment, then, is an attempt to see if the prediction holds true. Bearing in mind that a scientific theory can be proven to be incorrect but never definitively correct, an even better question to ask when developing a hypothesis may be, "What can I do to demonstrate that the theory is wrong or incomplete?"

THE NULL HYPOTHESIS AND ITS ALTERNATIVES

Experiments are set up to test hypotheses. The language with which hypotheses are described, however, can sometimes cause considerable confusion among new researchers. In general terms the hypothesis is the expected result of an experiment. If the researcher investigating two pain treatments expects treatment A to be better than treatment B, then the hypothesis is that treatment A is better than B. In presenting the hypothesis of a study in a thesis report or presentation the hypothesis may be stated in this way. However, the statistical analyses that are usually a part of experimental studies are formally designed to test hypotheses stated in what is called the *null* form. The *null hypothesis* (previously discussed in Chapter 3) is that there is no difference between or among treatments. The results of a statistical analysis of most experiments are used to either accept or reject the null hypothesis.

When the null hypothesis is rejected it means that there is a difference, at least in a probabalistic sense, between or among the treatments used in the experiment. However, there are two ways in which such differences may be anticipated to occur and, therefore, there are two possible alternatives to the null hypothesis. One alternative to the null hypothesis is the prediction that treatments will produce results that are different but with no anticipated direction to that difference. The other is that differences will be in one direction only. Consider for example, a study comparing two soft drink formulas for sweetness. The null hypothesis is that there is no difference in sweetness. If soft drink formula A is compared to formula B with the expectation that if the null hypothesis is rejected it will be because A will taste sweeter than B, that is a directional alternative hypothesis. If they have the same sweetness, or if B is sweeter, then the null hypothesis will be accepted. On the other hand, if there is no expectation concerning which formula will taste sweeter if the null hypothesis is rejected, that is a non-directional alternative hypothesis. The null hypothesis will be rejected if either drink is sweeter than the other. The directionality or lack thereof of the alternative hypothesis does not affect the design of an experiment, except at the point of statistical analysis of the resulting data. When treatment groups are compared statistically the null hypothesis will be accepted or rejected on the basis of some kind of statistical test that may be *one-tailed* or *two-tailed*. One-tailed tests are used with directional alternative hypotheses. Two-tail tests are used when the alternative is non-

Figure 8.2   Design notation.

R	O_1		O_2
R	O_1	X_1	O_2
R	O_1	X_2	O_2

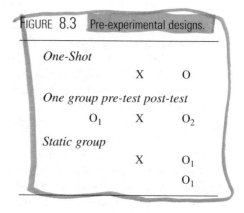

Figure 8.3   Pre-experimental designs.

One-Shot

X   O

One group pre-test post-test

O_1 X O_2

Static group

X O_1

O_1

directional or when directionality is uncertain. The concept of one- and two-tailed statistical tests is discussed further in Chapter 15.

NOTATION FOR RESEARCH DESIGNS

Figure 8.2 is a representation of a research design using a simple shorthand widely used for describing experimental and experimental-like research designs. Each of the three rows in this design notation represents a different set or group of subjects used in the experiment. There are three groups in this design. The letter R preceding each group indicates that subjects are assigned to groups by a random process. The letter O is used to represent an **observation** or *measurement of some kind* and the letter X represents a **treatment** or *experience of some kind.* In some texts, the letter T is used instead of X to designate a treatment. The lack of an X for the first group indicates the group is a control group, although the symbol X_C is sometimes used. Subscripts are used to distinguish between different observations and treatments. Notice that the measurements taken at the beginning and at the conclusion of the experiment are the same for all three groups, but that the treatments given to each group are different.

PRE-EXPERIMENTAL DESIGNS

Figure 8.3 shows several research designs designated as *pre-experimental.* These designs are characterized as **pre-experimental designs** because *although they closely approximate the concept of an experiment, studies using them do not really qualify as experiments.* None of these designs is able to eliminate sources of outcome variation other than variation in the independent variable and random chance.

The so-called **one-shot design** consists simply of *exposure of a single group of subjects to a treatment or procedure of some kind followed by a measurement.* No research project should ever intentionally use the one-shot design. The design does not permit any changes occurring in the subject group to be attributed to the treatment. Indeed, because there is not even a pre-treatment measurement it is not even possible to determine whether any change has actually occurred. However, the one-shot design may be the only design possible when measurements are made following an unexpected event. For example, measurements of the blood pressure of a group of people 30 minutes after they experience a magnitude 8.5 earthquake would constitute a one-shot design. If their blood pressures are rather high, common sense would suggest that the cause of their hypertension was the earthquake, even though the design of the study cannot eliminate other possible causes.

The *one-group* **pre-test post-test** design involves one group that is *subjected to a measurement both before and following a treatment or procedure*. The use of the pre-test means that change can be detected and quantified. However, the fact that there is only one group means that such changes cannot be attributed to the treatment. It is possible that change would occur with or without the treatment and it is even possible that changes might be greater in the absence of the treatment.

The **static group comparison** design involves two groups of subjects. *One group is exposed to a treatment or procedure while the other is not, and then both groups are measured.* Because this design employs two groups of subjects it is possible to detect and quantify differences between the two groups at the conclusion of a study. However, the design does not provide any information about the initial status of either group, and there is no basis for assuming the initial equality of the two groups. Therefore, differences between the two groups following exposure to differing treatments cannot be attributed to the different treatments. The differences may have been present from the beginning.

TRUE EXPERIMENTAL DESIGNS

True experimental designs are those that really do provide a good degree of confidence that variations in the outcome are due to either differences in treatment or to random chance, although they may not completely eliminate all other sources of variation.

The *pre-test post-test randomized groups* design involves two or more groups created by random assignment. All groups are measured before treatment, subjected to different treatments, and then measured again. It is probably most appropriate when the number of subjects available for each group is small (less than about 15), limiting the ability of the randomization process to provide initially equivalent groups. It is also appropriate when there is a specific need to measure *change* rather than final status in the dependent variable. However, if the number of subjects in each group is sufficient, there is really no need for the pre-test. Properly applied, randomization assures that, from a statistical point of view, the groups may be assumed to be initially equal.

FIGURE 8.4   Pre-test post-test randomized groups.

R	O_1	X	O_2
R	O_1		O_2

FIGURE 8.5   A randomized groups design. In this case there are two treatment groups and one control group.

R	X_1	0
R	X_2	0
R		0

FIGURE 8.6   Solomon Four and Three Group Designs are used to control the possible effects of pre-tests.

Four Groups					Three Groups			
R	O_1	X_1	O_2		R	O_1	X_1	O_2
R	O_1		O_2		R	O_1		O_2
R		X_1	O_2		R		X_1	O_2
R			O_2					

A potentially serious weakness of the pre-test post-test randomized groups design is that the use of the pre-test introduces the pre-test itself as a possible source of variation. This is particularly important when one of the groups is actually a control group; that is, the treatment given the group is actually no treatment. In such cases the very fact of being exposed to a pre-test may change the behavior of subjects in the control group, making that group different from a proper control group.

The difficulties caused by the pre-test in the above design are eliminated in the *randomized groups* design which is also simpler and usually more efficient. The randomized groups design is the same as the pre-test post-test randomized groups design except that no pre-test is administered. Figure 8.5 shows a three-group randomized design with one group serving as a control; however, the simplest and most commonly employed version of the randomized groups design uses only one treatment group plus a control. The lack of a pre-test may seem to some as a weakness as less information is made available to the researcher. However, just the opposite is true. As long as subjects are actually assigned randomly and subject groups are large enough (generally more than about 15 subjects per group) so that the chance assignment of one or a few atypical subjects should not have a significant effect, the randomized groups may be assumed to be initially equivalent through **randomization.** That is, *the initial variation present between and within the groups is made random with respect to those groups by the randomness of the assignment of subjects to groups.* If there is any concern that the existence of a pre-test will have an effect on subject behavior during treatment, as is likely in any study involving human subjects who are aware of being pre-tested, the randomized groups design should usually be preferred.

Another approach to controlling the effects of pre-testing is to select a design that treats the pre-test itself as a second independent variable. This can be accomplished using designs known as the *Solomon Four Group* and *Solomon Three Group* designs (see Figure 8.6). The Solomon Four Group design starts with the random assignment of subjects into four different groups. The first two groups are given both pre- and post-treatment tests. Of these groups, one group receives the experimental treatment and the other serves as a control. Groups three and four are handled exactly the same as groups one and two, respectively, except that no pre-test is given. The Solomon Four Group design acts as a control for the effects of pre-testing both by itself and in combination with the treatment. Additionally, statistical analysis applied to the data can partition and quantify the variation in the dependent variable which can be attributed to the treatment, pre-testing, and the interaction of pre-testing with treatment.

The Solomon Three Group design is the same as the Four Group design except that the group receiving neither pre-testing nor treatment is omitted, reducing the total number of subjects required by 25 percent. The group receiving pre-testing with no treatment and the group receiving treatment without pre-testing act as controls for the direct effects and some of the interactive effects of the treatment with pre-testing. However, it will fail to control for situations in which either pre-testing or the treatment leads to the same or opposite outcome as treatment and pre-testing together. Fortunately, such situations are not common.

All of the designs presented above, with the exception of the Solomon Four Group design, enable the researcher to test the effects of a single independent variable. In the Solomon Four Group design it may be argued that the presence or absence of a pre-test is a second independent variable. Real world phenomena, however, are rarely so simple. Real phenomena tend to be governed by multiple factors, many of which may interact with each other in complex ways. Learning to swim, for example, may be affected by body density, water density, gender, age, the type and quality of instruction, the availability and use of learning aids, water temperature, water clarity, bottom conditions, environmental distractions, learning ability, desire to learn, prior experience, and probably many other factors. Furthermore, some of these factors, such as type of instruction and age, may interact with each other so that not everyone is affected in the same way. An instructional approach in which relaxation and ease of effort are emphasized may not work as well in cold as in warm water.

For the researcher investigating complex phenomena it is almost always more desirable to arrange experiments that examine the effects of more than one independent variable at a time. *Designs that examine two or more independent variables in a true experiment* are called **factorial designs.**

Factorial designs are named and described according to the number of *factors* and the number of *levels* of each factor. Each factor is a different independent variable. The levels of each factor are the different attributes or treatments of a factor being studied. For example, a study might be constructed to examine the effectiveness of two different methods of teaching, and the effects of gender and age on the learning of a skill. The three factors in such a study are method, gender, and age. There are two levels of method and two of gender, whereas age can be categorized into any desired number of levels. If age is treated as a variable with three levels then the design would be correctly described as a $2 \times 2 \times 3$ *factorial* design.

A factorial design enables the researcher to test the effects of several independent variables and their interactions on a dependent variable. The statistical analysis applied in such studies attempts to estimate how much of the variation in the dependent variable can be attributed to each of the independent variables and each of the possible interactions. The *variation attributable to each independent variable* is called the **main effects** of that variable and the *variations attributable to each interaction* are called the **interaction effects.** The outcome variation in a factorial design with two independent variables will be attributable to two main effects plus one interaction effect. In a factorial design with three independent variables the outcome variation will be attributable to three main effects and four different interaction effects. A study with four independent variables will produce four main effects and eleven interaction effects.

FIGURE 8.7   A 2×2 factorial design. Simple factorial designs can be described using the notation system on the left. More complex factorial designs, however, will be easier to understand when shown using the table format on the right. The notation and table describe the same 2×2 design.

R	X_1	X_1	O_1
R	X_1	X_2	O_1
R	X_2	X_1	O_1
R	X_2	X_2	O_1

		Variable 1	
		Level A	Level B
Variable 2	Level A	Group 1	Group 2
	Level B	Group 3	Group 4

A 2×2 factorial design requires four groups of subjects. A 2×3×6 factorial design requires 36 groups of subjects. Clearly, the expansion of factors or levels of factors cannot proceed very far before the number of subject groups becomes quite unwieldy. With a minimum group size of 15 the 2×3×6 factorial design requires at least 540 subjects. There are several possible solutions to this problem, including the covariance design, nested factorial designs, or other partial factorial designs.

OTHER DESIGNS

The factorial design uses independent (either true independent variables or classification variables treated as independent) variables or factors that are nominal or categorical in scale. That is, from the standpoint of the design and the subsequent statistical analysis, the different levels of each independent variable are simple categories. Quite often, however, the categories or levels of a factor are artificially created from the range of values found in a continuous variable. For example, the categories of teenager, young adult, adult, middle aged, and senior citizen might be artificially defined for the continuous variable of age. In such cases, because it uses actual data on each subject rather than the grouping of subjects into groups with certain ranges of data values, the use of a *covariance design* can be used to reduce, sometimes substantially, the necessary number of subject groups. If the six-level factor in the 2×3×6 factorial design discussed in the previous paragraph is a continuous variable then the use of a covariance design will reduce the number of subject groups from 36 to 6. The **covariance design** is the *same as the factorial design except that data for the covariate (or covariates) is simply obtained by measurement of each subject and is not explicitly expressed in the design of the experiment.* If *the covariate is a pretreatment measurement of the dependent variable* such a design may be referred to as a **repeated measures** design. Such designs are often used in educational situations in which the pre-existing grouping of student subjects precludes their random assignment to treatment groups. A simple example would be a study of two methods of teaching arithmetic in which the same test of arithmetic competency is used before and after a year of instruction. A somewhat more complex example would be a similar study but with additional administrations of the test during instruction or a year after the end of instruction. The covariance design also requires a slightly different statistical analysis

FIGURE 8.8   A Covariance or repeated measures design. The design shown is a two-way repeated measures factorial design if the covariate, shown as O_1, is the same as the dependent variable. If the covariate is different from the dependent variable, the design should be called a two-way covariance design.

R	O_1	X_1	Y_1	O_2
R	O_1	X_2	Y_1	O_2
R	O_1	X_1	Y_2	O_2
R	O_1	X_2	Y_2	O_2

FIGURE 8.9   A nested design. A different set of three levels of age are nested under each level of method. The table shows there are 15 subjects assigned to each of the 12 groups or cells in the design.

	METHOD A			METHOD B		
Age	10–12	25–27	16–18	19–21	22–24	13–15
Male	15	15	15	15	15	15
Female	15	15	15	15	15	15

called an analysis of covariance, or, if all independent variables are continuous, a regression analysis.

There are often research situations in which a complete factorial design is impractical, undesirable, or even impossible. Consider, for example, a study of the effectiveness of three different methods for teaching basic swimming with the classification variables of gender and six different levels of age. Using the complete factorial design this is a $3 \times 2 \times 6$ factorial and requires 36 groups of subjects. If some information about the effects of age or the interaction of age with gender and method of instruction can be sacrificed, the number of subject groups can be reduced significantly by using a **nested design** with *the age variable nested under method of instruction*. In the example already introduced, three levels of age could be nested under one method of instruction and the other levels of age nested under the other method. The number of subject groups is reduced to 12. Although such a design may fail to detect or control the main or interaction effects of the nested variable, it can still be useful for examining the effects of the other variables, and the effects of the nested variable may be controlled if the levels of the nested variable are nested randomly.

When classification or other extraneous variables are necessarily present in a study but their main or interaction effects with the independent variable under study are not of interest, the effects of those variables can be controlled through use of designs in which subjects with each classification (level) are counterbalanced in their exposure to levels of the independent variable. A Latin square is

Figure 8.10   A Latin square of letters.

A	B	C	D	E
D	A	B	E	C
B	C	E	A	D
E	D	A	C	B
C	E	D	B	A

Figure 8.11   A Latin square design used in a study of three methods of fitness instruction at three different times of day with three different class sizes. Subjects are randomly assigned to one of nine groups, each of which receives one combination of method, time of day, and class size. Such a design should be considered quasi-experimental.

	MORNING	MIDDAY	EVENING
Method A	Small	Medium	Large
Method B	Medium	Large	Small
Method C	Large	Small	Medium

Figure 8.12   The Latin square design applied to a study of three methods of fitness instruction at three times of the day. Each of three groups of students is given each type of instruction at each time of day. The Latin square is used to assure that each group receives each method of instruction and that each method is applied equally at each time of day.

	MORNING	MIDDAY	EVENING
Group A	Method A	Method C	Method B
Group B	Method B	Method A	Method C
Group C	Method C	Method B	Method A

a square arrangement of items such that each item may be found once, and only once in each column and row. For example, the letters A, B, C, D, and E may be arranged in the 5×5 array of letters shown in Figure 8.10 to form a Latin square. The **Latin square design** is *a design in which subject groups or levels of one variable are distributed using a Latin square pattern*. It may be used to control the effects of two extraneous or classification variables or to control the effects of the order of treatments or measurements in studies in which subject groups are exposed to multiple treatments or measurements.

In any study using a Latin square design it is possible to superimpose a second Latin square of the same dimension on the first so that the levels of two variables are distributed according to the Latin square pattern. Such a design is referred to as a Graeco-Latin square design.

QUASI-EXPERIMENTAL DESIGNS

In many fields of study, including education and the social sciences, the use of a true experimental design is often difficult or impossible. For example, researchers in education looking at factors affecting teaching or learning are often forced to use existing classes as subject groups. As students are not typically assigned to specific classes at random, none of the designs based on random assignment of subjects to treatment groups can be used. In such cases, a quasi-experimental design may be an acceptable substitute for a true-experimental design. The **quasi-experimental designs** *tend to provide most of the controls offered by the true-experimental designs, though often at the expense of requiring a more complicated statistical analysis.* The following are examples of quasi-experimental designs.

The **non-equivalent control group design** is *identical to the pre-test post-test randomized group design except that there is no random assignment of subjects to groups.* Two or more subject groups are pre-tested, subjected to different treatments, and then post-tested. The design is called non-equivalent because without the random assignment step there is no basis for any assumption of initial equivalence between or among the treatment and control groups. Initial differences among the groups are detected by the pre-test, and the statistical analysis technique called the analysis of covariance can then be used to correct for these differences. However, the use of a pre-test, and analysis of covariance should NOT be viewed as a perfect substitute for a randomized design. Although initial differences in the parameter measured by the pre-test will be controlled, there may very well be other differences among groups that will go undetected.

A **time series design** is one in which *one or several groups of subjects or even a single subject is tested or measured repeatedly at constant or measured intervals both before and after treatment.* These designs are called *single group time series* designs if only one subject or group of subjects is used and a *two (or more) group time series* if more groups are used. The idea is to control subject maturation through the actual measurement of the rate of change within the

FIGURE 8.13   Non-equivalent control group design. This approach employs a pre-test to compensate for the absence of random assignment of subjects to groups.

O_1	X_1	O_2
O_1	X_2	O_2
O_1		O_2

FIGURE 8.14   Time series design.

O_1	O_2	O_3	O_4	X_1	O_5	O_6	O_7	O_8

FIGURE 8.15   A single subject time series or reversal design.

O_1	X_1	O_2	O_3	X_1	O_4	O_5	X_1	O_6

subject group prior to treatment rather than through use of an untreated control group. The time series design is a useful approach in situations in which the researcher wants to see if the naturally occurring rate of change in some parameter is affected by the treatment. For example, a time series could be used in a study to see if exposure to moving air from a fan affects the rate of growth of tomato plants in a greenhouse. The rate of growth of a group of plants could be measured every day for a week with the fan off, for several days with the fan on, and then for a week after the fan is turned off. If the fan has any effect on growth, then the rate of growth should change when the fan is turned on but then return to its original rate when the fan is turned off. Time series designs can also be used in situations in which only a small number (as few as one) of subjects is available. Such a situation might occur when investigating the effectiveness of a new drug in treating a very rare disease for which only a single subject might be available to the researcher at one time. After an initial measurement the new drug would be administered and another measurement taken after an appropriate interval. The drug would then be withheld for some period of time after which the process of measurement, treatment, and measurement would be repeated. If the drug is effective then there should be a change (hopefully an improvement) in the measurements taken before and after each administration of the drug and either no change or a decline in the two measurements taken between each administration of the drug. Such a *design, in which changes occurring in concert with an effective treatment are expected to be reversed when the treatment is withheld,* is called a **reversal design.**

An **ex post facto study** uses a design that appears, in its simplest form, to be the *same as the pre-experimental static group comparison design.* However, such designs have the exception that subjects are not assigned to groups by the researcher, randomly or otherwise. Instead, *subjects are assigned to groups because they are different on some characteristic.* For example, two groups might be composed of swimmers and non-swimmers or of healthy adults and heart attack patients of the same age. Typically such studies seek to find factors that indicate to which group a subject belongs or which correlate well with group membership. In the study of swimmers and non-swimmers, such factors as body density, lung capacity, or foot flexibility might be investigated to see if they discriminate between the two groups. Studies of this type can only suggest a link between such factors and group membership; a true experiment is needed to test the hypothesis that a link is present.

META-ANALYSIS

In recent years the methods of meta-analysis have achieved increasing use in exercise science and allied fields. Although meta-analysis is more properly described as a systematic, statistically supported approach to the review of scientific literature, it is discussed here because it is most commonly applied to the review of studies of an experimental or quasi-experimental nature and because it is generally applied to research questions that are best addressed experimentally. Aspects of meta-analysis are also discussed in Chapters 1 and 12.

Meta-analysis is a systematic approach to the integration of findings from multiple, independent studies, using the result from each included study as a single data point in a larger study. Suppose, for example, a researcher has identified a hundred or so independent research studies examining the effects of caffeine on reaction time. If each study were identical to every other study in such matters as the dosages of caffeine, the measure of reaction time, all subject characteristics, the number of subjects, and all other factors, then their integration should be quite simple. All the studies (with exceptions few enough to be attributed to random error) should show the same thing and the effects of caffeine on reaction time should be so well documented that there would be little need for further study. In the real world, however, there will be many differences among the various studies and their results may not appear to be entirely consistent. Some studies may show more or less of an effect on reaction time. On the other hand, some studies may have used subject groups with different age or gender compositions, different caffeine dosages, different measures of reaction time, or may appear to differ in other ways. Whereas a traditional literature review requires the researcher to subjectively evaluate or explain the impact of such differences, the techniques of meta-analysis provide a somewhat more objective basis for such judgments.

The initial step in a meta-analysis is to identify and obtain reports for all available studies on the topic of interest. In general this search process should be an exhaustive one. That is, the researcher should attempt to obtain every report published in research journals (including those in other languages, where feasible) dissertations, theses, papers read at scientific meetings, and those available through other sources. The procedures used to search the literature and any decisions made regarding the inclusion or exclusion of items must be consistently applied and explicitly identified in the meta-analysis.

The next step is to identify each possible *comparison* or *effect* that was made in each study. Each study will involve at least one effect but may involve several effects. A simple two-group experiment, for example, involves a single effect. An experiment with two treatment groups and a control group, however, will have three effects, each treatment to the control and the treatments to each other. Each of the effects found constitutes one case in the meta-analysis. Such effects, however, may be reported in the literature in a wide variety of ways. The authors of the various reports may have reported the statistic known as the effect size, but often the only information provided are the means and standard deviations of treatment and control groups, values of group comparison or correlation statistics, or perhaps only a statement that differences between groups were, or were not, significant at some level of confidence. (Some of these concepts are discussed in subsequent chapters.) In order to permit the integration of studies in a meta-analysis, each of these reported effects must be converted or transformed into a common form called the **effect size.** *It is the effect reported in a study expressed in a common form that can be compared to effect sizes from other studies.* Chapter 12 provides several transformations for this purpose when effect sizes are not already available. In addition to the effect size, the data recorded for each effect should include every identifiable characteristic of the study providing the effect that could conceivably be relevant to that effect. This may include such miscellaneous factors as the mode of publication, whether or not a peer review preceded publication, or even the professional status of the author.

Once effect sizes and study characteristics for each effect have been assembled there are at least two approaches that may be taken in the meta-analysis. The first is to treat each effect size as the dependent measure for a subject in a single study having the characteristics associated with that effect. Of the 100 or so effect sizes found concerning caffeine effects on reaction time, for example, some of the effects may have involved only subjects within a particular age range, some may involve other age ranges, and others may involve groups of mixed or unreported ages. The meta-analyst using such data might choose to isolate those effect sizes that are associated with each age range and attempt to assess whether there is any effect on reaction time produced by the interaction of age with caffeine intake. That is, the meta-analyst might want to determine whether caffeine affects reaction time differently with age. If there were 23 effects identified with the 15- to 20-age range, 27 effects identified with the 21- to 25-age range, and 17 effects identified with the 26- to 30-age range, then the effect sizes for the 67 studies of subjects within particular age ranges would be treated as measures of reaction times from 67 subjects in a study of caffeine effects on subjects in three different age ranges.

The second approach to meta-analysis is to attempt to look for associations between effect sizes that appear to be inconsistent with the general trend and particular study characteristics. Noticing that effect sizes from the studies of caffeine effects on reaction time are not consistent in magnitude, for example, the researcher might isolate those that cluster around similar values and discover the presence of a trend relating to age. This approach to meta-analysis should not be a mere "fishing expedition" looking exhaustively for relationships in the absence of any underlying theoretical basis for the expectation of a relationship. Rather, it should be an attempt to explain any inconsistencies that may be present in the assembled effect sizes. For example, if the relationship between caffeine intake and reaction time is a simple one, one that does not involve any interactions with subject characteristics such as age or gender, and if all of the studies are carried out in a manner that does not affect the outcome in any way, then the effects and the effect sizes should be extremely consistent. The only differences should be due to random error. If, on the other hand, some characteristic of subjects or experimental procedure, such as gender or a weak, pre-experimental design, does affect the outcome of some studies, then the effect sizes for the affected studies should vary in magnitude from those that are unaffected. The very presence of anomalous effect sizes suggests (though it does not confirm) the presence of some such characteristic. The discovery of such characteristics may be useful in the elaboration of the theoretical understanding of a phenomenon or in establishing a basis for the exclusion of studies whose results are inconsistent with theory.

TERMS

covariance design	*ex post facto* study
effect size	factorial design
experimental design	interaction effect
Latin square design	pre-experimental design
main effect	quasi-experimental design
nested design	randomization
non-equivalent control group design	repeated measure design
observation	reversal design
one-shot design	static group comparison
pre test	time series design
post test	treatment

EXERCISES

1. Find several research articles with hypotheses stated in the null form. Restate these in the directional form.
2. Find several research articles with hypotheses stated in the directional form. Restate these in the null form.
3. Find examples in the research literature of as many as possible of the designs explained in this chapter.

ADDITIONAL RESOURCES WITH ANNOTATION

Thomas, J.R. & French, K.E. (1986). The use of meta-analysis in exercise and sport: A tutorial. *Research Quarterly for Exercise and Sport, 57*, 196–204.
An introduction and tutorial in the technique of meta-analysis, including an example of a study from the field of exercise science.

HISTORICAL
RESEARCH METHODS

History is defined by Barzun and Graff (1985) as "the story of past facts." Their definition, however, lends itself to several, very different interpretations, as Barzun and Graff themselves point out. One interpretation is to place emphasis on the word "facts"—that is, to define history as the facts of things that happened in the past. History, therefore, is the truth of what happened in the past. Such a definition is ultimately inadequate because what happened in the past is ultimately unknowable in its full detail and any attempt to recite or write the story of what happened in the past in its full detail would be unimaginably tedious.

A second interpretation is to place emphasis on the word "story"—that is, to define history as the story we know or tell about things that happened in the past. History, then, is what we say or believe happened in the past. This is also an inadequate definition of history, at least for most of us, because it fails to require a connection between the story and the facts of what happened. History then becomes propaganda or ideology. It may then become unstable, shifting over time according to prevailing needs and ideas rather than in response to new discoveries of fact, or it may become dogmatic, immune to criticism arising from new discoveries of fact. Barzun and Graff's definition must be taken as a whole, with a balance of emphasis on both "story" and "facts." Thus, history is the story that is understood, told, or written about the facts of what happened in the past. In telling the story of the past, the historian edits out incomprehensible and irrelevant detail—admittedly a task requiring subjective judgment—and tells a story of the past. At the same time, the story that is told is required to be consistent with all of the available facts. For example, historians of baseball may write different stories about the origin of the game as new evidence is discovered but such stories may never portray Abner Doubleday as the inventor of the game because there is clear evidence to the contrary.

SCHOLARLY WORK IN HISTORY

Although history may be defined as the telling of the story of the facts of what happened in the past, there are a variety of approaches to scholarly work in history. The most fundamental approach is what may be termed **descriptive history**. Most of the history taught in schools is principally descriptive in nature. Descriptive history *tells the story of what happened, usually in a narrative form*. Descriptive history may be about a particular event, an individual, a period of time and place, a series of related events or people, and so on. Examples from the world of sport may include the invention of basketball, a

FIGURE 9.1   The long road of history.

biography of Babe Ruth, the evolution of Negro baseball leagues in the American South, or the political aspects of the Olympic Games. Another approach to historical research is termed *analytical history*. **Analytical history** *attempts to answer questions about why things in the past happened the way they did.* Clearly, this approach is highly vulnerable to error from biases of all sorts, especially when the events under study are recent or directly involve the researcher, and any explanation of a historical event can never be adequately tested. Nevertheless, there is a strong argument that the real lessons of history are those that come from understanding why events happened the way they did and perhaps the details of what happened are, in the long run, of considerably lesser interest. This is what is meant when it is said that those who do not know history are condemned to repeat it. Some examples of research questions from the world of sport that might be answered through analytical history include why organized sports appeared where and when they did, why the ancient Olympic Games were founded and later abolished, why certain sports are popular in the U. S. while others are not, and why professional athletics were racially segregated as long as they were.

Another form of historical research involves the collection, documentation, and preservation of historical documents and artifacts. Merely *collecting historical documents and artifacts* is called **antiquarianism**, but the historian is also interested in preserving information about the objects or documents collected. For example, much of the value of such artifacts as pottery shards and arrowheads found in pre-Columbian settlements in the American Southwest lies in information to be found in their in-situ context (in their original surroundings), not in the artifacts themselves. Closely related to the collection and preservation of artifacts is the prevention of their loss due to age, decay, or even the act of their study. For example, many of the ancient tombs of Egypt that have survived intact during thousands of years of burial are now rapidly decaying as a result of changes brought about by their discovery. Another closely related type of study is the preservation of knowledge held by living persons by transforming it into tangible form, such as transcripts of interviews, audio, video, and film recordings, and the like. The knowledge so preserved may be the individual's life story or their experience of some event, or it may be a form of raw information such as the vocabulary of a rare or dying language, the sound of a folk song, or the rules or procedures of a childhood game.

Another approach to historical research might be called forensic history. **Forensic history** *seeks to answer such questions as the identity of an artifact, the author of a document, or the creator of a work of art.* For example, a ball purported to be the one that was hit for the sixty-first home run by Roger Maris in 1961 might be verified as the genuine article by forensic research.

HISTORICAL METHODS

The study of history deals with discovery and explanation of things that happened in the distant or recent past. By the very fact of their having already taken place, questions of history cannot be answered using experimental methods. Historians cannot construct a controlled experiment comparing different versions of the 1960s to test hypotheses concerning the causes of the Vietnam War. Historians, paleobiologists, archaeologists, and others engaged in the study of events in the past will often use the methods of experimental, descriptive, or other kinds of research, but the discovery and interpretation of historical evidence requires the use of methods and concepts of historical inquiry.

Sources of Historical Data

Events in history are not available for direct measurement by the researcher. The historical researcher must rely on indirect sources of information such as official records and documents, artifacts, personal memories, eyewitness reports, and other forms of evidence created by others in the past. Because of this heavy dependence on indirect evidence, the historian evaluating the meaning of historical evidence must pay close attention to its source.

Historical evidence may be obtained from *primary* or *secondary* sources and may be written or unwritten in form. Official government records, transcripts or proceedings of meetings, personal diaries, eyewitness accounts, newspaper reports actually written or recorded by a direct witness to an event, audio or video recordings that have not been edited, and other *original documents created by persons actually observing an event* are **primary sources.** Artifacts, such as old arrowheads and pottery shards, antiques, fossils, ocean bottom cores, and pieces of trash dug up from old landfills may also serve as primary sources in unwritten form, although the information they contain may be more difficult to decipher. Newspaper reports by a reporter interviewing eyewitnesses, interpretations of primary materials by other researchers or non-witnesses, and other *materials that have been edited or filtered through non-witnesses* are **secondary sources.** In a study of the fairness or unfairness of the boxing judging at the 1992 Summer Olympics, for example, an official record of the blow-by-blow scoring by each judge would be primary evidence whereas statements by coaches or other boxers who were in the locker room during the bouts in question would be secondary sources. In the field of law, secondary source testimony is often called *hearsay* evidence. Primary source evidence should always be given more weight than evidence from secondary sources.

External and Internal Criticism of Evidence

External criticism of some element of evidence refers to *evaluation of the authenticity of the evidence.* The researcher must answer the question, "Is this evidence really what it seems to be?" Researchers engaged in the study of controversial issues or issues in which there are individuals or organizations with a strong vested interest in the outcome need to be especially alert to the possibility of encountering deliberately fraudulent or misleading evidence. For example, a letter containing material embarrassing to a candidate for political office which is found just prior to an election is likely to turn out to be a fake planted by an opponent in hopes of affecting voter decisions.

External criticism, however, is more than just distinguishing genuine from fraudulent evidence. Obviously, if a piece of evidence is fraudulent there is no reason for further evaluation. However, a document or artifact may be quite genuine, yet not be what it seems to be. For example, until recently the oldest known copies of the books of the Old Testament were actually made more than a thousand years after the occurrence of the events they describe. Although these documents are certainly genuine their faithfulness to the original remains an open question. They are, after all, handwritten copies of handwritten copies as well as translations from the Hebrew or Greek in which the originals were written. Recent (1948) discoveries of much more ancient manuscripts called the Dead Sea Scrolls promise to resolve the issue.

External criticism may also involve attempting to establish the degree to which a document is a genuine representation of the truth. Such criticism is likely to become increasingly important in evaluating photographs, films, audio and videotape recordings, and digital recordings of all kinds in which original materials have been edited. An editing process that removes irrelevant or duplicate material, or that eliminates segments of poor recording quality—but in which the sequence of events or their context is essentially unchanged—will produce a document that qualifies as genuine. However, an editing process in which the content or sequence of events is changed, or their context altered, produces a document that is not genuine—not an authentic representation of the truth.

The external criticism of a document or artifact must recognize that certain aspects of a document may be genuine while others are not. For example, a letter written by a sailor present at the attack on Pearl Harbor and describing the attack could be quite genuine

---

The Piltdown Man—The Case of the Missing Link That Wasn't

When evaluating evidence of a historical nature the researcher must be scrupulously careful to avoid allowing that evaluation to be influenced by wishful thinking or personal bias. The case of the Piltdown Man discovery provides an excellent example. Near the turn of the twentieth century a skull was reportedly discovered in England that had characteristics of both humans and apes. At the time, the height of British colonial power, it was widely believed that evolution was a process that led purposefully toward greater and greater advancement and that mankind (specifically white mankind and even more specifically British, white mankind) was the ultimate and final expression of that process. The discovery of a so-called missing link in England seemed to confirm what to many seemed inevitable: that mankind must have evolved somewhere near England. Although the skull was a fraud constructed by attaching an ape jaw to a human skull, the fact that many scientists wanted to believe it was real prevented the detection of the fraud for many years.

FIGURE 9.2   Caves at Qumran where the Dead Sea Scrolls were found. Analyses so far available suggest that currently accepted versions of the Old Testament are not radically different from those found in the caves.

in the sense that it really is a letter written by that sailor and that it describes the real, first-hand experience of the attack, yet not be genuine with respect to the date of the letter. The letter could have been written months or years after the attack, yet dated December 7, 1941. Aside from an attempt to create a fraudulent document, perhaps the sailor was simply trying to create an effect on the recipient of the letter by back dating it to the date of the attack.

External criticism of a document or artifact often involves examination of a range of factors that *must* be true if the document is genuine. If any factor is clearly demonstrated as false, then the document cannot be genuine. For example, suppose a letter is discovered bearing the signature of Abraham Lincoln. If the letter is genuine, then the paper and the ink must be of a type manufactured during or before Lincoln's time. If the ink turns out to be toner from a photocopier, then the letter is clearly established as not genuine, although it could also be a photocopy of a genuine letter. Sometimes the content of a document can also be tested for such consistency. For a somewhat simplistic example, a coin claimed to be of ancient Roman origin and bearing the date 33BC is clearly a fake. No genuine document or artifact could ever legitimately bear a date of origin with reference to a future event. Similarly, a painting purported to be by Rembrandt but portraying the faces of Winston Churchill, Franklin Roosevelt, and Joseph Stalin is obviously not genuine.

Once a piece of evidence is established as genuine the evaluation process can shift to its contents and meaning. A piece of evidence may be genuine yet still contain information that is untrue or misleading. For example, an eyewitness account of the attack on Pearl Harbor could be quite authentic but still contain errors in details such as the exact time of the attack. If a document is shown to contain many errors or if well-known, key elements of fact are missing, then other details of the document's accuracy are called into question even though the document itself is genuine. *Evaluation of the contents of a document or artifact and interpretation of its meaning* is called **internal criticism.** In such evaluation of evidence the historical researcher must pay careful attention to the context, both written and historical, of the evidence, to the perspective of the author if the evidence is a written document, to the accuracy of detail within the document, and to the interpretive biases of the researcher.

Context

Politicians frequently complain of being quoted "out of context" by opponents and the news media, not always without justification. Their complaint is that a quotation is accurate as to specific words spoken or written but inaccurate or misleading because its isolation from its surrounding situation (its context) completely changes its meaning. Consider, for example, the following quotation: "I aimed right at him and hit him as hard as I could. I knocked him unconscious." On first glance this might be taken as a confession of an attempted murder or an assault. Its meaning completely changes, however, in the following quotation, in which the context is obvious: "It was third and 20. I aimed right at him and hit him as hard as I could. I knocked him unconscious."

The historical researcher must be careful to preserve the meaning of a piece of written evidence with respect not only to its internal context—that is, the wording or style of the document itself—but also to the historical context in which it was created. Both aspects of context may be illustrated using the Second Amendment to the Constitution of the United States, which reads, "A well-regulated militia being necessary to the protection of a free people, the right of the people to keep and bear arms shall not be infringed." If the second clause is taken out of the context of the wording of the full amendment, it constitutes an absolute protection of the right to bear arms. In the larger context, on the other hand, the infringement of the right to bear arms is prohibited only so long as a well-regulated militia is necessary. Even the full amendment must be evaluated in its historical context. What, for example, did the framers of the Constitution mean by a well-regulated militia? What did they mean by "keep and bear" arms? Today, "to keep arms" means to maintain possession and "to bear arms" means to carry them on one's person. It is arguable, however, that at the time the Constitution was written, "to keep arms" may have meant to train in the use of arms and that "to bear arms" meant to serve in an armed militia. Thus, it may be argued that the Second Amendment really protects every citizen's right to serve in the armed forces.

Perspective

Much of the evidence examined by the historian consists of documents and artifacts created by people and can, therefore, only be reliably understood with knowledge and understanding of the perspective of their creators. This should be obvious with written documents involving the observations or opinions of people, such as personal letters, minutes of meetings, diaries, and newspaper articles. Certainly the observations of persons with a strong, vested interest in the events observed must be evaluated differently from those whose interest is less subject to bias. For example, the observations of the officials of a game of football are generally given greater credence than those of the players or coaches, at least insofar as violations of the rules are concerned. Even seemingly clear-cut evidence such as simple observations of fact must be evaluated in light of the perspective of those recording them. For example, a review of literature showing the use of tobacco to be harmless but overloaded with studies controlled by the tobacco industry should be given considerably less weight than one controlled by more independent researchers.

Researcher bias

Just as historical documents may be biased by the perspective of their authors, so might their interpretation be biased by the perspective of the historian. The historian's description of events or historical evidence may be similarly biased. Such bias has always been a significant, and sometimes unrecognized, problem in the study of history. Western or European history books, for example, are nearly always written from the western or European point of view rather than from Native American, African, or Asian perspectives, any of which would very likely place different emphasis on certain key events even when telling the same stories. In the field of sport history, the history of baseball is rather different when told from the points of view of management or player, or from those of black or white players.

Researcher bias sometimes is manifested in the language used in writing or reciting history. For example, in a history of European colonization of the Americas, descriptors such as "discovery," "exploration," and "wilderness" clearly reflect the bias of the European perspective, whereas the Native American history would probably favor terms such as "invasion" or "land." Researcher bias can probably never be eliminated completely, but it may be minimized through self recognition of its potential and through disclosure of recognized biases to the reader.

Accuracy of details

Obviously, the fact that a document is genuine does not guarantee the accuracy of its contents. Personal letters, checks, and even legal documents may be back- or post-dated for various reasons ranging from accident to intentional fraud. Statements of fact may be in error. Information recorded in documents may even be completely accurate and still be misleading. A hotel register bearing the name of George Washington, for example, could be completely truthful but refer to someone other than the first president, making the claim "George Washington slept here" truthful yet quite misleading. Thus, the contents of historical documents must be examined or evaluated very carefully with respect to the accuracy of their details.

The most obvious method of evaluating the accuracy of details in historical documents is called *triangulation.* The term comes from the land surveyor's method of plotting the exact location of a distant object by measuring the direction to the object from two locations a known distance apart. The line drawn between the two locations and the lines drawn from each known location to the object form a triangle with the object at its vertex. In the evaluation of the accuracy of information in a historical document, **triangulation** refers to *obtaining the same information from two (or more) independent sources.* If two or more independent sources are in agreement as to an assertion of fact or other item of information, then that information is more likely to be accurate. However, in much historical research this is not as simple as it may appear. That two documents agree on specific points of detail is usually fairly obvious, but it is often not so easily demonstrable that the two documents are independent. For example, stories from two different newspapers about the play-by-play events of a football game may both have been written with the aid of information from a wire service. If an error was made by the wire service it might well be replicated in both newspaper stories. Although the two stories may appear to be independent, primary sources of information, in fact they are neither independent nor primary. Even when two documents qualify as primary sources, they may not be independent. If the two stories of the football game in the above example were written by writers actually in attendance but sitting next to each other, their own discussion of the events they observe prior to writing their stories renders the independence of their stories questionable at best.

Information in a document might also be triangulated to some extent through correspondence with other information that would be expected to be true if the document is accurate. A newspaper article stating that a baseball game was canceled due to rain might be corroborated by weather reports indicating poor weather at the time and place of the game.

Another method for judging the accuracy of details in historical documents or artifacts is **confirmation,** which refers to *the agreement between the details of the document and some form of independent, physical evidence.* For example, a claim that the writer of a letter had been present when the New York Jets beat the Baltimore Colts in Super Bowl III would be substantially confirmed by a ticket stub from that game among that person's memorabilia. The ticket stub could, of course, have been obtained by means other than attendance at the game, but unless the letter writer had a clear motive for misleading its recipient, the probability is very strong that the claim to have attended the game is truthful.

Frequently there will be many elements of information in a document, some of which may be triangulated or confirmed and some of which may defy all efforts of verification. In such cases the historical researcher may be forced to rely solely on the apparent credibility of those creating the documents in question. Such credibility may often be subjectively judged in reference to facts known about the individuals involved or in reference to those elements of information that can be verified. If the individuals involved can be established as reliable chroniclers of elements of information in other documents, or if those elements that can be verified turn out to be highly reliable, then there is a good, though far from certain, chance that the unverifiable elements are, in fact, accurate.

 TERMS

analytical history	forensic history
antiquarianism	internal criticism
confirmation	primary source
descriptive history	secondary source
external criticism	triangulation

EXERCISES

1. Obtain several descriptive news stories about the same event from local newspapers or magazines. Check each stated fact for consistency across all sources. If inconsistencies are found, speculate on how the truth might be determined.

2. Identify several individuals who were witnesses to some event, such as a controversial call in a basketball game, that you did NOT witness. Interview each witness and record opinions about what happened. Do not forget to record information about matters such as likely biases and the conditions under which each witness observed the event. From the information thus gathered, attempt to determine what really happened.

3. Interview several people who were witnesses to some event of which you were not a part. Alternatively, obtain several pieces of primary evidence about such an event. Write a paper of three or four pages presenting a descriptive history of the event and documenting every assertion of fact.

4. Consider a document or artifact supplied by your instructor, from a museum display, provided by a classmate, or from some other source. Speculate on how you might decide whether or not the item is genuine.

5. Consider a document or artifact supplied by your instructor, from a museum display, provided by a classmate, or from some other source. Discuss the "story" behind the artifact that may be deduced from the evidence of the artifact itself and whatever contextual information is available.

ADDITIONAL RESOURCES WITH ANNOTATION

Park, R.J. (1992). The rise and demise of Harvard's B.S. program in anatomy, physiology, and physical training: A case of conflicts of interest and scarce resources. *Research Quarterly for Exercise and Sport, 63* (3), 246–260.
An example of a historical study in the field of physical education. This article also may serve as a source of examples of referencing style in the field of history.

10

EXPLORATORY AND QUALITATIVE RESEARCH METHODS

On the first page of this book research was described as a self-directed effort to find answers. That description may be somewhat too limited, depending upon what one means by "answers." The very existence of the possibility of an answer implies that there must be a question, so research must also be a search for questions—at least for those questions for which answers are scientifically possible. While it be argued that a distinction between a search for a question and a search for an answer is unnecessary since the question, once found, is really an answer (to the question, "What is the question?"), if such a distinction is made then it is appropriate to make a corresponding distinction between research methods as exploratory and as confirmatory in nature. Confirmatory methods are those techniques of research that serve to test hypotheses or to eliminate alternative explanations. Experimental designs, methods of sampling, objective measurement, and many statistical analytical techniques principally serve such purposes. Exploratory methods, on the other hand, are those that serve to help the researcher develop hypotheses or explanations by becoming familiar with the subjects, behaviors, materials, or methods under study, discovering apparent relationships or phenomena, or just finding items or artifacts that might be worthy of further study. Qualitative research, observational research, and creative research are often primarily exploratory in nature, although it would be wrong to view exploratory and confirmatory research as mutually exclusive or antagonistic.

The term **qualitative research** is applied, perhaps somewhat loosely, to *approaches to scholarly inquiry that seek to discover or reveal new knowledge through processes of detailed description and interpretation rather than through more objective methods.* Although the term might seem to imply research dealing with immeasurable, or non-quantitative, aspects of the universe, qualitative research is not totally devoid of measurement or numbers any more than quantitative research is completely free of the non-quantitative. The term *qualitative research* does not name a particular method of research. Rather, it describes a method of *knowing* that is different from other ways of knowing. According to Locke (1989) the qualitative researcher *knows* something through a process of personal experience: "I know because I have been there." The qualitative researcher does not claim to know truth in any absolute sense but, rather, claims to know truth as experienced or interpreted by the researcher. This way of knowing is contrasted by Locke to that employed by the quantitative researcher: "I know because I have carefully employed the methods of science," or the theologian: "I know because the Bible tells me so."

FIGURE 10.1   Spelunkers inside a cave—
"Because It's There." Exploratory research may
be conceptualized as a systematic effort to
identify questions.

Data collection in qualitative research often involves prolonged observation of complex phenomena, but mere observation does not constitute research of any kind. The observation and data collection conducted should be planned, systematic, and as detailed as possible. Although the researcher may want to record observations of events that were unanticipated in the planning stage, the data to be recorded concerning anticipated events should be planned and made as objective as possible. A researcher wishing to record interactions between a coach and members of a team, for example, should invest considerable planning time defining the behaviors to be recorded. To the degree that the researcher is a participant in the study, this is especially important as a control against various forms of expectation effects.

Another very important aspect of data collection in qualitative research, given the absence of controls usually found in experimental research, is the avoidance of spurious data and of the cross-contamination of data.

Spurious data refers to the recording of observations of events that did not occur, or grossly inaccurate versions of events that did occur. Such errors can occur in many ways, of which intentional falsification is only one. When an observer misses a portion of an event, perhaps because of a momentary diversion of attention, there is a tendency for the mind to fill in the missing details with a rational explanation of what "must have occurred." Witnesses to automobile accidents, for example, often give conflicting versions of the event for this reason. Further, the details filled in by the minds of several witnesses are likely to be biased in the direction most advantageous to each witness, not because of conscious intent to misrepresent the facts but because in filling in missing details the mind unconsciously gives greater weight to desirable hypotheses of those missing details than to undesirable ones. In the absence of experimental controls, the effects of such spurious data are best controlled by triangulation or confirmation. Triangulation, in this case, refers to the concept of giving greater weight to data that can be obtained from two or more independent sources than that which cannot. For example, a disagreement between two football referees over whether or not a player was out of bounds could be settled by triangulation using a third referee or a television replay. Confirmation refers to giving greater weight to information that is in agreement with physical evidence. In the case of differing descriptions of an automobile accident, for example, physical evidence in the form of vehicle damage or skid marks might tend to support one witness's description over another's.

Whenever added credence is given to data because it is obtained from multiple sources, it is of critical importance that those sources be independent. This is especially true when the data is such that it could be affected by variations of human judgment, but, as was classically demonstrated by Asch (1955), the cross contamination of data can occur even in cases involving data that would appear to be highly objective (see discussion of Asch experiment in Chapter 6). In cases involving data of a subjective nature, such as the evaluation of the work performance of a coach or teacher, cross contamination must be scrupulously avoided. In a qualitative study in which several researchers were to use journals to record their interpretations of some experience, they would be well advised to avoid discussing their experiences or sharing their journals until the data collection process is completed. For the same reason, jury members are always instructed to avoid discussing their case, either amongst themselves or through external sources, until all evidence has been heard.

Qualitative research is essentially descriptive in output and must be regarded as predominantly exploratory with respect to the advancement of knowledge. It is a valuable technique for gaining insight or developing hypotheses about many kinds of complex phenomena, but is of little value in testing or confirming such insight or hypotheses.

That research is of a qualitative nature does not imply that it is free of objective data or even that it is free of numerical data. The data collection process is not haphazard. Indeed, the absence of experiment-like controls and the fact that most qualitative research is conducted under field rather than laboratory conditions may require a very high degree of systematization and planning for data collection. Researchers doing qualitative research may use a variety of methods to gather data, although none is unique to this type of research. Some of the methods most commonly used are discussed in the following sections.

THE FOCUS GROUP INTERVIEW

There are many occasions in which the researcher is interested in the views, problems, ideas, impressions, needs, or other more or less subjective characteristics of a group of people. Use of a questionnaire with scaled response items, checklists, or multiple choice items may be an appropriate approach if the researcher can define one or more very specific research questions. However, there are many cases in which the researcher is more interested in a general exploration to discover the views, ideas, or needs, of a group rather than in quantifying them. A marketing manager for a minor league ice hockey team, for example, might be interested in exploring the problems encountered by

Suggestions for Coordinating a Focus Group Interview

DO
Keep things simple
Keep things specific
Be flexible

DON'T
Use leading questions
Ask questions or make statements that
    might be intimidating or constitute a
    challenge to the group member.
Force subjects to respond

fans attending a game. An advertising director might want to explore potential customers' reactions to a new form of packaging. A school administrator might want to explore the real needs of teachers before investing in a new computer system. For such exploratory work, the technique of the focus group interview may be appropriate.

The focus group usually consists of 8 to 12 people. As a rule, subjects are selected to be part of a group not by any process of randomization but because they fit some profile the researcher is interested in. That is, the members of a focus group should be as homogenous as possible. (For the quantitatively oriented researcher it may be helpful to consider that it is the *group* being interviewed and not the individual subjects.) However, members of a focus group should be selected independently. Groups should not be assembled from already established groups such as families, classes of students, or colleagues at work. Pre-existing relationships among members of such groups will tend to modify the contribution of each group member, biasing the result.

The focus group interview is conducted by a coordinator or moderator who asks questions and keeps the group on task. Typically a small number of pre-planned questions will be asked and then more probing questions will follow group members' initial responses. Although the members of the group must be kept focused on their task, the interviewer must be extremely careful to avoid any question or action that might act to influence responses. Anything that indicates a desired or expected response, or any reaction of an evaluative nature (positive or negative) may tend to influence both subsequent responses and subsequent willingness to respond. Leading questions, those that provide a description or answer within the question itself and merely request confirmation or denial, must also be avoided. Such questions tend to restrict the range of responses likely to be made and may often tend to bias responses in the direction respondents perceive to be desired.For example, in a focus group exploring the positive and negative experiences of fans attending minor league baseball games, the subject of seating is likely to be brought up. If a group member were to make the comment, "I like the seats near third base," the coordinator would probably want to probe more deeply for specifics. Questions such as, "You like the color?" or "Are they comfortable?" are leading questions because they force the response to focus on a particular characteristic of the seats that may or may not have anything to do with the perceived advantage of seats near third base. The preference for seats near third base may be related to some characteristic of the seating itself or it may be a personal preference for that location. A better follow-up question to the comment about third base seating would be to use the subject's own words: to prompt, without influencing, an elaboration For example, "You prefer the seats near third base?"

The potential data obtained through a focus group interview consists of everything that can be detected as having occurred within the context of the interview. This includes member responses to questions, failures to respond, facial expressions, body language, interactions between the coordinator and the group or portions of it, and interactions within the group. Methods of recording data may be as varied as the imagination of the researcher and may include written notes, audio and video recordings, counts and durations of specific, pre-determined events (such as positive and negative adjectives used to describe a product) or even post-interview reflections by group members or the coordinator. The selection and use of a data recording method, however, must be tempered by an understanding of how different methods may tend to produce biased or edited results. For example, audio recordings may fail to record data adequately from individuals not favorably placed with respect to microphones or whose speech is difficult to follow. Video recordings may tend to favor the responses of individuals facing the camera and the presence of a television camera may tend to reduce the impact of shy group members.

Although the researcher may enjoy great freedom in the data collection and recording process, great caution must be exercised in analyzing or interpreting such data. It must be constantly be kept in mind that the data can only be regarded as exploratory or suggestive in nature, never as confirmatory. Even when quantitative data is generated, its interpretation outside the delimitations of the focus group itself must be handled with great caution. In general, analysis should be limited to summarization of the interview itself, identification of themes or trends that apparently emerge during the interview, clearly labeled subjective interpretation of the interview, and perhaps some rudimentary quantitative analysis such as the number or duration of certain clearly defined events.

THE IN-DEPTH INDIVIDUAL INTERVIEW

There are occasions in which the researcher is interested in the same kinds of questions for which the focus group interview is appropriate except that the use of a group environment is awkward, inconvenient, or inappropriate for various reasons. The focus group interview is used quite frequently in product marketing studies, for example, but if the product under study is a condom or a piece of lingerie, some subjects may feel uncomfortable in a group setting. On other occasions the researcher might be interested in examining how certain events or phenomena are experienced by different individuals. For example, a sport psychologist might want to try to understand the experience of winning (or losing) the Super Bowl. Or a researcher in geriatric psychology might want to understand

FIGURE 10.2   A Brief Excerpt from an Individual In-Depth Interview. Note that the follow-up questions are not pre-planned. Rather, they are derived from subject responses to initial questions. Note also that the initial question is extremely open-ended, designed to initiate a response rather than to obtain specific information.

Initial Question:	What is it like to win the Super Bowl?
Response:	Oh, it's a trip!
Follow-up:	A trip?
Response:	Yea, You know, it's like being somewhere really special you thought you'd never get to. This game can end for anyone on any play. I could get hurt on the first day of spring practice and never play again, but that doesn't matter now.
Follow-up:	It doesn't matter now?
Response:	I've been to the mountaintop, and nothing can change that. No matter what happens from now on, I know I made it all the way to the top.
Initial Question:	. . .

something of the experience of abandonment among nursing home residents. In such cases an individual in-depth interview approach may be appropriate.

In most respects an individual in-depth interview is little different from the focus group interview other than the participation of only a single subject at a time and, often, the nature of the questions being explored. Typically, the interviewer asks a short series of open-response questions and then seeks to probe more deeply with follow-up questions derived from the subject's initial responses.

Although the individual in-depth interview is very similar in most respects to the focus group interview, the individual interview may sometimes be facilitated using certain specialized techniques that would be difficult or impossible in a group setting. For many years, for example, the field of psychoanalysis has used various projective techniques in which a client is shown an abstract drawing or object of some kind and asked to describe it. In theory, at least, such descriptions may provide clues regarding unresolved concerns or conflicts bothering the client. A similar approach may occasionally be useful in areas of research such as product marketing or sociological issues. A potential consumer, for example, might be given a package decorated in patterns of various colors but unlabelled and asked to describe the product. Alternatively, the consumer might be given two packages that are decorated differently and asked which product is better. Another approach might be to ask a subject to draw and then explain a picture (or construct a model) of some abstract construct such as the Olympic Games or the experience of being cut from a team.

The results of an interview may be recorded verbatim using video or audiotape (with appropriate permission) or in the form of concurrent notes taken by the researcher. Such recording allows for repeated review of the contents of the interview and thereby helps control for expectation effects and other researcher biases that might lead to unconscious *selective editing* of what is heard in an interview. Although the record of an interview constitutes the raw data of the study, the real information of interest may remain to be extracted in some way, such as reviewing the transcript of the interview for specific instances of certain predetermined items. This extraction process can sometimes be used to produce data of a numerical nature. For example, in a study of the experience of high school football players the researcher might review the transcript of each player interview and count the number of comments characterizable as optimistic or pessimistic.

SYSTEMATIC OBSERVATION

One of the chief limitations on any form of research in which data is collected by a human observer is the potential for the nature of unaided human observation to introduce bias. Most people can determine the temperature of a cup of water with reasonable accuracy when aided by a thermometer, for example, but may be wildly inaccurate using only their built-in senses. One person with nearly frostbitten hands and another with normally warm hands will report the temperature of a stream of 50-degree (F) water as painfully hot and cool, respectively.

In addition to bias due to such subjectivity, the human observer is frequently unable to pay equal attention to all potentially observable events, especially in the absence of limitations on the events to be observed. The attention of the human observer must be given some form of direction and there is often a tendency to detect events that are desired or expected in favor of those not desired or expected.

Systematic observation may be understood as *an attempt to objectivise and standardize processes of data collection mediated through human observation.* Generally it involves the construction of an **observer system** in the form of *a set of definitions of exactly what is to be observed and how that is to be recorded or measured.* What is to be observed may derive from theoretical arguments or from earlier, more informal, observation. For example, many hours of informal classroom observation might suggest to a researcher in pedagogy that certain teacher behaviors associated with asking children questions might convey some expectation of the child's ability to answer correctly and thereby affect the child's response. The researcher might then reason that such behaviors might involve variations in voice inflection or tone, facial expressions, or other kinds of body language. From such ideas the researcher might then construct an observer system. Each identifiable characteristic of voice, expression, and body language would be defined and given a name. Rules would then be constructed to define when a behavior has occurred in association with a question directed at particular children and when it has not. The researcher would also make decisions about how such behaviors will be recorded.

> In qualitative research the data to be collected should be carefully planned in advance. However, unanticipated events may still be important to record. For example, a researcher using qualitative methods to study the emotional impact of the 1976 Olympic opening and closing ceremonies on spectators in the stadium could hardly have been expected to have anticipated the intrusion of a streaker, yet the impact of that incident might still be worth recording.

A similar process might be used to assess children's responses to questions. Such an observer system might call for the observer to record the voice inflection, facial expression, and body language, if any, and correctness of pupil response for each incidence of a question being directed at an individual child.

Before attempting to collect actual data using an observer system, the researcher must establish the validity and reliability of that system and those using it. Validity refers to the degree to which the observer system really records or measures what it is supposed to record or measure. The observer system described above, for example, might be low in validity if the questions asked of pupils differ systematically in difficulty. Reliability refers to the ability of the observer system and the observer to produce consistent results. If the observer is poorly trained in the use of the system, if the system is so complex that a significant portion of relevant data is missed, or if the observer is inconsistent in ability to observe relevant events because of variations in placement, fatigue, observing conditions, or other factors, the reliability is likely to be impaired. Reliability may also be problematic among observers if two or more different observers are used.

Validity is usually established through a process of expert review. A panel of experts is used to carefully review a videotape of whatever is being observed, the data obtained using the proposed observer system, and then make a judgement concerning the apparent validity of the system.

Reliability of an observer system is often established in a similar manner. Using a videotape, the system is repeatedly used to record the same events, with enough time elapsing between viewings that memorization of events is unlikely.

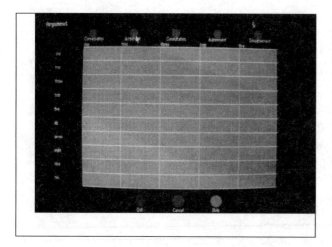

FIGURE 10.3 A Computer System for Observer System Data Collection. In this program, called *Eventlog*, data collection is accomplished by using the mouse to point and click on the array of buttons shown above. Each button is both an event counter and an event timer, depending on which mouse button (right or left) is used. The program will display such an array of any dimension up to 10 by 10. Columns and rows may be labelled by the user to customize the observer system to almost any application. The program also provides for recording incidental comments during the data collection process.

If the results are consistent the observer system is judged to be reliable. The reliability of an observer system across multiple observers (its inter-rater reliability) may be established by having multiple observers use the system while observing the same events on a videotape. **Inter-rater reliability** is *the degree to which different observers produce the same results.*

Systematic observation is fairly widely used in teacher training, animal behavior studies, and in other complex behavioral studies. Observer systems specifically developed for applications in education or physical education include the Flander's Interaction Analysis System (Flanders, 1970) the Cheffer's Adaptation of Flander's Interaction Analysis System (Cheffers, Amidon, and Rogers, 1974) the dyadic adaptation of Cheffer's Adaptation of Flander's Interaction Analysis System (Martinek, and Johnson, 1979) and the Academic Learning Time–Physical Education (Seidentop, Tousignant, and Parker, 1982). In most observer systems, and in all of the above mentioned systems, the data collected consists of counts and/or durations of certain events or behaviors. In some cases the events recorded may be keyed to specific individuals within a group or to some sub-group of individuals. For example, the data might consist of the number of times or the total amount of time a teacher engaged in interacting with each pupil in a class. Data is frequently collected manually by writing marks or some kind of shorthand code on paper and then later transcribing it into a computer for analysis. Data is also sometimes collected using specialized electronic devices consisting of an array of switches and some kind of recording mechanism such as a tape cassette or memory chips. Such devices may provide for a direct display or printout of data or they may be able to transfer data to a computer for display and analysis. Data may also be collected directly by computer, permitting analysis to be available almost immediately. Earlier computer programs for this purpose tended to use the keyboard and a potentially complicated encoding scheme for input, but more recent programs use the mouse to point to an array of virtual counters and timers on the video display.

PARTICIPANT AND NON-PARTICIPANT OBSERVATION

In the field of physical education and sport science qualitative research is applicable to a variety of research problems of a descriptive nature, often concerning the meaning or interpretation of some experience by those participating in the experience. Such studies might be concerned, for example, with the meaning of such experiences as being a student in a junior physical education class, learning to swim, trying out for a football team, student teaching, teaching in a university, playing a sport, serving as an official in the Special Olympics, being a spectator at the Olympic Games, or climbing a mountain. The goal of such studies is understanding the phenomenon through detailed, or *rich,* description. In such studies the researcher is often a participant in the phenomenon under study. That is, the researcher is part of and may affect the outcome of his or her own study. Sometimes the researcher may be a major participant, as would be the case in a study of the researcher's own experiences as a university teacher. When *the observer is an actual participant in the experience under study,* the observer is known as a **participant observer.** More often, the researcher participates only to the extent that his or her presence as an observer may affect the behavior of the major participants. For example, in a qualitative study of experiences of athletes on a high school football team, those experiences may be altered by very facts of the researcher observing practices, interviewing players, and otherwise being a part of the experience. When *the observer is not an actual participant in the event under study,* the observer is known as a **non-participant observer**. Even when the observer can blend in to the environment to the point of invisibility, however, it is critical to recognize that the observer remains a participant in the experience to the extent that the qualitative approach involves the researcher's interpretation of it.

When a qualitative study is conducted by a non-participant observer, data is quite commonly collected by extensively interviewing the participants using interviewing methods such as those described in this chapter for focus groups and the individual in-depth interview. Thus the researcher looking at the meaning of membership on a high school football team might collect data by periodically interviewing team members throughout the course of a season. Such an interview might ask very general questions such as, "What is it like to make a tackle?" or "Tell me about the referees during a game," which would be followed by more probing questions based on initial responses.

Data for qualitative studies may also be obtained from documents created by the participants (which may include the observer) such as journals, diaries, drawings, artwork, stories, songs, games, and so on. Any written document of a reflective nature and written concurrently or episodically with the events documented might be called a journal or diary. Often a diary refers to a document of a relatively personal nature, not intended to be read by others, and a journal refers to something of a more public nature. Journals are commonly employed in qualitative research using both participant observer and non-participant observer approaches. The researcher acting as a participant observer may keep a journal (the terms *research logbook* or *field notebook* might also be applied here) in which very detailed observations and reflections are recorded frequently and regularly during the experience under study. For example, when the author George Plimpton participated in the Detroit Lions training camp as a quarterback candidate, it is very likely he recorded his thoughts and experiences on a regular, probably daily, basis in some form of journal. Otherwise, he would have had to rely solely on memory when later writing his book *Paper Lion* (1966).

What I Learned in Class Beyond What Was Taught

In this class we were taught a lot of skills useful for outdoor adventure activities and we went on several field trips where we tried out our skills for real. The most important thing I learned, however, was that I could do, and actually enjoy, a lot of things I thought I would never even think of doing. Going in the cave, for example. Until I took this course I would never have considered going underground in a cave. Even when I agreed to go I was worried I would get claustrophobic the minute we got inside, but the fact is I wasn't scared at all. . . .

An excerpt from a study assignment to write about anything learned in a course other than anything that was explicitly taught. Such papers might serve (with proper permission) as a form of raw data in a qualitative study.

Journals or other items produced by subjects under study may also be used commonly in qualitative research. Subjects participating in some experience being studied might be asked to maintain a diary (they must be appropriately informed in advance if these are to be shared with the researcher) in which they record and reflect upon their experiences on a regular basis. For example, a group of age group athletes from different and mutually hostile backgrounds but selected to play and live together on a touring soccer team might each be asked to keep a reflective diary and eventually to share that diary with the researcher interested in detecting and examining changes in social attitudes. Alternatively, participants may periodically be asked to write essays or answer in writing specific questions posed by the researcher. Pupils in an adventure-oriented physical education course, such as canoeing or rock climbing, for example, might be asked in a mid-semester or final course evaluation to write a paragraph or essay in which they are instructed to "describe something you have learned in the course *other than* that which was explicitly taught."

CONTENT ANALYSIS

Written and other documents in permanent form (video and audiotapes, phonograph records, films, etc.) are materials that may be involved in qualitative studies. The researcher might be interested in such matters as children's interpretation of television violence, or the impressions of readers or viewers concerning racial, ethnic, or gender bias in sports reporting, for example. Such studies may often employ the method of **content analysis,** which is *the systematic, objective review of the content of various kinds of documents.*

Briefly, content analysis involves the generation of a set of operational definitions of the particular aspects of the content of a document to be measured and the systematic review of that document to quantify those aspects of its content. For example, in a study of gender bias in the sports reporting of a campus newspaper, the researcher might want to review the sports pages of a three-month series of newspaper issues. Specific aspects of content that might be quantified may include the number of column inches devoted to men's and women's teams, the number of such column inches placed on each page of the sports section, the proportion of articles or column inches devoted to positive and negative aspects of men's and women's sports teams, and the number of articles or column inches reporting simple results versus those of greater depth for each gender.

TERMS

content analysis	participant observer
inter-rater reliability	qualitative research
non-participant observer	systematic observation
observer system	

EXERCISES

1. Interview several classmates concerning their interpretations of the purposes of the research requirement in your current curriculum.

2. Obtain several newspaper sports page stories concerning a recent or forthcoming game. Analyze their content to determine the number of superlatives used per column inch.

3. Spend several days in close observation of a physical education class, an athletic team practice, a hospital emergency room, or some other human experience of which you are NOT a participant. Write a detailed interpretation of the experience of the participants. When you have finished writing, share what you have written with several participants. Ask about and record their comments about the accuracy and completeness of your interpretations.

ADDITIONAL RESOURCES WITH ANNOTATION

Al-Enad, A.H. (1991). Counting items versus measuring space in content analysis. *Journalism Quarterly, 68* (4), 657–662.
An easily readable discussion of some potential sources of bias in content analysis research.

Buchanan, D.R. & Lev, J. (1989). *Beer and fast cars: How brewers target blue-collar youth through motor sport sponsorships.* Washington, DC: AAA Foundation for Traffic Safety. (ERIC Document Reproduction Service No. 333 299)
An example of a study employing a focus group interviewing process.

Graber, K.C. (1991). Studentship in preservice teacher education: A qualitative study of undergraduate students in physical education. *Research Quarterly for Exercise and Sport, 62* (1), 41–51.
An example of a qualitative study in which the researcher was a non-participant observer. Participants, however, were aware of the researcher's purpose for being present in their environment.

Harris, J.C. & Hills, L.A. (1993). Telling the story: Narrative in newspaper accounts of a men's collegiate basketball tournament. *Research Quarterly for Exercise and Sport, 64* (1), 108–121.
An example of a qualitative study in which the subject was the content of newspaper accounts of a sporting event.

Schutz, R.W. (1989). Qualitative research: Comments and controversies. *Research Quarterly for Exercise and Sport, 60* (1), 30–35.
A response to the article by Locke (cited in above references) calling attention to some important limitations of qualitative research methods and to the occasional tendency of researchers to seek research problems to fit their chosen method of inquiry rather than to choose methods that fit the research question.

Scott, D.K. & Gobetz, R.H. (1992). Hard news/soft news content of the national broadcast networks, 1972–1987. *Journalism Quarterly, 69* (2), 406–412.
A simple example of research using content analysis.

Silverman, S., Devillier, R. & Ramirez, T. (1991). The validity of academic learning time-physical education (ALT-PE) as a process measure of achievement. *Research Quarterly for Exercise and Sport, 62* (3),319–325.
An example of a study using the ALT-PE observer system.

Williamson, K.M. (1993). A qualitative study on the socialization of beginning physical education teacher educators. *Research Quarterly for Exercise and Sport, 64* (2), 188–201.
An example of a qualitative study in which the researcher was a principal participant.

11

DATA PRESENTATION

Human beings are not very good at comprehending large volumes of data presented as huge arrays of numbers. In the modern world computers can process such arrays thousands of times faster than the human brain and with far less chance of making an error, but, in the end, *comprehension* of the meaning of such data requires a human brain. How can large volumes of data be arranged so that its meaning can be understood by and shared among people? One skill in which the human brain is still far superior to the computer is in the interpretation of images. The alert human mind can grasp at once the information in a photograph, for example, while the computer struggles just to locate boundaries or distances between objects in it. The human mind can quite readily read and understand a handwritten essay (if it is at least reasonably legible) while the computer may fail even to decipher single characters printed in an unfamiliar type style.

Pictures, therefore, are often the most effective and efficient means of transmitting information to other people. Photographs, paintings, videos, three-dimensional models, computer-generated animation, diagrams, blueprints, sketches, graphs, and tables are all examples of different kinds of pictures that can serve as powerful media for the transmission of ideas and information to people. This chapter is intended to provide the student with an overview of some basic methods of graphic data presentation likely to be encountered in professional practice and research literature.

BAR CHARTS

A **bar chart** or bar graph is *a simple graph in which quantity is represented as the length of a bar, line, or line of symbols.* Figure 11.1 is a very simple bar chart showing the first quarter sales figures for several sporting goods stores and shows the basic elements of a bar chart. Construction of a bar chart begins with the establishment of a base line. This serves as a common zero point or starting line for each of the bars and helps the eye recognize that all of the bars do, in fact, have a common starting point. In Figure 11.1 the base line is drawn horizontally but could just as easily have been drawn vertically. A vertical base line could also be drawn on either side, and a horizontal base line could be drawn at the top of the graph, but base lines are usually drawn at the bottom or left of the graph. The next step is the addition of a scale line perpendicular to the base line. The scale is marked in the appropriate units of measure and should usually be constructed so that its full range is slightly larger than the largest quantity to be expressed in the graph. Note that the scale could have been drawn on the left or even in the center. Next, the bars are drawn with lengths proportional to the values of the variables they represent. Finally—and

FIGURE 11.1   A simple bar graph.

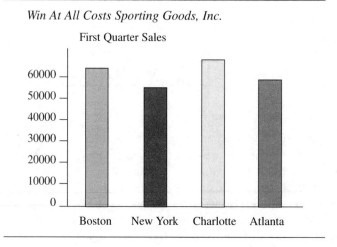

Win At All Costs Sporting Goods, Inc.

First Quarter Sales

FIGURE 11.2   A bar graph using bars constructed of meaningful symbols.

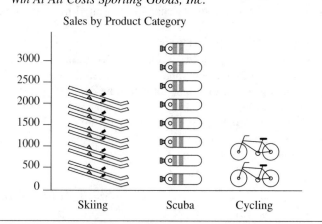

Win At All Costs Sporting Goods, Inc.

Sales by Product Category

this point is often forgotten by inexperienced students—the graph must be properly labeled and given a suitable heading.

To aid in interpretation, the bars of a bar chart may use different colors or *tiling* patterns, or they may be composed of repeating symbols representative of the categories whose quantities are being expressed. Figure 11.2, for example, shows sales of skiing, bicycling, and scuba diving equipment using bars composed of little pairs of skis, bicycles, and scuba tanks.

Figure 11.1 showed the first-quarter sales figures for a chain of stores. Suppose we are interested in examining sales figures for the second, third, and fourth quarters as well as the first. We could produce three more graphs like the one in Figure 11.1, but these would be a lot of work to produce and would require the reader to look at four separate graphs, making comparisons among graphs difficult. We could also make a single bar chart with 20 bars arranged in five repeating sets of four bars, but this would be very cluttered and hard to read.

FIGURE 11.3   A stacked bar graph. Note the different tiling patterns representing each quarter.

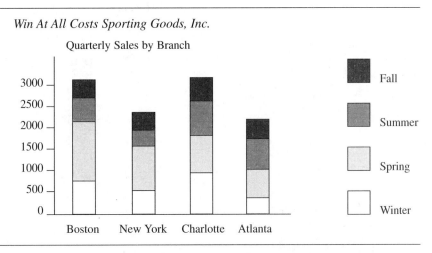

To make things easier for everyone we can combine the data from all stores for all quarters and produce a single graph called a **stacked bar chart,** as is done in Figure 11.3. A stacked bar chart is simply *a bar chart display of two dimensions at once, in which the bars for each dimension are stacked on top of each other rather than beginning on a common base line.* For example, in Figure 11.3, the four bars represent the four different stores and the four segments of each bar represent sales figures for each quarter. The use of a stacked bar chart makes direct comparison of the stacked data difficult since a common base line is not present. However, the stacked bar chart also displays additional information not readily obtained from separate charts. In Figure 11.3, for example, the overall length of each bar shows the yearly sales totals for each store.

An alternative to the stacked bar chart which overcomes the problem of the missing common base line for the stacked data is to use the principles of perspective to produce a projected image of a three dimensional bar *model.* In effect, such a graph consists of several bar charts superimposed on each other in layers with each deeper layer slightly offset vertically and horizontally. This can be very difficult to do properly by hand but many computer software packages are now available that can produce such charts in a few seconds.

PROPORTIONAL GRAPHS

A **proportional graph** is *one in which the components of some whole are represented as proportional areas of a figure.* The most commonly used form of proportional graph is the **pie chart.** Figure 11.4 is a pie chart showing first quarter sales figures for a chain of stores—the same data used to make the bar chart in Figure 11.1. The total sales for the year are represented by the circle, or *pie,* and the slices show the contribution of each quarter toward the total.

Construction of a pie chart begins with a circle of appropriate size with a radius to serve as a starting point. Most often the starting radius is drawn in the 12 o'clock position. Additional radii are then drawn to produce sections

FIGURE 11.4   A simple pie chart.

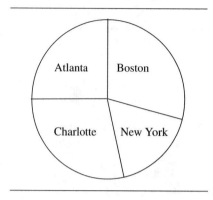

FIGURE 11.5   Thermometer graph.

FIGURE 11.6   Football graph.

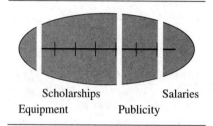

FIGURE 11.7   Hourglass graph.

FIGURE 11.8   Clock graph.

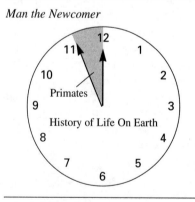

(slices) proportional to the quantities being expressed. Usually, the sections are then filled in with contrasting colors, different tiling patterns, or symbols of some kind. Finally, an appropriate heading and labels or a legend are added to complete the chart.

There are many common variations on the idea of a pie chart in which some shape symbolic of the meaning of the chart is used instead of a single circle. A thermometer graph, for example, uses a drawing of a thermometer. Thermometer graphs are quite often used in fund-raising events to display the amount

FIGURE 11.9   Ring graph.

FIGURE 11.10   Exploded pie graph.

Seasonal Sales for Four Stores

Winter   Spring   Summer   Fall

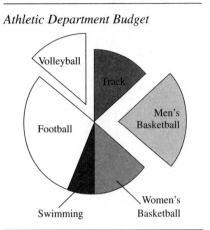

Athletic Department Budget

raised to date relative to the total goal. The idea is to encourage donors to make pledges in order to raise the *temperature* to the top of the thermometer. Another symbolic proportional graph could be made for budgetary information using a drawing of a dollar bill or dollar coin. Similarly, the budget for a football team might be expressed using a football shaped graph. Concepts such as the time remaining or spent on various components of a job or task may be expressed using a graph in an *hourglass* shape or with a *clock* graph. A clock graph is really the same as a pie chart but includes a clock face as a cue to the reader that the variable being expressed is time.

A *ring chart* is a variation of a pie chart that can be used to show two data dimensions in a single chart. A ring chart is to a pie chart what a stacked bar chart is to a bar chart. In a ring chart, one dimension is represented by a series of concentric rings, and each of these is divided into sections to represent the second dimension. Figure 11.9 displays in ring chart form the same data used to make the stacked bar chart in Figure 11.3.

Another pie chart variation which can be useful to call attention to one or more of the components represented by pie slices is the *exploded pie chart*. An exploded pie chart is one in which one or more of the slices have been moved outward from the center.

SCATTER DIAGRAMS

A **scatter diagram** (sometimes called a scattergram, scatter plot, or dot plot) is *a graph that uses dots plotted on a Cartesian coordinate system* to represent **bivariate data values.** That is, *each point plotted shows the measurements on two variables of one subject or case under study.* Figure 11.11 is a scatter diagram of the 100-meter and 1,500-meter run times for each member of a class of 36 students. Each of the 36 dots on the diagram represents one of the 36 students and the *x* and *y* coordinates of each dot are the run times.

The area of a scatter diagram occupied by *most* of the points form what is commonly referred to as a *cloud.* If there are enough points so that the area occupied by the cloud of points is readily distinguishable from the area not

FIGURE 11.11   A scatter diagram of performances in two running events for 36 members of a physical education class. Each dot represents the values of two different variables for one case or subject. In this case the downward (moving from left to right) slope of the cloud of dots suggests an inverse relationship between performance in short-distance events and performance in long-distance events.

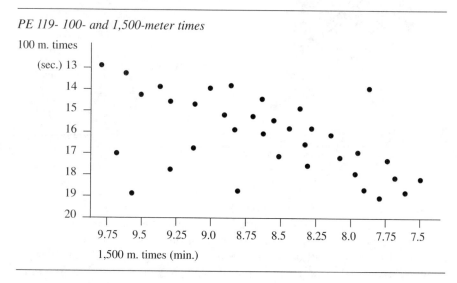

PE 119- 100- and 1,500-meter times

occupied, then the general shape of the cloud can provide useful information about the relationship between the two variables plotted in the diagram. If those variables are independent of each other (that is, if they have no relationship to each other) then the cloud of points will be approximately circular in shape. If there is a perfect linear relationship between the two variables then all of the points will fall on a line. The line will slope upward if the relationship is positive and downward if the relationship is negative or inverse. If there is some relationship between the two variables then the cloud will have a lenticular or football shape. Figure 11.11 shows a moderate, inverse relationship between times for the 100- and 1,500-meter runs.

LINE GRAPHS

A **line graph** is *a diagram of the trajectory or path of a variable as a second variable changes or is manipulated.* For example, Figure 11.12 is a line graph showing the trajectory of the Dow Jones stock average during a day of trading. The second variable (represented by the horizontal axis) is time.

Notice that the line graph is not the same as a scatter diagram with the dots connected. In the scatter diagram one point is plotted for each subject or case under study. In a line graph there are a series of points plotted for a single subject or case, representing a series of measurements on that subject. The data plotted in Figure 11.12 is the measurement known as the Dow Jones average (a weighted average of several important stocks) repeated every hour from 9 A.M. to 4 P.M. Since time is really a continuous variable, it is reasonable to interpolate stock average values between the actual measurements by connecting

FIGURE 11.12   A simple line chart tracking the Dow Jones Average, a popular index of stock market prices, for a day of trading.

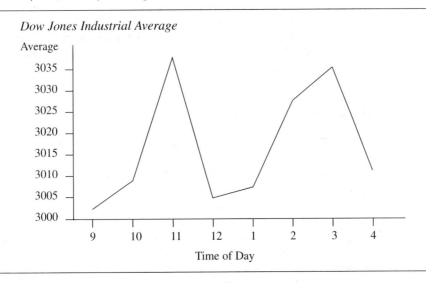

Dow Jones Industrial Average

FIGURE 11.13   A compound line chart showing quarterly sales for stores in each of four cities. If available, lines may be drawn in color or using different arrangements of dashes or other symbols.

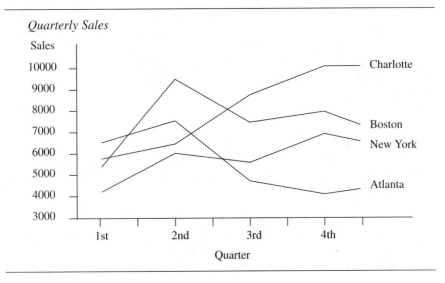

Quarterly Sales

the dots with straight lines. In truth, of course, the stock average does not change so smoothly but usually has many peaks and valleys within the period of an hour.

The sporting goods sales figures displayed earlier in this chapter in bar chart and pie chart form can also be displayed as a line graph. The sales figures for each quarter of the year result from a measurement repeated over time periods of three months, and, since time is a continuous variable, a line may be drawn connecting those measurements. To compare the sales of several stores over the same time period, we could draw several line graphs or we can draw several lines on a single line graph as is done in Figure 11.13. To aid in interpretation the area under the lines or between lines may be filled in with different colors or tiling patterns, or the lines themselves may be drawn using different patterns of dots, dashes, and other marks. When areas are filled in this type of graph is sometimes called a *layer* graph or chart.

TREE DIAGRAMS

Hierarchical relationships, such as the lines of command in an organization, the file and directory structure on a computer disk, or the evolutionary history of a species or organization, are often best displayed using a **tree diagram.** Following the metaphor of a tree, *such a diagram consists of a single root or stem which branches successively as one moves away from the root.* Some tree diagrams may have two or more roots. From any location on any branch of a diagram having a single root there is *one and only one* path back to the root. Also, any two branches are connected to each other through one and only one path and that path passes through some point between the branches and the root (or through the root itself). These attributes may not always hold for tree diagrams having two or more roots.

The root of a tree diagram is often placed at the top with the branches dividing downward when the diagram is used to display a command or authority relationship. Placing the root at the top is consistent with the notion of an authority figure as being in a superior position. However, the kind of information commonly displayed in a tree diagram, such as organizational structures, could as well be displayed with the root at the bottom, to either side, or at the center. Placing the root at the center is consistent with the concept of a chief executive as playing a coordinating role rather than one of a command.

There may be cases in which branches of a tree diagram may be drawn as disconnected from the root as a reflection of missing information. A tree diagram of the evolution of early man or of the dinosaurs, for example, might contain such gaps where the ancestor of two or more divergent species is unknown. If a connection is to be shown as hypothesized but unconfirmed, some variation of the diagram, such as a different color or shading, or the use of dotted rather than solid lines might be used.

FIGURE 11.14   A simple tree diagram for a college administrative structure. Note the placement of the president at the top of the diagram, suggesting a position of superior rank.

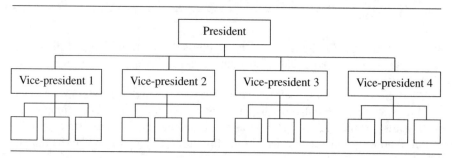

FIGURE 11.15   This tree diagram shows the same administrative structure as above but with the president placed in the center, suggesting a role of coordination rather than superiority.

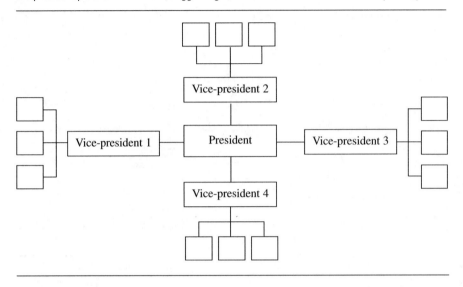

FIGURE 11.16   A partial family tree for the royal house of 16th-century England. A family tree is a tree diagram with multiple roots, convergence, and divergence.

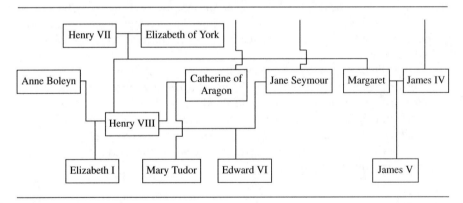

Most tree diagrams show either a divergence from a common root or a convergence toward a common outcome. A diagram of the assembly of increasingly larger companies into a single huge conglomerate would be an example of convergence. However, in situations in which there are more than one root, such as in a family tree, both divergence and convergence may occur simultaneously. In a family tree the earliest known ancestors are the roots, and members of the most recent generations are represented by the branches. Moving distally from the roots, the lines of the diagram then converge and rediverge as individuals with different roots come together and produce offspring. Similarly, the history of various mergers and divestments of a corporation could be illustrated using a tree diagram that would include multiple roots, convergences, and divergences.

FIGURE 11.17   A simple flow chart for preparing for an exam.

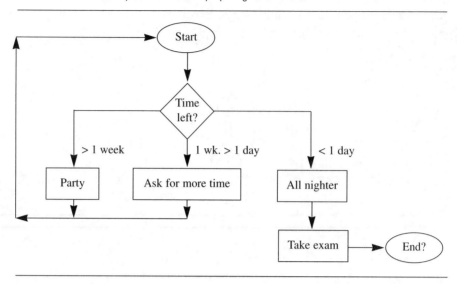

FLOW CHARTS

A **flow chart** is *a diagram showing a sequence of decisions or steps leading from some starting point to the end of some process.* Although they are commonly associated with the description of computer programs, flow charts can be used to describe such processes as the steps for baking a batch of cookies, assembling an automobile, conditioning a football team, or the sequence of decisions leading to a medical diagnosis.

A flow chart may be as simple as a few words identifying a linear sequence of steps or procedures connected by lines indicating the direction of flow or it may consist of hundreds of steps and conditional decisions with connecting lines that branch and loop back upon themselves with substantial complexity. The special symbols used by computer programmers for elements such as the entry and exit points, conditional decisions, and so on, may be helpful in preparing complex flow charts for any process.

MAPS

Maps are a familiar part of everyday life. Few people in the modern world are unfamiliar with road maps, globes, shopping mall locator displays, and treasure maps on which "X marks the spot." But a map is far more than a guide for finding how to get *there* from *here*. It is a powerful and flexible tool for communicating a wide range of information about anything that can be spatially conceptualized.

We usually think of a map as a two-dimensional representation or diagram, drawn to scale, of some two- or three-dimensional feature of geography. Road maps, political maps, television weather maps, and topographic maps all fit this description and a quick look at the pages of any atlas will reveal many more examples. Maps of this type portray the shapes of major features, such as land forms, bodies of water, roads, rivers, and political boundaries more or less

FIGURE 11.18   A map is a model or representation of information in two or more dimensions.

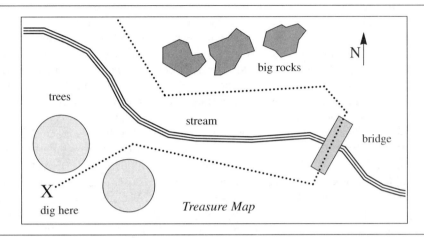

accurately, at least insofar as the scale of the map permits and, of course, only in two dimensions. Other features, such as houses, schools, churches, and even towns in larger scale maps, are indicated using more or less standardized symbols. Some types of maps also use special kinds of marks to indicate such features as land altitude, water depth, forest, marsh, or mountains. The *contour lines* on topographic maps, for example, indicate hills and valleys in the map area by connecting areas of equal altitude. Similar lines are used on weather maps to show areas of equal barometric pressure or temperature, and on oceanographic charts to show depth.

All maps are diagrams drawn to some kind of scale. However, the scale used is not always that of the physical dimensions of the objects or places portrayed. The scale can be that of some feature or characteristic of the objects portrayed. For example, in a traditional map of the United States the area of each state relative to that of the whole country is proportional to the actual area of the state relative to the nation. However, a map could be drawn with the area of each state adjusted to reflect some characteristic of the states other than area. Of course, the shape of each state has to be modified in such a map but the shape usually remains similar enough to be recognizable. Computers with sophisticated graphics or animation software are particularly useful tools for generating distorted maps of this kind.

There are several extensions of the idea of a map which can be very useful for conveying complex information or ideas, and such extensions are likely to become increasingly easy to use with the aid of computer technology. A three-dimensional model, for example, has long been used in sculpture and architecture to convey three-dimensional or spatial information. If adequate computer technology is available, maps can be drawn on the computer screen as projections of three-dimensional objects and then rotated around any point to be viewed from different angles. Color, motion, sound, and animation techniques can even be used to create maps that display information in four or more dimensions. For example, when a television weather report shows an eight-hour radar loop of an area of thunderstorms, the graphic sequence is actually displaying

An animated stick figure sequence of an athlete performing a skill is a kind of map.

five dimensions of data; time, two dimensions of land surface area, rainfall intensity, and presence of wind turbulence. A color code is used to show rainfall intensity, and flashing colors are used to indicate turbulence.

Advances in technology in recent years have led to some incredible advances in mapping and the kinds of information that can be displayed in maps. Cameras attached to satellites, for example, are used to generate maps of weather systems, geologic formations, oceanic water temperature patterns, vegetation patterns, and many other surface and even sub-surface features that can be studied in no other practical way. Similar equipment has even mapped the surface features of the moon, Mars, and, to a limited extent, Venus. Computers and various kinds of special sensing equipment are regularly used to generate maps of features inside solid or living objects noninvasively. For example, hospitals and medical centers regularly use magnetic resonance imagery (MRI), computerized axial tomography (CAT), and other methods to map both physical structures and physiological functions inside living patients (even deep inside the brain) without surgery or even anesthesia. Such apparatus has even been used to examine fossils still embedded in solid rock. Images generated from reflected pulses of sound are used in medicine to observe fetuses in utero, and in geology to observe layers of rock and oil deposits deep underground.

TABULAR PRESENTATION OF DATA

Tables should be used as part of a research report whenever they are the clearest or most effective method of data presentation. They should not be used merely to repeat information readily and clearly incorporated into the text of a report.

Any orderly arrangement of related items of data in columns and rows (and sometimes layers) is a table. Most tables found in research reports are rectangular in arrangement, consisting of columns and rows of cells containing data, although cubic arrangements, consisting of columns, rows, and layers of cells, are also possible. The computerized spreadsheet should be a familiar example of a rectangular table. Tables may also be arranged in circular or other patterns but such arrangements are rarely found in formal research reports.

FIGURE 11.19   A simple table showing quarterly staffing levels for stores in each of four cities and totals for each quarter. Data is arranged in a rectangular array of columns and rows.

Staffing Levels				
STORE/CITY	**WINTER**	**SPRING**	**SUMMER**	**FALL**
Boston	8	6	7	12
Charlotte	6	9	6	11
New York	7	10	6	15
Atlanta	8	13	8	13
Totals	29	38	27	51

FIGURE 11.20   A simple cross-tabulation table using numerals to represent quantities. A cross tabulation looks superficially like a data table. However, in a cross tabulation the quantities displayed represent frequencies of occurrence of some measure or response. In a table, the quantities displayed represent actual measures or responses. A cross-tabulation table is also sometimes known as a contingency table.

Baseball Bat Preferences of Players from Three Regions of the United States			
REGION	**BAT PREFERENCE**		
	Wood	Metal	Plastic
North	20	17	23
South	22	16	22
Central	13	25	22

FIGURE 11.21   A cross tabulation using hash marks instead of numerals. The data displayed is the same as in Figure 11.20.

Baseball Bat Preferences of Players from Three Regions of the United States			
REGION	**BAT PREFERENCE**		
	Wood	Metal	Plastic
North	‖‖ ‖‖ ‖‖ ‖‖	‖‖ ‖‖ ‖‖ II	‖‖ ‖‖ ‖‖ ‖‖ III
South	‖‖ ‖‖ ‖‖ ‖‖ II	‖‖ ‖‖ ‖‖ I	‖‖ ‖‖ ‖‖ ‖‖ II
Central	‖‖ ‖‖ III	‖‖ ‖‖ ‖‖ ‖‖ ‖‖	‖‖ ‖‖ ‖‖ ‖‖ II

The variations of tabular data presentation that may be used are limited only by one's imagination and the admonition that the table should not be more complicated or busy than is necessary to display unambiguously the information that must be presented. A review of current journals and books in the student's field may be helpful in suggesting ideas for constructing tables. Edward Tufte's recent books entitled *Envisioning Information* (1990) and *The Visual Display of Quantitative Information* (1983) also should be consulted for some excellent suggestions on all kinds of graphical data presentation.

Preparation Instructions for Tables

Guidelines for manuscript preparation, such as the *Publication Manual of the American Psychological Association* (1994), give detailed instructions on how tables should be prepared in manuscripts of research reports submitted to research journals. More often than not, academic departments which have a student research requirement specify the use of such guidelines in the preparation of those papers.

In general, the instructions given in a publication manual for the preparation of graphs and tables should be followed exactly, and any deviation from those instructions should be approved by the student's research committee.

However, both the student and the research committee should understand that current publication manuals are written with the assumption that manuscripts will be prepared using a typewriter or word processor. One of the principal purposes of the guidelines prescribed in such manuals is to avoid ambiguity in the manuscript submitted to the publisher's typesetters. Unlike a manuscript submitted to a journal, a dissertation, thesis, or other student research paper is a final product which will be archived and used by others in the form in which it is finally submitted by the student. If the resources are available, it may be to the advantage of everyone for tables and graphs (as well as the main text) to be prepared in a manner more consistent with a book, journal, or other typeset document. If the student has access to a computer equipped with a laser or other very high-resolution printer, a typesetting software package may be used to create typeset-quality text and simple graphs and tables. More sophisticated graphs and drawings may be made using drawing or paint software packages, and scanning devices and software may be used to incorporate photographs or existing illustrations into a document prior to typesetting. Illustrations of various kinds can even be produced and printed in color if a printer or plotter with color capabilities is available.

DATA PRESENTATION MEDIA

Although student research usually does not require the presentation of research findings in formats other than the written research report or oral defense, the successful completion of a research study frequently leads to the opportunity to do so. Professional group meetings, specialized seminars, and even meetings of non-professional groups and clubs all serve as potential outlets. Oral or spoken presentations are usually limited in length to from 10 to 90 minutes and, therefore, must be carefully constructed so as to avoid boring the listener or concealing relevant information behind layers of irrelevant details. A variety of audiovisual aids can often be very helpful in presenting both specific data and general concepts as well as in structuring and pacing the presentation.

Slides and Transparencies

Projection slides and overhead projector transparencies are the traditional media used to project an image onto a screen which can be viewed by relatively large audiences. Slides are made using transparency film in a standard camera. After the film is developed, the images are individually mounted in cardboard, plastic, or metal frames. The slides (the film and mounting frame) are then arranged in a tray from which they can be fed automatically into a projection machine. The projection machine shines a very bright light through the film onto a highly reflective screen to create the image seen by the audience. Transparencies are made by drawing or photocopying an image directly onto an 8 1/2"×11" sheet of transparent plastic. The plastic sheet may then be mounted in a cardboard frame or used without a frame. Transparencies are then placed by hand on the working surface of a machine called an overhead projector which projects an image in essentially the same manner as the slide projector.

Slides are clearly the better choice for projecting an image when photographic quality or color images are required or when there are more than just a few images to be projected. Slides can be sorted and placed into trays well in advance and under controlled conditions whereas transparencies must be manipulated during the presentation (usually with the lights turned off). Transparencies, on the other hand, may be preferable if projectable images are needed very quickly. It is also possible to write directly on the transparency during a presentation.

If slides or transparencies are to be used to make a professional presentation of any kind their quality must be sufficiently high as to avoid distracting from the presentation itself. All photographs should be properly exposed and sharply focused, and it is essential that any text or small details be clearly readable by everyone in the audience. It is much better to use more slides than to use too small a type size in the attempt to put too much into a slide.

> ### Making Slides of Computer Displays
>
> Although special machines are available that can produce slides of considerably better quality, slides of monochrome or color computer displays may be made with any good quality single lens reflex camera. Use slide film with a speed of at least ASA 400, set the camera on a tripod, focus carefully, and use a lens speed no faster than one thirtieth of a second.

Computerized Slides

Both slides and transparencies are physical objects that must be sorted and oriented prior to or during a presentation. Anyone who has ever been to a slide presentation has probably seen at least one image projected upside down, sideways, backwards, out of focus, or out of sequence. Such mistakes may be a minor annoyance to those in the audience but may be a major distraction to the presenter, especially when time for the presentation is severely limited.

Although the technology is still rather new and not widely available, the above problems can be avoided through the use of computer-generated slide presentations. Computerized slides are digitized images stored on a computer disk, CD-ROM, or other storage device. They may be created using special electronic cameras, captured from video sources, scanned into a computer with a page scanner, or generated within the computer itself (Rash, 1990). A series of such images can then be assembled, sorted into any order, and displayed through any type of computer display, including devices designed to project the image onto a reflective screen. The computer may be used to display a collection of such slides in sequence or to permit their random selection during a presentation. Also, the computer may be used to generate a variety of special effects such as fades, wipes, and dissolves, or even to combine slides with animated sequences.

Videotape and Disk

The use of videotape or videodisk replay adds the dimension of motion to presentations. Television sequences may be recorded using a videocamera, transferred from movie film, or generated by computer. They may then be edited in a variety of ways and combined with one or more sound tracks, and even subjected to various forms of computerized image enhancement. Images stored on videotape can be played back in sequence, freeze framed, played back in slow motion, or rewound and played back again at will during a presentation. Images on a videodisk or CD-ROM can even be accessed randomly under computer control. Video is a peerless tool for presenting ideas and information, but one that requires substantial experience and some relatively sophisticated equipment to use well. Poor image quality, and especially poor sound quality, are very distracting and will ruin a video presentation. The student would be well advised to seek expert assistance with the preparation of video materials.

TERMS

bar chart

bivariate data values

flow chart

line graph

pie chart

proportional graph

scatter diagram

stacked bar chart

tree diagram

EXERCISES

1. Using data obtained from your own measurements, from an almanac, or from other sources, construct a variety of bar charts, pie charts, line graphs, and tables by hand.

2. Find one or more sets of data presented in the form of tables or graphs of various types. Re-present the same data using different forms of graphs. Discuss with your classmates which forms convey the meaning of the data most clearly.

3. Use a computer and spreadsheet or graphics software to produce computerized versions of the charts and graphs made in exercise 1.

4. Use a copy machine to transfer a graph done on paper onto a transparency.

ADDITIONAL RESOURCES WITH ANNOTATION

Jaret, P. (1991). The disease detectives. *National Geographic, 179* (1), 114–140.
    Includes current and classic examples of how mapping is used to discover the causes of epidemics. Includes a brief discussion of mapping by John Snow in 1854 in London that led to the discovery that cholera is spread by contaminated water. Also includes coverage of epidemiological efforts to study influenza, Lyme disease, and AIDS.

O'Neill, T. (1993). New sensors eye the rain forest. *National Geographic, 181* (3), 118–130.
    Provides examples of maps made using a variety of remote sensing devices.

Rash, W. (1990). Down to business: Picture this. *Byte 15* (10), 111–112.
    Discusses using slides and computer generated images for illustrating presentations.

Sochurek, H. (1987). Medicine's new vision. *National Geographic, 171* (1), 2–41.
    Provides examples of modern imaging systems including MRI, PET, DSA, CT, sonography, and other mapping techniques.

Ward, F. (1989). Images for the computer age. *National Geographic, 175* (6), 718–751.
    Provides examples of computer-generated imaging techniques used in engineering, scientific research, medicine, and other fields.

12

ELEMENTARY STATISTICS

LEARNING STATISTICS

Statistics. A word that strikes fear into the hearts of students everywhere faced with a course requirement and revulsion in many having completed such a course.

Many students experience difficulty in courses or parts of courses dealing with statistics, but it does not have to be that way. Statistics are extremely valuable and powerful tools widely used in every profession and academic discipline, and a working understanding of these tools is vital to successful mastery in every field of study. Any student can learn to use and interpret a basic repertoire of statistical tools and methods. The subject is not really all that difficult, but effective learning tends to demand greater attention to certain study behaviors than other subjects. The following paragraphs are intended to provide some guidance regarding study habits and attitudes which have proven effective in the past.

A Positive Attitude

All too frequently, students begin a course in statistics already convinced that they will do poorly or fail. They complain to anyone who will listen, "I know I'm going to fail," or "I can't do math." Such words often become self-fulfilling prophesies because they serve as excuses that let students give up before they have started. How many basketball games would a team win if it began each game believing it had no chance? What these students fail to realize is that their fears are largely unfounded. Taught from an applied point of view, no mathematics in a beginning level statistics course will be higher than ordinary arithmetic and some very simple algebra. It is true that some rather formidable-looking symbols and formulas involving Greek letters, subscripts, and superscripts may appear in textbooks, including this one, and chalkboard discussions, but these are not really essential to understanding.

Development and nurturing of a positive attitude may well have a significant impact on your success in a statistics course. Make up your mind that you can and will succeed in statistics!

Any statistical summary or analysis of a set of data is only as good as the data itself. If the data is contaminated through weak design, sloppy or biased measurement, inadequate precision, or other causes, it cannot be decontaminated by statistics.

Hand Computation

A question often asked by students (and many professors also) in courses in statistics is whether it is necessary to perform computations of the statistics being learned. The modern researcher, they argue, would simply submit a set of data to a computer and let the machine do the computations. That the researcher would use a computer to compute statistics is indisputable. However, that researcher must have a genuine understanding of statistical tools and methods in order to direct the computer to compute the appropriate statistics and to understand the meaning of those statistics after they are computed. Actually computing statistics, at least those for which the computation is not excessively tedious or complicated, is an excellent way to gain such understanding. Thus, it is highly recommended that the student diligently complete all assigned exercises that require the step-by-step, manual computation of each statistic. Although some computational exercises are provided at the end of this chapter it is assumed that additional exercises will be provided by the course instructor. Unless directed otherwise by your instructor, calculators may be used to perform arithmetic computations required as steps in computing a statistic but calculator functions capable of computing the statistic directly should *not* be used.

Computer Computation

Although hand computation of statistics can be a very helpful exercise for developing understanding, in the real world most statistical computations are done by computer. This is especially true for complicated statistical analyses and even for simple analyses when data sets are large. Thus, the student should endeavor to gain some experience in computerized statistical computation, ideally using a variety of different software packages on both mainframe and micro-computers.

Depending on the types of computers available, most colleges and universities have a variety of different statistical software packages available for use by students. These may range from very simple, if somewhat limited, public domain and shareware programs running on small micro-computers to very powerful, and sometimes complex, commercial products running on more powerful micro-computers, mini-computers, or mainframes. Some of the more powerful products in widespread use in university settings include SPSS (Statistical Packages for the Social Sciences), SAS (Statistical Analysis System), and Systat. Each program has its own procedures for handling and defining data and specifying the analyses to be performed. While these are not extremely difficult, they are exacting enough that some practice will be required to achieve proficiency.

Relating to Real World Applications

Asked to calculate a simple ratio, some students experience difficulty. Many of these same students, however, can quickly compute the batting average of a baseball player or the free-throw shooting percentage of a basketball player. The computation is the same in all three cases. The difference is that the batting average or the free-throw percentage make sense to the student and the ratio does not. The batting average and the free-throw percentage have, in the mind of the student, a connection to the real world, while the ratio is an abstraction.

The student, therefore, should find it an effective learning strategy to attempt to make a connection between each statistical tool and a familiar, real world application of that tool. Examples of such applications from the worlds of education and sport are provided throughout this book. Students will benefit by spending some time pondering these examples and speculating amongst themselves about additional ones.

PARAMETRIC AND NON-PARAMETRIC STATISTICS

The validity of specific statistics often depends on the validity of certain assumptions about the variables and data with which they are used. For example, it will be demonstrated very shortly that the arithmetic mean is an appropriate measure of central tendency for sets of data that are distributed normally but inappropriate for data sets containing very extreme values. Indeed, the mean cannot even be calculated for data sets that are nominal in scale.

Statistics that are based on the assumption that the data under analysis is distributed normally (in a pattern resembling the normal curve) or are distributed according to some other known distribution are called **parametric**. Although such statistics are often quite robust with respect to reasonable deviations from this assumption, their use when such violations are significant can lead to misleading results.

Statistics that do not require assumptions with respect to the distribution of data are called **distribution-free** or **non-parametric**. (From the statistician's or mathematician's point of view these terms are not quite synonyms but in general they are used interchangeably.)

Non-parametric methods are often less powerful but should be used in place of parametric techniques whenever data varies significantly from normality (or from some other distribution for which appropriate techniques are available). Such methods should also be used when the data to be analyzed consists of proportions, categorical counts, or ranks rather than interval or ratio scale measurements.

BASIC DESCRIPTIVE STATISTICS

Large arrays of data, such as the skin fold measurement data shown in Figure 12.1, are not easily understood by most people, even mathematicians. There is often much information present in such an array but it is hidden among the mass of data. The meaning of the array is concealed by the mass of numbers just as a forest is concealed by trees. The basic, descriptive statistics described in this section are tools for expressing the important characteristics of arrays or groups of data. These characteristics include central tendency, variability, symmetry, and kurtosis.

Central Tendency

Figure 12.1 is a table showing skin fold measurements (a test that measures the amount of fat in the body) for four groups of college students. Which group is fatter than the others? Clearly group A has the fattest student, but the leanest student is also in group A. How can the fatness of each *group* be expressed? Is there some way in which the "class fatness" could be expressed as a single number—a value that would be the best estimate of the fatness of the class as a whole?

Figure 12.2 shows an archery target with several holes made by arrows. (All the holes were made by the same archer under the same conditions and attempting to hit the center of the target.) Suppose you could win a large sum of money if you could correctly predict where the next arrow would strike. Where would you predict the arrow would strike? Obviously, the bull's eye would not be a very good guess as the archer has not even come close to it yet.

FIGURE 12.1   Skin fold measures for four groups.

GROUP A		GROUP B		GROUP C		GROUP D	
15	35	20	35	20	35	20	30
20	35	20	35	25	35	25	30
20	35	20	40	25	35	25	35
25	35	20	40	30	35	25	35
25	40	25	40	30	35	25	35
25	40	25	40	30	35	25	35
30	40	30	40	35	35	25	40
30	40	30	40	35	35	25	40
30	45	30	45	35	40	25	45
30	45	30	45	35	40	30	50
35	45	30	50	35	40	30	
35	50	30	50	35	45	30	
35	50	35	50	35	45	30	
35	55	35	50	35	50	30	

Also, anywhere on the left side of the target does not appear to be a very good prediction; all the hits so far have been on the right side. Is there some way in which the most likely location of the next hit could be expressed?

The concept of reducing a set of data—skin fold thicknesses, target strike locations, or any other kind of information—to a single data element (usually a number) is the concept of **central tendency.**

The central tendency of any real phenomenon is a very real characteristic of that phenomenon. In the skin-fold thicknesses of the group of students shown in Figure 12.1, there really is a thickness that is most representative of the group. That real point, however, can never be known with certainty. It can only be *estimated.* There are quite a few different statistics for estimating the central tendency of a set of data. Each represents a different method or formula, and, under the right circumstances, each is as valid and as potentially misleading as any other. Statistics for estimating central tendency which are discussed in the following pages include the mean, median, mode, harmonic mean, geometric mean, and interquartile mean.

The Mean

One way in which we might try to estimate the central tendency of the archery target data shown in Figure 12.2 would be to find a location such that the total of the distances between that location and each of the actual hits is smaller than for any other location. In fact, if we treated the distance to hits above and to the right of each proposed central tendency location as positive and those below and to the left as negative we could eventually find a location where the sum of all

FIGURE 12.2   An array of hits to an archery target.

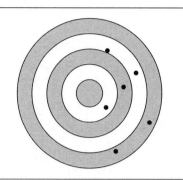

FIGURE 12.3   The algebraic formula for the mean. The actual computation is not as formidable as the equation.

$$\overline{X} = \sum \frac{X_i}{n}$$

the distances would be zero. We would have found the mean. We could do the same thing with the skin fold measurements in Figure 12.1.

The mean of a set of data is a number such that the sum of the deviations of each member of the set from that number is zero. Often known as the arithmetic mean or average, the **mean** is *calculated by adding together all of the elements of a set and then dividing the sum by the number of elements in the set.* (In some situations in which means are calculated as part of another statistic or as a step in some procedure of a more complex statistical analysis, the sum may be divided by one less than the number of members.)

The mean is certainly the most commonly used method for estimating central tendency. It is considered appropriate for estimation of central tendency when the data is ratio or interval in scale. The mean can be calculated when the data is ordinal in scale but the usefulness of such a statistic is questionable in most situations. The mean can become very misleading as an estimate of central tendency when the data set includes one or more **outliers** or *very extreme scores* because a single extreme score can have such a strong influence on the mean that the mean may misrepresent the real tendency of the group. The mean should never be used as an estimate of central tendency for data consisting solely of means (or other summary statistics) unless it is known that the means represent groups of equal size. Instead, a weighted mean or average may be computed for this type of data. Also, the means of two or more dissimilar measures or dimensions should never be combined. For example, to combine the means of student ratings of a teacher's clarity of speech with those of the teacher's subject knowledge is nearly meaningless.

The Median

Another approach to estimation of central tendency is to find the member of the data set that falls exactly in the middle of the set; that is, the member for whom there are an equal number of members with higher and lower values. Such an estimate is not affected by outliers or extremely high or low members of a data set, as is the mean. In the skin fold data in Figure 12.1, for example, there is one student in group D with a very high score, at least in relation to the others in the group, indicating a condition of obesity. Each group has at least one member with such a high score and group A has a member with an even

FIGURE 12.4   Skin fold data—group means.

GROUP	SUM OF SKIN FOLDS	N	MEAN
A	980	28	35
B	980	28	35
C	980	28	35
D	780	26	30

FIGURE 12.5   Effects of outliers on the mean. The mean of hits on each target is at "X." Clearly, the mean for target B is a poor representation of the archer's tendency.

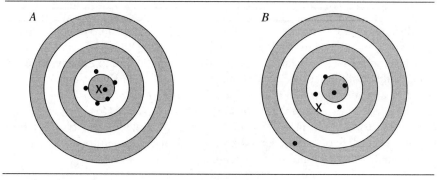

FIGURE 12.6   Skin fold data—group medians.

GROUP	N	MEDIAN
A	28	35
B	28	35
C	28	35
D	26	30

higher score. This extreme score causes the mean of the whole group to suggest that the members of that group have more fat than they really do. The median is not affected at all by extreme scores and would, in this case, be a better indicator of the central tendency of the group.

The **median** is *the middle member of a data set when the members are arranged into rank order.* The median is calculated by arranging or sorting the members of a data set into rank order (descending or ascending) and then finding the member in the center. This is very simple whenever there is an odd number of members. If, for example, there are 11 members in a set, the median is the sixth member counting from either the highest or lowest member. When there are an even number of members, computation is complicated by the fact that there is no middle member. Instead, in a set with 12 members there are two members (numbers 6 and 7 counting from either end) who are closest to the

FIGURE 12.7   Computation of the median when *n* is even.

NO TIES PRESENT	TIES PRESENT
8	12
9	13
11	15
13	15
15	15
17	18
18	18
20	20
22	23
25	26
(15 + 17)/2 = 16	(15 + 15 + 15 + 18 + 18)/5 = 16.2
Median = 16	Median = 16.2
n = 10	*n* = 10

middle. Also, the computation may be further complicated if one or both of the middle members is involved in a tie with other members. In such cases the median is found by computing the weighted mean of the midmost members.

The median should be the method of choice for estimation of central tendency of data sets that are noticeably skewed in distribution or that contain one or more extreme members. For most circumstances also, it is the only meaningful measure of central tendency for ordinal scale data.

The Mode

Data which is nominal in scale (or which does not involve numbers at all) cannot be appropriately used as the basis for most numerical computations. It would be meaningless, for example, to compute the mean or the median of jersey numbers of the members of a softball team. Similarly, for a data set consisting of the preferences of such players for wood or metal softball bats, computation of a mean or median is impossible. In such cases, central tendency can sometimes be expressed using a statistic called the *mode*. The **mode** is simply *the most frequently occurring member of a data set.*

The mode for any data set may be found by simply counting the frequency of each different data element. With some data sets, in which no two data elements are the same, there is no mode. In other cases, the data set may be bi-modal (two modes), tri-modal (three modes), or multi-modal (many modes).

The mode is an appropriate estimate of central tendency for nominal or categorical data. (The letters chosen by a group of students on a multiple choice format test is an example of a data set with categorical data.) Though the mode may be found for ratio, interval, or ordinal scale data sets, it may prove to be

FIGURE 12.8   A bi-modal distribution has a shape like a two-humped camel.

FIGURE 12.9   Modes of data distribution.

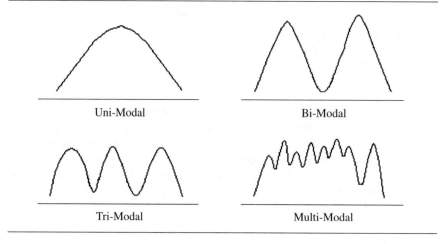

Uni-Modal

Bi-Modal

Tri-Modal

Multi-Modal

very misleading, depending upon the use to which it is applied. For example, if the number of points scored by a football team in a season were 36, 24, 0, 28, 34, 56, 22, 0, 32, and 44, the mode would be 0. Zero points, however, is certainly not a very good indication of the central tendency of the offensive performance of such a team. It would be, on the other hand, the best bet for a gambler who could only win by guessing the exact number of points that would be scored in the next game.

The Harmonic Mean

The **harmonic mean** of a set of data is *the reciprocal of the mean (arithmetic mean) of the reciprocals of the members of the set.* (The reciprocal of any positive number is equal to 1 divided by the number.) The harmonic mean is a kind of weighted average that can be useful in certain situations in which data is in the form of a frequency or rate, such as miles per hour, meters per second, or revolutions per minute. Consider, for example, a round trip automobile drive of

FIGURE 12.10   Computation of the harmonic mean.

Find the harmonic mean of 60 and 90

1/Hm = (1/90 + 1/60) /2

1/Hm = (5/180)/2

1/Hm = 5/360

Hm = 360/5

Hm = 72

180 miles done at 90 miles per hour outbound and 60 miles per hour on the return. The arithmetic mean of the velocities (90 mph and 60 mph) is 75 mph. This answer, however, is *wrong* as a computation of the overall rate of travel because it does not account for the fact that the two legs of the trip require different durations. The correct computation of the mean requires each velocity to be multiplied by the time required.

$$\frac{(90 \text{ miles} + 90 \text{ miles})}{(1 \text{ hr} + 1.5 \text{ hr})} = \frac{180 \text{ miles}}{2.5 \text{ hrs}} = 72 \text{ mph}$$

Fortunately this rather tedious computation can be avoided by computing the harmonic mean of the outbound and inbound velocities. The harmonic mean is computed by first converting each member of the data set to its reciprocal. The arithmetic mean of the reciprocals is then computed and the result is converted to its reciprocal.

The Geometric Mean

The geometric mean is the appropriate statistic for estimating central tendency of data sets consisting of measures on a geometric progression. The pH scale used to measure the acidity of solutions (such as swimming pool water) is an example of a geometric progression. On that scale, each change of 1 unit (such as a change from pH 6.0 to pH 7.0) represents a 10-fold change in acidity. The decibel scale used to measure sound intensity and the Richter scale used to measure the power of earthquakes are additional examples. The geometric mean uses all of the information contained in a set of data, as does the arithmetic mean, but it makes adjustment for the fact that the data form a geometric progression.

The **geometric mean** *of any set of* n *members is the nth root of the product of all the members of the set.* It may be calculated by first multiplying together all of the members of the data set and then finding the nth root of the product. A calculator or computer is highly recommended for such a calculation, particularly for finding the nth root. If one is not available, the geometric mean may also be found with the aid of log–anti-log tables. The geometric mean is the anti-log of the arithmetic mean of the logarithms of the members of the data set.

The Interquartile Mean and The Trimean

The interquartile mean and the trimean are two central tendency statistics which represent compromises between the strengths and weaknesses of both the mean

FIGURE 12.11   Geometric mean of swimming pool pH measures.

pH Measures [6.9, 7.2, 7.5, 7.2, 7.3, 7.0, 7.2 ,7.0]

$$Gm = \sqrt[8]{(6.9)\,(7.2)\,(7.5)\,(7.2)\,(7.3)\,(7.0)\,(7.2)\,(7.0)}$$

$$Gm = \sqrt[8]{6909184.4\ldots}$$

$$Gm = 7.16\ldots$$

and the median. Both are affected somewhat by asymmetry in the data set but much less than the mean. Both are affected by asymmetry only if the data set is so skewed that even the middle 50 percent of the data set is skewed.

The **interquartile mean** of a data set is *the mean of the middle 50 percent of the members of the set.* It is computed by sorting the members of the set into rank order, eliminating those members that fall into the upper and lower 25 percent, and then finding the mean of the remaining members. The **trimean** is computed as *the weighted mean of the first, second (taken twice), and third quartile scores.* The second quartile score (the median) is counted twice to give it more weight on the justification that members of the original data set tend to cluster in greater frequency around their median than around the upper and lower quartile scores.

THE CENTRAL TENDENCY OF VECTOR AND MATRIX DATA

Any of the central tendency statistics mentioned above may be computed for data sets consisting of vector or matrix data. (The student should refer to more specialized texts on vector or matrix mathematics if the nature of vector or matrix data is not understood.) The vectors or matrices of such data sets must, of course, all be of the same dimension. That is, all the vectors in a vector data set must have the same number of elements, and all of the matrices of a matrix data set must have the same number of rows and columns. The result of such a computation is always a vector or matrix having the same dimension as the members of the original set.

The computation of a central tendency statistic for a set of vectors or matrices is the same as the computation of that statistic for a set of scalars, except that the computation is repeated for each set of corresponding elements of the vectors or matrices.

VARIABILITY

In the skin-fold thickness data of Figure 12.1, the means of three of the groups are exactly the same. Does this mean that those three classes are identical in fatness? Clearly they are not. The members of group A seem to be more different from each other than are the members of the other groups. Both the fattest and the leanest student in all four groups are in group A. Group C, on the other hand, seems to be very homogeneous with respect to body fat. Obviously, central tendency does not tell the whole story. Groups can have the same central tendency but differ in the way members of the group vary from their central tendency. Is there some way the differences in body fat among the members of each group could be expressed as a single number?

The concept of reducing a set of data to a single number or descriptor that expresses the degree to which the members or elements of the set differ is the concept of **variability.**

There are several different statistics for estimating the variability of a set of data. As with the central tendency statistics, each represents a different formula. Each is equally as valid and as potentially misleading depending upon the circumstances. Statistics for estimating variability include the mean absolute deviation, variance, standard deviation, range, interquartile range, and quartile deviation.

Range

The **range** is a crude but very simple statistic for estimation of variability. It is simply *the difference between the two most extreme (high and low) members of a data set.* The range is calculated by subtracting the lowest value in a set of scores from the highest value. A major weakness of the range as an estimate of variability derives from the fact that only two members of a data set are used in its calculation, and the two most extreme scores at that. As the total number of data elements increases in a set of data, the occurrence of very extreme values becomes more likely. Thus, the range tends to increase with the size of the data set even when the actual variability of the data does not change.

The range may perhaps be more useful as a direct descriptor of a set of data rather than as an estimate of variability. For example, a survey of the salaries of professional hockey players might reveal high and low figures of $1,500,000 and $30,000 for a range of $1,470,000. Such a statistic does not really provide much insight into the real nature of the differences in hockey players' salaries, but the information about the range itself might still be useful.

Mean Absolute Deviation

The difference between a member of a data set and the mean of the data set is called a **deviation score**. Intuition might suggest that variability could be estimated by finding the mean of the deviation scores of each member of a data set. The mean of the set could be subtracted from each member to obtain a set of deviation scores which could then be summed and divided by the number of members. Unfortunately such a computation does not work. The deviations greater than zero and those less than zero exactly cancel each other so the sum, and therefore the mean deviation, is *always* zero.

FIGURE 12.12   Computation of the range statistic—skinfold data. The range is computed as the highest value minus the lowest value.

GROUP	A	B	C	D
High	55	50	50	50
Low	15	20	20	20
Range	40	30	30	30

FIGURE 12.13   The mean absolute deviation—sit-up scores of seven students.

SIT-UPS	DEVIATION	ABSOLUTE DEVIATION
102	2	2
106	6	6
94	–6	6
96	–4	4
100	0	0
104	4	4
98	–2	2
$\Sigma = 700$	$\Sigma = 0$	$\Sigma = 24$
$n = 7$	$n = 7$	$n = 7$
$\overline{X} = 100$	$\overline{X} = 0$	$\overline{X} = 3.43$

One method for dealing with the problem of self cancellation by positive and negative deviation scores is to convert each deviation score to its **absolute,** or *positive,* **value,** by dropping the sign. These *absolute values can then be summed and divided by the number of members in the data set* to produce a statistic called the **mean absolute deviation.** The mean absolute deviation is a valid statistic for estimation of variability but it is not commonly used, largely because alternative statistics, specifically the variance and the standard deviation, are computationally more convenient and useful as components of more complex analytical statistics.

The mean deviation is always zero because the mean itself, by definition, is that point about which the sum of deviations is zero.

Variance and Standard Deviation

An alternative to the absolute value function as a method for dealing with the self-cancellation of positive and negative deviation scores is to use the *squaring* function. When either a positive or a negative real number is squared (multiplied by itself) the result is always a positive. This procedure leads to two statistics useful as estimates of variability; the *variance* and the *standard deviation.*

The **variance** of a data set is *the mean of the squared deviation scores.* Once a set of deviation scores have been found, the variance is calculated by squaring each deviation score, summing the squares, and dividing the sum by the number of members in the set. This computational procedure gives an estimate for variability that is slightly smaller than it should be and is sometimes referred to as a *biased* estimate. Most statisticians and just about all statistical software perform the final step above by dividing by one less than the number of members of the set. This yields an *unbiased* estimate of variability.

The variance is a perfectly good statistic for estimation of the variability and is the basis of a variety of analytic statistical procedures. However, the variance statistic itself is not very appealing as a descriptive statistic because the numerical value of the variance of any non-trivial data set is generally not

FIGURE 12.14   Computation of the variance and standard deviation statistics—sit-up scores.

SIT-UPS	DEVIATION	SQUARED DEVIATION
102	2	4
106	6	36
94	–6	36
96	–4	16
100	0	0
104	4	16
98	–2	4
$\Sigma = 700$		$\Sigma = 112$
$n = 7$		$n = 7$
$\overline{X} = 100$		
		VAR = 16
		SD = 4

intuitively reasonable as a measure of variability. The process of squaring each deviation score leads to a variance value that is quite commonly (though not necessarily) larger than the largest deviation score in the data set. This problem is eliminated by taking the *square root of the variance* to obtain a new statistic called the **standard deviation.**

Interquartile Range and Quartile Deviation

Both the variance and standard deviation are appropriate estimates of variability for data sets consisting of ratio or interval level data. Like the mean, however, they are highly affected by outliers or extreme data elements. One method of dealing with the problem of outliers is to eliminate their effects by inventing a new statistic that is computed without them or that is minimally affected by them. The interquartile range and quartile deviation are two such statistics for estimation of variability.

The **interquartile range** is *the difference between the first and third quartile scores* and is found by subtracting the smaller of the two from the larger. The **quartile deviation** is *one-half of the interquartile range.* Both the interquartile range and the quartile deviation are considered to be more representative of the data set as a whole than the range. Even though only two members of the data set, the first and third quartile scores, are used in computation of these statistics, all of the other members of the data set are required to find those scores. Either statistic may be preferable to the standard deviation in situations in which the median is chosen as a measure of central tendency because of the presence of extreme members in the data set.

SYMMETRY AND KURTOSIS

Central tendency and variability are not enough to fully describe the contents of a data set. In two of the groups of student skin-fold measures shown in Figure 12.1, the means and standard deviations are exactly the same even though the data are obviously not the same. How are the skin-fold measures in Figure 12.1 distributed? Are they arranged in a balanced pattern above and below their central tendency or is the distribution unbalanced? Are most of the members of the data set clustered tightly together around their central tendency or are they spread out widely?

The balance of distribution of members of a data set around their central tendency is the concept of **symmetry** or **skewness**. A distribution in which the majority of members are above their central tendency as measured by the mean is said to be *negatively skewed*. When the majority are below the mean the distribution is said to be *positively skewed*. Negatively and positively skewed distributions are also commonly referred to as left and right skewed, respectively, but such terminology is only correct when the distribution is displayed graphically with values increasing to the right.

Symmetry is estimated using a statistic called *skewness*. Skewness is zero if the distribution is perfectly symmetrical. It is greater than zero if the distribution is skewed to the right and less than zero if it is skewed to the left. Skewness is calculated by finding the mean of cubed deviation scores and dividing by the cube of the standard deviation.

The degree to which the members of a data set cluster around their central tendency is the concept of **kurtosis.** *A distribution in which the majority of members are more tightly clustered around their central tendency than those of a normal distribution* is called a **leptokurtic distribution.** *One in which the members are less tightly clustered than a normal distribution* is called a **platykurtic distribution.**

Kurtosis is estimated using a statistic that is also called *kurtosis*. The statistic is zero when the members of the data set are normally distributed. It is greater than zero for a leptokurtic distribution and less than zero when the distribution is platykurtic. Kurtosis is calculated by finding the mean of the fourth powers of the deviation scores, dividing by the square of the variance (or the fourth power of the standard deviation), and then subtracting 3.

FIGURE 12.15   Variations of data distributions from normality.

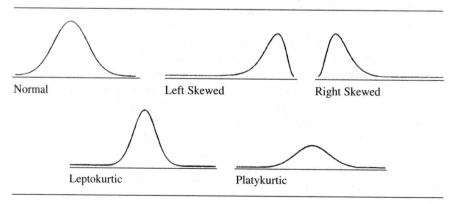

Normal   Left Skewed   Right Skewed

Leptokurtic   Platykurtic

TRANSFORMATIONS OF DATA

The student may recall from elementary algebra that if the two sides of an equation are both subjected to the same mathematical operations their equivalence is not affected. If we have the equation:

a = b

and we multiply both sides by 6x, we get the result:

6ax = 6bx.

The equation has been transformed. Also, the student may recall that no information has been lost because the inverse operation, dividing both sides by 6x, reverses the process and restores the original equation. Multiplying both sides of an equation transforms the equation into a different form but does not affect the relationship between the sides of the equation.

Transformations can also be performed on the elements of a set, such as a set of measurements of some variable in a research study. All of the elements of a set can be multiplied or divided by a constant, added to or subtracted from a constant, raised to a power, or subjected to other mathematical operations without affecting their relationships to one another. For example, a set of data consisting of the heights of a group of basketball players could be multiplied by 2.54 without affecting the relationships within the data set. Multiplying each height by 2.54, incidentally, is exactly what would be done to transform a set of heights measured in inches into a set of heights measured in centimeters.

Research data usually consists of sets of related elements, which may be scalar numbers, complex numbers, strings of text, or some other kind of information. Sometimes such data may be in a form that makes analysis, presentation, or comparison difficult. For a simple example, one set of measurements may be in inches and another in centimeters. In such cases it may be possible to use a data transformation to convert a set or sets of data into a more useful form. The following sections describe some common data transformations and their applications in measurement and research.

Arithmetic Transformations

A set of data may be transformed by adding or subtracting a constant, by multiplying or dividing by a constant, or by performing various trigonometric, logarithmic, and other functions. Any arithmetic operation for which the inverse operation will return the original data value can be used. (Note that the inverse of the operations of raising to a power and finding a root may not always return the original value.)

Multiplying or dividing by a constant is a very common kind of transformation used to convert data from one unit of measure to another. In the example given above, data in inches was multiplied by 2.54 to transform it into centimeters. Dividing centimeters by 2.54 would convert the measures into inches.

Adding or subtracting a constant is frequently used in the preparation of graphs. For example, we could subtract the recommended percentage of body fat for males from the actual body fat measurements of a set of males to produce a graph showing how much each *differs* from the recommended value.

A logarithmic transformation (converting a raw score to its natural logarithm) may sometimes be used to convert a set of scores that have a non-linear relationship to one with a linear relationship. The Richter scale, used to express the amount of energy released in earthquakes, the pH scale, used to express the strength of acids and bases, and the decibel scale, used to express the loudness of sounds, are all examples of logarithmically transformed data.

z-Score Transformation

Figure 12.16 shows the scores of eight graduate students on two parts of a standardized national exam. There are two scores for each student, one for the practical skills part of the exam and one for the knowledge portion. What can we learn by comparing these two sets of scores? Did all the students do very well on the practical skills part and very poorly on the knowledge portion? The truth is that we cannot compare these two sets of scores directly because the two tests are scored on different scales. The practical skills exam is scored on a scale ranging from 250 to 990 and the knowledge exam uses a scale of 600 to 699.

Attempting to compare scores directly is akin to comparing apples to oranges. Dissimilar items, such as apples and oranges, inches and centimeters, or quarters and dimes, can only be compared or combined meaningfully after being converted or transformed into units representing their commonality. In mathematical terms this is called the greatest common denominator. Apples and oranges can be combined as *pieces of fruit*.

Two sets of scores on different scales can be compared directly if they are both transformed to a common scale using a technique such as the z-score transformation. In the **z-score transformation** *each element of the original data set is converted into units of standard deviation above or below the mean.* First, the mean and standard deviation of the data set must be calculated. Each element is then transformed into a deviation score by subtracting the mean and finally into a standard score (also called a z-score) by dividing the deviation score by the standard deviation. Scores on a z-score always have a mean of zero. Raw scores above the mean will be converted into positive z-score values and raw scores below the mean will become negative z-score values.

FIGURE 12.16   National exam scores for eight graduate students.

TEACHER	PRACTICAL SKILLS	KNOWLEDGE
A	550	609
B	780	640
C	830	670
D	810	663
E	470	605
F	510	643
G	544	610
H	476	602

T-Score and Related Transformations

The z-score transformation permits two or more sets of paired or linked measures to be compared even when the measures have been made using different scales. The data, however, is converted into a form that is not of the same order of magnitude as the original measurement or within a range that is intuitively meaningful. For most measures for which the original data is normally distributed, the vast majority of transformed values will always be decimal numbers between –3.0 and 3.0. To make the data more intuitive, or simply to eliminate confusion caused by the negative and fractional values, it is often useful to perform a second transformation on a set of z-scores. Negative values may be eliminated by adding a constant larger than the most negative z-score value. Decimal fractions in the z-scale values may be eliminated or made less significant by multiplying each z-score value by a constant. The T-scale transformation, for example, adjusts scores so that they have a mean of 50 and a standard deviation of 10. **T-scale scores** may be *obtained by multiplying z-scores by 10 and adding 50*. Standardized IQ and some other tests are commonly converted to a scale with a mean of 100 and a standard deviation of 15.

Effect Size Transformations

A relatively new technique in research is an approach to the interpretation of multiple, independent studies in which the results of each study are treated as individual data points in a single study called a meta-analysis. For example, and with some simplification, 20 separate experimental studies on the effects of caffeine on reaction time might be combined in a meta-analysis. If each of the separate studies involved a single treatment group and a control group, then the meta-analysis would constitute a study with a similar design and 20 subjects in each group. In most cases meta-analytic studies turn out to be more complicated than this, however, as the various component studies vary in design and other factors.

Data-based research studies generally involve one or more controlled comparisons between pairs of groups of subjects or cases. Within each study comparisons may usually be made by examining the difference between central tendencies of each group relative to the variation within groups. (This is discussed in greater detail in Chapter 14). In a meta-analysis, however, there are many reasons that data from different studies cannot be compared directly to data from other studies. Such reasons include differences in the sizes of experimental groups, differences in the variability of group data, and differences in the data reported for each study. For an example of the latter difference, some studies of caffeine effects might report the means and standard deviations of experimental groups whereas others might report only t or F test values (see Chapter 14 for an explanation of these terms) and others still might report correlation coefficients (see Chapter 13).

Although a meta-analytic study may involve many additional steps, an important early step is the transformation of the data reported for each included study into a common form called an effect size. In its simplest form the **effect size** is simply *a z-score transformation of the difference between group means*. This, however, makes the assumption that group means are known or can be computed, that group variability is known or can be computed, that

FIGURE 12.17   Some common effect size transformations. The transformation for *F* ratio values (g) is for two group *F* values only. The transformation for Chi-square values (h) is only for those from 2×2 contingency tables. Transformation (a) should be used whenever a genuine control group design has been used. Use transformation (e) for effects between two non-control treatment groups.

a) transformation from group means and standard deviations. Subscripts refer to treatment (x) and control (c) groups.

$$ES = \frac{M_x - M_c}{SD_c}$$

b) correction for above when effect sizes are obtained from small samples

$$ES_{corrected} = ES_{uncorrected} \left(1 - \frac{3}{4(N_1 - 9)}\right)$$

c) transformation from Student's *t*

$$ES = 2\frac{t}{\sqrt{df}}$$

d) transformation from coefficient of correlation

$$ES = \frac{2r}{\sqrt{1 - r^2}}$$

e) weighted transformation from group means and standard deviations, for use when there is no real control. Subscripts refer to alternative treatments.

$$ES = \frac{M_1 - M_2}{\sqrt{\dfrac{SD_1^2(N_1 - 1) + SD_2^2(N_2 - 1)}{N_1 + N_2 - 2}}}$$

f) correction for above when effect sizes are obtained from small samples.

$$ES_{corrected} = ES_{uncorrected} \left(1 - \frac{3}{4(N_1 + N_2 - 2) - 9}\right)$$

g) transformation from *F* ratio

$$ES = 2\frac{\sqrt{F}}{\sqrt{df\,(error)}}$$

h) transformation from chi-square, for use only with chi-square values obtained from 2×2 contingency tables.

$$ES = 2\frac{\sqrt{\dfrac{x^2}{n}}}{\sqrt{1 - \dfrac{x^2}{n}}}$$

group variabilities are equal, and that the sizes of groups are equal. Such assumptions often do not hold. Therefore, meta-analysts have developed a variety of computational techniques for effect size transformations to transform different forms of statistical information and/or to adjust for other inconsistencies in available data. Entire textbooks are available that deal with the intricacies (as well as unresolved controversies) of meta-analysis and these should be consulted by anyone considering such a project using studies for which effect sizes are not reported.

Percentile Scores and Ranks

Many kinds of measurement data are used to make comparisons between or among individual cases. For example, scores on the Physical Education Specialty exam portion of the National Teacher's Exam (NTE) are often used to make comparisons among applicants for teaching positions. In such cases it is often more useful to compare an individual's score to the scores of the entire population taking the test than to make comparisons of the raw scores of a few individuals. Such comparisons may be made using percentile scores and ranks.

A **percentile score** is defined as *a raw score that is better than a specified percentage of cases.* For example, a score of 770 on the Physical Education Specialty Exam mentioned above is the 99th percentile score because it is better than the scores of 99 percent of those taking the test. A **percentile rank** is defined as *the percentage of cases that are lower than a specified score.* To continue the previous example, the percentile rank of a score of 770 on the Physical Education Specialty Exam is the 99th.

Percentile ranks of raw scores are calculated using the formula:

$$P = 100 \left(\frac{R - .5\,N}{N} \right)$$

where P = the percentile rank
R = the average rank of the raw score
N = the total number of raw scores

The average rank is the number of raw scores that are equal to or lower than the raw score for which a percentile is being calculated. If, for example, a particular score occurs three times and there are 10 lower scores, then the average rank for that score is 12 (the average of 11, 12, and 13). Note that although the above formula makes percentile ranks of 0 and 100 impossible, some computer programs may include rounding procedures which occasionally result in such values.

Along with percentile ranks and scores, quartile and decile ranks and scores are also sometimes used in describing the placement of an individual score within a group of scores. The first, second, third, and fourth quartile ranks are the same as the 25th, 50th, 75th, and 100th percentile ranks. Similarly, the decile ranks correspond to every 10th percentile ranks. Finally, the 2nd quartile score, the 5th decile score, the 50th percentile, and the median all mean the same thing.

Recoding

Data transformations need not always be mathematical. **Recoding** may be defined as *a logical, rather than mathematical, transformation of a set of data.* Data elements are recoded by two or more logical evaluations in the form:

If A then B

in which A is some kind of test of each member of the original data set for which the result will vary between true and false according to the original data, and B is the re-coded data. Figure 12.18, for example, shows the original and recoded data for eight subjects in a study of pizza topping preferences. The original data, in the form of names for favorite pizza toppings, has been transformed into a numerical code according to rules shown to the right of the figure. Such recoding can serve to permit analysis using computer software that is unable to handle textual data. Recoding may also be used to reduce numerical data from a continuous scale to a discrete or categorical scale. We do this almost automatically when we express the variable of age, which is clearly continuous, using the discrete units of years, or when we further reduce age to categories such as teenage, adult, and middle aged. Recoding using a transformation that cannot be reversed without knowledge of a difficult-to-ascertain countertransformation forms the basis of encryption procedures used to protect sensitive information from unauthorized access.

FIGURE 12.18   Recoding is the *logical* transformation of data.

Pizza Topping Preferences			Recoding Logic
SUBJECT	**TOPPING SELECTION**	**RE-CODED TOPPING**	If topping is Cheese then Recode as 1
1	Cheese	1	If topping is Pepperoni then Recode as 2
2	Anchovy	6	If topping is Pepper then Recode as 3
3	Pepperoni	2	If topping is Tomato then Recode as 4
4	Cheese	1	If topping is Onion then Recode as 5
5	Peppers	3	If topping is Anchovy then Recode as 6
6	Pepperoni	2	If topping is Other or Unknown then Recode as 0
7	Cheese	1	
8	Cheese	1	

TERMS

absolute value	outlier
central tendency	parametric statistics
deviation score	percentile rank
distribution-free statistics	percentile score
effect size transformation	platykurtic distribution
geometric mean	quartile deviation
harmonic mean	range
interquartile mean	recoding
interquartile range	skewness
kurtosis	standard deviation
leptokurtic distribution	symmetry
mean	trimean
mean absolute deviation	*T*-scale scores
median	variability
mode	variance
non-parametric statistics	*z*-score transformation

EXERCISES

1. Using a set or sets of data obtained from an almanac, your own measurements, or from your instructor, compute several means, medians, standard deviations, and ranges using only hand computation or a calculator.

2. Use a computer and statistical analysis software to compute the same statistics done by hand in exercise 1. Compare answers with those found in exercise 1 and attempt to explain any differences.

3. Identify what statistical analysis software is available for use on computers on your campus. Make an attempt to use each package to compute some basic statistics.

4. Convert the exam scores in Figure 12.16 to z-scores and T-scale scores. Make the conversion by hand if appropriate computer software is unavailable.

5. Using the skin fold data in Figure 12.1, determine the first and third quartile scores for groups A and B. Make the conversion by hand if appropriate computer software is unavailable.

6. Using the skin fold data in Figure 12.1, determine the first, second, third, and fourth decile scores for groups C and D. Make the conversion by hand if appropriate computer software is unavailable.

7. Use a computer statistical analysis program to compute skewness and kurtosis statistics for the skinfold data in Figure 12.1.

8. Identify and share with your classmates examples of variables in your school environment with various non-normal distributions.

RELATIONSHIPS AMONG VARIABLES

MULTIVARIATE DATA

Data is said to be **multivariate** whenever *two or more input and/or output variables are observed or measured for each subject or case under study.* If, for example, we measure the height and weight and categorize by gender each subject, the data is multivariate. Whenever *exactly two variables are observed or measured or when two variables at a time are examined even when more data has been collected,* the data is said to be **bivariate** or **paired.**

ASSOCIATION OF BIVARIATE DATA

If two people or things are *associated* with each other, then they tend to be found or to do things together. Two paired variables may also be associated with each other.

In the game of football it is common for coaches or analysts to say that the team that can consistently gain five or more yards on first down will win the game. Do they mean that gaining five yards on first down is *how* football games

FIGURE 13.1 A table of paired measurements: SAT and GRE scores of applicants to graduate school. The table shows the results of two measurements for each of nine students.

STUDENT	SAT (BEST COMBINED)	GRE
A	720	930
B	750	1005
C	690	895
D	810	1100
E	780	925
F	800	925
G	975	1020
H	720	1125
I	910	965

FIGURE 13.2   Scatter diagram of the SAT and GRE scores of nine students applying to graduate school. Notice the shape of the cloud of dots, which indicates a positive but not perfect
relationship between these two measures.

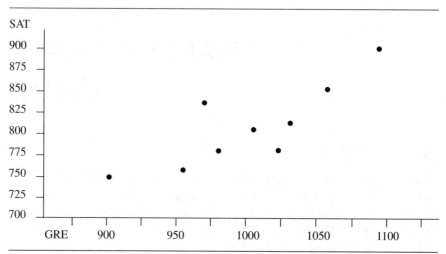

are won? Do they think that gaining five yards on first down *causes* a team to
win? Of course not! They mean that doing well on first down is *associated* with
winning in football. They mean that teams that win tend to gain more on first
down than teams that lose. Yards gained on first down and victory or defeat are
two paired variables that appear to be associated with each other.

The idea of two paired variables being related to each other is the concept
of association. The *degree or amount of association between two paired variables* is estimated using statistics that produce a **correlation coefficient.** There
are a variety of such statistics for use with various kinds of variables. Each correlation statistic is always a decimal number between 1.0 and –1.0. The
absolute value of the correlation statistic indicates the degree of association
between the two variables. A value of 1.0 (or –1.0) indicates a perfect association and a value of 0 indicates no association. The sign of the correlation
statistic shows the direction of the association. A positive correlation coefficient stands for a positive or *direct* association in which an increase in one
variable is matched by an increase in the other. A negative correlation coefficient stands for a negative or *inverse* association in which an increase in one
variable is matched by a decrease in the other.

CORRELATION VS. CAUSATION

If correlation statistics are computed for a wide variety of pairs of variables
some rather odd, even bizarre, associations will be found. It is, therefore,
important to recognize that the existence of an association between two variables, even a strong association, does not mean there is any kind of cause and
effect relationship between those variables. For example, using 7- to 14-year-
old children as subjects, a very strong association will be found between height
and ability in reading. Clearly, growing taller does not cause the learning of
reading any more than learning to read causes growth in height. Both variables

FIGURE 13.3   A data table showing ten different measures for each of 10 rookie basketball referees. Any combination of two of the above measures may be considered as paired with each other and used to compute a correlation statistic or to produce a scatter diagram. The age, weight, height, written test, and practical test measures are interval measures. The two rankings consist of ordinal data; notice that the referee's ranking contains a tie. Gender is a true dichotomy. The need or lack of need for eyeglasses is commonly considered as a dichotomy but is really a false dichotomy since the breakpoint that defines the boundary beyond which eyeglasses are needed is arbitrary. Prior playing experience is also a false dichotomy because the amount of such experience could be quantified. Different correlation statistics are available for each possible combination of types of data.

Rookie Referee Data and Ratings											
REFEREE	AGE	GENDER	HEIGHT	WEIGHT	PLAYING EXPERIENCE	GLASSES	WRITTEN TEST	PRACTICAL TEST	COACH'S RANKING	REFEREE'S RANKING	5-YEAR RATING
1	26	M	72	175	N	Y	85	90	9	10	85
2	24	M	74	185	N	Y	80	100	10	9	83
3	23	F	69	175	Y	N	75	80	7	2	75
4	28	M	75	200	Y	Y	95	65	8	8	73
5	30	F	68	165	N	N	100	80	6	2	93
6	33	F	69	165	N	Y	90	85	5	7	85
7	24	M	72	190	Y	Y	70	65	4	4	69
8	43	M	73	200	Y	Y	65	70	3	1	73
9	27	F	67	160	Y	N	80	85	2	5	84
10	50	M	65	175	N	Y	95	85	1	6	86

are, in fact, the result of maturation. Children tend to grow taller and to increase their reading ability between the ages of 7 and 14.

CORRELATION STATISTICS

Figure 13.3 is the data from a fictitious study of a class of 10 rookie basketball referees. It includes descriptive data such as age, gender, height, weight, and the need to wear corrective lenses, and evaluative data including scores on written and practical officiating examinations, and rankings by fellow officials and coaches. The table includes ratio, ordinal, dichotomous, and false dichotomous data. A cursory inspection of the data would suggest that there is some association between some pairs of variables and reason would also suggest that some associations should be present. Because there are several different kinds of data present, several different correlation statistics are needed to estimate the degree of correlation between each pair of variables. These, and a few other related statistics, are described in the following sections.

Pearson's Product-Moment Correlation

Pearson's product-moment correlation, named after the statistician Karl Pearson who invented it, is appropriate for estimation of linear correlation of paired variables when both are ratio or interval in type and measured as such. Also known as Pearson's *r* correlation, it is probably the most well-known and commonly used correlation statistic.

Pearson's *r* correlation is defined as *the sum of the products of the paired variables after conversion to standard form, divided by one less than the number of pairs.* This may be written as the equation:

$$r = \frac{\sum z_a z_b}{N - 1}$$

where z_a and z_b are the paired values of the variables being correlated expressed in standard form, and N is the number of pairs of measures. Chapter 12 provides a discussion of the z-score transformation used to transform raw data sets into standard form.

If hand computation of Pearson's *r* correlation is necessary, the following formula produces the same result as that in Figure 13.4 and avoids the necessity for preliminary computation of the means and standard deviations of each variable.

$$r = \frac{N\sum AB - (\sum A)(\sum B)}{\sqrt{[N\sum A^2 - (\sum A)^2]\,[N\sum B^2 - (\sum B)^2]}}$$

where A and B are the raw data and N is the number of pairs of data.

Although this equation appears quite complicated the computation is actually fairly simple, as is illustrated in Figure 13.4

Spearman's Rho Correlation

Spearman's rho is *used to estimate the association between two sets of ordinal or ranked measures* such as the ratings by officials and coaches in Figure 13.3. It is actually a special case of Pearson's *r* correlation and gives the same result if the rankings do not include ties.

The formula for Spearman's rho is

$$\rho = 1 - \frac{6\sum (x-y)^2}{N(N^2-1)}$$

where x and y are paired ranks and N is the number of pairs of ranks.

Computation of Spearman's rho is illustrated in Figure 13.5 using the coach's and referee's rankings from the rookie referee data given in Figure 13.3.

Kendall's Tau Correlation

Kendall's tau correlation may be *used to estimate association between two sets of ordinal data* such as the ratings by officials and coaches in Figure 13.3. It is also used with one set of ordinal data and one set of dichotomous data. The previous playing experience and need for eyeglasses variables in Figure 13.3 are both dichotomous. It is probably more appropriate than Spearman's rho when one or both measures contain many ties, as is certain to be the case when a ranking is correlated with a dichotomy.

FIGURE 13.4   Hand computation of Pearson's r correlation. The raw data for the two variables to be correlated, labeled A and B, appears in the second and third columns above. The first computational step is to find the squares of each raw score. These are placed in columns four and five. Computation of the products of each pair of raw scores is the next step and is shown in column six. The columns of raw scores, squared raw scores, and products of paired raw scores are then summed, as is shown at the bottom of each column. Finally, these values are plugged into the equation and solved as is shown at the bottom of the table. The r coefficient of correlation is equal to .200 which indicates a very low degree of association between the two sets of scores.

REFEREE	WRITTEN TEST SCORES	PRACTICAL TEST SCORES	A²	B²	AB
1	85	90	7225	8100	7650
2	80	100	6400	10000	8000
3	75	80	5625	6400	6000
4	95	65	9025	4225	6175
5	100	80	10,000	6400	8000
6	90	85	8100	7225	7650
7	70	65	4900	4225	4550
8	65	70	4225	4900	4550
9	80	85	6400	7225	6800
10	95	85	9025	7225	8075
Totals	835	805	$\Sigma A^2 = 70925$	$\Sigma B^2 = 65925$	$\Sigma(AB) = 67450$

$$r = \frac{10 \times 67450 - 835 \times 805}{\sqrt{(10 \times 70925 - 835^2)} \times (\sqrt{10 \times 65925 - 805^2})} = \frac{2325}{\sqrt{12025} \times \sqrt{11225}} = .200$$

There are two different equations for Kendall's tau, depending on whether or not ties are present. The equation for Kendall's tau when ties are not present is

$$\tau = \frac{S}{\frac{1}{2}N(N-1)} \quad \text{or} \quad \tau = \frac{2S}{N(N-1)}$$

where N is the number of paired rankings and S is the sum of ranks of one variable that are in natural order minus the sum of ranks of that variable not in natural order when the paired rankings are sorted into natural order according to the second ranking.

When ties are present the equation for tau is

$$\tau = \frac{S}{\sqrt{[\frac{1}{2}N(N-1) - T_x][\frac{1}{2}N(N-1) - T_y]}}$$

where S and N are as defined above, and

FIGURE 13.5   Computation of Spearman's rho correlation. Notice that the one pair of tied ranks (referee's rankings for rookies number 3 and 5) have been replaced by the average of the tied ranks, leaving no rookie ranked as second or third. If there had been three referees tied for third they would have been given new ranks of third and no one would be ranked second or fourth. Note, however, that if ties are numerous the use of Spearman's rho may be inappropriate.

REFEREE	COACH'S RANK x	REFEREE'S RANK y	$x-y$	$(x-y)^2$
1	9	10	−1	1
2	10	9	1	1
3	7	2.5	4.5	20.25
4	8	8	0	0
5	6	2.5	3.5	12.25
6	5	7	−2	4
7	4	4	0	0
8	3	1	2	4
9	2	5	−3	9
10	1	6	−5	25
$N=10$				$\sum(x-y)^2 = 76.5$

$$\rho = 1 - 6\frac{76.5}{10(10^2-1)} = 1 - \frac{459}{990} = .536$$

T_x and T_y are $\frac{1}{2}\sum t^2-t$

in which t is the number of ties in each set of ties in the x and y rankings respectively.

The computation of Kendall's tau when ties are present is illustrated in Figure 13.6 using the coach's and referee's rankings from Figure 13.3.

Kendall's Coefficient of Concordance

Particularly in the world of sport there are many situations involving data consisting of several (three or more) sets of rankings that ought to be highly consistent. In springboard diving, figure skating, gymnastics, and many other sports in which the victor is determined by scores or rankings assigned by a panel of judges it is highly desirable that there be a high degree of consensus among judges with respect to the scores or placement of the performers. Even allowing for reasonable differences in subjective judgment, angle of view, and other variables, there should not be a great deal of variation in the order of finish if the judging is fair and competent.

The degree of agreement among three or more sets of ranks may be estimated using Kendall's coefficient of concordance, called "W." Kendall's W is a number between 0 and 1 with 0 indicating maximum disagreement among judges and 1 indicating perfect agreement. Note, however, that whereas perfect

FIGURE 13.6   Computation of Kendall's tau when ties are present. Notice that the tied ranks (the referee's rankings of rookies 3 and 5 have been converted to their average rank of 2.5 and no one is ranked second or third.

REFEREE	COACH'S RANK	REF'S RANK	REFEREE REFEREE'S RANK	10 6	9 5	8 1	7 4	6 7	5 2.5	3 2.5	4 8	1 10	2 9
10	1	6		x	x	x	x	x	x	x	x	x	x
9	2	5		−1	x	x	x	x	x	x	x	x	x
8	3	1		−1	−1	x	x	x	x	x	x	x	x
7	4	4		−1	−1	1	x	x	x	x	x	x	x
6	5	7		1	1	1	1	x	x	x	x	x	x
5	6	2.5		−1	−1	1	−1	−1	x	x	x	x	x
3	7	2.5		−1	−1	1	−1	−1	0	x	x	x	x
4	8	8		1	1	1	1	1	1	1	x	x	x
1	9	10		1	1	1	1	1	1	1	−1	x	x
2	10	9		1	1	1	1	1	1	1	1	−1	x

$$S = 29 - 15 = 14$$

$$T_x = 0 \qquad \sqrt{\tfrac{1}{2}N(N-1) - T_x} = \sqrt{\tfrac{1}{2}10(10-1) - 0} = \sqrt{45} = 6.71$$

$$T_y = 1 \qquad \sqrt{\tfrac{1}{2}N(N-1) - T_y} = \sqrt{\tfrac{1}{2}10(10-1) - 1} = \sqrt{44.5} = 6.67$$

$$\tau = \frac{14}{6.71 \times 6.67} = .313$$

agreement (all judges give the same rankings) is possible, perfect disagreement cannot occur as with more than two judges there has to be some degree of correlation between some of the rankings. Note also that unlike other correlation statistics, Kendall's W can never be negative in value. Finally, it is important to recognize that certain patterns of rankings, such as two identical sets of exactly or almost exactly opposite rankings, will produce values indicating no agreement even though there is an obvious relationship among the rankings.

With no ties present the equation for Kendall's W is

$$W = \frac{12S}{m^2(N^3 - N)}$$

where m is the number of rankings (judges), N is the number of ranks, and S is the sum of squared deviations of rank sums from the mean sum of ranks.

If a set of rankings contains only a few ties the above equation may be used with averaged ranks assigned in place of the original tied ranks. If there are many ties, however, the equation for W is changed to

$$W = \frac{S}{\tfrac{1}{12}m^2(N^3 - N) - m\sum T}$$

FIGURE 13.7   Computation of the concordance statistic for the rankings of six skaters by five judges.

SKATER	JUDGES' RANKINGS							
	US	GB	FR	CH	AR	SUM	d	d^2
A	+1.5	2	1	2	1	7.5	−13.5	182.25
B	3	1	2	1	2	9	−12	144
C	+1.5	3	3	3	3	13.5	−7.5	56.25
D	4	4	4	4	5	21	0	0
E	5	6	5	5	4	25	4	16
F	6	5	6	6	6	29	8	64

$\sum$sums=105 $S = \sum d^2 = 462.5$

$\sum \dfrac{\text{sums}}{N} = 21$

$W = \dfrac{12S}{m^2(N^3-N)} = \dfrac{12 \times 462.5}{5^2(6^3-6)} = \dfrac{5478}{5225} = .958$

where m, N, and S are as defined above and

$$T = \frac{\sum(t^3 - t)}{12}$$

where t is the number of tied rankings in each set of ties.

Figure 13.7 shows the rankings assigned by six judges to five figure skaters and the computation of W. One judge has assigned tied rankings to two skaters but there are no other ties. Consequently, although the ranks of the two tied skaters are converted to their average rank, W is computed without the correction factor for ties.

OTHER LINEAR CORRELATION STATISTICS

Figure 13.3 includes a variety of types of variables, including interval, ordinal, dichotomous, and false dichotomous measures, and meaningful associations may exist between any pair of these variables. In sports officiating, for example, it might be claimed that experience as a player is an advantage in becoming a competent official, or that a need for eyeglasses is a disadvantage. Also, it might be hoped that rankings of new officials by coaches would be approximately the same as rankings by experienced officials. There are a variety of other correlation statistics that may be used with ranks, dichotomies, or other kinds of data. However, these are really just simplified computational formulas for computing the Pearson statistic with certain kinds of data. They were developed at a time when computations had to be done manually and computation of Pearson's r can be quite tedious. The Pearson equation will produce the same result and is generally more readily available in statistical software packages.

The following sections briefly describe several of these statistics that may be encountered in the literature and the kinds of data for which they are used.

Biserial and Point Biserial Correlation

Biserial and **point biserial correlation** formulas are *used to estimate association between a continuous, interval or ratio scale variable and a dichotomous variable.* Biserial correlation is used when the dichotomy is false and point biserial is used with a true dichotomy. In Figure 13.3 the need for eyeglasses and previous playing experience variables are both false dichotomies and gender is a true dichotomy.

Phi Correlation

The **phi correlation** formula is *used when one variable is a continuous measure and the other is a dichotomy.* The correlation between the written test scores and gender in Figure 13.3 could be estimated using the phi coefficient.

Tetrachoric Correlation

The **tetrachoric correlation** formula can be *used to estimate association between two variables that are false dichotomies* such as the need for eyeglasses and prior playing experience variables in Figure 13.3.

IS AN ASSOCIATION REAL?

All of the correlation statistics described above with the exception of Kendall's *W*, which is a measure of agreement but not correlation, always give a value between –1 and 1. In general it is correct to say that a positive value indicates a direct association in which an increase in the value of one variable is associated with an increase in the other, that a negative value for the correlation statistic indicates an inverse association, and that a correlation of zero indicates no association. However, this is a bit simplistic. A correlation of exactly zero will rarely occur even when data values are generated completely at random. A high correlation statistic can occur even when no real association exists and a correlation statistic near zero can occur even when a strong association exists, but the opposite is *more likely*.

There is no statistical method to determine with certainty whether a correlation coefficient computed for any pair of variables represents a genuine association or is due to chance. However, it is possible to compute the *probability* that any particular value of the correlation coefficient could occur by chance alone when no genuine association exists. For example, in Figure 13.3 the rankings by coaches and referees have a Spearman's rho correlation of .536. Without going into the computational details, with 10 pairs of data points the probability of obtaining a Spearman's rho correlation of .536 by chance when no association is present is slightly more than .05. That is, a correlation of .536 should be expected by chance alone a bit more often than 5 out of every 100 or 1 out of 20 times. Stated alternatively, a Spearman's rho correlation coefficient of .536 indicates a genuine association a bit less than 19 out of 20 or 95 out of 100 times. A coefficient of .564 or higher should occur by chance five percent of the time. Thus, we can say we are less than 95 percent certain that the association between the officials and coaches ratings is real. In the jargon of research the correlation coefficient of .536 is "not significant at the .05 level of confidence."

It is generally unnecessary to perform any computations to determine the significance of a correlation coefficient. If the output of the computer software used to compute the correlation coefficient itself does not include an indication of significance, then significance may be found using tables included in many statistical references and textbooks.

THE VARIANCE INTERPRETATION OF CORRELATION: IS AN ASSOCIATION MEANINGFUL?

If two variables are associated with each other then some portion of the variation found for one variable should be explainable in terms of the variation found in the other variable. Such explanation may be accomplished through the variance interpretation of the correlation coefficient. Height and weight, for example, are fairly closely associated in the human population. In the rookie referee data the Pearson's r correlation between height and weight is .781, a figure that is expected to occur by chance less than 1 percent of the time in a sample of 10 paired measurements. Some of the variation in weight may be accounted for by variation in height and some of the variation in height may be accounted for by variation in weight. But how much?

Although the mathematical reasoning involved is beyond the scope of this book, the square of the correlation coefficient represents the proportion of the variation in one variable that may be attributed to or explained by variation in the other. Multiplying the squared correlation coefficient by 100 converts the proportion to a percentage. Thus, the correlation of .781 between the heights and weights of the rookie referees means that 60.1 percent ($100 (.781 \times .781) = 60.1$) of the variation in weight can be attributed to (explained by) variation in height. Also, 60.1 percent of the variation in height can be explained by variation in weight. (Remember that such explanations or attributions do *not* necessarily imply any causal relationship.)

Because the probability of obtaining any non-zero correlation coefficient by chance alone decreases as the number of data points (subjects or cases) increases, correlation statistics must be interpreted carefully. It is quite common to obtain correlations that are significant (that is, unlikely to be due to chance) but virtually meaningless. If there had been 100 rather than 10 subjects in the rookie referee study (Figure 13.3), a correlation of .254 would be considered significant at the .01 level (such a correlation would occur by chance less than 1 percent of the time). However, a correlation that explains only $.254 \times .254 = .065 = 6.5$ percent of the variance in the data is not generally very useful. The remaining 93.5 percent of the variance is unaccounted for.

COMPARING AND COMBINING CORRELATION COEFFICIENTS

Because correlation coefficients computed for randomly generated data are not normally or even symmetrically distributed, it is misleading to attempt to compare or combine coefficients directly. For example, it would be improper to compute an average of two or more correlation coefficients. It would be similarly improper to attempt to express the difference between two or more correlation coefficients in terms of the coefficients themselves.

Correlation coefficients can be combined or compared by first using a transformation called Fisher's z transformation. Such transformed values have an approximately normal distribution. The transformation equation is

$$z_r = \frac{1}{2} \log_e \frac{(1 + r)}{(1 - r)}$$

Tables of transformed correlation coefficients are available in many statistics texts for those lacking access to computers and appropriate software. (A Mathcad program for this transformation is provided in Appendix C.5.)

Figure 13.8 provides a summary of data from five studies of the relationship between hours spent watching television and a test of academic achievement. These are then transformed using the Fisher z formula, weighted according to the degrees of freedom associated with each study (N–3), and then averaged. The average z_r value is then converted back to a correlation coefficient that is appropriate for expressing the relationship between the two variables across all five studies.

The z transformation can also be used for a test of the significance of the difference between two correlation coefficients. A statistic z is computed using the equation

$$z = \frac{\frac{1}{2} \log_e \frac{(1+a)}{(1-a)} - \frac{1}{2} \log_e \frac{(1+b)}{(1-b)}}{\sqrt{\frac{1}{n_1-3} + \frac{1}{n_2-3}}}$$

This is then evaluated using the z-test described in Chapter 14. Using the data for groups A and B in the previous example, the value for z works out to .334 which is less than the value of 1.96 required for significance at the .05 level.

FIGURE 13.8   Data from a study of the relationship between hours spent watching television and academic achievement. Use of the Fisher z transformation to find the average of several correlation coefficients. Note that the result here is the same as a simple arithmetic average of the correlation coefficients, but this is simply coincidence.

GROUP	N	r	z	df(N–3)	z (df)
A	26	−.65	.775	23	−17.825
B	34	−.70	.867	31	−26.877
C	37	−.72	.908	34	−30.872
D	27	−.68	.829	24	−19.896
E	30	−.60	.693	27	−18.711
Totals				139	114.181

$$\bar{z} = \frac{114.181}{139} = .821 \qquad\qquad \bar{r} = .676$$

NON-LINEAR ASSOCIATIONS

Figure 13.9 is a scatter diagram showing the performance of athletes under varying degrees of stress. If a Pearson's *r* correlation is computed for this data the result will be close to zero. Clearly, however, there is a definite relationship between stress and performance. Performance improves as stress increases to a certain point and then declines as the level of stress increases further. The difficulty lies in the fact that the relationship or association between stress and performance is not a *linear* one. The correlation statistics that have been discussed in this chapter are all designed to express linear relationships only. Thus, a zero or low correlation coefficient means only that there is little or no linear association between two variables and not that there is no association between them. Although there are statistics for detecting non-linear relationships, the best approach is simply to visually examine a scatter diagram.

THE REGRESSION LINE

If a perfect, linear relationship exists between two paired variables then all of the points on the scatter diagram of those variables fall on a straight line. If the relationship is strong but less than perfect then the points of the scatter diagram fall approximately, but not exactly, on a line. The points deviate somewhat from a line. As the relationship becomes weaker, the cloud of points become arranged less and less on a line. The deviations of the points from a line become greater.

With a perfect correlation between two variables, the line formed by the points of the scatter diagram defines the relationship between the two variables. The equation for the line, in the form

$$y = mx + b$$

where *m* is the slope and *b* is the *y* intercept may be used to determine the value of *y* for any value of *x* or to determine the value of *x* for any value of *y*. Such a line is called a **regression line.**

When the correlation between two variables is high but not perfect it is intuitively obvious from inspection of the scatter diagram that there must be a line

FIGURE 13.9   Scatter diagram of athletic performance vs. stress. A non-linear association.

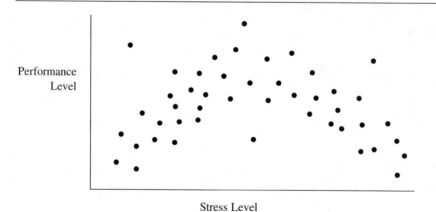

Performance
Level

Stress Level

whose equation describes the relationship between the variables but exactly where that line should be is uncertain. In Chapter 12 the mean of a set of data was described as a point from which the total deviation of all the elements of the set is less than for any other point. Extending that idea provides a method for producing a regression line for paired data sets. The regression line may be defined, therefore, as a line from which the total deviation of all the paired elements is less than for any other line. Alternatively stated, the regression line for any set of paired data elements is the line whose equation (in the form y= mx+b) best represents the relationship between those data elements.

The regression line is a line having the formula:

$$y = mx + b$$

where m is the slope and b is the y intercept. The y intercept is defined as the value of y when the value of x is zero. The value for the slope m may be found by solving the equation:

$$m = r \times \frac{z_y}{z_x}$$

where r is the Pearson's r correlation of the paired variables, z_y is the standard deviation of the variable plotted on the y axis, and z_x is the standard deviation of the variable plotted on the x axis. Once the slope m has been calculated, the y intercept b may be found by using the equation:

$$b = \overline{X}_y - \overline{X}_x \times m$$

FIGURE 13.10   The mean is a point on a number line closer to all members of a set of numbers on that number line than any other.

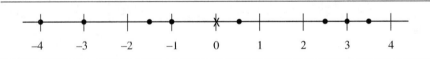

FIGURE 13.11   The regression line is a line across a plane closer to all members of a paired data set than any other.

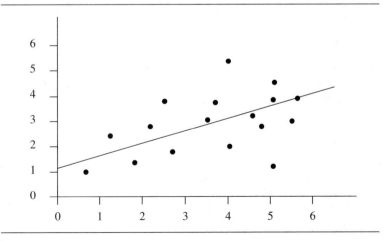

in which X_y is the mean for the variable plotted on the y axis, X_x is the mean of the variable plotted on the x axis, and m is the slope.

Once the slope and y intercept have been computed the regression line can be plotted on a graph. The y intercept is one point on the line when the value for x is zero, and any second point can be found using the regression equation. Once two points are plotted they may be connected by a straight line which may be extended as desired.

The R.M.S. Error for a Regression Line

A regression line and its equation for any set of paired variables may be viewed as a kind of central tendency statistic. The regression line represents the central tendency of the relationship between the two variables. In Chapter 12 it was demonstrated that central tendency statistics alone were not enough to summarize the information in a set of data. A second statistic was necessary to express the variability within the data set, and the same is true for sets of paired data.

Figure 13.12 shows a regression line drawn within a scatter diagram of data points. Some data points fall directly on the regression line but most do not. They vary from the regression line. Each point not on the line is either above or below the line.

The distance above or below the regression line is the amount by which each data point varies from the regression line and may be quantified by measuring the distance from the data point to the regression line along a line parallel to the x *or* y *axis.* These variations are called **residuals.** *Collectively, the residuals from each data point constitute a measure of the variation within the set of paired data from their central tendency.* This collective variation is summarized by the statistic called the **root mean square (r.m.s.)** error of the regression which is in essence the central tendency of the errors. It is defined by the equation:

$$rms = \sqrt{\frac{\Sigma(R^2)}{N}}$$

where *rms* is the r.m.s. error, R is the residual for each data point, and N is the number of data points.

The r.m.s. error for regression may be found by solving the above equation or using the following equation:

$$rms = \sqrt{1 - r^2} \times Z_y$$

where *rms* is the r.m.s. error, r is the Pearson's r correlation coefficient, and Z_y is the standard deviation of the y axis variable. The r.m.s. error is to a regression line what the standard deviation is to a mean.

Plotting Residuals

The residuals to a regression line may be plotted on a graph. The graph is drawn using the same x axis as the scatter diagram or regression line, but the y axis is adjusted so that the residual values for the y axis variable may be plotted rather than the raw data values. Figure 13.13 shows a scatter diagram and regression line above and the corresponding residuals plot below.

FIGURE 13.12   The length of a line drawn parallel to the *y* axis from a data point to the regression line is the amount by which the data point varies from the regression line. That variation is called the residual.

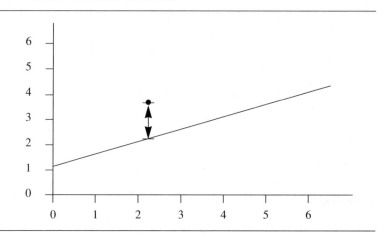

If the linear relationship expressed by the linear regression line is an accurate description of the relationship between the two variables involved, the residuals plot should be oval and symmetrical in shape. Such a shape is described by statisticians as **homoscedastic** which means "same spread." *If the residuals plot is asymmetric or has a shape other than an oval* it is termed **heteroscedastic.** A heteroscedastic residuals plot may indicate that the relationship between the two variables involved is non-linear and that use of a linear regression line may be inappropriate. The plotting of residuals to a regression line for a set of paired data elements is analogous to computing the skewness and kurtosis of a set of individual data points.

PARTIAL AND MULTIPLE CORRELATION AND MULTIPLE REGRESSION

The idea of finding the equation for a line that describes the relationship between two variables can be extended in several powerful ways. Although a discussion of the details and procedures of such techniques is well beyond the scope of this book, many of the more powerful computer programs for statistical analysis of data contain procedures that provide them almost automatically.

One extension is to compute a **partial correlation coefficient** which *adjusts a simple correlation coefficient for the effects of additional independent variables.* Another is to attempt to find *an equation for a line that describes the relationship between two or more independent variables and one dependent variable.* Called **multiple regression,** the result is an equation in the form:

$$y = MA + NB + C$$

where *A* and *B* represent values of independent variables, *M* represents the relationship between *A* and *y* after correcting for the effects of *B*, *N* represents the relationship between *B* and *y* after correcting for the effects of *A*, and *C* is the *y* intercept.

FIGURE 13.13   Scatter diagram with regression line and a corresponding residuals plot.

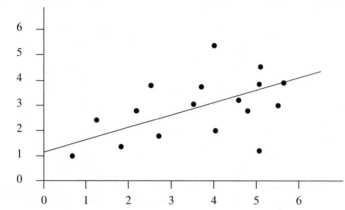

Scatter diagram and regression line

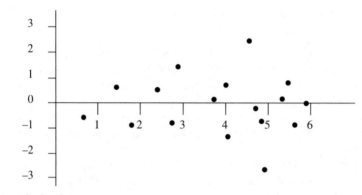

Residuals plot

To illustrate these techniques, consider Figure 13.3. The correlations between each of the two test scores (written and practical) and the independent ratings five years later are .681 and .684, both of which are significant at the 95 percent confidence level. Both tests explain approximately 46 percent (.68 ×.68 = .46) of the variance in the five-year ratings. Notice, however, that although the correlation between the two tests is very low, only .200, the two tests together cannot explain 92 percent (46 + 46) of the variance in the five-year ratings. Some of each test, and therefore the portion of the five-year ratings explained by each, has already been explained by the other test. The technique of partial correlation involves computing the correlation between two variables (such as the written referee test and the five-year rating) after the effects of a third variable (the practical referee test in this case) have been removed. Multiple correlation attempts to compute the correlation between a combination of two or more independent variables (the written and practical tests) with a dependent variable (the five-year rating). *Computing a correlation between two or more independent variables and a dependent variable while controlling for the effect of one or more additional independent variables* is called **multiple-partial correlation. Multiple regression** involves *attempting* *to find an equation with weightings that most efficiently combine two or more independent variables to predict a dependent variable.*

POLYNOMIAL REGRESSION

Another extension of the concept of a regression equation or line, called **non-linear** or **polynomial regression,** is to find an *equation for a curve, rather than a line, that best fits the relationship between one or more independent variables and a dependent variable.* Although the mathematics of polynomial regression are formidable, most of the better statistical computer programs are able to perform such regressions quite easily.

TERMS

biserial correlation

bivariate data

correlation coefficient

heteroscedastic

homoscedastic

Kendall's tau correlation

multiple-partial correlation

multiple regression

multivariate data

Pearson's *r* correlation

phi correlation

point biserial correlation

polynomial regression

regression line

residuals

root mean square

Spearman's rho correlation

tetrachoric correlation

EXERCISES

1. Collect several sets of measurements, such as height, weight, need for eyeglasses, and others, from members of your class. Prepare scatter diagrams for several pairs of these measurements.

2. For several pairs of the measurements obtained for exercise 1 above, determine the most appropriate correlation statistic. Compute these statistics using a computer and statistical analysis software.

3. Using any of the rankings in the rookie referee data (Figure 13.3) given in this chapter or any other sets of rankings, compute coefficients of correlation using the Pearson, Spearman, and Kendall equations. Compare the results.

4. With two of the sets of measurements (use measurements of continuous variables) use a computer software package to plot a scatter diagram and regression line.

5. Continue the analysis begun in exercise 3 above by preparing a residuals plot. Explain the resulting residuals plot.

6. Use a computer software package to perform a multiple regression using the rookie referee tests and five-year ratings given in Figure 13.3.

7. Use a computer software package to perform a polynomial regression using the rookie referee tests and five-year ratings given in Figure 13.3.

MAKING GROUP COMPARISONS

Nearly all experimental and many descriptive and other types of studies involve comparisons between two or among several groups. In a typical experiment, two groups of subjects are created and equated by random assignment, given treatments that differ in only one way, and then observed or measured in some way. If the groups are different following treatment it is evidence that the difference in the treatments given has had an effect. On occasion the difference between groups is obvious and beyond dispute. For example, if each member of one group of 50 students in a swimming class can swim between 150 and 300 meters and each member of a second group can only swim between 10 and 25 meters, then it is quite obvious that the two groups are different in swimming ability. No further statistical or other analysis is needed. If the two groups were created at random as part of an experiment evaluating two methods of swimming instruction it would be quite obvious which method was superior.

Sometimes, however, the differences between or among groups are not so clear. Suppose that the second group of swimmers in the above example could swim between 125 and 250 meters. The average distances the students in each group can cover are different but there is considerable overlap. The stronger swimmers in the weaker group can outperform the weaker members of the stronger group. Because the mean distances for the two groups are closer to each

FIGURE 14.1 These performances of two groups of swimmers are clearly different. They have almost no overlap.

FIGURE 14.2 That the performances of these two groups of swimmers are different is not so obvious. There is considerable overlap between the two groups.

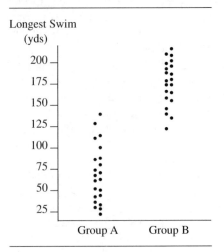

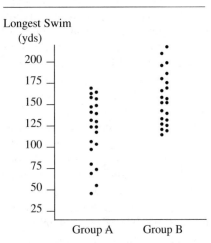

other and because of the overlap between the two groups it is now not so obvious that the groups are really different. The numerical difference between the mean swimming distances could be real or it could be simply random variation.

How can we decide if the differences in the means of two sets of measurements, such as the swimming distances, are real or simply random variation? With certainty, the answer is we cannot! Regardless of the differences between the two sets, we can never be absolutely certain the difference is not due to chance. However, it is possible to make reasonable decisions about observed differences between or among groups by computing the probability of obtaining such differences by chance alone. If we can determine that the probability is 1 percent that chance alone could produce an observed result then we can say that we are 99 percent certain that the difference is not due to chance.

There are a variety of statistical techniques for comparing means of two or more groups. Some are used only with very simple kinds of designs whereas others can be generalized to a wide variety of complex designs. The proper use of each requires that certain assumptions hold true about the type and distribution of the data being analyzed. There are also a variety of analogous techniques for comparing medians or frequencies. This chapter is intended to introduce the student to some of these techniques in terms of their general concept and use. Some formulas and computational examples are included for the simplest ones as a vehicle for becoming familiar with the general idea of each statistic. However, as these techniques are extremely simple to obtain using many readily available computer programs on any computer from a mainframe to a simple PC, a complete set of computational examples is not given here.

TYPE I AND TYPE II ERROR AND SELECTION OF THE ALPHA LEVEL

Experiments and many quasi-experimental studies are set up to evaluate a hypothesis or hypotheses concerning differences between or among groups following differing treatments. Although hypotheses may predict either a difference or no difference, they traditionally are stated and statistically evaluated in the *null* form, which states that there will be no difference. For example, in a study of the effectiveness of a new antibiotic drug, in which one group is given the new drug and the other a placebo, the null hypothesis would be that the effectiveness of the new drug would be the same (presumably little or no effect) as the placebo.

For any hypothesis stated or statable in the null form there are two possibilities. The null hypothesis may be correct or it may be incorrect. Therefore, in evaluating or making a decision about the truth of a hypothesis there are two ways we can be in error. We might *reject the null hypothesis when it is true,* or we might *accept the null hypothesis when it is false.* The former is called a **type I error** and the second is a **type II error.**

The Greek letters [α] and [β] are often used to symbolize the alpha and beta levels of a statistical test.

Statistical procedures for comparing groups lead eventually to the computation of the probability that the data actually obtained in a study will occur strictly by chance when there are, in fact, no differences between the groups compared. In a research report a probability of less than .035 percent would be written in notational form as (p ≤.035). This probability is then compared to *a pre-determined value,* called the **alpha level,** to decide whether to accept or reject the null hypothesis.

FIGURE 14.3   Type I and II errors. A type I error is the rejection of a null hypothesis that is, in fact, true. A type II error is the acceptance of a null hypothesis that is, in fact, false.

TRUTH	DECISION	
	ACCEPT NULL	REJECT NULL
Null is correct	correct decision	Type I error
Null is false	Type II error	correct decision

If the probability of the obtained data occurring by chance is less than the alpha level, the null hypothesis is rejected. If it is greater than alpha, then the null hypothesis is accepted.

Good scientific practice demands that the alpha level be set during the design phase of an experimental study and not during the process of statistical analysis of experimental results. To do otherwise is to risk the temptation to choose an alpha level such that the results of the study will result in rejection of the null hypothesis rather than accepting or rejecting that hypothesis on the basis of the data and alpha level.

It is fairly common in education and the social sciences for researchers to set alpha rather arbitrarily to .05. Differences with a probability of chance occurrence of less than 5 percent are then reported as *significant* and the null hypothesis is rejected whereas those with more than a 5 percent chance of occurrence are called *non-significant* and the null hypothesis is accepted. To arbitrarily set alpha to .05 (or any other level) is really to ignore issues related to the alpha level and to risk increasing the potential for damage resulting from an incorrect conclusion. Although there are several factors that may affect the selection of an alpha level (Franks and Huck, 1986) the most important is probably consideration of the relative consequences of making a type I or type II error. As illustrated in Figure 14.3 a type I error refers to the rejection of the null hypothesis when it is true and a type II error refers to acceptance of the null hypothesis when it is false. To illustrate, consider a study of the effects of a new idea in physical training (a new method or drug) thought to have potential for promoting muscle development. A controlled experiment is conducted to evaluate two null hypotheses—first, that the treatment (the method or drug) has no effect on muscle development and, second, that it has no effect on long-term health. Either null hypothesis may be, in fact, true or false independently of the other. The experiment may also result in acceptance or rejection of either hypothesis, also independently of the other. The possible conclusions and the resulting consequences of the study are shown in Figure 14.4. In four cases the conclusions would be correct and should lead to consequences that would be as predicted by the study, and in four cases incorrect conclusions would lead to unexpected consequences. In the case of the effectiveness of the treatment in producing muscle development the consequences of an incorrect conclusion range from unexpected failure to develop muscles when the treatment is used but does not work to failure to develop muscles when the treatment is not used when it might have been effective. It is a close judgment call which is the more serious or harmful consequence of error. In the case of the effects of the treatment on long-term

FIGURE 14.4   Consequences of type I and type II errors on different hypotheses. Clearly the consequence of a type II error with the effect on health variable is much more serious than any of the others.

TRUTH	DECISION	EFFECT ON STRENGTH		EFFECT ON HEALTH	
		Error	Consequence	Error	Consequence
Null is true	Reject null	type I	useless method used	type I	useless method used
	Accept null	no error	—	no error	—
Null is false	Reject null	no error	—	no error	—
	Accept null	type II	useful method not used	type II	long-term health damage

health, however, the consequences of error range from failing to develop muscles when the treatment might have been effective to long-term health damage. Clearly the latter consequence is potentially more harmful and much more important to avoid. Therefore, the researcher directing such a study has a roughly equal interest in avoiding type I and II errors for the first hypothesis but should have a much greater interest in avoiding a type II error for the second hypothesis. An alpha level of .05 might be appropriate for the first hypothesis but the second might require an alpha level of only .20 or even .30.

Power and Beta Level

The **power** of a statistical comparison of groups is *the probability of correctly rejecting a false null hypothesis.* As the *probability of a type II error (accepting a false null hypothesis)* is called **beta** (β), the power of a statistical test is expressed as one minus beta $(1-\beta)$. The probability of a type II error is related to alpha in that use of a smaller alpha level tends to increase beta. However, beta can be made smaller (and the power thereby increased) by means other than using a less stringent (higher) alpha. The most direct method is to increase the number of subjects in the groups to be compared. Beta can also be decreased by using measurement instruments that minimize the variance due to measurement error, and by selecting study populations that have less variance because they are more homogeneous. An overly homogeneous study population, of course, limits the degree to which study results may be generalized to more heterogeneous populations.

TESTS OF SIGNIFICANCE: ALTERNATIVE HYPOTHESES

All tests of the significance of differences between or among groups involve two alternative hypotheses, one of which must be true and the other false. One hypothesis is the null hypothesis, that there is no difference between groups. The other is that there is a difference. However, this alternative to the null hypothesis may take either of two forms. The alternative hypothesis may be that the two groups are different, without regard for directionality of the difference, or it may be that one group will be different from another in a specific direction. For example, if a researcher wishes to test whether two groups of shoppers at a mall carry the same number of credit cards, the non-directional alternative hypothesis is appropriate. On the other hand if the researcher wants to test whether shoppers at one store carry more credit cards than those at a second store then the directional alternative is appropriate. The non-directional alternative hypothesis requires what is called a *two-tailed* test of significance. The directional alternative requires a *one-tailed* test. Each of the statistical tests described in the following sections involves comparison of a statistic expressing the difference between or among groups to a value for that statistic expected to occur at any particular alpha level. The one- or two-tailed version of each test involves an adjustment of the value of that expected statistic. If the researcher is in doubt, selection of the two-tailed test cuts the probability of a type I error in half.

THE *z*-TEST

In Chapter 12 the *z*-score transformation was illustrated as a conversion of data from different measures into common units that could be directly compared. Measurements were converted into units of their own standard deviation, or *z* units. A *z* value of zero represented the mean, a value of 3 meant three standard deviations above the mean, –3 meant three standard deviations below the mean, and so on. A similar computation provides the foundation for a test of the difference between two means called the *z-test*.

If a sample is drawn at random from a larger population then it should be expected that the sample will have the same mean as the original population. Chance may result in the two means being different but if such samples are drawn repeatedly those differences should be small *most* of the time and increasingly larger differences should be increasingly rare. If samples are drawn an infinite number of times and the original population is normally distributed then the differences in means should also be normally distributed. With the distribution of sampling means known to be normal it becomes possible to compute the likelihood of occurrence by chance of any mean and this forms the basis for the *z*-test.

The **z-test** is *a procedure for estimating the probability that the difference between a population mean and a sample mean could occur by chance when no real differences actually exist.* It can also be used to test the difference between two group means. It is a parametric test that requires a normal or approximately normal distribution of data and knowledge of the population variance. Also, the *z*-test is only appropriate when the number of subjects or cases in the sample (or in each group if there are two) is large (30 or more).

In the *z*-test the value of *z* is computed using the equation

$$z = \frac{O - E}{SE} \quad \text{or} \quad z = \frac{\overline{X} - \mu}{SE}$$

where O and $\overline{X}$ are the observed or sample mean, E and μ are the expected or population mean, and SE is the standard error of the population.

If the mean of a sample is being tested to see if it is the same as that of a larger population the standard error is computed as

$$SE = \sigma \sqrt{N}$$

where σ is the standard deviation of the population, and N is the size of the sample.

If two samples are being tested, the standard error is computed as

$$SE = \sqrt{x_1{}^2 + x_2{}^2} \text{ or } SE = \sqrt{SD_1 / \sqrt{N_1} + SD_2 / \sqrt{N_2}}$$

where $x_1{}^2$ and $x_2{}^2$ are the standard errors of the samples, SD_1 and SD_2 are the standard deviations of the samples, and N_1 and N_2 are the sizes of the two samples.

The expected value is the value that would occur in a perfect world if the null hypothesis is correct. In a comparison of a sample mean to a population mean, the expected value for the sample mean is the mean of the population. In a comparison of two samples it is the mean of the other group. The standard error is the standard deviation of the population multiplied by the square root of the sample size.

The computation of the value of z is illustrated in Figure 14.5 and is really nothing more than a z-score transformation of the difference between the means being compared. Once z is calculated it is evaluated by finding the probability of its occurrence by chance. This may be done in any of several ways, all of which are functionally equivalent to the others. A "table of areas under the normal curve" found in many texts on statistics may be used to look up the area for the nearest available value of z. A z value of 2.00, for example, encompasses 95.45 percent of the area under the curve for a two-tailed test, meaning that a z value greater than or equal to 2.00 should occur by chance only 4.55 percent $(100 - 95.45 = 4.55)$ of the time. Therefore, the probability of occurrence by chance is less than .05 ($p <= - 05$). Another method for evaluating z is to use an equation solver software package to find the area, or integral, under the curve. The integral of the normal curve from -2.00 to 2.00 is 95.45 percent of the total

FIGURE 14.5   Computations for a z-test. All 4,715 students in a school system were weighed in October. Weights were normally distributed with a mean and standard deviation as shown above. After all students were given instruction in weight control, a random sample of 103 were weighed in March with the results as shown. Computation of z produced a value of -3.88 which has a chance probability of occurrence less than .001. Therefore, we can be very confident that a change really has occurred.

	MEAN (LBS)	STANDARD DEVIATION (LBS)	NUMBER TESTED
October fitness test	157	10.5	4715
March fitness test	153	10.5	103
Difference	-4		

$$z = O - \frac{E}{SE} = \frac{153-157}{10.5/\sqrt{103}} = \frac{-4}{1.03} = -3.88$$

area, the same answer obtained from the table. Appendix B.1 provides a sample program for doing this using the equation solver called Mathcad. Computer programs that perform z-tests may also provide these areas, or the derived p values, automatically.

THE t-TEST

Two very important limitations of the z-test are that it requires knowledge of the population variance and it is appropriate only when sample sizes are large ($N=\geq 30$). In the t-test the problem of small samples ($N<30$) is addressed through use of **Student's t distribution** in place of the normal distribution. The t distribution is *symmetrical around the mean and looks very much like the normal curve but is somewhat flatter in order to adjust for smaller sample sizes.* Actually there are different t curves for each value of N, each one increasingly platykurtic (flat) as N becomes smaller. The t-test solves the problem of unknown population variance by a process of estimation.

The name Student's does not imply that the t-test is for use by those still in school. It was the pen name of the curve's inventor.

The t-test is appropriate for the evaluation of the difference between two means when sample sizes are small and when the sample distributions are normal or approximately normal. It is relatively robust with respect to deviations from normality but large deviations warrant at least use of a more stringent alpha level in order to avoid a type I error. The t-test is essentially equivalent to the z-test when samples are larger than 30.

The t-test may be used to compare two independent sample means, to compare an independent sample to a population mean, or to compare two dependent means. Here the term dependent mean is used to indicate the means of two different measurements of the same group of subjects, as occur when a single group of subjects is measured before and after some treatment, or the means of two different groups selected by a process of matching rather than a random process. The t-test has also been used, and may occasionally still be used, in studies involving more than two groups or more than two measurements of one group but such use is considered obsolete and inferior to more sophisticated methods such as the analysis of variance.

A t-test is conducted by calculating the value of the statistic t and then evaluating the probability of obtaining at least that value, expressed as p. As was the case for the z-test, t may be compared to values obtained from a "table of critical values of t" found in many statistics texts, or p may be obtained mathematically by using an equation solver software package or some other method to find the area under the t curve. Tests may be one-tailed or two-tailed. Appendix B.2 provides an example of how this may be done using Mathcad. The equations for t are rather complex, making errors likely if hand computation is attempted. Fortunately, statistical computer software packages are widely available and nearly all offer t-tests for every situation likely to be encountered. Such programs usually include computation of exact p values.

ANALYSIS OF VARIANCE

Figure 14.6 shows the raw data from a study of the effects of caffeine ingestion on a measure of reaction time involving a simple decision-making process.

FIGURE 14.6   Data from a study of caffeine effects on reaction time.

	CAFFEINE 200 MG (N=12)		CAFFEINE 100 MG (N=12)		PLACEBO 0 MG (N=12)		COMBINED
REACTION TIMES	143	140	145	136	138	142	
	145	144	144	145	145	144	
	134	140	134	144	143	149	
	135	137	136	138	145	150	
	147	145	155	159	149	151	
	146	134	165	130	151	139	
MEAN	140.83		144.25		145.50		143.52

Three groups, each consisting of 12 subjects, were created by random selection from a class of 36 students. One group served as a control, undergoing all the same experiences related to the study as the treatment groups but receiving a placebo in the form of caffeine-free coffee in place of the regular coffee given to the treatment groups. A double-blind procedure was used to control for expectation effects. Even in such a simple and well-controlled experiment, however, there is still more than one source for the variation found in the dependent variable. The experiment was designed to examine the effects of caffeine ingestion—the independent variable—so clearly that is one source of variation in the dependent measure. Other sources of variation in this experiment are random variation in the dependent measure and error in various forms.

The analysis of variance (ANOVA) is an approach to data analysis that seeks to *partition* the variance that exists within the dependent measures of a study in order to quantify the proportion of that variance that may be attributed to each source of variation. Although its application is limited to parametric data and to dependent variables that may safely be assumed to have a normal or approximately normal distribution, it is a powerful data analysis technique. Although it is mathematically related to the *t*-test it is not restricted to situations involving only two groups of subjects, nor is it restricted to studies of only a single independent variable.

An analysis of variance is conducted much like any other statistical group comparison test. First the variance is partitioned into the various categories permitted by the study's design by dividing the sum of squares for that category by the possible degrees of freedom for that category to obtain the mean square or *variance estimate* for that category. For a simple study with one independent variable and two or more groups of subjects the categories are called *between groups variance* and *within groups variance*. The between groups variance is the variation that is considered the main effect of the independent variable. The within groups variance is not attributable to any source within the design of the study and so is attributed to error. For more complex designs there may be several between group comparisons, called the *main effects* of each independent variable, and several combinations of *interactive effects* of two or more independent variables. Next, the value of a statistic, this time called *F*, or the *F* ratio, is computed

FIGURE 14.7   The concept of variance partitioning. The idea of variance partitioning is illustrated by the following three sets of scores. In set 1 all the scores are the same so there is no variance
to partition. In set 2, there is considerable variance between groups A, B, and C but no variance at
all within any of the groups. In set three there is variance both between and within groups.

SET 1			SET 2			SET C		
A	B	C	A	B	C	A	B	C
80	80	80	60	80	100	78	82	80
80	80	80	60	80	100	82	80	82
80	80	80	60	80	100	76	84	84
80	80	80	60	80	100	83	79	81
80	80	80	60	80	100	85	78	86
80	80	80	60	80	100	81	77	83

as the ratio of the variance estimate for a category to the estimate for error.
Finally, the probability of obtaining such a value by chance is obtained from a
table available in most statistics texts or calculated directly. A Mathcad program
for this is provided in Appendix C.3. A value of F is obtained for each separate
source of variation built into the study design. The degrees of freedom for each F
ratio are the degrees of freedom of the numerator and denominator of the F ratio.

For the one-way design the equation for the F ratio is

$$F = \frac{Var.Est._b}{Var.Est._w}$$

where $Var.Est._b$ and $Var.Est._w$ are the variance
estimates for the between and within groups
variances.

The equations for the variance estimates
are

$$Var.Est._b = \frac{\sum \frac{(\sum X_g)^2}{N_g} - \frac{(\sum X)^2}{N}}{k-1}$$

and

$$Var.Est._w = \frac{\sum X^2 - \sum \frac{(\sum X)^2_g}{N_g}}{N-k}$$

where X stands for the raw scores, N is the
number of subjects in a group or overall, g
stands for the group number, and k is the
number of groups.

The equations for the degrees of freedom
for the F ratio are $k-1$ for the numerator and
$N-k$ for the denominator.

SOURCES OF VARIANCE

One-Way Design
Main Effects of Variable A
Error

Two-Way Design
Main Effects of Variable A
Main Effects of Variable B
A×B Interaction
Error

Three-Way Design
Main Effects of Variable A
Main Effects of Variable B
Main Effects of Variable C
A×B Interaction
A×C Interaction
B×C Interaction
A×B×C Interaction
Error

As the design of a study increases in complexity, involving multiple independent variables, multiple levels of independent variables, repeated measurements of dependent variables, or other design attributes, the computation of an analysis of variance can quickly become quite complex and certainly pass well beyond the scope of this text. The general concept, however, is illustrated in the examples that follow for one-way and two-way analyses. In practice such computations will almost always be performed by computer using a statistical analysis package.

ONE-WAY ANALYSIS OF VARIANCE

A one-way analysis of variance is used with designs involving one independent variable expressed in the design as two or more categorical *levels*. In the study of caffeine effects on reaction time there are three levels—200 mg, 100 mg, and 0 mg—of the independent variable of caffeine use. In such a design there are two sources of variance for the dependent variable of reaction time that may be isolated, the variance that occurs between different levels of the independent variable and the error variance that occurs within each level. (Note that it is possible that the calculated error variance is not all due to error, but as there is nothing in the design to partition the variance any further it must be *assumed* to be all error.) The ratio of the between groups variance to the within groups variance is the value of F. The F ratio has degrees of freedom of the number of groups minus one for the numerator and the number of subjects minus the number of groups for the denominator.

Figure 14.8 shows the computations for a one-way analysis of variance using the data from the study of caffeine effects on reaction time. The result is presented in the *ANOVA Summary Table* at the bottom; everything else is either raw data or one of the intermediate computational steps. (Computer programs will generally print or display only the summary table.) The column labeled *variance estimate* (sometimes called the mean square) shows the variance attributable to each source in the table. The ratio of the between and within groups variance estimates is the value of the F ratio and is approximately 1.385. For 2 and 33 degrees of freedom this fails to exceed the critical value of F at the .05 level (the actual probability of occurrence by chance is 27.7 percent) so it may be concluded that the difference between groups is very unlikely to be real.

TWO-WAY ANALYSIS OF VARIANCE

A two-way analysis of variance is used with designs involving two independent variables, each of which is expressed in the design as having two or more categorical levels. Suppose, for example, that in the study of caffeine effects on reaction time subjects were also classified according to gender. Even though subject gender is not a true independent variable, because it is not actually manipulated by the researcher, it is treated as such in the analysis. In such a design there are four sources of variance in the dependent variable that may be isolated: the variance attributable to the three different levels of caffeine use, the variance attributable to the two levels of gender, the variance attributable to the interaction of caffeine use and gender, and the variance attributable to error. The analysis, which is called a *3 by 2 analysis of variance,* produces three different

FIGURE 14.8   Computations for a one-way ANOVA.

CAFFEINE 200 MG				CAFFEINE 100 MG				PLACEBO			
Scores		Squares		Scores		Squares		Scores		Squares	
143	140	20449	19600	145	136	21025	18496	138	142	19044	20164
145	144	21025	20736	144	145	20736	21025	145	144	21025	20736
134	140	17956	19600	134	144	17956	20736	143	149	20449	22201
135	137	18225	18769	136	138	18496	19044	145	150	21025	22500
147	145	21609	21025	155	159	24025	25281	149	151	22201	22801
146	134	21316	17956	165	130	27225	16900	151	139	22801	19321

Group Sums of Scores			Squared Sum of Scores/N
$\sum X = 1690$	$\sum X = 1731$	$\sum X = 1746$	$\dfrac{(\sum X)^2}{N} = 741608$

Squared Group Sums/Group N			Squared Sum of Scores/N
$\dfrac{(\sum X)^2}{N_1} = \dfrac{1690^2}{12}$ $= 238008$	$\dfrac{(\sum X)^2}{N_2} = \dfrac{1731^2}{12}$ $= 249697$	$\dfrac{(\sum X)^2}{N_3} = \dfrac{1746^2}{12}$ $= 254043$	$\sum \dfrac{(\sum X)^2}{N}$ $= 741748$

Group Sums of Squares			Sums of Squares
$\sum (X^2_1) = 238266$	$\sum (X^2_2) = 250945$	$\sum (X^2_3) = 254268$	$\sum (X^2) = 743479$

Number of Subjects = $N = 36$ Number of Groups = $k = 3$

Between Groups   Sum of Squares = $\sum \dfrac{(\sum X)^2}{N_g} - \dfrac{(\sum X)^2}{N} = 741748 - 741608 = 140$

degrees of freedom = $k-1 = 2$

Within Groups   Sum of Squares = $\sum X^2 - \sum \dfrac{(\sum X)^2}{N_g} = 743479 - 741748 = 1731$

degrees of freedom = $N-k = 33$

Total   Sum of Squares = $\sum (X^2) - \dfrac{(\sum X)^2}{N} = 743479 - 741608 = 1871$

degrees of freedom = $N-1 = 35$

ANOVA Summary Table MEAN SQUARE				
SOURCE	**SS**	**DF**	**VAR. EST.**	**F**
Between Groups	140	2	70	1.385
Within Groups	1730	33	52.4	
Total	1871	35		

CRITICAL $F_{2, 33}$

.05 - 3.29

.01 - 5.31

FIGURE 14.9   Two-way analysis of variance. This figure shows the raw data and the analysis of variance table but omits the intermediate computations, which are almost always left to the computer.

SUBJECT GENDER	CAFFEINE 200 MG		CAFFEINE 100 MG		PLACEBO	
Male	143	140	145	136	138	142
	134	140	134	144	143	149
	147	145	155	159	149	151
Female	145	144	144	145	145	144
	135	137	136	138	145	150
	146	134	165	130	151	139

Analysis of Variance Table				
SOURCE	SUM OF SQUARES	DF	MEAN SQUARE	F
Caffeine	140.056	2	70.028	1.231
Gender	12.250	1	12.25	0.215
Caffeine-Gender Interaction	12.167	2	6.083	0.107
Error	1706.5	30	56.88	

F ratios, one for each independent variable (main effects) and one for the one possible interaction effect. Each is the ratio of the mean square or variance estimate for the corresponding main effect or interaction and the mean square for error. The degrees of freedom will be 2 for the main effect of caffeine use, 1 for the main effect of gender, and 2 for the interaction effect.

Figure 14.9 shows the analysis of variance for a two-way design using the same data used for the one-way example but with the added information on subject gender. The intermediate computations are omitted as these will almost always be left to the computer. None of the F ratios are significant at the .05 level.

FIXED, RANDOM, AND MIXED EFFECTS IN ANOVA

In any analysis of variance involving two or more independent variables, the computation of the F ratio varies slightly depending on the particular *model* being tested. The models being tested may be *fixed* effects, *random* effects, or *mixed* effects. A **fixed effects model** is one in which *all of the independent variables are truly categorical or one in which, even though one or more independent variables are actually continuous, the researcher is only interested in the effects of the particular levels used.* Gender is clearly categorical. The dosage of a drug that is manufactured in only 5, 10, and 15 milligram tablets is an example of a continuous variable that might be of interest only at those

FIGURE 14.10 The ANOVA summary table for the data given in Figure 14.9 using a mixed effects model. The *F* ratio for the random variable (caffeine dosage) is computed by dividing the mean square for caffeine effects by the mean square for interaction. The computation of other *F* ratios is unaffected.

Analysis of Variance Table				
SOURCE	SUM OF SQUARES	DF	MEAN SQUARE	F
Caffeine	140.056	2	70.028	11.51
Gender	12.250	1	12.25	0.215
C/G Interaction	12.167	2	6.083	0.107
Error	1706.5	30	56.88	

specific levels. A **random effects model** is one in which *all of the independent variables are truly continuous and the researcher's interest is not limited only to the specific levels used.* Subject age is frequently reduced to a few categories, for example, but is generally of interest as a continuous variable. A **mixed effects model** is simply one in which *at least one independent variable is fixed and at least one is random.*

The two-way ANOVA shown in Figure 14.9 uses the computation for a fixed effects model. The *F* ratios are computed by dividing the mean square for a variable or interaction by the mean square for error. If the researcher in this study were interested in treating caffeine dosage as continuous the proper computation would be as a mixed effects model. In such circumstance the *F* ratio for the main effect of caffeine would be the mean square for caffeine divided by the mean square for interaction of caffeine with gender. (In three or higher way ANOVA designs all of the interactions involving the variable treated as random would be summed in the denominator of the *F* ratio.) The recomputed ANOVA table for the mixed effects model is shown in Figure 14.10. In a random effects model, interaction effects involving each variable are included in the denominator of each corresponding *F* ratio. The computation of *F* ratios for interaction effects is not affected.

MULTIPLE COMPARISONS

A significant effect for an independent variable in an analysis of variance means that significant (unlikely to be due to chance) differences are present that may be attributable to differences in the levels of that variable. If there are only two levels of that variable then it is clear just where the difference lies. We can attribute, with the indicated degree of confidence, the difference in the two groups to the difference between the two levels of the independent variable. When there are three or more levels of the significant variable, however, it is not yet clear where the difference lies. Suppose, for example, that an experiment involving lecture, guided discovery, and cooperative learning as categories (levels) of teaching method shows a significant effect. Is the lecture method different in effect from guided discovery? Is it different from cooperative learning? Is guided discovery different from cooperative learning? It is quite possible that some *but not all* such comparisons are significant. Further analysis is needed to determine which comparisons are significant.

One approach to finding the significance of two-group comparisons after a multiple group ANOVA has shown overall significance is to perform separate analyses (such as *t*-tests) on each two-group comparison. However, such an approach leads to an inflated alpha level unless some kind of correction is included. Three separate *t*-tests with an apparent alpha level of .05 for each leads to an actual probability of at least one type I error of .143 (rounded figure). Some method of correction must be employed if the intended alpha is to be maintained.

Common methods for making such multiple comparisons include tests known as orthogonal comparisons, Scheffè, Tukey, Newman-Keuls, and Duncan, all but one named for their inventors. The computations involved in each method are beyond the scope of this text and are almost always performed by computer in any case. However, a brief review of the concept and application of each is in order.

The **orthogonal comparison** approach is essentially *an extension of the analysis of variance that may be used to test the differences between independent groups or combinations of groups.* The idea is that the total variance between *k* groups can be partitioned into *k–1* portions, each attributable to a different comparison. Because this allows only certain combinations of comparisons to be tested, the orthogonal comparison methods are considered appropriate only for testing comparisons that have been identified in advance (a priori) and not for locating the sources of differences after overall significance has been established. As in the analysis of variance, a sum of squares is found for each orthogonal comparison and a standard *F*-test is used to determine the significance of each.

If the independent variable of interest is interval or ratio in scale, in reality the orthogonal comparison approach may be extended to make an analysis of trend. Although the details are beyond the scope of this text, a *trend analysis* is an attempt to determine the shape of the relationship between the independent and dependent variable across the tested levels.

The Scheffè, Tukey, Newman-Keuls, and Duncan methods are all able to examine all possible comparisons irrespective of orthogonality. Of these, the Scheffè test, which is based on use of the F distribution, is the most flexible and the most rigorous in its power to avoid a type I error. The Scheffè method can be performed when groups are unequal in size and can be used to test combinations of groups as well as pairs of single groups. The other three methods are based on the t distribution and are limited to comparisons of pairs of single groups of equal size. The order of decreasing resistance to type I error is Scheffè, Tukey, Newman-Keuls, and Duncan.

ANALYSIS OF COVARIANCE

The alert student may have noticed in the previous section that in an analysis of variance each independent variable must vary across only a small number of levels. In the illustrated computations, for example, the variable of gender varied across just two levels and the variable of caffeine ingestion, which in the real world is a continuous variable, varied across just three levels. The analysis of variance operates under the requirement that the independent variables are all

FIGURE 14.11   Analysis of covariance for a study with two categorical independent variables and one continuous independent variable. The method and gender variables are categorical; age is continuous.

SUBJECT	METHOD	GENDER	AGE	DISTANCE SWAM (YDS)
1	Crawl	M	21	25
2	Breast Stroke	M	18	115
3	Breast Stroke	F	23	135
⋮				
129	Breast Stroke	M	17	100
130	Crawl	F	25	35

Analysis of Covariance Summary Table				
SOURCE	SUM OF SQUARES	DF	MEAN SQUARE	F
Age	1178.22	1	1178.22	0.095
Gender	5985.18	1	5985.18	0.482
Method	307550.44	1	307550.44	24.76
Interactions	10749.77	1	10759.77	0.86
Residual (Error)	1565044.75	126	12420.99	

categorical or that they are treated as such. Furthermore, good design requires a certain minimum number of subjects receiving each combination of levels of the independent variables and that the number of subjects in each *cell* be approximately equal. Meeting such requirements is often undesirable or inconvenient for several reasons. First, studies involving several independent variables can quickly become unwieldy and expensive in terms of subject assignment to cells, particularly when classification rather than true independent variables are involved. A study involving three levels of caffeine use, two levels of gender, and five levels of age would require $3 \times 2 \times 5 = 30$ cells, each with perhaps 15 subjects using an analysis of variance. Second, creating a small number of categories for a variable that actually varies across a broad range of values creates a loss of information. All subjects within a category are treated as though they are all equal for that variable when, in fact, they may vary considerably from one another. Subjects within an age category of 25 to 30, for example, may actually range in age from 25 years and 0 days to 30 years and 364 days. Finally, there are many research situations that involve variables, such as pre-test scores, that are clearly likely to have an effect on the dependent measure but that cannot be controlled or reduced to a few categories. The researcher cannot control for variation in pre-test scores, for example, if a main effect of or an interaction effect with pre-test scores is desired.

Situations involving one or more independent variables of a continuous nature *and* one or more categorical independent variable may be analyzed using the technique of analysis of covariance. The analysis of covariance, abbreviated as ANCOVA, is essentially the same as the analysis of variance but uses the technique of regression to account or adjust for variance in the dependent measure attributable to the continuous independent variable or variables.

Figure 14.11 above shows an abbreviated table of raw data and the analysis of covariance summary table for a study involving the effects of the continuous independent variable of age and the categorical independent variables of gender and content of instruction on a measure of success in learning to swim. As the intermediate computations are rather complex and would almost certainly be done by computer they are not shown. The resulting F values are significant for the main effects of content of instruction and gender and not significant for main effects of age or any interactions.

REGRESSION ANALYSIS OF VARIANCE

Data from studies in which *all* of the independent variables are continuous rather than categorical may be analyzed using the technique of regression analysis of variance. Technically, any analysis of variance or analysis of covariance is actually a special case of regression analysis of variance in which at least one (ANCOVA) or all (ANOVA) independent variables are reduced to categories. Given otherwise identical data, a regression analysis of variance using data in which one variable occurs in just a few values and an analysis of variance treating the same variable as the same number of categories or levels will produce the same results.

The complexities of regression analysis are not covered here as they go far beyond the purpose of this book, and, indeed, will fill a far larger book.

MULTIVARIATE ANALYSIS OF VARIANCE AND REGRESSION

Each of the statistical tests discussed thus far is designed for use in studies involving only a single dependent variable, but many studies employ several dependent measures. For example, the caffeine effect study described previously could have used several different measures of reaction time, such as simple reaction time, decision reaction time, and so forth. If the number of dependent variables is very small (such as 2 or 3) and a fairly stringent alpha level is chosen, the researcher may be relatively safe simply treating the data as if it were from several entirely different studies. The researcher would then simply perform separate analyses for each dependent variable. However, any increase in the overall number of dependent variables increases the chance that a type I error may be made. A test statistic (t, x^2, F, or other) that just achieves significance at the .05 level is, by its own definition, expected to occur by chance about 5 percent of the time. Thus, the researcher doing an analysis involving one dependent variable and choosing the .05 alpha level has one chance in 20 of falsely rejecting the null hypothesis. However, the chances of such an error are nearly doubled (the exact figure is 9.75 percent) and nearly tripled (the exact figure is 14.2625 percent) when there are two or three independent variables. In order to maintain the desired level of confidence, there must be some adjustment in the computations to account for the changes in probabilities brought about by additional dependent variables. The techniques of multiple analysis of variance (abbreviated as MANOVA) and multiple regression analysis make these adjustments. Although the computations involved are far too complex for inclusion in this text, they are included in most major statistical software packages.

NONPARAMETRIC TESTS

When the data permits, the parametric tests already discussed in this chapter are preferable to the nonparametric methods that follow. Parametric tests tend to have more power than nonparametric methods but make more assumptions about the distribution and type of data under analysis. Even though the parametric methods are relatively resistant toward violations of assumptions about data distribution they are not invulnerable. Parametric methods also require data that is interval or ratio in scale. Nonparametric methods are the order of the day whenever the distribution of measurement data is not in conformance with parametric assumptions or is unknown or when that data is not interval or ratio in scale.

CHI-SQUARE

Although a full discussion of its derivation is well beyond the scope of this text, the distribution of the statistic chi-square (x^2) forms the basis of a variety of nonparametric tests. **Chi-square** is *a theoretical distribution that is used in essentially the same way as the* t *or* F *distributions.* The value of chi-square for a set of observed data is computed and then evaluated, using direct computation or a table of pre-computed values to determine its probability of occurrence by chance, exactly as is done in the *t*-test. Appendix C4 provides a program for computing critical values of chi-square using Mathcad.

Chi-square is usually used in the analysis of data consisting of counts or frequencies or data that has been converted to frequencies. Chi-square tests are used to evaluate the *independence* of two or more sets of frequencies and as tests of the *goodness of fit* of a set of frequencies to some theoretical distribution. A study examining the preferences of sports writers for the designated hitter in baseball and the three-point shot in basketball is an example involving a test of independence. If preferences are independent then knowledge of a writer's preference for one rule tells us nothing about that writer's preference for the other. A test for goodness of fit would be used in a study to see if the incidence of handedness and eye dominance among professional baseball players is the same as in the general population.

The value of chi-square for any set of frequency data may be computed using the equation

$$\chi^2 = \sum \frac{(O-E)^2}{E}$$

where O is the observed frequency, and E is the expected frequency.

CHI-SQUARE TEST OF INDEPENDENCE

Figure 14.12 shows the results of a study of bat material preference among softball players. One hundred softball players in a municipal league were selected

Figure 14.12   Bat material preference of 100 softball players.

GENDER	MATERIAL	FREQUENCY
Male	Wood	39
Female	Wood	19
Male	Metal	22
Female	Metal	20
TOTAL		100

Figure 14.13   Computations for chi-square test for independence.

a) Observed Bat Preferences				b) Expected Bat Preferences			
	MALE	FEMALE	TOTAL		MALE	FEMALE	TOTAL
Wood	39	19	58	Wood	35.4	22.6	58
Metal	22	20	42	Metal	25.6	16.4	42
Total	61	39	100	Total	61	39	100

c) Chi-Square Computation				
O	E	$O-E$	$(O-E)^2$	$\dfrac{(O-E)^2}{E}$
39	35.4	3.6	13	.37
19	22.6	−3.6	13	.58
22	25.6	−3.6	13	.51
20	16.4	3.6	13	.79

$$df = 1 \qquad \chi^2 = \sum \frac{(O-E)^2}{E} = 2.25 \quad \text{(Not significant)}$$

at random and asked if they preferred to use metal or wood bats. Data on subject gender was also recorded. A chi-square test of independence may be used to determine the probability that bat preference is independent of gender.

Figure 14.13a shows the bat preference data rearranged into a 2-by-2 contingency table. The four cells of the table represent the four possible combinations of gender and bat preference. If "plastic" had been an option for players to choose, then the contingency table would be 2-by-3 cells. Figure 14.13b shows the expected frequencies for each cell if the null hypothesis (complete independence) is true. Expected cell frequencies are computed using the equation

$$\frac{R \times C}{N}$$

where R and C are the row and column totals, and N is the total number of subjects to adjust each variable for variation in the other.

The computation of chi-square is shown in Figure 14.13c. The value for chi-square is 2.25. In this case the number of degrees of freedom is 1 as once the frequency for one cell is determined the marginal totals fix the other three. The computed value of chi-square fails to reach the critical value of 3.84 for 1 degree of freedom and the .05 level. Therefore it must be concluded that bat preference is independent of gender.

CHI-SQUARE TEST FOR GOODNESS OF FIT

Figure 14.14 shows data from a study of the distribution of hits to field (left, center, and right) at a baseball park and for all other parks in the league. The team owners are concerned that the prevailing wind or the distance to the out-field fences may be causing a distortion in the distribution of hits. There have been 510 hits over the past two seasons. A survey of other parks shows that 41 percent of all 3625 hits have been to centerfield, 35 percent to left, and 24 percent to right. If the null hypothesis that the distributions of hits are not different is correct then the 510 hits should have gone approximately 41 percent to center, 35 percent to left, and 24 percent to right. That is, the observed frequencies for the park should fit the pattern predicted by the other parks. Therefore the observed number of hits to each field must be compared to these expected values. The computation of chi-square in this case is shown in Figure 14.15.

FIGURE 14.14   Hits to field for selected fields and league average.

	LOCAL PARK	LEAGUE TENDENCIES
Right	133	870
Center	178	1486
Left	199	1269
Total	510	3625

FIGURE 14.15   Chi-square computation for goodness of fit of hits to field data. Note that a significant chi-square here means a poor fit—the distribution of hits is different from that of the league.

O	E	O–E	$(O–E)^2$	$\dfrac{(O–E)^2}{E}$
133	122	11	121	.9918
178	209	−31	961	4.598
199	179	20	400	2.234

$$df = 2 \qquad \chi^2 = \sum \frac{(O–E)^2}{E} = 7.824 \quad (p<=.05)$$

THE VALIDITY OF CHI-SQUARE

Chi-square is a powerful and widely used statistical tool for many situations in which the assumptions required by the parametric statistics do not hold, but it is not entirely free of assumptions.

Chi-square is for use with frequencies or counts or with other forms of data that have been converted to frequencies. It is not appropriate for use with data consisting of ratios or proportions. For example, in the example given above for the goodness of fit test it would not be appropriate to use the percentage or proportion of hits to each field as the observed or expected values because proportions and percentages are independent of sample size. The actual number of hits to each field must be used. Chi-square is also inappropriate in situations in which the categories to which observations are assigned are not independent or not mutually exclusive. If, for example, a survey was conducted asking patrons of a concession stand their preferences in beverages and more than one response was recorded from all or some subjects, then some observations in the data would not be independent because they would come from a common source.

The chi-square statistic itself can be somewhat biased in favor of a type I error when one or more of the *expected* cell frequencies are small. With designs involving only one degree of freedom, expected cell frequencies less than 10 (some statisticians say 5) can produce significant bias; the problem is less important with 2 or more degrees of freedom in the data. When designs with 1 degree of freedom are employed and there are small expected frequencies for some cells, the computation of chi-square should be modified by using *Yate's Correction for Continuity*, which is to subtract .5 from each observed count that exceeds its expected value and to add .5 to each count that is less than its expected value. Statistical software packages that perform chi-square tests will often invoke the Yate's correction automatically when small expected frequencies are encountered.

SIGN TESTS

The parametric tests are inappropriate when their required assumption of normally distributed data is not met. In such circumstances it may be desirable to convert interval or ratio scale data into frequency data and use a test based on the chi-square statistic to compare groups. Sign tests are tests employing the transformation of data points into the categories of positive, negative, or zero, usually on the basis of the data point's position relative to the group median.

The Median Test (Sign Test for Independent Samples)

Figure 14.16 shows the weights of two samples of subjects selected at random from clients concluding a smoking cessation program. The samples are independent because they are composed of different people. Notice that there is a substantial difference between the group means. But is this difference, large as it is, real or due to chance? The *t*- and *F*-tests are often used to evaluate the difference between group means, but in this case, even though the data is ratio in scale, the assumption of normality is not met. The mean weight of one group is severely skewed to the right by the presence of one very obese individual.

FIGURE 14.16   Post treatment weights of two groups of subjects. The difference between means appears quite large and could be evaluated for significance with a *t*- or *F*-test. However, the mean of group 1 is seriously skewed by one very extreme score. Therefore, a sign test for independent groups (median test) is more appropriate.

Post Smoking Cessation Weights of Two Groups of Clients	
GROUP 1	**GROUP 2**
(155 158 444 170 145)	(175 182 137 160 157 172)
(180 175 162 163)	(163 193 171 167 175)
$\bar{X} = 194.6, Md = 163$	$\bar{X} = 168.4, Md = 171$

FIGURE 14.17   Computations for the sign test for independent groups (median test). The chi-square value of 0 is obviously not significant. Therefore, the group medians are not significantly different. Note that Yate's correction for continuity was used. Even without Yate's correction, however, chi-square is still not significant.

Group 1
$(--++-)$
$(++--)$

Combined Median = 168.5

Group 2
$(++---+)$
$(-++-+)$

	Observed				*Expected*	
	GROUP 1	**GROUP 2**		**TOTAL**	**GROUP 1**	**GROUP 2**
+	~~4~~ 4.5	~~6~~ 5.5		10	4.5	5.5
−	~~5~~ 4.5	~~5~~ 5.5		10	4.5	5.5
Total	9	11		20		

O	*E*	*O–E*	$(O–E)^2$	$\dfrac{(O–E)^2}{E}$
4.5	4.5	0	0	0
5.5	5.5	0	0	0
4.5	4.5	0	0	0
5.5	5.5	0	0	0

$$\chi^2 = \sum \frac{(O-E)^2}{E} = 0$$

Determining the statistical significance of the difference between two means makes little sense when the mean itself is misleading as a measure of central tendency. In such situations it is more appropriate to evaluate the difference between the two-group medians using a sign test for independent samples, also known as the *median* test.

The median test converts each measurement value into a + if it is greater than the combined median or a − if it is less than the combined median. (Perhaps more simply, the scores in each group that are above and below the combined median are counted.) The null hypothesis, that each sample has the same number of scores above as below the combined median, is evaluated using chi-square. The computation is shown in Figure 14.17.

Sign Test for Correlated Samples

The sign test may be extended to correlated or paired samples by examining the sign of the difference between each pair of measures. (The two measures must have a common scale.) If the null hypothesis, that the two samples are not different, is correct, then the two samples should have the same median. If this is true then there should be an equal number of positive and negative differences between pairs of observations as each sample will have an equal number of observations above and below the median.

Figure 14.18 shows a set of paired measurements of golf scores for 12 golfers playing 18 holes on each of two successive days, and the computations for a sign test to evaluate the difference in medians for the two days. The null hypothesis is that the difference between the medians is due to chance only. In this case there are 8 positive and 4 negative differences. Had any pairs of values

FIGURE 14.18   Sign test for two correlated samples.

GOLFER	DAY 1 SCORE	DAY 2 SCORE	DAY 1–DAY 2	SIGN
A	82	81	1	+
B	90	88	2	+
C	88	89	−1	−
D	79	84	−5	−
E	85	86	−1	−
F	82	84	−2	−
G	81	86	−5	−
H	80	84	−2	−
I	86	80	6	+
J	81	82	−1	−
K	80	81	−1	−
L	82	81	1	+

O	E	$O-E$	$(O-E)^2$	$\dfrac{(O-E)^2}{E}$
4.5	6	−1.5	2.25	.375
7.5	6	1.5	2.25	.375

$$\chi^2 = \sum \frac{(O-E)^2}{E} = .75$$

been equal their difference would be zero and they would be dropped from the computation. Using Yate's correction, chi-square is used to determine the chance of obtaining 8 pluses and 4 minuses with expectations of 6 and 6. With 1 degree of freedom the calculated chi-square value of .75 is not significant at the .05 level. Therefore, the null hypothesis cannot be rejected.

An alternative method of computation for this test is to use the equation

$$\chi^2 = \frac{2\,[n_+ - n_-] - 1}{\sqrt{n_+ + n_-}}$$

where n_+ and n_- are the numbers of pluses and minuses.

Sign Test for Three or More Independent Samples

The two independent sample sign test can be applied to studies involving three or more samples. The computation is essentially the same as for the two-sample test. First the median across all samples is found. The number of scores above and below this median in each sample is then counted. The observed counts of pluses and minuses in each sample are then compared, using chi-square, to the equal distribution that would be expected under the null hypothesis that the sample medians are the same as the overall median. Finally the computed value of chi-square is compared to the critical value for n-1 (where n is the number of samples) degrees of freedom. Figure 14.19 shows the computations for this test for four sets of bowling scores. In the example the chi-square value of 8.52 is significant at the .05 level.

RANK TESTS

In the study of sport in particular there are many occasions involving ranked or ordinal data. The order of finish in competitive events, seeding arrangements for tournaments, and the rankings of teams by sports writers are all examples. There may also be frequent occasions when data collected using an interval or ratio measurement scale may be transformed into ordinal data as when actual scores or times are reduced to first place, second, third, and so on. Differences in samples consisting of ranks may be evaluated using chi-square based tests known as *rank tests*.

Wilcoxon Rank Sum Test
for Two Independent Samples of Ranks

Any two samples drawn at random from a single set of rankings should be expected to have approximately the same medians and approximately the same distribution around their medians. (Note that the medians and distributions are described above as only approximately equal because if ties are not present they cannot be exactly equal.) If the medians and distributions are, in fact, equivalent, then the sums of each sample will also be about equal. The Wilcoxon rank sums test compares the actual rank sums of two independent samples of ranks to their probability of occurrence by chance to test the null hypothesis that the difference between the two sums is due only to chance. The computations are illustrated in

FIGURE 14.19   Sign test for three or more independent samples. Here the sign test is applied to four samples of bowling scores to determine if the sample medians differ significantly from each other.

GROUP 1	GROUP 2	GROUP 3	GROUP 4	ALL GROUPS
186 184 177 182	178 186 179 182	148 176 197 172	169 175 172	
179 135 181 132	180 142 182 187	150 196 195 157	143 196 158	
180 155	181 139	191 161 158	174 175	
$n = 10$	$n = 10$	$n = 11$	$n = 8$	$n = 39$
$Md = 80.5$	$Md = 80.5$	$Md = 72$	$Md = 73$	$Md = 78$
$\bar{X} = 72.1$	$\bar{X} = 73.6$	$\bar{X} = 72.8$	$\bar{X} = 70.25$	
$+ = 7$	$+ = 7$	$+ = 4$	$+ = 1$	
$- = 3$	$- = 3$	$- = 7$	$- = 7$	

O	E	$O–E$	$(O–E)^2$	$\dfrac{(O–E)^2}{E}$
7	5	2	4	.8
3	5	–2	4	.8
7	5	2	4	.8
7	5	–2	4	.8
4	5.5	–1.5	2.25	.41
7	5.5	1.5	2.25	.41
1	4	–3	9	2.25
7	4	–3	9	2.25

$$df = 4–1 = 3 \qquad x^2 = \sum \frac{(O–E)^2}{E} = 8.52 \qquad (p<=.05)$$

Figure 14.20 using times for members of two cross country running teams in a five-mile race. The raw scores (the running times) are first converted to overall ranks using average ranks in cases of ties, and the sums of ranks found for each sample. In the example the sums are 96.5 and 55. The sum for the smaller sample (team B) is then evaluated in either of two ways to determine the probability of obtaining that or an even smaller value by chance alone. If the sample sizes are both 25 or less, the sum of ranks (the smaller of the two sums) may be evaluated by direct computation or by using a table of pre-determined critical values available in many statistics texts. A computer program for the direct computation for total sample sizes of up to about 16 is provided in Appendix C.4. With the data given in the example, significance is not quite achieved at the .05 level. Alternatively, if the sample sizes are each 8 or higher, the difference in rank sums may be evaluated using a z-test with z calculated using the equation

$$z = \frac{|R_1 - \bar{R}_1| - 1}{\sqrt{\dfrac{N_1 N_2 (N_1 + N_2 + 1)}{12}}}$$

FIGURE 14.20   Sum of ranks computation for the Wilcoxon or Mann Whitney U tests. The smaller of the two sums is evaluated for statistical significance.

Team A		Team B	
TIME	**OVERALL RANK**	**TIME**	**OVERALL RANK**
25:14	10	25:10	7
26:10	17	24:49	2
25:22	11.5	24:52	3
25:13	8.5	24:59	5
25:35	14	25:13	8.5
24:41	1	25:22	11.5
25:49	15	24:53	4
25:32	13	25:06	6
26:03	16		
	$N_1 = 9$		$N_1 = 8$
	$R_a = 96.5$		$R_b = 55$

where (N_1) and (N_2) are the numbers of ranks in each sample, (R_1) is the smaller sum of ranks, and $(\overline{R}_1)$ is a mean defined as

$$\frac{N_1(N_1 + N_2 + 1)}{2}.$$

If there are a large number of ties among the ranks, z is calculated with a correction factor using the equation

$$z = \frac{|R_1 - \overline{R}_1| - 1}{\sqrt{\frac{N_1 N_2}{N(N-1)} \left(\frac{N^3 - 1}{12} - \sum \frac{(t^3 - t)}{12}\right)}}$$

in which N is the number of ranks in both samples combined, t is the number of ties in each set of ties, and N_1, N_2, $\overline{R}_1$, and R_1 are as defined above.

Mann Whitney U Test for Two Independent Samples of Ranks

Another test for two independent samples of ranks is the Mann Whitney U test. In actuality the Mann Whitney U test is the same as the Wilcoxon test and values of U may be obtained from the Wilcoxon sum of ranks using the transformation

$$\text{Smaller of} \quad U = N_1 N_2 + \frac{N_1(N_1 + 1)}{2} - R_1$$

$$\text{or} \quad U = N_1 N_2 + \frac{N_2(N_2 + 1)}{2} - R_2$$

where N_1, N_2, R_1, and R_2 are as defined for the Wilcoxon statistic. This test may be useful when Mann Whitney tables are available but those for the Wilcoxon test are not.

FIGURE 14.21   Computations for the Wilcoxon matched-pairs signed-ranks test.

Pre- and Post-Treatment Fitness Test Scores				
PRE-TEST	**POST-TEST**	**DIFFERENCE**	**SIGN**	**MARK**
73.3	84.0	10.7	+	3.5
90.6	77.0	13.6	+	7
87.7	75.2	12.5	+	6
70.1	78.3	8.2	–	2
87.4	80.0	7.4	–	1
72.0	86.1	14.1	+	8
87.4	76.1	11.3	–	5
85.8	75.1	10.7	–	3.5

$\sum R_+ = 24.5$ $\sum R_- = 11.5$ Not significant at .05 level

Wilcoxon Matched-Pairs Signed-Rank Test for Two Dependent Samples

The Wilcoxon matched-pairs signed-ranks test is useful as an alternative to the dependent samples t-test. (Note that although it is called a rank test, this test requires interval or ratio scale data and cannot be used with data consisting originally of ranks.)

The matched-pairs signed-ranks test involves the computation of the sums of ranks of the absolute positive and negative differences between paired measurements. The smaller sum is then evaluated to determine its probability of occurrence by chance by either direct computation or using predetermined values from a table available in many statistics texts.

The computations involved are illustrated in Figure 14.21 using pre- and post-treatment test scores on a fitness test given to a group of eight students. First, the absolute values and signs of the difference between each pair of scores are found. Any cases of tied measurements are dropped from the computation. Second, overall ranks are assigned according to the magnitude of each difference but without regard for the sign. Next, the sums of ranks for each sign are found. The smaller of these is then evaluated for significance. In the example, the smaller sum is 11.5 which is not significant at the .05 level.

Kruskal-Wallis Test for Three or More Independent Samples of Ranks

If the members of any set of ordinal numbers are assigned by a random process (such as drawing numbers from a hat) to two or more subsets, then there is no difference in the probability that any subset will receive any particular number. Further, each subset should be expected to receive about an equal assignment of low, intermediate, and high numbers. Therefore, if the sums of the numbers assigned to each subset are compared they should be expected to be about equal. On the other hand, they should be expected to be unequal if something other than chance is involved in the assignment process. This is the basis of the Kruskal-Wallis test for independent samples of ranks.

The Kruskal-Wallis test may be used whenever data consists of three or more subsets of a *single* ranking or when interval or ratio scale measurement data has been reduced to such data. It is not used to compare sets of independent rankings. The test is performed in two steps. First, the statistic H is computed according to the equation

$$H = \frac{12}{N(N+1)} \sum \frac{S_g^2}{n_g} - 3(N+1)$$

where N is the total number of ranks, and S_g and n_g are the sum of ranks and number of ranks for each group or subset.

The distribution of H is approximately equal to the chi-square distribution for k–1 degrees of freedom (where k is the number of subsets) so H is evaluated as a chi-square for that number of degrees of freedom.

For an example of the Kruskal-Wallis test computation consider the 60-second sit-up test scores for five groups of children shown in Figure 14.22. Because the data is skewed by a few very fit and very unfit children the use of a parametric test may be inappropriate so the actual scores are converted to overall ranks. Notice that average ranks are used in cases of tied scores. The H statistic is computed and evaluated as a chi-square with four $(5-1)$ degrees of freedom. As the value of H is less than the critical value, the null hypothesis cannot be rejected.

IS A DIFFERENCE MEANINGFUL?

Statistical tests provide the researcher with an estimate of the probability that numerical differences between or among groups represent actual differences or are due to chance, but they do not provide any information about whether such differences are meaningful. A significant difference is one unlikely to occur by chance, not one that is noteworthy or important. The question of meaningfulness of a difference between groups or sets of data may be approached contextually or statistically in several ways.

Meaningfulness may be subjectively evaluated in any context by answering the question, "Does this difference make any difference?" For example, consider an experiment showing that some exercise treatment can produce an average improvement in reaction time of .01 second in athletes. Does such an improvement make any difference? To a competitor in the 100 meter sprint it certainly does! To a marathon runner, however, an improvement of .01 second, in an event that takes more than two hours even at the highest level, is relatively meaningless.

Meaningfulness may also be evaluated statistically. One approach is to use the ω^2 statistic to estimate the meaning of a difference between means in terms of the proportion of variance explained by or attributable to that difference. Consider, for example, a study showing that two different methods of flexibility training produce improvement in sit and reach scores averaging 1.25 and 1.5 inches, a significant difference. The ω^2 statistic provides an estimate of the

FIGURE 14.22   Computations for a Kruskal-Wallis test of three or more independent samples. Here the test is applied to sit-up scores of five groups of children.

	GROUP 1	GROUP 2	GROUP 3	GROUP 4	GROUP 5
Scores	55 60 49 58 65 61	53 57 62 63 57 64 52	60 66 63 59 54 53 58	75 58 65 53 56 61 57	38 55 60 54 59 62 62 65
Ranks	26.5 15 34 20 4 12.5	31 23 10 7.5 23 6 33	15 2 7.5 17.5 28.5 31 20	1 20 4 31 25 12.5 23	35 26.5 15 28.5 17.5 10 10 4
S_g (Sum of Ranks)	112	133.5	121.5	116.5	146.5
S_g^2	12544	17822.25	14762.25	13572.25	21462.25
n_g	6	7	7	7	8
$\dfrac{S_g^2}{n_g}$	2090.6	2546.0	2494.6	1938.9	2695.3

$$N = 35 \quad df = 4 \quad \sum \frac{S_g^2}{n_g} = 11765.4$$

$$H = \frac{12}{35(35+1)} \cdot 11765.4 - 3(35+1) = \frac{12}{1260} \cdot 11765.4 - 108$$

$$= 112 - 108 = 4.0 \qquad \text{Not significant at .05 level}$$

percentage of the difference in scores that can be explained by the difference in training methods. We might find, for example, that only five percent of the difference can be explained by the method of training and the rest must be attributed to other, unknown factors. Ultimately, however, only the individual undergoing the training can decide whether the gain from the more productive method is *worth* whatever additional costs (time, pain, risk of injury, etc.) may be associated with that method. The ω^2 statistic is commonly available in statistical computer software packages as part of t-test, analysis of variance, and other group comparison procedures. If not, and if the comparison involves a relatively simple t-test or analysis of variance, it may be hand calculated using one of the equations given in Figure 14.23, depending on what statistics are available.

A third approach to statistical estimation of meaningfulness is to compute the size of the difference between group means in standard units to create a statistic known as the *effect size* (ES). The equation for effect size is

$$ES = \frac{M_1 - M_2}{s}$$

where M_1 and M_2 are the group means, and s is the standard deviation.

The standard deviation in the above equation may be that of the control group in studies involving a control group, the pre-treatment scores in studies comparing a single group of subjects before and after some treatment, or a combined or *pooled* standard deviation using the equation

FIGURE 14.23 Equations for computing omega squared. a) Following *t*-test, b) Following analysis of variance. (Equations from Tolson, 1980)

a) With *t*-test

$$\omega 2 = \frac{t^2 - 1}{t^2 + N_1 + N_2 - 1}$$

where *t* is the *t* statistic, and N_1 and N_2 are the number of subjects in each group

b) With ANOVA

$$\omega^2 = \frac{[F(g-1)] - (g-1)}{[F(g-1)] + (N-g) + 1}$$

where *F* is the *F* ratio, *g* is the number of groups, and *N* is the total number of subjects

Reproduced with permission from the American Alliance for Health, Physical Education, Recreation, and Dance, Reston, VA 22091.

$$s = \sqrt{\frac{s_1^2(n_1 - 1) + s_2^2(n_2 - 1)}{n_1 + n_2 - 2}}$$

where s_1 and s_2 are the standard deviations of the two groups, and n_1 and n_2 are the number of subjects in each group.

Some research journals are now asking authors to report effect sizes whenever possible.

TESTS USED IN META-ANALYSIS

Meta-analysis was discussed previously in Chapters 1 and 8 and the transformation of results of independent studies into the common measure called the *effect size* was presented in Chapter 12 as well as, in a different context, earlier in this chapter. The raw data of a meta-analysis consists of the effect sizes and associated study characteristics from multiple studies of some phenomenon. The example used in all discussions of meta-analysis in this book has been a series of studies of the effects of the ingestion of caffeine on reaction time.

Once the raw data for a meta-analysis has been gathered, the meta-analyst may want to determine if the effect sizes all represent the effects of the original independent variable (caffeine, in our example) or if they have been influenced by particular characteristics present in certain studies. If the original independent variable of the various studies in the meta-analysis is the only factor affecting the dependent measures then all of the effect sizes may be said to have come from the same *population of effect sizes*. This is equivalent to the situation that would be in effect, and which could be assumed as a result of the design, if each of the effect sizes really represented a single case in a single experimental study.

The likelihood that a set of effect sizes does, in fact, represent cases from a common population may be tested using the test of homogeneity described originally by Hedges (1982). Hedges' test of homogeneity begins with the computation of the statistic *Q* using the equation below.

$$Q = \sum ES^2 \cdot \frac{1}{v} - \frac{(\sum ES \cdot \frac{1}{v})^2}{\sum \frac{1}{v}}$$

where *ES* are the corrected effect sizes, and *v* are the variances of each effect size.

The value of Q is then evaluated as a chi-square with $(n - 1)$ degrees of freedom. If the value of Q is evaluated as not significant, then the effect sizes come from a common population and their weighted mean may be used to represent the effect of the independent variable across all studies. If Q is evaluated as significant, then the next step in the meta-analysis should be to attempt to identify or explain the lack of homogeneity in terms of differences in study characteristics. The first may be described as a kind of analysis of variance because it attempts to partition the Q statistic into portions attributable to study characteristics. The set of effect sizes is divided into groups according to levels of the categorical study characteristic hypothesized to be responsible for the lack of homogeneity and the Q statistic calculated for each subgroup. If, for example, it is hypothesized that subject gender is the source of the lack of homogeneity in the full data set then a Q statistic would be computed for studies using male subjects and for those using female subjects. The sum of these Q statistics would then constitute a within groups Q. The total Q minus the within groups Q would constitute the between groups Q. These Q statistics are then evaluated as chi-squares with p –1 (p is the overall number of effect sizes) and p–k (k is the number of levels of the variable being evaluated) degrees of freedom. This approach, illustrated in Figure 14.25, is appropriate if all of the study characteristics that have any effect are categorical in nature and if there are not many of them. The second approach is to use the technique of weighted regression to attempt to explain deviations from homogeneity. This approach is more appropriate than the former when there are multiple study characteristics affecting the dependent measure or in any case involving continuously variable characteristics. Details on the use of these techniques may be readily found in Hedges and Olkin (1985).

FIGURE 14.24   Test of homogeneity of effect sizes from nine studies. The value of Q is evaluated as a chi-square with eight degrees of freedom. In this case significance is achieved (p < .001).

ES	VARIANCE (v)	$\frac{1}{v}$	$ES \cdot \frac{1}{v}$	$ES^2 \cdot \frac{1}{v}$
1.54	.245	4.08	6.28	9.68
2.40	.150	6.67	16.01	38.42
1.75	.190	5.26	9.21	16.11
3.45	.210	4.76	16.42	56.66
2.10	.255	3.92	8.23	17.29
1.80	.175	5.71	10.28	18.50
1.40	.125	8.00	11.20	15.68
0.50	.180	5.56	2.78	1.39
1.90	.250	4.00	7.60	14.44
degrees of freedom = 9 – 1 = 8		$\sum = 47.96$	$\sum = 88.01$	$\sum = 188.17$

$$Q = 188.17 - \frac{(88.01)^2}{47.96} = 26.67$$

FIGURE 14.25   Partitioning of the homogeneity statistic in an ANOVA-like analysis. Note that although the computation closely resembles that of an analysis of variance and produces a comparable table, the resulting ratios are tested as chi-squares and not as F ratios. Degrees of freedom for between genders is the number of gender classes minus one. Degrees of freedom for within genders is the number of male studies minus one plus the number of female studies minus one. Degrees of freedom for each gender class is the number of studies of that gender minus one. Degrees of freedom for total is the number of studies minus one.

Studies with male subjects				Studies with female subjects			
ES_m	$\frac{1}{v_m}$	$(\frac{ES}{v})m$	$(\frac{ES^2}{v})m$	ES_f	$\frac{1}{v_f}$	$(\frac{ES}{v})f$	$(\frac{ES^2}{v})f$
1.54	4.08	6.28	9.68	1.80	5.71	10.28	18.50
2.40	6.67	16.01	38.42	1.40	8.00	11.20	15.68
1.75	5.26	9.21	16.11	0.50	5.56	2.78	1.39
3.45	4.76	16.42	56.66	1.90	4.00	7.60	14.44
2.10	3.92	8.23	17.29				

$$\sum \frac{1}{v_m} = 24.69 \quad \sum(\frac{ES}{v})m = 56.15 \quad \sum(\frac{ES^2}{v})m = 138.16$$

$$\sum \frac{1}{v_f} = 23.27 \quad \sum(\frac{ES}{v})f = 31.86 \quad \sum(\frac{ES^2}{v})f = 50.01$$

$$Q_{wm} = 138.16 - \frac{(56.15)^2}{24.69} - 10.47 \qquad Q_{wf} = 50.01 - \frac{(31.86)^2}{23.27} = 6.39$$

$$Q_w = Q_{wm} + Q_{wf} = 10.47 + 6.39 = 16.86$$

$$Q_B = Q_T - Q_w = 26.67 - 16.86 = 9.81 \quad (Q_T \text{ is the total Q statistic from Figure 14.24})$$

Summary of Fit Table		
SOURCE	**Q**	**DEGREES OF FREEDOM**
Between Genders	$Q_B = 9.81$	1
Within Genders	$Q_w = 16.86$	7
Within Gender Male	$Q_m = 10.47$	4
Within Gender Female	$Q_f = 6.39$	3
Total	$Q_T = 26.67$	8

TERMS

alpha level	random effects model
beta level	Student's *t* distribution
fixed effects model	type I error
mixed effects model	type II error
orthogonal comparison	*z*-test
power	

EXERCISES

1. A student once asked, "How many subjects do I need in my experiment?" The thesis advisor responded, "How confident do you want to be in your results?" Explain the advisor's answer.

2. Use a statistical software package to perform the analyses in the figures in this chapter.

3. Use the Mathcad programs given in Appendices B.1 through B.4 to compute the significance or lack thereof for the tests performed in exercise 2.

ADDITIONAL RESOURCES WITH ANNOTATION

Thomas, J.R., & French, K.E. The use of meta-analysis in exercise and sport. *Research Quarterly for Exercise and Sport, 57* (3), 196–204.
  An easily readable tutorial in the conduct of a meta-analysis, but does contain some errors that could be confusing.

15

ETHICAL ISSUES IN RESEARCH

During the Second World War, some Nazi doctors in Germany were interested to know how long airmen might be expected to survive immersed in cold water if their plane went down. They conducted a simple test. They forcibly immersed concentration camp inmates and prisoners of war up to the neck in water only a few degrees above freezing, using life jackets to prevent drowning, and measured the time until they died. Over eighty victims of these and similar experiments were killed outright and several hundred more who survived the experiment itself were executed later. From the point of view of experimental design these experiments seem sound. Ethically, however, they were completely unacceptable, amounting to nothing less than a form of murder, and the perpetrators who were captured after the war were executed.

Good research requires attention to more than just scientific methodology. Though most of the issues are not as dramatic or as clear cut as the case described above, researchers, even students engaged in simple projects to fulfill a course or degree requirement, have a responsibility to conduct their research in a manner that conforms to currently accepted ethical (and legal) standards. This chapter seeks to introduce several ethical issues that may be encountered by students or researchers involved in conducting or publishing the results of a research project.

PLAGIARISM

Plagiarism is *the intentional or negligent misrepresentation of work done by someone else as one's own.* It includes such academic infractions as copying from someone else on an exam or term paper, quoting or using the words of someone else in a paper or speech without proper attribution (use of quotation marks and an adequate bibliographic citation), and paraphrasing substantial portions of another person's work even though small changes in wording or style are made.

Plagiarism is universally viewed by academic and professional organizations as a very serious offense whether committed by students, faculty, or staff. Penalties to students guilty of plagiarizing on course assignments range from automatic failure of the course in which the infraction occurs to automatic, permanent expulsion from the institution for the first offense. A faculty member committing such an offense is likely to be dismissed.

Many incidents of plagiarism by students are due to negligence or ignorance regarding the need for citation when the work of another is used. It is, after all, perfectly all right to *use* small portions of someone else's work; what is wrong is to claim or misrepresent that work for oneself. (Note that using *large* portions of another's work, even with proper attribution, could constitute an infringement of copyright.) While misuse of a phrase or two on occasion may be excused as accidental, there is no defense when major portions of an assignment or paper are plagiarized. For purposes of illustration and discussion of some of the ways in which plagiarism occurs, perhaps inadvertently, the following are provided as genuine examples of incidents of plagiarism.

- A graduate student, pressed for time to write a hypothetical research proposal, copied portions of a literature review and nearly all of a methods section from a research article published in a journal, changing the tense of the methods section from past to future.

- An undergraduate student, asked to answer some questions dealing with the subject matter of a reading assignment, located the appropriate sections of the assignment and copied the major points word for word without attribution.

- A researcher who had co-authored a journal article used portions of the review of literature section, which had been written by the other author, without attribution, in a subsequent work.

- A graduate faculty member used a major portion of a literature review done by a student as part of a thesis in an article he/she later wrote on a related topic.

- An academic dean used major portions of editorials written by syndicated columnists in a graduation speech without attribution.

- A candidate for president of the United States repeatedly gave speeches including passages substantially taken from famous speeches by major historical figures without attribution.

CHEATING

Most students are familiar with the concept of cheating as it applies to examinations and academic exercises. In such an environment, cheating is the offense of not participating in accordance with the rules. Obtaining the answers to exam questions by methods not permitted, either explicitly or by common practice, is cheating. Usually such methods as looking at another's answers, referring to concealed notes (crib sheets), or leaving the examination room and looking up answers in a textbook are considered to be forms of cheating, although exams could be designed and conducted to permit any or all such practices. Plagiarism is also a form of cheating.

Most students are well aware that cheating can sometimes be a serious problem in the classroom environment. They might be more surprised to find that other forms of cheating can also sometimes be a problem in the larger academic and professional community. The scientific community has, for example, been shaken in recent years by several scandals involving various forms of cheating by researchers. Such cheating by researchers has involved the fabrication of data for experiments that were never actually conducted, the destruction of experimental data contrary to the results expected by the researcher, attempts to obtain grants by falsely making it appear that other grants had been awarded, and attempts to influence grant giving by making unfounded claims of an emergency situation. Cheating has also occurred by individuals, businesses or institutions making grants to support research. For example, companies making products thought to be potentially harmful or useless have occasionally attempted to influence the findings of research into the safety or application of their product by making the continued funding of such research contingent upon a favorable finding or by suppressing negative findings. Also, some special interest and extremist groups have been known to establish grant-making foundations to fund research that is promised to support their views.

COPYRIGHT INFRINGEMENT

A copyright is a legal ownership of the rights of reproduction of a creative work. Many kinds of works can be copyrighted including books, periodical articles, poems, stage and screen plays, computer programs, and recordings. Even the "look and feel" of a computer program can be given copyright protection if it is original.

Whether or not it is unethical for a researcher or research institution to accept grant money from organizations with extremist viewpoints or other special interests is debated. Although different institutions may have differing policies for such matters, the acceptance of funds is generally considered unethical if any coercion is involved regarding the outcome or dissemination of the results. Even when no coercion is involved some institutions may feel that acceptance of funds from organizations with abhorrent objectives is improper because the institution may become associated with those objectives.

A copyright is established by the creation of a work in some kind of permanent form and the placement of a notice of copyright in some form within the work. A copyright may be registered, giving the owner an additional level of protection, but registration is not necessary to establishment of the copyright itself. Owning a copyright means ownership of all rights regarding reproduction of the copyrighted work in all forms. This means, for example, that the copyright owner of a novel also owns the rights to translations into other languages, movie and television rights, rights of conversion into electronically or mechanically readable form, and so on. In the case of a script for a stage or screen play, the copyright owner controls the rights to performance of the play.

The symbol © on a document of any kind means "Copyright."

Copyright infringement means *copying or reproducing a copyrighted work by any means or in any form without permission of the copyright owner.*

RIGHTS OF HUMAN AND ANIMAL SUBJECTS

It was not very long ago that scientific (or pseudo-scientific) research was carried out regularly without any sort of formal or institutional effort to protect the rights of either human or animal subjects. Such protection was left to the judgment of the individual researcher. Though many scientists were careful to avoid unnecessary harm to the subjects of their experiments, abuses did occur both to human and animal subjects. The horrible example of the Nazi experiments in hypothermia has already been cited. Other famous events of human subject abuse have ranged from the highly disturbing case of deliberately withholding treatment for syphilis (Jones, 1993) in order to study the disease progression to the relatively benign case of allowing subjects to be exposed to verbal and physical abuse by other subjects (Zimbardo, 1972) in a study involving a simulated jail environment.

Today there are laws designed to prevent research practices that violate the rights of human subjects and to hold both the researcher and the institution supporting the research responsible for damages resulting from such violations. To assure compliance with such laws most universities and other institutions in which research is conducted have established procedures for reviewing and approving all research projects involving human (or animal) subjects. Researchers are required to inform subjects carefully and accurately of their rights relative to participation as research subjects and of the potential risks of participation. Usually there is an oversight committee which must review and approve the procedures of all studies involving human subjects before the study can begin.

In any study in which human subjects are exposed to risk, including the risk of death or injury, embarrassment, pain, financial cost, or other hardship, the prior *informed consent* of each subject must be obtained. **Informed consent** by a subject of a study means that *the subject agrees to serve as a subject in the full knowledge of the nature and degree of the risks involved.*

The process of obtaining informed consent must begin with a careful and complete disclosure to the prospective subject of the purposes of the study, the risks involved, and the steps to be taken to minimize those risks. This disclosure must also include a review of the subject's rights concerning participation in the study, including the rights not to participate or to withdraw from participation at any time. Disclosure information should be given to subjects in writing but should also be carefully explained in person, especially if the subject's reading comprehension may be limited. The researcher will need to be especially careful if the subject has a limited command of English.

Once subjects have been informed of the potential risks of participation and have agreed to participate they are generally asked to put that agreement in writing by signing (after reading) an informed consent form. This is principally for

---

*Study Characteristics Requiring Special Attention
to the Rights of Subjects*

Although the researcher should never shy away from an important study because human subjects' approval is difficult, the following study characteristics are likely to require extra attention to assure that the rights of subjects are not abused.

- Studies involving subjects who are vulnerable to coercion, including students of the researcher, prisoners, or candidates for employment.

- Studies involving significant risk of long-term or serious injury to the subject.

- Studies involving the collection of sensitive information such as sexual behavior, illegal behaviors, financial resources, political or religious beliefs, or evaluations of job performance.

- Studies involving subjects who are particularly vulnerable to injury or harm, including children, pregnant women, the terminally ill, or the emotionally ill.

- Studies involving subjects unlikely to fully comprehend the nature of the study or the risks involved, including young children and subjects with mental impairments.

the protection of the researcher and the sponsoring institution, as it serves as documentation that informed consent has been given, but is also of value to the subject as it serves as a reminder of the risks involved and of subjects' rights concerning such matters as terminating participation.

The informed consent form should provide a concise summary of information concerning the purpose of the study, risks involved, rights of subjects to withdraw, and whom to contact for additional or clarifying information. It should then provide a statement which the subject may sign to indicate that the risks are understood and accepted. The form should not include any language disclaiming the responsibility of the researcher or sponsoring institution for the consequences of negligence or through which the subjects' rights are waived.

The above paragraph notwithstanding, anyone engaged in studies involving human subjects must bear in mind that procedures for protecting the rights of research subjects (human or animal) may be affected at any time by changes in the law, changes in administrative interpretation of the law at any level, or by decisions arising from legal cases. Thus the researcher must take care to assure that the procedures that are followed in any study conform to current standards.

SCIENTIFIC RITUAL

There is a well worn joke (source unknown) that tells of a husband who asked his wife of several years why she always cut off the end of a roast beef before cooking it. She was not sure but she said she learned to do this from her mother. When asked, her mother also could not explain the practice but was certain that the practice had been learned from her mother. When the grandmother was asked she laughed and explained very simply, "In my day the oven was too small for a whole roast so we cut it to fit."

The story of the roast beef, of course, is really about doing things ritualistically and without any understanding, and serves to illustrate a problem that can sometimes happen in research. In every field of study research is often quite methodologically oriented. Most introductory courses in research, in fact, include the word "methods" in the course title and have content focused on the methods or procedures of research. Sometimes this can lead inexperienced scientists or students to behave as though the methods of research *are* the research. That is, as though what is most important is the correct execution of the chosen methodology rather than the answering of a question of knowledge. One manifestation of such thinking is likely to be a very well-designed study answering a completely trivial question or one for which the answer is already well known such as a laboratory experiment to see if the presence or absence of sunlight affects whether or not grass will grow. Another is the liturgical repetition of studies done previously (by the same researcher or others) with endless minor changes in subjects or conditions without any identifiable reasons for such repetitions. For example, a study looking at the effects of nicotine ingestion on the reaction time of baseball players might be repeated using football players, women volleyball players, visually impaired junior high debate team members, and so on ad infinitum even though no theoretical basis for the existence of any relevant differences between such groups has been hypothesized.

Over-commitment to methods and procedures also tends to lead to studies being seen by the researcher as completed when data has been collected and

Cargo Cult Science

In his book, *Surely You're Joking Mr. Feynmann*, Nobel prize-winning physicist Richard Feynmann discusses the problem of researchers blindly following a procedure by comparing them to the so-called "Cargo Cults" of Micronesia following the Second World War. For many years following the war certain natives of those islands, having been impressed with the wealth of goods that accompanied the American soldiers, ritualistically tried to mimic the behaviors of the radio operators who had guided in the supply ships and planes in the hope that they might cause those ships and planes to come again and bring them more supplies.

analyzed, as opposed to when the research question has been answered to the researcher's satisfaction. Such a mistake may manifest itself as a series of research reports about the isolated results of single, small experiments being submitted (probably without success) to journals or conferences when a single report showing the implications of a coordinated or evolving series of such experiments would be much more meaningful and, probably, successful in gaining acceptance.

All of the above is not meant to suggest that correct methodology is unimportant. Incorrect methods will render worthless any attempt at research. It is to assert that the methods used should be determined by the nature of the problem being researched and that those methods are not ends unto themselves. The researcher must not forget that research is an effort to find answers, not the recapitulation of a procedure. The methods of research—experiments, surveys, statistical analysis, and so on—are used because they serve usefully in solving research problems. Finally, it is to suggest that the blind devotion to research methodology is unethical because it is a form of deluding oneself if not others.

ENVIRONMENTAL PROTECTION

As the human population of the earth grows ever larger and economic development around the world results in increasing consumption, even on a per capita as well as absolute basis, humankind is becoming more and more of a threat to the very environment in which we all live. We have already caused the extinction of large numbers of plant and animal species and many others are threatened. We are already capable of wiping out most of the life on the planet along with civilization as we know it in a single rash act of nuclear suicide and our slower but seemingly inexorable destruction of tropical rainforests (Wilson, 1991) at least theoretically has a similar if more gradual potential for rendering the planet uninhabitable.

Though the protection of the environment on a global scale is clearly a governmental matter and most of the really serious air, water, noise, and other forms of pollution of the environment come from industrial and agricultural activity, concern for environmental protection is not outside the concern (or responsibility) of the individual researcher. Ethical practice demands that the researcher in any field be cognizant of and take appropriate steps to avoid or minimize any negative environmental impact from their conduct of research. Failure to take such steps may leave the researcher financially liable for any environmental damage caused and possibly even subject to criminal prosecution for willful violation of environmental protection laws.

We usually tend to think about environmental damage in the context of large-scale disasters such as the Exxon *Valdez* oil spill in Prince William

Sound in Alaska or the chemical pollution at Love Canal in New York. However, serious damage also occurs on a small scale through the ill-considered actions of individuals. Such actions as the improper use of fertilizers or pesticides, or the improper disposal of hazardous chemicals, such as dumping a tray of photographic chemicals or a quart of used motor oil on the ground, can produce damage and should be considered unethical—if not illegal—if done intentionally.

Prior to the initiation of any research project in which there is any question of environmental impact, a review similar to that regarding the rights of human or animal subjects should be conducted. Such a review attempts to identify the environmental impact that will or may occur, to determine procedures for minimizing or eliminating such impact, and to weigh the benefits of proceeding with the project against the environmental costs. In cases in which wetlands, watershed areas, or areas that are the habitats of endangered species are involved, approval may be needed from the Federal Environmental Protection Agency or other governmental units before the project may proceed, and such approval may be quite difficult to obtain.

CONFLICTS OF INTEREST

The term **conflict of interest** refers to *a situation in which a person or institution has two or more interests that are mutually exclusive, either wholly or in part.* That is, a circumstance in which the satisfaction of one interest directly denies or impedes the satisfaction of another. For example, a coach whose own son or daughter tries out for the team has one interest in placing the best available players on the team and another interest in doing what is best for his or her own child. Unless the child is one of the best available players, any decision that achieves one interest automatically precludes the other, and the dilemma is very likely to influence the coach's judgment of whether the child is one of the best, or is not.

There are many ways in which conflicts of interest may occur for a researcher, some specifically associated with the conduct of research and others that are merely incidental and may affect anyone in any line of work. One obvious conflict of interest occurs when a researcher compromises the professional relationship that must exist between researcher and subject by becoming socially or sexually involved or interested in a subject. Another occurs when a researcher becomes involved in research evaluating a product or service in which he or she has a financial interest. A third, and more subtle, conflict of interest may occur when the researcher's long-held beliefs (scientific, religious, or otherwise) are challenged by research results. A closely related conflict may be encountered when the researcher's commitment to truth requires the researcher to announce findings that are likely to produce an angry (sometimes violently so) response from others. A fourth, and very difficult conflict of interest can occasionally arise when the need to publish or otherwise act upon a researcher's findings is (or appears to be) against the public interest. The "great cranberry affair" ("The Cranberry Affair," 1959) provides an illustration of this kind of situation. Just before Thanksgiving (when most cranberries are eaten) in 1959 the Secretary of Health, Education and Welfare issued a warning that some cranberries had been contaminated with a carcinogenic chemical. Not surprisingly, sales of cranberries plunged. The warning was issued in spite of the fact that the dosage of the offending chemical that had produced cancer in mice was equivalent to what a person would consume from eating 7.5 tons of cranberries every day for several years, because the law was interpreted to mean that no amount of a carcinogenic chemical could be allowed.

There are a variety of ways of dealing with different kinds of conflicts of interest. One simple approach, but one that is probably of limited effectiveness and may even create additional conflicts, is to simply operate under policies designed to prevent conflicts of interest from occurring. For example, companies concerned about relationships among employees possibly interfering with supervisory functions (it is hard to discipline an employee whom one is dating) may attempt to establish a policy prohibiting employees from dating other employees. These types of policies, of course, tend to drive such relationships underground rather than prevent them. Furthermore, in at least some states such policies may even be contrary to law. Probably a more effective control for conflict of interest, at least in professional practice, is to proactively educate people about the ways in which conflicts arise and ask them to avoid conflicts by taking themselves out of decision-making situations when conflicts do appear. For example, the coach with a child trying out for the team could assign the decision of who makes the team to someone else—and to someone not subject to disciplinary action from the coach. Perhaps the players themselves might play a role in such a decision. *The practice of disqualifying oneself because of an actual or perceived conflict of interest* is called **recusement.** A third approach to controlling conflicts of interest is the establishment of a review board or oversight committee to watch for cases of conflict or potential conflict and intervene when they occur.

AUTHORSHIP AND PUBLISHING STANDARDS

Particularly in higher education institutions, but also in other places of professional practice, the authorship of research papers, presentations, and other forms of scholarly publication is a prime route to professional prestige and advancement. Rightly or wrongly, in fact, the quantity and *perceived* quality of publications will sometimes determine whether a faculty member is even retained as a faculty member.

Because researchers in institutions of higher education are usually under intense pressure to publish and because such researchers often work in teams rather than as isolated individuals, questions often arise as to who should or should not be listed as an author of an article and how two or more authors should be listed.

As a general rule, all persons making a significant professional contribution toward the design or execution of the research being reported or toward writing the research report itself should be included as authors. This includes those responsible for the identification of the research problem, design, statistical analysis, or interpretation of results. It does *not* include those playing only a supportive role, such as providing advice on design or statistical analysis, typing or proofreading, data collection, computer operation, and similar services. A thesis or dissertation advisor is ordinarily not listed as an author on the basis of the advice provided. However, such an advisor might be properly considered an author if the research problem was developed and provided by the advisor, if the study design was done by the advisor, or if some other critical aspect of the study was the work of the advisor. A thesis or dissertation advisor should *never* be listed as a primary author.

When there are two or more authors, then that person making the most significant contribution is listed first and other authors are listed according to their contribution in decreasing order. Authors may also be listed in alphabetical order if their contributions are equal. Determination of the order of authorship is the responsibility of the authors themselves, and it is best for such questions to be resolved as early as possible.

In addition to these general guidelines, educational and other institutions involved in the support of research may have their own rules or procedures for determining authorship, especially when persons of unequal power or rank are involved. Such procedures may be needed to reduce the potential for abuse, or the accusation of abuse, by senior faculty against those of junior rank or by faculty against students.

In order to balance the sometimes conflicting needs of authors, publishers, and consumers of research, there are certain procedural standards that must be adhered to when submitting a research article for publication or presentation or when serving as a reviewer for such articles. Failure to do so is generally considered a breach of ethics and could result in professional sanctions if flagrant.

When submitting an article to a journal or for presentation at a conference, **simultaneous submissions** *(submitting one manuscript to more than one publication at the same time)* are generally not considered acceptable. Some editors, however—particularly those of some popular magazines—will accept simultaneous submissions as long as they are informed at the time of submission. When a journal will not allow a simultaneous submission it has an obligation to the author to review the submission and arrive at a publication decision expeditiously, although the review process does commonly take several months. If a journal is unable to make a decision within a reasonable period (three to six months is not unreasonable or uncommon with many journals) and the journal editor is unresponsive regarding the status of the submission, an author may be justified in withdrawing the submission and resubmitting it to another journal. The editor of the first journal should, of course, be notified in writing of the withdrawal and given a reasonable time to respond (two to three weeks) before the article is resubmitted.

Most research journals require authors to grant all rights to accepted articles to the journal prior to publication. This means that the copyright to the article is transferred to the journal and any subsequent publication of the same article or a substantially similar article requires the permission of the publisher. Secondary publication of an article may be permissible, however, if more limited rights are given to the primary publisher. For example, popular magazines commonly acquire first worldwide serial rights, which merely gives the magazine the right to be the first publisher of the material anywhere in the world, or first North American serial rights, which means the right to be the first publisher of the material in North America. Whenever an article that has been published is submitted a second time it is essential to make full disclosure of the article's history to the secondary journal editor.

The more prestigious research journals always use a blind review process to assure that publication decisions are not affected by the reputation or lack of reputation of the author. On occasion, a reviewer may become aware of the identity (or the probable identity) of the author of a manuscript under review. This may occur when the article deals with a line of research in which only a very small number of researchers are engaged, when the reviewer has been consulted or otherwise involved in discussions concerning the research study, when the reviewer is able to deduce the identity of the author from reference citations or other information within the manuscript, or in other ways. When a reviewer is aware of the identity of an author for a review that is supposed to be blind, the journal editor should be contacted for advice on how to proceed. In some cases, especially when an alternate reviewer can be easily secured, it may be best to return the manuscript unreviewed so an alternate reviewer may be used. In other cases it may be necessary to proceed with a non-blind review but such a decision should be left to the journal editor.

TERMS

conflict of interest

copyright infringement

informed consent

plagiarism

recusement

simultaneous submissions

EXERCISES

1. Debate with other classmates several research-related ethical dilemmas such as the use of only partially tested drugs for the treatment of an otherwise untreatable, fatal disease, and how to discipline a distinguished public figure found to have plagiarized portions of a thesis many years ago.

2. Write a brief summary of or make a presentation to your class about a recent case of alleged scientific misconduct.

3. Prepare an annotated bibliography, in chronological rather than alphabetical order, of newspaper or magazine articles about a recent case of alleged misconduct, showing the progress of the case or public opinion related to the case.

4. Obtain copies of all relevant forms and policies regarding the protection of human research subjects at your institution.

5. Obtain copies of all relevant forms and policies regarding the protection of animal research subjects at your institution.

6. Obtain copies of all relevant forms and policies regarding the protection of the environment during research projects at your institution.

ADDITIONAL RESOURCES WITH ANNOTATION

Annas, G.J., & Grodin, M.A. Eds. (1992). *The Nazi doctors and the Nuremberg Code: Human rights in human experimentation.* New York: Oxford University Press.

A review of the atrocities committed by Nazi doctors in the name of research during the German Third Reich.

Blinderman, C. (1986). *The Piltdown Inquest.* Buffalo, NY: Prometheus Books.
An analytic history of the Piltdown Man case of scientific forgery.

Blum, D.E. (July 27, 1988). Plagiarism in speeches by college presidents called "capitol offense" and "ultimate sin." *The Chronicle of Higher Education,* A11–A12.
A report on the issue of plagiarism (often accidental) in college presidents' speeches.

Fanning, D. (Producer) (1993). *Prisoners of Silence* [Video]. Boston, MA: WGBH Educational Foundation.
An episode of the Frontline television program concerning the debate over facilitated communication and illustrating the potential for self-deception by scientists. A transcript of the video may be obtained from Journal Graphics, Inc. of Denver, CO.

Fields, C.M. September 14, 1983). Professors' demands for credit as co-authors of students' research papers may be rising. *The Chronicle of Higher Education,7,* 10.
A news report of an increase in the incidence of professors demanding to be listed as authors of their students' research papers. Includes the APA policy statement concerning joint authorship of research papers.

Jones, J.H. (1993). *Bad blood: The Tuskegee syphilis experiment.* New York: Free Press.
An expanded and updated edition of an earlier (1972) book with the same title, this book tells the story of the Tuskegee syphilis experiment and analyzes its legacy. A chapter is devoted to the effects of the revelation of the experiment on conspiracy theories among some African-Americans concerning the AIDS plague in particular and health care workers in general.

Marso, L. (1992). Scientific fraud. *Omni 14* (9); 38–43, 82–83.
A discussion of recent incidents of data falsification, data fabrication, and plagiarism and the reasons why such incidents seem to be increasing. This article includes an enumeration of ten of the most famous cases of scientific fraud.

Muller, K. (1974). Tanna awaits the coming of John Frum. *National Geographic, 145* (5), 706–715.
An account of the cargo cult phenomenon on the island of Tanna.

National Association of College Stores, Inc. (1990). *Questions and Answers on Copyright for the Campus Community.* Oberlin, OH: Author.
Provides answers to commonly asked questions regarding the fair use of copyrighted materials in educational settings.

Schachman, H.K. (1993). What is misconduct in science? *Science 261,* 148–149, 183.
A review of the evolution of governmental concern over scientific misconduct from matters clearly relating to the practice of science to matters only peripherally related.

Thompson, K.S. (1991). Piltdown Man: The Great English Mystery Story. *American Scientist, 79,* 194–201.
A review of the Piltdown Man fraud and recent theories of who was involved.

Wheeler, D.L. (August 14, 1991). Researchers debate ethics of payments for human subjects. *The Chronicle of Higher Education,* A7–A9.
A discussion of the issue of paying finder's fees to physicians or others who refer patients to become subjects of research studies.

APPENDIX A

QUICK MATH REVIEW

Students faced with a requirement to complete a research project are often very much afraid of the mathematical demands of such a project. Stories told in Hollywood movies and television sometimes tend to create an image of researchers as an elite few who can digest mountains of numbers or as human computers who learned calculus in the second grade. Stories told by some more advanced students also may portray the statistics associated with many kinds of research as indecipherable gibberish and a terror to be avoided at all costs.

Research does require a certain amount of mathematical ability, but not nearly as much as Hollywood and recent students tend to imply. Research does require the researcher to think in an organized, systematic manner and to solve problems by applying reason to evidence.

Research also may require the student to understand and use a variety of mathematical techniques, particularly from the branch of mathematics called statistics. However, except for the use of statistics, the conduct of most kinds of research inquiry and most research in the fields of physical or health education, sports, sports management, and exercise science do not really require any significant use of mathematics beyond that ordinarily covered in a one-year college algebra course and a good high school geometry course. (A few advanced types of research and some topics involving complex relationships of variables, however, may be much easier for students who have had some exposure to calculus.)

This appendix is included as a quick review of a range of research-related mathematical concepts and procedures not covered elsewhere in this book. The student who has done well in a full-year, college algebra course and a high school course in geometry should find everything quite familiar. The student who has not completed a full-year, college algebra course may find it constructive to devote significant attention to concepts or techniques that are unfamiliar and may need to consider additional tutoring with specific topics as well.

PROBABILITY AND RANDOMNESS

People deal with probability daily in their language and behavior, though not always wisely or with real understanding. We use the concept in our speech with such words or phrases as "probably," "my best guess," "chances are," "an even bet," and "it's a long shot." Decisions unconsciously involving probability are made all the time when a student makes an "educated guess" of the answer to a test question, when a coach decides to use a particular play, or when a driver chooses a particular route where the traffic ought to be lighter. We may be more aware of the involvement of probability when we play roulette, bet on a horse, or drop a coin into a slot machine, although most people's behavior with respect to such activities would suggest either they know little about the mathematics involved or they believe in magic.

A fundamental principle of science is that we live in a deterministic universe, one in which every event is the consequence of pre-existing conditions (at least as far back in time as the origin of the universe as we understand it in the "big bang"). This is not to say, however, that every event is predetermined or preordained irrespective of our own actions or free will, although it may be argued that such actions, or lack thereof, are also deterministic. This is a question of philosophy or religion inappropriate for discussion here. However, it is clear that even in a deterministic universe there are many events that are, from our point of view at least, quite unknowable in advance. Such events are described as *random*. Many things in our lives, the daily weather conditions, the transfer of genes at conception, test scores for individuals in a large population, the roll of a pair of dice, etc., are either truly random or *appear to be* random and thus may be treated as such. Phenomena that are entirely deterministic but that are useful for simulating genuine randomness, such as the sequence of numbers generated by a computerized random number generator are called *pseudo random*. An example of such a program is provided in Appendix C.1. Phenomena that are deterministic but that depend on unknowably small differences in pre-existing conditions or upon an incomprehensible number of variables of pre-existing conditions are referred to as *chaotic*.

The probability of an event happening is the ratio of the number of times the event actually occurs to the number of opportunities for occurrence, expressed either as a percentage or as a proportion, when the number of opportunities is infinite. The probability of an event happening makes no predictions about whether or not the event will *actually* happen in a single opportunity or even in a series of opportunities. Probability tells us nothing, for example, about whether a single toss of a coin *will* come up heads, nor even about whether a roulette wheel *will* come up even

---

The Butterfly Effect

At one time researchers in meteorology believed the development of a computer program for long-range prediction of weather conditions was feasible. The computing power required would be immense and the necessity for input of huge quantities of data would be daunting but it would eventually be achieved. In the early 1960s, however, in what at first appeared to be a computer error, Edward Lorenz at MIT discovered that extremely small differences in the numerical values of input data in the equations needed for weather prediction led to radically different long-range results. The iterative equations describing the evolution of weather conditions eventually amplified tiny differences in initial conditions until the resulting predictions diverged dramatically. Eventually it was realized that because it would never be possible to know every detail of initial conditions down to the last decimal point, long-range, small-scale weather prediction would never be possible. Perhaps because a map of the chaotic behavior of these equations had a shape (known as a strange attractor) that resembled a butterfly, it is sometimes said that Lorenz showed that the flap of a butterfly's wings in the midwest might, in a few days, lead to a tornado on the east coast (Briggs and Peat, 1989).

---

at least once in eight tries. It does, however, tell us how many times we may *expect* heads to come up in a series of tosses or about how many times to *expect* at least one even result in eight spins of a roulette wheel. If we toss a fair coin 100 times, probability tells us to expect heads to come up approximately 50 times. Such predictions tend to become increasingly accurate as the number of opportunities increases.

PERMUTATIONS AND COMBINATIONS

An understanding of the likelihood of many kinds of events depends on understanding how many different outcomes are possible. For example, the 50 percent probability that a coin toss will land as "heads" derives from the fact that there are exactly two possible and equally probable outcomes. The probability that a three will appear when a die is rolled is one chance in six because there are six possible and equally probable outcomes. Further, the probability that the total of two dice will be six is five chances in 36 because there are 36 possible outcomes and five of them would produce a total of six.

Depending on how the possible different outcomes are defined, the number of such outcomes is often the number of *permutations* or *combinations* of some number of items.

A permutation is a unique arrangement or sequence of items. The letters A, B, and C can be arranged into six different sequences: ABC, ACB, BAC, BCA, CAB, and CBA. Often, what is of interest is the number of possible arrangements that can be made from a set of items when some smaller subset of those items is used each time. For example, a baseball coach with five players judged to have the ability to lead the batting order might be interested in determining how many permutations of "first three hitters" can be made (There are 60).

The number of permutations of t things taken s at a time is written as

$$P_s{}^t$$

and the general equation for finding the number of such permutations is expressed as

$$P_s{}^t = \frac{t!}{(t-s)!}$$

where t is the total number of items that may be selected and s is the number of items selected in each permutation.

Thus, the number of three-player sequences that may be made from a set of five players is computed as

$$P_s{}^t = \frac{t!}{(t-s)!} = \frac{5!}{2!} = \frac{5 \times 4 \times 3 \times 2 \times 1}{2 \times 1} = 60$$

A combination is a unique set of items. A combination is different from a permutation in that different arrangements of the same items constitute different permutations but they all represent the same combination. Whereas there are 60 different three-player permutations that may be made from five players, there are only 10 three-player combinations that may be made.

The number of combinations of t items taken s at a time is written as

$$C_s{}^t$$

and the general equation for finding the number of such combinations is expressed as

$$C_s{}^t = \frac{t!}{s!(t-s)!}$$

where t is the total number of items that may be selected and s is the number of items selected in each combination.

Thus, the number of combinations of 3 baseball players that can be selected from a list of 5 players is computed as

$$C_s{}^t = \frac{t!}{s!(t-s)!} = \frac{5!}{!3!(5-3)!} = \frac{120}{6(2)} = 10$$

The number of combinations of 5 basketball players that can be made from a roster of 14 is

$$C_s{}^t = \frac{t!}{s!(t-s)!} = \frac{14!}{!5!(15-5)!} = \frac{87178291200}{43545600} = 2002$$

THE NORMAL CURVE

If a coin is not *loaded* or weighted so that its center of mass is closer to one face or part of the edge than to the other, then it is said to be *fair*. If a fair coin is "tossed" it has an equal chance of landing *heads* side up or *tails* side up. It is said that the coin has a 50-50 chance of landing heads or tails which means that the coin is expected to come up heads *about* 50 percent of the time and tails *about* 50 percent of the time.

In the sentence above the word *about* is italicized because it is very important to recognize that the 50 percent occurrence of heads and tails is an approximation and not an exact figure. Suppose a coin is to be tossed 100 times. Can the exact number of heads be predicted? The best guess is 50 heads but it will certainly *not* come up 50 heads every time. Sometimes there will be 49 or 51 heads, sometimes 48 or 52. In fact, if the 100 toss exercise could be repeated enough times it might even come up 0 or 100 heads.

How often would each possible number of heads come up? If the 100 toss exercise were repeated several hundred times a graph could be constructed to show how many times each possible outcome actually occurred. If the coin used is a fair one, 50 heads will occur more often than any other count. Counts of 49 and 51 heads will occur about the same number of times and will be greater than any other count except 50. The next greatest frequency will be for 48 and 52 heads. Counts of 0 or 100 would be very rare indeed!

Suppose we tried a similar experiment using a pair of dice. We could prepare a similar graph showing how many times in 100 rolls the sum came out even. The graph would look the same as that obtained tossing the coin. In fact, it would be *almost exactly* the same as long as we repeated the experiment enough times. We could repeat the experiment using *any* phenomenon whose

FIGURE A.1   Though not essential to understanding or application, this is the rather formidable formula for the normal curve. The area under the curve between any two points on the horizontal axis is the integral of the equation between those two values and may be found quite easily by using an equation solver computer program such as Mathcad. A Mathcad program for doing this is given in Appendix B.1.

$$d(x) = \frac{100}{\sqrt{2\pi}} e^{\frac{-x^2}{2}}$$

outcome is determined only by chance and the graph of the results would have the same shape. That graph is called the *normal curve* and is a very important concept in statistics.

The normal curve is the graph of random variation. It is the approximate shape of the distribution of variability of many phenomenon when the only factor controlling such variation is chance. Measurement of a large number of cases of any phenomenon for which all variation is random will produce a distribution with such a shape. The same shape will occur for deterministic phenomena for which the determining factors occur randomly or in a manner that approximates randomness. Such phenomena include adult height and most other physical characteristics, IQ, some standardized test scores, most weather conditions for any date, and many other things of common experience. This is so consistent that notable deviation from normality of distribution in any set of data is a clear sign that some factor other than chance is present.

Properties of the Normal Curve

Figure A.2 is a graph of the normal curve. The baseline of the graph is marked in units of standard deviation away from the mean. (These statistics will be explained in another chapter.) The vertical axis is unlabelled but represents an increase, away from the axis, in frequency of occurrence. That is, the higher the frequency of occurrence, the higher on the vertical axis. The frequency is highest for the mean or average and declines as values deviate either above or below the mean. Notice that the normal curve is symmetrical around the mean. This means that in a normal curve, and in any data set which is *normally distributed*, the mean, median, and mode are all the same. Incidentally, all the other estimates of central tendency are the same as well.

Because the mean and the median are the same in a normal distribution, the number of cases falling above the mean will be the same as the number falling below the mean. Because the curve is symmetrical, the same is true for any distance from the mean. For example, the number of cases falling higher than the 75th percentile will be the same as the number falling below the 25th percentile. The number of cases more than 1 standard deviation above the mean will be the same as the number falling more than 1 standard deviation below the mean.

The above characteristics will apply to any symmetrical frequency curve, normal or otherwise, although the proportion of cases within a given distance of the mean will be different for each curve. Because the normal curve is derived from the mathematical laws of probability, however, we can also know the exact percentage of cases falling above, around, or below any distance from the mean. Indeed, we can determine the percentage of cases between any two points, symmetrical about the mean or otherwise. For example, it can be shown that 68.26 percent (the figure is rounded) of all cases will fall within 1 standard deviation of the mean and that 95 percent of all cases will fall within 2 standard deviations of the mean. Some additional percentages are shown in Figure A.2.

An understanding of the basic properties of the normal curve is important because the parameters of many real-world phenomena closely resemble the normal curve in distribution and the properties of that curve can be used to make inferences about those phenomena. For example, the distribution of adult height is approximately normal in the human population. Using the normal curve, one

FIGURE A.2   Areas under the normal curve. The vertical lines mark the locations of the mean and 1, 2, and 3 standard deviations above and below the mean. The areas of the zones created by these lines represent the frequency with which randomly variable events will vary by 1, 2, or 3 standard deviations (or less) from their own mean.

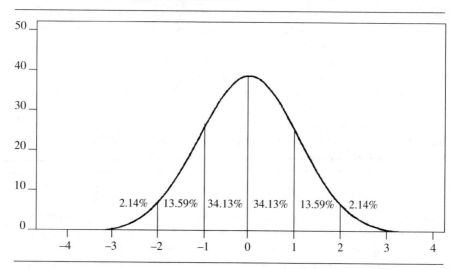

can infer that in the adult population, and also in any random sample of that population, approximately 68 percent of the individuals will be within 1 standard deviation of the mean in adult height. Similarly, we can infer that any group of people for whom approximately 68 percent of the individuals are not within 1 standard deviation of the mean is *probably not* a representative or random sample of the population as a whole. Also, we can say that an adult individual whose height is 1 standard deviation above the mean is taller than 84 percent of all adults.

We can even make a statistical estimate of the likelihood that the group is or is not a representative sample of the population as a whole if we also know the size of the group and its mean, but this is covered in another chapter.

TYPES OF NUMBERS

At one time in history there was a need for only a few numbers. Indeed, even today in some very small, isolated cultures it would not be possible to explain the meaning of a "dozen" donuts because "twelve" would have no meaning. The language of the Wayanas of the Amazon basin of South America contains words for only eleven numbers—one through ten, and "many" (DeVillers,1983).

Our world is a bit too complex for only eleven numbers so we have had to invent more. In fact, we have repeatedly had to invent new *kinds* of numbers in order to deal with ever more complex needs. The numbers in our world cannot be listed completely on a sheet of paper or even on millions of sheets of paper. We have to deal with an *infinite* number of numbers. Our numbers can only be described as groups or *sets* of objects or symbols which conform to certain rules or characteristics. The following sections describe the major types of numbers with which the student should be familiar.

Natural Numbers or Positive Integers

The natural numbers are the numbers used for counting things. The set of natural numbers, also called the positive integers can be written as (1,2,3, . . .). While the set continues indefinitely (indicated by the 3 dots) in units of 1, it does not include zero, negative numbers or any kind, or any fractional values such as 1/2 or 4.4.

Integers

The set of natural numbers cannot express the idea of zero or of negative quantity. To address such ideas the number zero was added and a minus sign was invented as an addition to a natural number to represent what we call a negative quantity. The integers, therefore, are the set of all positive and negative whole numbers, and zero. The set of integers may be written as (. . . –3, –2, –1, 0, 1, 2, 3, . . .).

Rational Numbers

A limitation of the integers is that they do not provide for the idea of a fractional quantity. With only integers, for example, how would you describe the serving you would get if you and another person decided to share a pie equally? The idea of dividing an object, such as a pie, into two parts so that each of two people can receive *one* of the *two* parts led to the numbers being written as a ratio. One part of two was written as 1/2 and the fraction was invented. It is because what we call a fraction really represents a *ratio* that such numbers are called *rational*. The rational numbers, therefore, are all numbers that can be expressed as the ratio of two integers. (Note: There is one exception to this definition. The expression 1/0 or any other integer over zero, appears to be a ratio of two integers. However, such an expression has no quantitative meaning.)

Real and Irrational Numbers

Figure A.3 shows a number line from -4.0 to 4.0. The idea behind a number line is that it represents *all* of the numbers between the two points at its termini. The set of all numbers that exist on a number line is the set of real numbers. It turns out that there are many points on a number line (that is, there are many numbers) that cannot be expressed as the ratio of two integers and are, thus, not rational numbers. Some numbers on the number line of Figure A.3 that are not rational include $\sqrt{2}$, $\sqrt{3}$, π, e, $\sqrt[3]{7}$, and $\sqrt[5]{5}$. These numbers are called *irrational* numbers. The term "irrational" means "not rational," that is, a number that cannot be expressed as a ratio of two integers. It does not mean that the numbers are "beyond reason."

FIGURE A.3   All real and irrational numbers fall somewhere on the number line. Imaginary numbers, however, may not.

–4	–3	–2	–1	0	1	2	3	4

FIGURE A.4   A number plane. The coordinates of the dot constitute a complex number that cannot exist on a number line but can be plotted on a number plane.

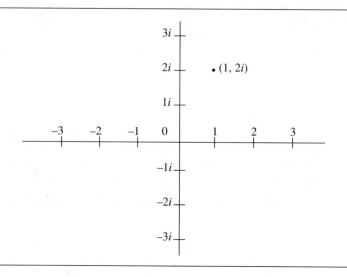

Complex and Imaginary Numbers

The real numbers are sufficient for most everyday purposes. However, there are other kinds of numbers that may occasionally be encountered and that can be extremely useful. One such kind of number is encountered when one attempts to find the square root of a negative number. Consider the square root of negative 4, for example. There is no point on a number line and, thus, no real number, that can be multiplied by itself to obtain any negative number. Therefore, the square root of -4 is not a real number. To deal with this kind of problem, the complex number was invented. A complex number cannot be plotted as a point on a number line but it *can* be plotted as a coordinate point on a number plane. A number plane is the plane defined by the intersection of two number lines at right angles to each other. A complex number may be written as consisting of two parts—a real part and an imaginary part. The real part corresponds to a point on one axis (called the real axis) of the number plane and the imaginary part corresponds to a point on the other axis (called the imaginary axis). The imaginary axis is a number line in units of i in which i represents the square root of negative 1. Thus a complex number may be expressed as an ordered pair of numbers in which the first is real and the second is imaginary or as a pair of coordinates on a number plane on which one axis is real and the second is imaginary.

Vectors and Matrices

All of the numbers described in the sections above may be used to express quantities of a unidimensional nature only. Such variables as height, weight, mass, speed, or a score on a test are all unidimensional, or scalar, but not all variables are so simple. None of the *scalar* numbers thus far described can be used to quantify such variables as the velocity of a cyclist, the potential of a basketball player, health status, or intelligence. Such variables are multidimensional.

Velocity consists of two dimensions: the magnitude or speed of movement, and the direction of movement. The potential of basketball players, health status, and intelligence cannot be definitively described in terms of a specific number of dimensions but certainly have several dimensions. Although we can certainly use several scalar numbers to individually represent values of different dimensions of a multidimensional variable, it is sometimes more convenient to combine those scalar numbers into a more complicated type of number. Vectors and matrices are numbers of this type.

A vector is defined as an ordered set of two or more scalar numbers. The simplest example of a vector is an ordered pair of scalar numbers in which each scalar represents one of two different dimensions. The coordinates of a point plotted on a Cartesian coordinate graph may serve as a familiar example. Vectors may also consist of ordered sets of three, four, or five or more scalars. Matrices are two-dimensional arrays of scalar numbers. That is, a matrix is an array of one or more columns and rows of scalar numbers.

MATHEMATICAL AND LOGICAL OPERATIONS

The term "operation" refers to any procedure that can be done on two or more elements of data to produce a third data element. An operation may be defined as mathematical if the data operated upon is a number or algebraic variable of some kind. Everyone is familiar with the basic arithmetic operations of addition and subtraction. The symbols "+" and "–" are used in mathematical expressions to indicate the operations of addition and subtraction and are placed between the two data elements upon which the operation is to be performed. The equals sign is used to indicate the result of the operation. Mathematical operations may be performed on a wide range of different kinds of mathematical data elements including scalar numbers, algebraic variables, vectors, matrices, and complex numbers. Figure A.5 shows a variety of mathematical operations and their associated symbols.

FIGURE A.5   Common mathematical operations and symbols.

OPERATION	SYMBOL(S)	EXAMPLE	MEANING
Addition	$+$	$a + b$	the sum of a and b
Subtraction	$-$	$a - b$	the difference between a and b
Multiplication	$\times$ or $\bullet$	$a \bullet b$	the product of a and b
Division	$/$ or $\div$	$a \div b$	a divided by b
Exponentiation	superscript	a^n	a multiplied by itself n times
Root	$\sqrt{}$	$\sqrt[n]{ax}$	the nth root of ax
Factorial	$!$	$a!$	the product of all integers from a to 1
Absolute value	$\mid\ \mid$	$\mid n \mid$	the unsigned value of n
Summation	$\sum$	$\sum_{0} i$	summation of i from 0 to infinity
Integration	$\int$	$\int_0^1 x dx$	the integral from 1 to 0 of the function of x

An operation performed on an element of data other than a number or algebraic value is commonly described as a logical operation. The student should note that the distinction made here between mathematical and logical operations depends on the kinds of data elements that are defined as numbers. Most of the operations described here as logical are also clearly mathematical and can be performed on certain kinds of numbers. Some common logical operations are described in the following sections.

- AND

    The AND operation is the combination of two sets in such a way as to produce a new set with membership consisting of only those elements found in both original sets. In the mathematics of sets, the AND operation is the *intersection* of two sets.

- OR

    The OR operation is the combination of two sets in such a way as to produce a new set with membership consisting of each of the elements found in either original set. In the mathematics of sets, the OR operation is the *union* of two sets.

- NOT

    The NOT operation is the combination of two sets in such a way as to produce a new set with membership consisting of all of the elements of the first original set except those which are also members of the second original set. In the mathematics of sets, the NOT operation is the *complement* of a set.

- exclusive OR (EOR)

    The exclusive OR operation is the combination of two sets in such a way as to produce a new set with membership consisting of all of the elements found in either, but not both, of the original sets. It is actually the combination of the AND operation followed by two NOT operations. In the mathematics of sets, the exclusive OR operation is the *complement* of the *intersection* of two sets.

FIGURE A.6   Logical operations.

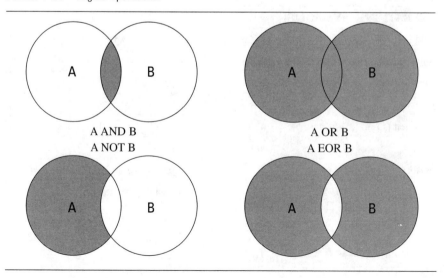

A AND B
A NOT B

A OR B
A EOR B

- Concatenation

Concatenation is the joining of two ordered sets into a single, longer, ordered set. For example, concatenation of the set {A,B,C} with the set {X,Y,Z} produces the new set {A,B,C,X,Y,Z}.

ROUNDING AND TRUNCATION

Chapter 6 included an example in which measurements of 1,500 feet, 1,250.7 feet, and 1,780.25 feet were added to produce a sum of 4,531 feet. The actual sum of these numbers, without the correction for significant figures in the various measurements, is 4,530.95 feet. The distance of 4,531 feet was obtained by a process called *rounding*.

Rounding is the process of adjusting the *least significant digit* according to the values to its *right*. For a discussion of what is meant by significant digits refer to Chapter 6. In the sum above, the 0 is the least significant digit because it is the fourth non-zero digit from the left and results from a computation that allows 4 significant digits. If the digit to the right of the least significant digit is a 5, 6, 7, 8, or 9, then the least significant digit is adjusted upward to the next highest value. If the digit to the right is a 0, 1, 2, 3, or 4, then the least significant digit is left unchanged.

Rounding is not the only method used to eliminate nonsignificant or trivial digits from numbers. An alternative method is *to drop the nonsignificant or unwanted digits so that the significant digits remain unchanged.* This method, called *truncation*, is often used in the retail business to handle sales of multiple unit items and should be familiar to anyone who has ever purchased a tank of gasoline. At a price of $ .99 9/10 per gallon, 15 gallons of gasoline comes to a total of $14.985. The process of rounding would result in a charge to the customer of $14.99. Truncation, on the other hand, simply drops the half cent so the customer is charged $14.98. Truncation results in a slightly larger average error than rounding but the direction of the error is always the same.

ORDER OF OPERATIONS

Most of the mathematical computations required for statistical treatment of research data involve solving equations that include several different operations that must be performed in the proper sequence. Most of the time the necessary arithmetic will be performed by a computer but for those occasions when hand computation is necessary the researcher must understand the rules that define the sequence with which operations are performed. Those rules are as follows.

1. The operations of multiplication and division are performed before those of addition unless parentheses or brackets direct otherwise.

   For example $2 + 3 \times 4 = 2 + 12 = 14$

   but $(2 + 3) \times 4 = 5 \times 4 = 20$

2. All operations enclosed by parentheses or brackets are performed before those not enclosed.

   For example $(2 + 3) \times (4 + 5) = 5 \times 9 = 45$

   but $2 + 3 \times (4 + 5) = 2 + 3 \times 9 = 2 + 27 = 29$

3. When operations enclosed by parentheses are themselves enclosed, the innermost sets of parentheses or brackets have priority.

For example $((2 + 3) - (4 + 5)) \times 6 = (5 - 9) \times 6 = -4 \times 6 = -24$
but $(2 + 3) - (4 + 5) \times 6 = 5 - 9 \times 6 = 5 - 54 = -49$

4. All operations under the radical or with parentheses or brackets raised to a power are performed before the root or exponentiation is performed.

For example $(4 + 12)^2 = 16^2 = 256$ and $\sqrt{4 + 12} = \sqrt{16} = 4$
but $4 + 12^2 = 4 + 144 = 148$ and $\sqrt{4} + 12 = 2 + 12 = 14$

SCIENTIFIC NOTATION

Scientific notation is a system for writing decimal numbers that is particularly useful for very large or very small values. All numbers are written as the product of two numbers in the form:

$$m \times 10^n$$

where *m* is a decimal equal to or greater than 1 and less than 10, and *n* is an integer. The first number (*m* in the above example) is called the *mantissa* and the second part (*n* in the above example) is called the *exponent*. The number 5,280, for example, is written in scientific notation as 5.280×10^3. Figure A.7 shows a variety of numbers in simple, decimal form and in scientific form. Any real number may be written using scientific notation. Writing numbers in scientific notation helps prevent misreading of numbers, especially when very large or very small decimal numbers are involved. Using scientific notation to express measurement data also reduces confusion concerning the precision of measurements. Sometimes the term *order of magnitude* is used for the exponents of numbers expressed in scientific notation. Thus the numbers 10,000 and 10, which in scientific notation are written as 1×10^4 and 1×10^1, are said to differ by 3 (4 − 1) orders of magnitude.

FIGURE A.7   Scientific notation permits very large and very small numbers to be written in a form that is much more easily understood.

DECIMAL NUMBER		SCIENTIFIC NOTATION
0.01234	=	1.234×10^2
5.67	=	5.67×10^0
345867.3	=	3.458673×10^5
−456.0	=	-4.56×10^2
3.1415 …	=	$3.1415 \ldots \times 10^0$

EXERCISES

1. Try tossing a coin 100 times (no cheating) and record the number of heads. Repeat this for a total of 5 sets of 100 tosses and combine your results with those of other students to build a bar graph. Compare this graph with the graph of the normal curve.

2. Use a mathematical computer program such as Mathcad to plot the normal curve from its equation. Use the integration function to find the area under the curve between various points.

3. Determine how many ways 9 baseball players could be assigned to the 9 field positions assuming each could play any position.

4. A typical combination lock has 48 numbers on its dial. Opening the lock requires entry of three of these numbers in the correct order. How many different locker combinations are possible?

5. In the game of roulette the probability that the number 00 will come up in one spin of the wheel is 1 chance in 38. What is the probability that 00 will come up in two spins? Hint: The answer is *not* 2 chances in 38.

6. Use an almanac to look up some statistics such as the U. S. population, the U. S. national debt, the Gross Domestic Product, or the number of people dying from smallpox for each year ending in 0 since 1800. (Or find some other such statistics involving very large or very small numbers.) Write these numbers in scientific notation.

ADDITIONAL RESOURCES WITH ANNOTATION

MathSoft, Inc. (1993). *Mathcad.* [Computer program]. Cambridge, MA: Author.
  A useful software package for learning and doing mathematics.

APPENDIX B

SAMPLE LETTER AND FORM

B.1 SAMPLE COVER LETTER FOR A SURVEY

UNIVERSITY OF HARD KNOCKS
School of Trial and Error

Use of letterhead adds credibility.

July 25, 1997

Dear Professor Smith,

Using a name rather than just a title adds a personal touch that increases the chance the questionnaire will be returned.

The incorporation of observations, internships, and other forms of practical experiences into the undergraduate physical education major is a widespread practice, but one that has received little formal study. As a graduate student in curriculum theory I have undertaken to conduct a descriptive study of practices with regard to such experiences as a dissertation topic. Successful completion of this project will form the basis of further study toward the aim of improving the training of future physical educators.

Explain the purpose of the study.

Your school has been randomly selected to take part in this survey from a comprehensive listing of schools offering an undergraduate degree in physical education. Your participation will require only about 15 minutes and is very important to the success of this study. Please complete the questionnaire as soon as possible and return it in the attached, postage-paid envelope by August 10, 1997.

Emphasize the importance of participation.

Sincerely;

Urge return within a specified period of time and call attention to the enclosure of the postage-paid return envelope.

A.P. Prenticeship

Personally sign each letter. Do not sign an original and make copies.

B.2 SAMPLE HUMAN SUBJECTS REVIEW FORM

Most institutions conducting research have their own human subjects review forms which will very likely be more detailed than the sample below. Studies involving invasive or dangerous procedures or that deal with sensitive topics, such as sexual or illegal behavior, may require substantially more detailed reviews than more benign studies.

I. Purpose and Objectives

Concisely describe why the study is being conducted and what will be gained by the successful completion of the study.

II. Subjects

Describe the subjects or subject groups to be used in the study and how they are to be recruited. In some studies it may be necessary to include a complete description of the criteria for inclusion or rejection of subjects. If subjects belong to groups that are especially vulnerable, describe why use of such groups is essential to the study.

III. Risks Involved

Describe in detail the potential risks that may be encountered by subjects, including risks of physical harm, embarrassment, invasion of privacy, and so on.

IV. Data Handling

Describe how data will be handled, including how data on individuals is to be protected from unauthorized disclosure. Include details of who will have access to data, how data will be stored, how long data will be stored, and when and how data will be destroyed.

V. Informed Consent

Describe how subjects will be informed of their risks and rights with respect to participation in this study, including how they will be informed of their right to decline to participate or withdraw from participation. Attach copies of the informed consent form to be used.

MATHCAD® PROGRAMS

C.1 AREA UNDER THE NORMAL CURVE

A Mathcad Program

x := 4, 3.99, . . . −4 Sets limits for the equation below.

Equation for the normal curve:

$$d(x) := \frac{100}{\sqrt{2 \cdot \pi}} \cdot e^{\frac{-x^2}{2}}$$

Graph of the normal curve:

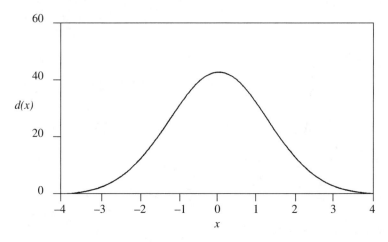

a := 3   b := −3 These values define the limits of the integral below.
Area under the normal curve between a and b:

$$\int_b^a d(x)\,dx = 99.73$$

The area under the normal curve bewteen any two points on the x-axis is found by taking the integral between those points. The integral above shows the area under the curve between the points defined as *a* and *b*. To find the area under the curve between any two points, simply re-define *a* and/or *b*.

C.2 THE *t*-TEST

A Mathcad program for Computing Areas Under the *t* Curve

$t = 10, 9.99, \ldots -10$ Defines range for the equation below.

    d := 8 Degrees of freedom.

    Intermediate computation:

$$c := 100 \cdot \frac{\Gamma\left(\dfrac{d+1}{2}\right)}{\sqrt{\pi \cdot d \cdot \Gamma\left(\dfrac{d}{2}\right)}}$$

    Equation for *t* distribution:

$$f(t) := c \cdot \left[\left(1 + \frac{t^2}{d}\right)^{-\frac{d+1}{2}}\right]$$

    Student's *t* curve for *d* degrees of freedom:

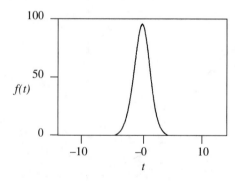

    Area under the entire curve:

$$y := \int_{-50}^{50} f(t) \, dt$$

a := 2.306   value of t,   b := 0 − a   value of *b* for two-tailed test.

Two-tailed test

Area under the curve from *a* to *b*:

$$x := \int_{b}^{a} f(t)\, dt$$

$\frac{x}{y} = 0.95$. Proportion of area under the curve between *a* and *b*.

$\quad p_2 := 1 - \frac{x}{y} \qquad p_2 = 0.05$ Probability of obtaining *t* by chance—Two-tailed test.

One-tailed test

Area under the curve from –50 to *a*:

$$z := \int_{-50}^{a} f(t)\, dt$$

$\frac{z}{y} = 0.975$. Proportion of area under the curve between –50 and *a*.

$\quad p_1 := 1 - \frac{z}{y} \qquad p_2 = 0.025$ Probability of obtaining *t* by chance—One-tailed test.

C.3 THE F TEST

A Mathcad Program for Computing Areas under the F Curves

$F := 20, 19.99, \ldots 0$ Sets limits for the equation below.

a := −12 numerator, b := 20 denominator, define degrees of freedom.

Equation for F distribution:

$$f(F) := \frac{\Gamma\left(\frac{a+b}{2}\right) \cdot \left(\frac{a}{b}\right)^{\frac{a}{2}} \cdot F^{\frac{a}{2}-1}}{\Gamma\left(\frac{a}{2}\right) \cdot \Gamma\left(\frac{b}{2}\right) \cdot \left(1 + \frac{a \cdot F}{b}\right)^{\frac{a+b}{2}}}$$

Graph of the F distribution:

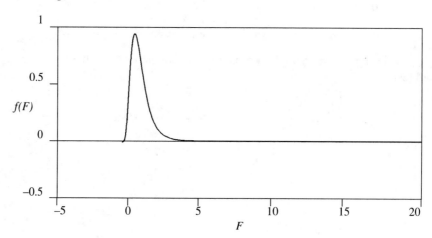

Area under the curve from 0 to F:

$$x := \int_0^{3.23} f(F) \, dF$$

Estimated area for the whole curve:

$$y := \int_0^{100} f(F) \, dF$$

$\frac{x}{y} = 0.98998$. Proportion of area from 0 to F.

$1 \cdot \frac{x}{y} = 0.010017896681404$ Probability of occurrence by chance is this value or less.

To test any F ratio first set the degrees of freedom above, then enter the value of F as the upper limit for the first integral above.

C.4 THE CHI-SQUARE TEST

A Mathcad Program for Computing Areas Under the Chi-Square Curves

$d := 7$ Define degrees of freedom

$x := 50, 49.99, \ldots 0$ Sets range of values for the equation below.

Equation for chi-square curves with d degrees of freedom:

$$f(x,d) := \frac{100}{\Gamma\left(\frac{d}{2}\right)} \cdot \left(\frac{1}{2}\right)^{\frac{d}{2}} \cdot x^{\frac{d}{2}-1} \cdot e^{-\frac{x}{2}}$$

Graph of chi-square curves:

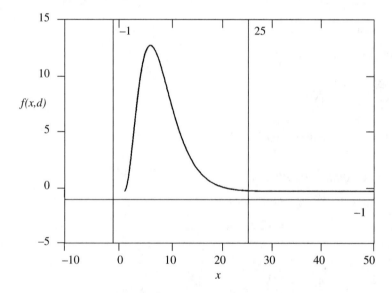

$b := 18.48$ Computed value of chi-square.

Area under the curve from b to 50:

$$z := \int_{b}^{50} f(x,d) \, dx$$

$z = 0.998$ $p := \dfrac{z}{100}$ Intermediate computations

$p = 0.009982$ Probability of occurrence of chi-square value by chance alone.

C.5 THE z-TRANSFORMATION OF THE CORRELATION COEFFICIENT

A Mathcad Program for Performing the z-Transformation of any Correlation Coefficient

Transformation r to z

r := .4973 Correlation coefficient

Equation for Fisher's z transformation:

$$Z := \frac{1}{2} \cdot \ln\left(\frac{1 + r}{1 - r}\right)$$

Transformed z value $z = 0.545713$

Reverse transformation z to r

zz := .8214 z value

Equation for reverse transformation:

$$r := \frac{-(-\exp(2 \cdot ZZ) + 1)}{(\exp(2 \cdot ZZ) + 1)}$$

Correlation coefficient r = 0.675831

z test for two correlation coefficients

a := .5760 Sample 1r   b := .4973 Sample 2r

n_1 := 12 Sample 1 size n_2 := 12 Sample 2 size

$$ZZZ := \frac{\frac{1}{2} \cdot \ln\left(\frac{1 + a}{1 - a}\right) - \frac{1}{2} \cdot \ln\left(\frac{1 + b}{1 - b}\right)}{\sqrt{\frac{1}{n_1 - 3} + \frac{1}{n_2 - 3}}}$$

Equation for z statistic

$$\sqrt{\frac{1}{n_1 - 3} + \frac{1}{n_2 - 3}} + 1 = 1.471$$

zzz = 2.55 Value for zzz (Evaluate using z test)

COMPUTER PROGRAMS

D.1 A COMPUTER PROGRAM FOR GENERATING RANDOM NUMBERS

For use on MS DOS computers using the BASICA interpreter or after compilation using Microsoft Quickbasic.

This program generates pseudorandom integers between any desired upper and lower limits. The user simply enters the desired number of random integers, a lower range limit, and an upper range limit, and confirms that the settings are correct.

The RANDOMIZE command uses the computer's internal clock to create a starting or seed value for its random number generator. The RND(1) command generates a pseudorandom decimal number greater than zero and less than 1. This value is then multiplied by the desired range defined by the upper and lower limits selected by the user. Finally, the generated number is converted by the INT command to an integer.

When using this program to generate a lengthy list of random numbers, it is important to recognize that the list of numbers produced is not genuinely random. All numbers generated are derived from the seed number that is produced within the computer at the moment the settings are confirmed. Thus, the first number generated may be treated as genuinely random, but all subsequent numbers are not truly random. This can be a problem when a very large number of random numbers must be generated. This problem may be avoided by using the program repeatedly to generate shorter lists.

```
'random number generator
' copyright 1997 by Charles F. Cicciarella

start: DIM count(100)
       CLS
       INPUT " Enter the number of desired random numbers >"; N
       INPUT "Enter the lower range limit for your random numbers >"; L
       INPUT "Enter the upper range limit for your random numbers >"; U
       PRINT "You have asked for "; N; " random integers => "; L; " and =< "; U
       PRINT "Please press <return> if this is correct, 'Q' to quit, or any other key if it is not"
       INPUT ""; x$
       IF x$ = "Q" OR x$ = "q" THEN END
       IF x$ <> "" THEN GOTO start:
repeat: RANDOMIZE TIMER
       FOR i = 1 TO N
          IF i MOD 10 = 0 THEN LOCATE 22, 20: INPUT "Press <Return> to continue"; x$
          LOCATE 10 + i MOD 10, 20: x = INT(RND(1) * ((U - L) + 1) + L): PRINT x
          count(x) = count(x) + 1
       NEXT i
       LOCATE 22, 20: PRINT "Done. Use <Return> to repeat, Q to quit, anything else to re-start"
       INPUT ""; x$
       IF x$ = "Q" OR x$ = "q" THEN END
       IF x$ = CHR$(13) THEN GOTO repeat:
       GOTO start:
```

D.2 A COMPUTER PROGRAM FOR ROOTS AND POWERS

For use on MS DOS computers using the BASICA interpreter or after compilation using Microsoft Quickbasic.

This program computes any desired power and any desired root of any positive number. The user simply enters a positive number and the desired power or root, and the answers are immediately displayed. This program computes positive roots only; it will not work with negative numbers.

```
'squares and roots
'Copyright 1997 Charles F. Cicciarella
start: CLS
      INPUT "Enter a value for N > "; n
      INPUT "Enter a value for your desired power and/or root > "; p
      LOCATE 10, 20: PRINT "N = "; n
      LOCATE 11, 20: PRINT "The "; p; " power of N = "; n ^ p
      LOCATE 12, 20: PRINT "The "; p; " root of N = "; n ^ (1 / p)
      INPUT "Press <Return> to repeat, anything else to quit"; x$
      IF x$ = "" THEN GOTO start
      END
```

D.3 A COMPUTER PROGRAM FOR COMBINATIONS AND PERMUTATIONS

For use on MS DOS computers using the BASICA interpreter or after compilation using Microsoft Quickbasic.

This program computes the number of permutations of *n* items taken *r* at a time and the number of combinations of *n* items taken *r* at a time. The user simply enters the number of items and the number of items to be used at one time in response to the prompts displayed on the screen. The answers are immediately displayed.

```
'permutations and combinations
'Copyright 1997 Charles F. Cicciarella
start: CLS
      INPUT "Enter the number of items > "; n
      INPUT "Enter the number of items to be taken at a time > "; r
      LOCATE 10, 20: PRINT "N = "; n
      np = 1
      FOR i = 1 TO n
        np = np * i
      NEXT i
      rp = 1
      FOR i = 1 TO r
         rp = rp * i
      NEXT i
      nrp = 1
      FOR i = 1 TO n - r
        nrp = nrp * i
      NEXT i
      p = np / nrp
      c = np / rp * nrp
      LOCATE 11, 1: PRINT "There are "; c; " combinations of "; n; " items taken "; r; " at a time."
      LOCATE 12, 1: PRINT "There are "; p; " permutations of "; n; " items taken "; r; " at a time."
      INPUT "Press <Return> to repeat, anything else to quit"; x$
      IF x$ = "" THEN GOTO start
      END
```

D.4 A COMPUTER PROGRAM FOR EXACT PROBABILITIES FOR THE WILCOXON RANK SUMS TEST

For use on MS DOS computers using the BASICA interpreter or after compilation using Microsoft Quickbasic.

This program computes exact probabilities (to the fourth decimal) for the Wilcoxon Rank Sums test for data sets consisting of two sets of rankings. There may be up to 15 cases in either ranking and up to 30 cases in the larger set of rankings. However, running time may be unacceptably slow when the size of the smaller data set exceeds eight or nine rankings. With data sets having nine and six rankings, for example, the running time should be approximately 13.5 minutes using a 33 MHz 486-DX based computer. With the same computer, the running time for eight and seven rankings will be approximately 2.5 hours.

The user simply enters the number of rankings in the larger data set, followed by the number of rankings in the smaller data set. When the necessary computations are completed, the program will display a table showing the sum, frequency, probability, and cumulative probability for each possible sum of ranks until a cumulative probability of .4 is reached.

To interpret a Wilcoxon Rank Sums test, the user simply locates the sum of ranks (for the smaller data set) obtained from the data in the "sum" column. The corresponding cumulative probability is the probability of obtaining that sum or a larger sum by chance. The "probability" column shows the probability of obtaining that sum exactly by chance.

```
'wilcoxon rank sums test
'program for computing exact probabilities for the Wilcoxon Rank Sum test
' smaller sample size limited to 15
'Running time may be unacceptably slow for values of smaller sample larger
' than about 8
'Rem out (preceed with ') For...Next loops below to control size of smaller
' group
'copyright 1997 Charles F. Cicciarella
CLS :
DIM poss(500)
INPUT "Number of subjects in the LARGER sample "; l: 'number in larger group
INPUT "Number of subjects in the SMALLER sample "; s: 'number in smaller group
n = l + s: 'n=total in both groups
FOR a = 1 TO n
PRINT "pass #"; a; " of "; n
x = x + a: 'sum of all ranks
FOR b = 1 TO n: IF b = a THEN GOTO newb
   IF s = 2 THEN GOSUB tabu:
   IF s <= 2 THEN GOTO newb:
FOR c = 1 TO n: IF c = a OR c = b THEN GOTO newc
   IF s = 3 THEN GOSUB tabu:
   IF s <= 3 THEN GOTO newc
FOR d = 1 TO n: IF d = a OR d = b OR d = c THEN GOTO newd
   IF s = 4 THEN GOSUB tabu:
   IF s <= 4 THEN GOTO newd:
FOR e = 1 TO n: IF e = a OR e = b OR e = c OR e = d THEN GOTO newe
   IF s = 5 THEN GOSUB tabu:
   IF s <= 5 THEN GOTO newe:
FOR f = 1 TO n: IF f = a OR f = b OR f = c OR f = d OR f = e THEN GOTO newf
   IF s = 6 THEN GOSUB tabu:
   IF s <= 6 THEN GOTO newf:
FOR g = 1 TO n:
   IF g = a OR g = b OR g = c OR g = d OR g = e OR g = f THEN GOTO newg
   IF s = 7 THEN GOSUB tabu:
   IF s <= 7 THEN GOTO newg:
```

```basic
FOR h = 1 TO n
   IF h = a OR h = b OR h = c OR h = d OR h = e OR h = f OR h = g THEN GOTO newh
   IF s = 8 THEN GOSUB tabu:
   IF s <= 8 THEN GOTO newh:
FOR i = 1 TO n
   IF i = a OR i = b OR i = c OR i = d OR i = e OR i = f OR i = g OR i = h THEN GOTO newi
   IF s = 9 THEN GOSUB tabu:
   IF s <= 9 THEN GOTO newi:
FOR j = 1 TO n
   IF j = a OR j = b OR j = c OR j = d OR j = e OR j = f OR j = g OR j = h OR j = i THEN GOTO newj
   IF s = 10 THEN GOSUB tabu:
   IF s <= 10 THEN GOTO newj:
FOR k = 1 TO n
   IF k = a OR k = b OR k = c OR k = d OR k = e OR k = f OR k = g OR k = h OR k = i OR k = j THEN GOTO newk
   IF s = 11 THEN GOSUB tabu:
   IF s <= 11 THEN GOTO newk:
FOR l = 1 TO n
   IF l = a OR l = b OR l = c OR l = d OR l = e OR l = f OR l = g OR l = h OR l = i OR l = j OR l = k THEN GOTO newl
   IF s = 12 THEN GOSUB tabu:
   IF s <= 12 THEN GOTO newl:
FOR m = 1 TO n
   IF m = a OR m = b OR m = c OR m = d OR m = e OR m = f OR m = g OR m = h OR m = i OR m = j OR m = k OR m = l THEN GOTO newm
   IF s = 13 THEN GOSUB tabu:
   IF s <= 13 THEN GOTO newm:
FOR nn = 1 TO n
   IF nn = a OR nn = b OR nn = c OR nn = d OR nn = e OR nn = f OR nn = g OR nn = h OR nn = i OR nn = j OR nn = k OR nn = l OR nn = m THEN GOTO newn
   IF s = 14 THEN GOSUB tabu:
   IF s <= 14 THEN GOTO newn:
FOR o = 1 TO n
   IF o = a OR o = b OR o = c OR o = d OR o = e OR o = f OR o = g OR o = h OR o = i OR o = j OR o = k OR o = l OR o = m OR o = nn THEN GOTO newo
   IF s = 15 THEN GOSUB tabu:
   IF s <= 15 THEN GOTO newo:

STOP
newo: NEXT o
newn: NEXT nn
newm: NEXT m
newl: NEXT l
newk: NEXT k
newj: NEXT j
newi: NEXT i
newh: NEXT h
newg: NEXT g
newf: NEXT f
newe: NEXT e
newd: NEXT d
newc: NEXT c
newb: NEXT b
NEXT a

oput: CLS : PRINT "sum          frequency   probability   cum probability"
FOR z = 1 TO INT(x)
IF poss(z) = 0 OR cum >= .4 THEN GOTO newz:
cum = cum + (poss(z) / count)
PRINT z, poss(z), INT(10000 * (poss(z) / count)) / 10000, INT(10000 * cum) / 10000
IF z MOD 20 = 0 THEN
   LOCATE 24, 1
   INPUT "Any key to continue"; z$
   CLS
END IF
newz: NEXT z
INPUT ""; z$
END
tabu:
   count = count + 1
   sum = a + b + c + d + e + f + g
   poss(sum) = poss(sum) + 1
RETURN
```

D.5 A COMPUTER PROGRAM FOR EXACT PROBABILITIES FOR THE SPEARMAN RHO CORRELATION

For use on MS DOS computers using the BASICA interpreter or after compilation using Microsoft Quickbasic.

This program computes exact probabilities (to the fourth decimal) for Spearman rho correlation coefficients for data sets with up to 10 data pairs. With data sets having greater than 9 data pairs, the running time may be unacceptably slow. Using a 33 MHz 486-DX based computer the running time should be approximately 10 minutes with 9 data pairs and nearly 2 hours with 10 data pairs.

The user simply enters the number of data pairs: an integer between 1 and 10. When the necessary computations are completed, the program will display a table showing the sum of d^2, frequency, cumulative frequency, probability, and rho correlation coefficient associated with each possible value of d^2. The last two columns are used in evaluating a rho correlation coefficient. The user simply finds the value of rho closest to that obtained from actual data. The corresponding value in the probability column is the exact probability of obtaining the matching value of rho. This program requires MS DOS 3.1 or later.

```
'Spearman Correlation test
'program for computing exact probabilities for the Spearman correlation coefficient
' Not for use with tied ranks
' for sample sizes up to 10
'Running time may be unacceptably slow for values of N larger than about 8

'copyright 1997 Charles F. Cicciarella
CLS :
DIM freqs(5000)
count = 0
INPUT "Number of pairs of subjects or cases"; N:
denom = .5 * (N * (N - 1))
FOR a = 1 TO N
PRINT "Pass "; a; " of "; N
r(1) = a
FOR b = 1 TO N: IF b = a THEN GOTO newb
   r(2) = b
   IF N = 2 THEN GOSUB tabu:
   IF N <= 2 THEN GOTO newb:
FOR c = 1 TO N: IF c = a OR c = b THEN GOTO newc
   r(3) = c
   IF N = 3 THEN GOSUB tabu:
   IF N <= 3 THEN GOTO newc
FOR d = 1 TO N: IF d = a OR d = b OR d = c THEN GOTO newd
   r(4) = d
   IF N = 4 THEN GOSUB tabu:
   IF N <= 4 THEN GOTO newd:
FOR e = 1 TO N: IF e = a OR e = b OR e = c OR e = d THEN GOTO newe
   r(5) = e

   IF N = 5 THEN GOSUB tabu:
   IF N <= 5 THEN GOTO newe:
FOR f = 1 TO N: IF f = a OR f = b OR f = c OR f = d OR f = e THEN GOTO newf
   r(6) = f
   IF N = 6 THEN GOSUB tabu:
   IF N <= 6 THEN GOTO newf:
```

```
FOR g = 1 TO N:
   r(7) = g
   IF g = a OR g = b OR g = c OR g = d OR g = e OR g = f THEN GOTO newg
   IF N = 7 THEN GOSUB tabu:
   IF N <= 7 THEN GOTO newg:
FOR h = 1 TO N
   r(8) = h
   IF h = a OR h = b OR h = c OR h = d OR h = e OR h = f OR h = g THEN GOTO newh
   IF N = 8 THEN GOSUB tabu:
   IF N <= 8 THEN GOTO newh:
FOR i = 1 TO N
   r(9) = i
   IF i = a OR i = b OR i = c OR i = d OR i = e OR i = f OR i = g OR i = h THEN GOTO newi
   IF N = 9 THEN GOSUB tabu:
   IF N <= 9 THEN GOTO newi:
FOR j = 1 TO N
   r(10) = j
   IF j = a OR j = b OR j = c OR j = d OR j = e OR j = f OR j = g OR j = h OR j = i THEN GOTO newj
   IF N = 10 THEN GOSUB tabu:
   IF N <= 10 THEN GOTO newj:
STOP
newj: NEXT j
newi: NEXT i
newh: NEXT h
newg: NEXT g
newf: NEXT f
newe: NEXT e
newd: NEXT d
newc: NEXT c
newb: NEXT b
NEXT a

oput: CLS : PRINT
PRINT "Sum of d^2    Frequency    Cum Frequency    Probability      rho"
FOR z = 0 TO 2000
cumfr = cumfr + freqs(z)

prob = INT(10000 * (cumfr / count)) / 10000
rho = INT(10000 * (1 - (6 * z / (N * (N ^ 2 - 1))))) / 10000

IF freqs(z) <> 0 AND rho <= 1 THEN
    PRINT z, freqs(z), cumfr, prob, rho
    IF z <> 0 AND z MOD 20 = 0 THEN
        INPUT "Press <Return> for more"; z$
        CLS
        PRINT "Sum of d^2    Frequency    Cum Frequency    Probability      rho"
    END IF
END IF
NEXT z

INPUT ""; z$

END
tabu:
s = 0
   FOR x = 0 TO N
      diff = r(x) - x
      s = s + diff ^ 2
   NEXT x
IF s > 0 THEN freqs(s) = freqs(s) + 1: 'freqs(s) contains the frequency of each possible s
IF s = 0 THEN freqs(0) = freqs(0) + 1
count = count + 1
RETURN
```

D.6 A COMPUTER PROGRAM FOR EXACT
PROBABILITIES FOR THE KENDALL'S TAU CORRELATION

For use on MS DOS computers using the BASICA interpreter or after compilation using Microsoft Quickbasic.

This program computes exact probabilities (to the fourth decimal) for Kendall tau correlation coefficients for data sets with up to 10 data pairs. With data sets having greater than 9 data pairs, the running time may be unacceptably slow. Using a 33 MHz 486-DX based computer, the running time should be approximately 30 minutes with 9 pairs and nearly 5 hours with 10 data pairs.

The user simply enters the number of data pairs: an integer between 1 and 10. When the necessary computations are completed, the program will display a table showing the value of the S statistic, frequency, cumulative frequency, probability, and tau correlation coefficient associated with each possible value of S. The last two columns are used in evaluating a tau correlation coefficient. The user simply finds the value of tau closest to that obtained from actual data. The corresponding value in the probability column is the exact probability of obtaining the matching value of tau.

This program requires MS DOS 3.1 or later.

```
'Kendall Correlation test
'program for computing exact probabilities for the Kendall correlation coefficient
' Not for use with tied ranks
' for sample sizes up to 10
'Running time may be unacceptably slow for values of N larger than about 8

'copyright 1997 Charles F. Cicciarella
CLS :
DIM freqs(500)
count = 0
INPUT "Number of pairs of subjects or cases"; n:
denom = .5 * (n * (n - 1))
FOR a = 1 TO n
PRINT "Pass "; a; " of "; n
r(1) = a
FOR b = 1 TO n: IF b = a THEN GOTO newb
    r(2) = b
    IF n = 2 THEN GOSUB tabu:
    IF n <= 2 THEN GOTO newb:
FOR c = 1 TO n: IF c = a OR c = b THEN GOTO newc
    r(3) = c
    IF n = 3 THEN GOSUB tabu:
    IF n <= 3 THEN GOTO newc
FOR d = 1 TO n: IF d = a OR d = b OR d = c THEN GOTO newd
    r(4) = d
    IF n = 4 THEN GOSUB tabu:
    IF n <= 4 THEN GOTO newd:
FOR e = 1 TO n: IF e = a OR e = b OR e = c OR e = d THEN GOTO newe
    r(5) = e
    IF n = 5 THEN GOSUB tabu:
    IF n <= 5 THEN GOTO newe:
FOR f = 1 TO n: IF f = a OR f = b OR f = c OR f = d OR f = e THEN GOTO newf
    r(6) = f
    IF n = 6 THEN GOSUB tabu:
    IF n <= 6 THEN GOTO newf:
```

```
        FOR g = 1 TO n:
          r(7) = g
          IF g = a OR g = b OR g = c OR g = d OR g = e OR g = f THEN GOTO newg
          IF n = 7 THEN GOSUB tabu:
          IF n <= 7 THEN GOTO newg:
        FOR h = 1 TO n
          r(8) = h
          IF h = a OR h = b OR h = c OR h = d OR h = e OR h = f OR h = g THEN GOTO newh
          IF n = 8 THEN GOSUB tabu:
          IF n <= 8 THEN GOTO newh:
        FOR i = 1 TO n
          r(9) = i
          IF i = a OR i = b OR i = c OR i = d OR i = e OR i = f OR i = g OR i = h THEN GOTO newi
          IF n = 9 THEN GOSUB tabu:
          IF n <= 9 THEN GOTO newi:
        FOR j = 1 TO n
          r(10) = j
          IF j = a OR j = b OR j = c OR j = d OR j = e OR j = f OR j = g OR j = h OR j = i THEN GOTO newj
          IF n = 10 THEN GOSUB tabu:
          IF n <= 10 THEN GOTO newj:
        STOP
        newj: NEXT j
        newi: NEXT i
        newh: NEXT h
        newg: NEXT g
        newf: NEXT f
        newe: NEXT e
        newd: NEXT d
        newc: NEXT c
        newb: NEXT b
        NEXT a

        oput: CLS : PRINT
        PRINT "S          Frequency   Cum Frequency    Probability        tau"
        cum = zeroes + negs
        FOR z = 1 TO 100
        cum = cum + freqs(z)
        cumfr = INT(10000 * (cum - freqs(z)) / count) / 10000
        prob = INT(10000 * (1 - (cum - freqs(z)) / count)) / 10000
        tau = INT(10000 * z / denom) / 10000
        IF z <= denom AND freqs(z) <> 0 THEN PRINT z, freqs(z), cumfr, prob, tau
        NEXT z

        INPUT ""; z$
        END
        tabu:
          count = count + 1
          s = 0
          FOR x = 1 TO n - 1
            FOR y = x + 1 TO n
          IF r(x) = r(y) THEN s = s + 0
          IF r(x) > r(y) THEN s = s - 1
          IF r(x) < r(y) THEN s = s + 1
          NEXT y
          NEXT x
          IF s > 0 THEN freqs(s) = freqs(s) + 1: 'freqs(s) contains the frequency of each possible s
          IF s = 0 THEN zeroes = zeroes + 1
          IF s < 0 THEN negs = negs + 1
        RETURN
```

REFERENCES

Achtert, W.S. (1985). *The MLA style manual.* New York: Modern Language Association of America.

Alexander, D. (1991). From the editor. *The Humanist, 51,* 2.

American Institute of Physics Publication Board. (1990). *AIP style manual.* (4th ed.). New York: American Institute of Physics.

American Psychological Association (1994). *Publication Manual of the American Psychological Association* (4th ed.). Washington, DC: Author.

Asch, S.E. (1955). Opinions and social pressure. In *Frontiers of psychological research.* San Francisco: W.H. Freeman & Co.

Barzun, J., & Graff, H.F. (1985). *The modern researcher* (4th ed.). San Diego: Harcourt Brace Jovanovitch.

Bernstein, C., & Woodward, B. (1974). *All the president's men.* New York: Simon & Schuster.

Blinderman, C. (1986). *The Piltdown inquest.* Buffalo, NY: Prometheus Books.

Boyer, E.L. (1990). *Scholarship reconsidered: Priorities of the professoriate.* Princeton, NJ: Carnegie Foundation for the Advancement of Teaching.

Bray, W. (1992). Under the skin of Nazca. *Nature, 358* (2), 19.

Briggs, J., & Peat, D. (1989). *Turbulent mirror: An illustrated guide to chaos theory and the science of wholeness.* New York: Harper & Row.

Cahalan, D. (1989). The Digest poll rides again! *Public Opinion Quarterly, 53,* 129–133.

Campbell, D.T., & Stanley, J.C. (1963). *Experimental and quasi-experimental designs for research.* Skokie, IL: Rand McNally.

Canfora, L. (1989). *The vanished library* (M. Ryle, Trans.). Berkeley: University of California Press. (Original work published 1987)

CBE Style Manual Committee (1983). *CBE manual: A guide for authors, editors, and publishers in the biological sciences.* Bethesda, MD: Council of Biology Editors.

Cheffers, J.T.F., Amidon, E.J., & Rogers, K.D. (1974). *Interaction analysis: An application to nonverbal activity.* Minneapolis, MN: Association for Productive Teaching.

Cicciarella, C.F. (1983). *The relative effectiveness of the crawl stroke and breast stroke sequences in the teaching of beginning swimming.* Unpublished doctoral dissertation, Boston University, Boston.

Cicciarella, C.F. (1992). *Directory of Periodicals in Sport.* Charlotte, NC: Persimmon Software.

Cicciarella, C.F. (1993). *Eventlog.* [Computer software.] Charlotte, NC: Persimmon Software.

Close, F. (1991). Cold fusion I: The discovery that never was. *New Scientist 129* (1752), 46–50.

The cranberry affair. (1959, November 23). *Newsweek 54* (21), 35–36.

Cureton, T.K. (1939). Standards for testing beginning swimming. *Research Quarterly, 10,* 54–59.

Darwin, C. (1859). *On the origin of species, by means of natural selection, or the preservation of favored races in the struggle for life.* London: John Murray.

Devillers, C. (1983). What future for the Wayana Indians? *National Geographic, 163* (1), 66–83.

Feynmann, R.P. (1985). *Surely you're joking, Mr. Feynmann.* New York: Quality Paperback Book Club.

Flanders, N.A. (1970). *Analyzing teaching behavior.* Reading, MA: Addison Wesley Publishing.

Franks, B.D., & Huck, S.W. (1986). Why does everyone use the .05 significance level? *Research Quarterly for Exercise and Sport 57* (3), 245–249.

Goodall, J. (1992). The chimpanzee: The living link between "man" and "beast." Edinburgh, U.K.: Edinburgh University Press.

Hedges, L.V. (1982). Fitting categorical models to effect sizes from a series of experiments. *Journal of Educational Statistics 6,* 107–128.

Hedges, L.V., & Olkin, I. (1985). *Statistical methods for meta-analysis.* New York: Academic Press.

Iverson, C. (Ed.) (1989). *American medical association manual of style.* (8th ed.). Baltimore, MD: Williams and Wilkins.

Jones, J.H. (1993). *Bad blood: The Tuskegee syphilis experiment.* New York: Free Press.

Ketteringham, J.M. (1987, July). People behind the wonders. *Reader's Digest, 131,* 134–138.

Likert, R. (1936). A technique for the measurement of attitude. *Archives of Psychology, 140.*

Locke, L. (1989). Qualitative research as a form of scientific inquiry in sport and physical education. *Research Quarterly for Exercise and Sport, 60* (1), 1–20.

Martinek, T., & Johnson, S. (1979). Teacher expectations: Effects on dyadic interactions and self-concept in elementary-age children. *Research Quarterly, 50* (1), 60–70.

Nideffer, R.M. (1974). *Test of attentional and interpersonal style.* Rochester, NY: Behavioral Research Applications Group.

Plimpton, G. (1966). *Paper Lion.* New York: Harper and Row.

Randi, J. (1984). Parapsychology: A doubtful premise. *The Humanist, 44,* 23–27.

Roethlisberger, F.J., & Dickson, W.J. (1939). *Management and the Worker.* Cambridge, MA: Harvard University Press.

Rosenthal, R., & Lawson, R. (1964). A longitudinal study of the effects of experimenter bias on the operant conditioning of rats. *Journal of Psychiatric Research, 2,* 61–72.

Segre, M. (1991). *In the wake of Galileo.* New Brunswick, NJ: Rutgers University Press.

Siedentop, D., Tousignant, M., & Parker, M. (1982). *Academic learning time—physical education, 1982 revisions: Coding manual.* Columbus, OH: School of HPER, Ohio State University.

Solomon, R.L. (1949). On extension of control group design. *Psychological Bulletin, 46,* 137.

Squire, P. (1988). Why the 1936 literary digest poll failed. *Public Opinion Quarterly, 52,* 125–133.

Thurstone, L.L., & Chave, E.J. (1929). *The measurement of attitude.* Chicago: University of Chicago Press.

Tolson, H. (1980). An adjunct to statistical significance: w^2. *Research Quarterly for Exercise and Sport, 51* (3), 580–584.

Tufte, E. (1983). *The graphical presentation of quantitative information.* Cheshire, CT: Graphics Press.

Tufte, E. (1990). *Envisioning information.* Cheshire, CT: Graphics Press.

Tushingham, A.D. (1958). The men who hid the Dead Sea Scrolls. *National Geographic, 104* (6), 784–808.

University of Chicago Press. *The Chicago manual of style* (1982). Chicago: Author.

Wilson, E.O. (1991). Rain forest canopy: The high frontier. *National Geographic, 180* (6), 78–107.

Zimbardo, P.G. (1972). The tactics and ethics of persuasion. In B.T. King, & McGinnis, E. (Eds.), *Attitudes, conflict, and social change.* New York: Academic Press.